Sydney Wooderson

A Very British Hero

Other runner biographies by the same author

The Little Wonder (Alf Shrubb)
Beer and Brine (Walter George)
Deerfoot (Louis Bennett)
Tea With Mr Newton (Arthur Newton)
Plimsolls On, Eyeballs Out (Jim Peters)

Sydney Wooderson

A Very British Hero

Rob Hadgraft

The Book Guild Ltd

First published in Great Britain in 2018 by
The Book Guild Ltd
9 Priory Business Park
Wistow Road, Kibworth
Leicestershire, LE8 0RX
Freephone: 0800 999 2982
www.bookguild.co.uk
Email: info@bookguild.co.uk
Twitter: @bookguild

Typeset in Aldine401 BT

Printed and bound in Great Britain by CPI Group (UK) Ltd, Croydon, CR0 4YY

ISBN 978 1912575 350

British Library Cataloguing in Publication Data.
A catalogue record for this book is available from the British Library.

This book is dedicated to all those ordinary club runners who, upon reaching middle age, look back at their running careers and realise they really ought to have done a bit less 'rubbish' mileage and paid more attention to running a fast mile.

I know exactly how you feel!

"He resembled an elderly, serious gentleman, stepping out on to the start line with shorts that reached nearly down to his knees, and a pair of glasses on his nose."

– Emil Zatopek's first impression of Sydney Wooderson, Oslo 1946

Contents

Foreword

by the Rt. Hon. The Lord Sebastian Coe, CH, KBE

(Double Olympic gold medallist, 12-time world record breaker)

SYDNEY Wooderson was without doubt one of the greatest British middle distance runners of all time. The bespectacled Blackheath Harrier, 5ft 6ins and 8st 13lbs, didn't have the look or physical stature of a winner but his tenacity, strength and willpower were more than a match for his contemporaries. Wooderson, the European 1500 metres champion of 1938, who overcame rheumatic fever to return to fitness at the end of World War II and take the 1946 title at 5000 metres, unluckily missed out on two Olympic opportunities, 1940 and 1944, editions which were cancelled due to the war. He had been unbeaten for two years prior to the first of those Games and, based upon his world records at the mile in 1937 and 800m in 1938, he would have toed the start line of the 1500m as the overwhelming favourite. That a broken bone in his ankle had prevented him from making the 1936 1500m final, the one Olympic Games he did contest, sums up his misfortune.

Wooderson, whose coach was Albert Hill, 1920 Olympic 800m and 1500m champion, holds the distinction of being the first British holder of the mile world record in the IAAF era. It's clear that had the war not intervened, with its poor food and lack of training opportunities, he would have pushed the record nearer to the 4-minute barrier than his personal best of 4:04.

Modest and shy, Wooderson, who has been described as "a tiger on the track", never gained the true fame that his prodigious athletics talent so richly deserved. A hero to a 15-year-old Roger Bannister, who was among a crowd of 54,000 watching him battle with Arne Andersson at the White City on August Bank Holiday 1945, Bannister later summed up the diminutive Englishman's appeal: "I admired him as much for his attitude to running as for the feats he achieved."

That Wooderson – the Mighty Atom, as he was dubbed by a public who adored him – inspired the man who was to become first to run a sub-4 mile, is the greatest testimony to his memory.

Sebastian Coe
IAAF President

Introduction

VEILED by a thin mist, the silence is eerily invaded by the distant sound of the school clock striking eleven.

Glistening playing fields stretch almost as far as the eye can see, but are completely deserted save for a single groundsman pottering quietly beside a far-off hedge. Mid-morning on this autumnal Thursday is clearly not games time at Sutton Valence, an independent boarding school in deepest Kent positioned majestically on the Greensand Ridge overlooking the Vale of Kent and the Weald.

Ahead of me sits a fenced-off, eight-lane running track, its brick-red synthetic surface and silver kerbing harshly incongruous in this verdant corner of the so-called Garden of England. The effect is exaggerated by the strange but irrefutable fact that the track has been built on sloping land. How often runners must curse that uphill back straight in the closing laps of a 10,000-metres race! The track was formally opened in 2009 by 80-year-old athletics legend Sir Roger Bannister, who spoke fondly that day of a certain Sutton Valence pupil who once ran in these fields. That boy had grown up to become a star, and it was he who inspired Bannister to take up running and make history as the first sub-four-minute miler.

Adjacent to the modern track is a field that for years housed the school's old track. This was a grass affair, with little protection from the elements, meaning the going was tough when windy. This was the place where the above-mentioned pupil learned to race the mile during a seven-year period between the two world wars.

This shy lad was short and skinny and ran in huge baggy shorts and thick, heavily-framed glasses. Based purely on appearance, a less-likely athletic champion would be impossible to imagine. But when he circled that grass track everything changed. His puny figure employed an unusually long stride for his size, and he clearly had staying power – and, best of all, a devastatingly fast finish. He would never blossom into a muscular, imposing athlete – but that didn't matter for he smashed world records anyway, becoming the most unlikely sporting hero the nation had ever produced.

The little fellow's name was Sydney Charles Wooderson.

Sydney attended Sutton Valence between 1926 and 1933, and for much of that time was overshadowed by the prowess of elder brother Alfred, an accomplished runner and all-round sportsman. For years Alfred was the undisputed star of school sports, but focus would slowly shift towards his little brother one wet and windy day in April 1930. Unlike the quiet, undemonstrative Sydney, Alfred was an outgoing, confident sort and at the annual school sports on this day nobody was surprised when he imperiously smashed the school's one-mile record by running 4 minutes and 49.8 seconds.

What did come as a shock was the sight, just a few strides behind, of the tiny figure of 15-year-old Sydney coming in third. No-one was more surprised than Sydney himself. It would prove a seminal moment: he was left slightly dazed by a heady excitement he'd never felt before and knew he'd discovered something he was very good at. From that moment he never looked back.

He learned how to race the quarter-mile, half-mile and mile here atop Kent's Greensand Ridge, and would be introduced to the rugged pleasures of cross-country running too. Within a few years of leaving school he'd become the world's fastest miler, the nation's favourite sportsman and a household name up and down the land.

In the 21st century Sydney Wooderson is a largely forgotten hero, his unique story never told in full until now. My decision to write his biography was made, purely by chance, on my 60th birthday. Knowing the year ahead would involve hefty amounts of research, much of it confined indoors, I decided to set myself a challenge: During my 12 months as a 60-year-old I would schedule visits to 60 of the venues at which Sydney raced during his career. It would allow me to check out the history, get a feel for the 'psychogeography' of these places and run a mile in Sydney's footsteps at each!

Hence, 48 hours later, 'Project Sydney' was underway and here I was pitching up in mid-Kent to have a run over these Sutton Valence fields,

Sydney's proving ground. Here he'd made himself the fastest schoolboy miler in history. My little jaunt on this cool, autumnal morning wouldn't be anywhere near that sort of pace, but then Sydney hadn't been encumbered by camera, notebook and pen!

Rob Hadgraft

1

A Delicate War Baby

SYDNEY Charles Wooderson was born at home in SE London on Sunday 30 August 1914, just 26 days after the start of the First World War. The second son of George and Jeanette ('Nettie') Wooderson, he breathed his first lungfuls in one of the six upstairs bedrooms of an impressive bay-fronted villa in Baldwin Crescent, Camberwell.

It may have been a warm and quiet Sunday in London, but just across the Channel the war was raging and lives were being lost on the western front. Horrific reports of British soldier deaths were tempered a little, however, by news that Paris was about to be saved and a major British counter-offensive was succeeding against invading German armies to the east of the French capital.

Life, on the surface, was somewhat less hectic in the well-to-do streets of Camberwell over the weekend of Sydney's birth, although just a few streets away injured men were being ferried back from continental battlefields via Waterloo Station to the Royal Herbert Military Hospital at Woolwich.

As a toddler growing up in Camberwell, the war would mean Sydney and other local children were denied access to one of the most attractive corners of the district – Myatts Fields Park – which was just 200 yards from the Woodersons' front door. Poet laureate Sir John Betjeman would later describe the park as "a strangely beautiful place" but around the time of Sydney's birth it was closed and requisitioned to help the war effort. It became an annexe to the First London General Hospital which was hastily created at the former St Gabriel's College building that loomed over the western end of the park. It was used to accommodate the soaring number of British casualties returning from battle, men in need of urgent surgery placed in beds crammed inside newly-erected wooden huts. Night-duty nurses slept in other huts in the park.

Sadly many soldiers breathed their last in this little park, and the sombre atmosphere would deepen on overcast days due to the dramatic and brooding presence of the enormous hospital building, formerly a happy place when occupied by carefree college students.

Sydney would be aged seven by the time the park was re-opened in 1921 for its original use. As he lived so close by, it's reasonable to assume this was where he did the first running of a life that would be defined by his achievements in the sport. During my visit to the area, the gates were welcomingly open and the well-kept paths beckoned me to run a few laps of the park. Imagining this must have been the scene of Sydney's first running steps, I took the bait.

I jogged past a handsome bandstand, past The Little Cat café incongruously blasting out Latin American music, and some council gardeners deep in discussion. Continuing out and around the corner, I stopped to examine the imposing bay-fronted villa, now called Monteagle House, in which Sydney was born. It was undergoing renovations following a recent sale for around £1 million. Next door stood a similar property which I was informed was once home to acclaimed author Dame Muriel Spark, the place in which she wrote her first eight novels.

The Wooderson family lived in relative comfort in their substantial house on account of the thriving business exploits of Sydney's father George. By the time Sydney was born, George was 49 and on his second marriage. The family wholesale fruit business based at Covent Garden was very well established, with George in charge of a warehouse and a team of employees in Long Acre. Nowadays that spot is occupied by a Paperchase store, coincidentally the company who randomly used an image of Sydney on some of their advertising material in 2015.

Sydney's father had been born in April 1865 in East London to Sarah and her husband Henry, owner of Wooderson's Fruit and Vegetable Merchants. The family then lived adjacent to the thriving Covent Garden marketplace and George inevitably followed his father, and grandfather, into the family business.

On Christmas day 1890 George married 19-year-old Caroline Cowlan in Peckham and within four years they had three children, Violet, George and Rhoda. With the business doing well, the family took a step up the housing ladder, moving from Lambeth to Herne Hill shortly after the turn of the century.

George sold a range of produce in the noisy, bustling environment of the wholesale marketplace, but his speciality was quality English apples grown on his own and other land around the Kent/Sussex borders. A splendid photo, taken during wartime, and now in the Imperial War Museum's archive, shows him engaged in friendly banter with a porter as they examine a basket full of apples, watched intently by other employees. With moustache and glasses, hat and smart overcoat, George looks in good health and of much stouter build than offspring Sydney.

Covent Garden Market had been central to London life since the 17th century, and the Woodersons had been prominent merchants for decades by the time of Sydney's birth. The main products were fresh produce and flowers brought in from local farms as well as by boat. It was the premier price-setting market in Britain, with an annual turnover of about a million tons. Its central London location meant there was little room to expand, resulting in growing congestion until it relocated in 1974.

Market life was unrelentingly hectic in George Wooderson's day, but success brought rewards and status, and accordingly he was admitted to the Freemasons, joining the Robert Burns Lodge in 1907. But, then, in 1909 tragedy struck: wife Caroline died at the age of 37, leaving George a widower at 44 with three teenage children to care for. He was hit hard by the loss and never quite recovered, despite re-marrying within two years.

His second bride, in a March 1911 ceremony on the Strand, was a 36-year-old spinster from the Lewisham area called Jeanette Tindall. Generally referred to as 'Nettie', his new wife moved into the established family home at 27 Holmdene Avenue, Herne Hill, joining George and the three children from his first marriage. Nineteen-year-old Violet was an assistant teacher, Rhoda, 18, an art student and George, 10, still at school. As the process of starting a second family with Nettie got underway, George moved them all to bigger premises less than two miles away in Camberwell.

Over subsequent years they would occupy premises in Baldwin Crescent and Calais Street, Camberwell, the family unit blossoming with the addition of three more sons in Alfred (December 1911), Sydney

(August 1914) and finally Stanley (October 1915). Added to the presence of domestic servant Elizabeth Shields, this took occupancy of their home into double figures for a spell. Sydney and Stanley shared a bedroom throughout the Camberwell years and would remain close throughout their lives.

The country was at war for Sydney's first four years of life but the biggest upheaval he would face in his younger years came in 1922 when George moved them all out of London and into the heart of rural Kent near Maidstone. Here were the orchards and fields that bore the fruit that passed through his Covent Garden business and, also importantly, on their doorstep would be an impressive independent school at which the three boys could receive a top education. Allowing the lads to grow up in the fresh air of the countryside was another factor behind the move: mum Nettie would reveal a few years later that Sydney had been a delicate baby. At one time it was thought he might not survive childhood, but he would thrive after the move into the country.

The 1920s and 1930s proved busy, but not altogether happy times for Sydney's father. It is said George never completely got over the death of his first wife, and even developed an interest in spiritualism in the hope of communicating with her. George and Sydney never developed an especially close relationship, although the opposite would be true with Sydney and his mother.

Simon Amos, grandson of Sydney's half-sister Rhoda, told me the house named 'Brookside' in the tiny village of Chart Sutton – around five miles south of Maidstone – was most likely built specifically for George Wooderson when he moved the extended family into Kent. Within a couple of years of the move, George gifted a small mixed farm ('Bungalow Farm', a few miles away near Cranbrook) to his daughter Rhoda upon her marriage to Christopher Pope. George's investments in Kent became a good source of apples and cherries for his business, but of course the Woodersons were not immune to the effects of the worldwide economic depression and by the mid-1930s Bungalow Farm would have to be sold, while the occupants of Brookside would also move out and return to SE London.

Before then, Sydney, on reaching the age of 11, along with younger brother Stanley, duly started at nearby Sutton Valence School on the rainy morning of Friday 5 May 1926. Established in the 17th century, this was an imposing establishment and the two small boys must have been grateful

The Woodersons moved to rural Kent in 1922 (Sydney, front right).

for each other's company in those nerve-wracking early days. They were initially day boys, coming in the short distance from home at Brookside (one mile across the fields, or a little more via the lanes). By now elder brother Alfred had already been at Sutton Valence for a full year and had made his mark, especially in sporting pursuits. Alfred was thus seen as a perfect role model for the shy Sydney, although the pair were very different temperamentally. All three Wooderson boys would later become boarders, accommodated within the school's Westminster House, Sydney moving there in 1931 upon entering the Sixth Form.

Sydney grew to love being outdoors, his interest in sports not precluded by his relatively small size and quiet personality. This will have been nurtured and encouraged by the school, whose sportsfields stood, and remain, amid beautiful countryside, and whose general philosophy included the proud message 'Sport is at the very heart of our enrichment journey.' Sydney would take part as keenly as any Suttonians in swimming, boxing and rugby sessions, as well as running.

2

The Die is Cast

SYDNEY was in awe of his elder brother's running talent but obediently agreed when Alfred one day insisted he ought to have a crack at the school's annual junior cross-country. Shedding his inhibitions, Sydney, then aged 12, went out and duly won the three-mile race. The die was cast.

School records indicate Sydney's first appearance in cut-and-thrust competition against other schools would come as a raw 14-year-old in March 1929. The Sutton Valence lads headed 20 miles eastward to Canterbury to face the boys of King's School in a Saturday afternoon cross-country over 4.75 miles. The home side was proudly hosting this fixture on its recently-acquired sportsfields near the city centre. Alfred Wooderson won and scrawny Sydney was a creditable 12th, a position that saw him beat a number of older and more experienced runners.

Almost exactly a year later, Sutton Valence welcomed the same opponents to their own fields for a midweek fixture, and although Alfred inevitably won again as the home side dominated, this time Sydney was an impressive fifth. The following Wednesday a local steeplechase course of 5.5 miles was set up for Sutton Valence pupils; Alfred drew away from the rest after the first water jump and won comfortably in 31:45 while Sydney overcame the demanding conditions to finish a plucky sixth. The annual School Sports followed in April of 1930, the swansong of Alfred, who duly ended his school days by winning the individual challenge cup, having triumphed in the 440 yards, 880 yards (2:09) and mile (4:49.8). The grass track was wet and runners buffeted by strong winds, but Sydney ran well to take third in both the 880 and the mile. Alfred would make his very last appearance in school colours a few days later, an impressive third at the Public Schools Championships at Stamford Bridge.

Pat Carslaw, one of Sydney's contemporaries at school, reminisced from his Oxfordshire home many years later about life at Sutton Valence alongside the Wooderson boys:

> "Sydney was a small, skinny junior in 1930 when I knew him. His elder brother was in the rugby XV with me, and both were good runners. Sydney's potential was noticed at an early age by our then music master Dr Russell, himself an Oxbridge long-distance blue. Thanks to Dr Russell, Sydney was prevented from competing with the seniors until properly mature, although he could have beaten most of them even when he was junior."

The School's archivist and historian David Pickard confirms that Dr Studley Leslie Lane Russell was music teacher from 1924 until 1934, throughout Sydney's school life, and also coached athletics. Russell, born 1901, had attended Christ Church, Oxford, where he was awarded the half-Blue for fives and athletics – this in addition to distinguished achievements in music, studying under Ralph Vaughan Williams and Malcolm Sargeant. Russell's astute assessment that little Sydney must not be rushed or pressurised into competing with older boys – despite his obvious potential – seems with hindsight to have been wise and effective, for Sydney's emergence as a top runner during schooldays was a steady and well-managed process. Russell knew he had a fine runner on his hands after testing Sydney's pace judgement: "Go and run a lap in 65 seconds," he told the boy, who promptly did exactly that without the aid of wristwatch, stop-watch or anything else.

Alfred Wooderson had undoubtedly been top dog until he departed in summer 1930, but from that point Sydney quickly blossomed into the school's best-ever runner. Academically, by his own admission, Sydney was "only average", and even failed his School Certificate first time round, but he would emerge from Alfred's shadow and exceed his brother's sporting achievements. By the time he was 16, Sydney had shed the role of plucky little runner-up and was winning things. A lightning-fast finish became his trademark and few could match him over any distance, although younger

Sydney, around the time he started at Sutton Valence School.

brother Stanley and the likes of Peter Barnett and Fenton Nunn did their utmost.

His development as a racer was clearly evident on the cool, bright afternoon of Monday 23 February 1931 when he represented the School in one of their regular matches with senior club side Blackheath Harriers. Visiting runner Adams won the contest across 5.5 miles of the Weald of Kent, but Sydney was an impressive third, pipping none other than elder brother Alfred, who was wearing Blackheath colours that day.

It was the first time Sydney had beaten his sibling in a serious race. It caused a stir at the Blackheath club, who published a glowing report in their *Gazette* newsletter, calling it "The surprise of the match." They noted the immense potential displayed by the tiny figure of Sydney and vowed to keep tabs on him. Inevitably he followed in his brother's footsteps and joined the club later in 1931. As if to underline the psychological importance of beating Alfred, Sydney went on to record outright victory in a proper race for the very first time just a fortnight later.

This landmark occasion was the annual school steeplechase – not a race for shrinking violets. Saturday 7 March was bitterly cold, with fierce easterly winds adding to the discomfort. Ironically that very same morning, the Amateur Athletic Association (AAA) general committee met in central London and one of the motions passed was to allow for the first time the wearing of sleeveless vests at all athletics events henceforth! Meanwhile, on the undulating fields south of Maidstone, Sydney and his schoolmates tackled the gruelling 5.5 miles of fences, mud and ditches, Sydney triumphing by a mere four seconds in 32:29. Poor Peter Barnett, pipped a year earlier by Alfred, now had to concede glory to the younger Wooderson too.

Emboldened by his steeplechase win, Sydney took centre stage at the schools' annual sports later the same month, competing in four different races. He won the lot and was the inevitable recipient of the cup for outstanding senior athlete. He was clocked at 11 seconds dead in winning the 100 yards dash, 57 seconds to win the 440 yards, 2:14 in the 880 yards and 4:56 for a very narrow mile victory. In each of the latter two events he pipped Geoffrey Nops, the opening batsman of the school's cricket team.

Sydney Wooderson had well and truly arrived at the age of 16. His sensational sequence of five wins out of five races during March 1931 raised his profile at school and naturally he represented Sutton Valence at the following month's prestigious Public Schools championships in London.

This annual, two-day event was at the huge Stamford Bridge stadium, a venue in the twilight of its era as the nation's athletics HQ. The AAA had recently decided to move out of Stamford Bridge to the White City Stadium less than four miles away in West London at the beginning of 1932. White City had been built for the 1908 Olympic Games but was mainly a greyhound racing venue until the AAA moved in and built a new quarter-mile running track. This was much-needed as Stamford Bridge's cinder circuit was by now suffering serious damage from the recently-introduced sport of speedway.

The Stamford Bridge that greeted Sydney in spring 1931 was of course a world away from the stadium we see in the 21st century. On an almost daily basis, matchday or not, football fans from near and far with rucksacks and ill-fitting jeans wander the concourse that encircles the ground, agog at the ostentatious display of wealth and glamour that is Chelsea Football Club. There's a megastore, a museum, restaurants and a luxury hotel to gawp at.

When Sydney arrived here in 1931 along with hundreds of teenage contemporaries, things were somewhat different. The 12-acre site had nothing to amuse or entertain tourists, indeed it was imposing enough to generate waves of fear and nervous tension in those about to perform here. The magnificent gloom of the huge Brompton Cemetery, right next door, won't have helped in this regard. Sydney must have been filled with nerves; he'd experienced nothing like this before, and was running competitively for the very first time outside of the school environment in peaceful Kent.

The whole two-day episode would prove quite an ordeal for such a greenhorn. The posh boys from other parts of Britain proved tougher nuts to crack than the opposition Sydney was used to. Most of them oozed the confidence that comes with a privileged upbringing, and most looked physically far superior to him, particularly those who were older. Take Lord John Hope, for example. This lanky figure, two years older than Sydney, roared to a spectacular record-breaking win in the half-mile, cheered on by fellow Etonians among the big crowd. This was a man who would later become a Major in the Scots Guards and cabinet minister in Harold MacMillan's government.

Conditions were relatively good on the opening day, Friday 17 April, sunshine making up for a brisk breeze that was of serious hindrance to the sprinters. The track had been rolled firmly following two days of speedway and held together well, with the heats of the mile providing the highlights of the day's racing. Sydney was among the younger and less experienced runners and it showed when he tackled his heat. Reports suggest he ran a poorly-judged race and qualified for Saturday's final only by the skin of his teeth, thanks to a desperate late sprint that brought him home seconds behind Tony Leach of Oundle (4:46.4). More than 500 excited boys had assembled for the championships but by 6pm on the Friday more than 300 had had their hopes shattered by defeat in the heats. Sydney's ability to finish strongly meant he wasn't one of them.

The correspondent of *The Times* dropped a clanger by reporting that Sydney had come third in the 1930 final a year earlier – when this was actually his elder brother Alfred. Believing Sydney to be more experienced than he was may explain the criticism he dished out in his report: he accused Sydney of running with poor judgement and being lucky to make the final. He was full of praise however for Samuel of Watford Grammar who won Heat Four with economy and panache and didn't need to scramble wildly like Sydney. This was Sydney's first coverage in the national press, and he was unlucky to be taken to task like this considering he was an unknown underdog who'd reached a final!

Stamford Bridge was not a cheerful place to be on the Saturday afternoon when the various finals were staged. There was a bitterly cold wind, the track cut up early on, and torrential rain made conditions thoroughly miserable. Wearing No.16 and an all-white kit of T-shirt and flapping shorts, it was easy to pick Sydney out as one of the youngest and smallest competitors involved. He and fellow four-lappers set off briskly in the race to become Public Schools mile champion. Pretty (Winchester) led off fast over the first quarter, pursued by More (Herbert Strutt, Belper). The strain soon began to show and poor More subsequently collapsed – exhausted by the effort of running two different events on the same day, a gamble various officials had advised him not to take. Pretty maintained his lead, passing halfway in 2 mins 13 secs with Samuel at his heels and the rest looking out of contention. Samuel made his bid for glory 220 yards from the end and for a while they were neck and neck. Samuel always looked the smoother and Pretty caved in 20 yards from home, Samuel winning in 4:37.4, the fourth-best time in the championship's 35-year history. Sydney was never in contention and came home buffeted by the wind in a rain-soaked sixth place.

Back at Sutton Valence, with spring underway, running was off the curriculum for another year and the school's sporting focus turned to other pursuits like cricket and rugby. The boys were expected to do their bit for the school on the rugby field and although Sydney possessed natural speed, he clearly had few of the other physical attributes normally required for the oval ball game. However, this was not necessarily viewed as a problem – indeed, school numbers in the 1930s were such that pupils were apparently told to take part, whether they liked it or not! Even if Sydney wasn't at home amid the crunching tackles he evidently didn't shirk his responsibilities, and before long would be awarded 2nd XV colours.

Around now, Sydney needed to turn away from sport and focus on getting through his School Certificate exams. The UK School Certificate, established in 1918 and later scrapped in favour of GCE 'O' levels, involved achieving one of four grades in the various subjects on the curriculum – fail, pass, credit or distinction. In his Lower Sixth year Sydney failed to get the six passes needed to obtain a certificate. He was able in 1932 to retake the subjects he failed, and this time made the grade. David Pickard, School archivist, says:

> "I think Sydney was being modest when he said he was only an average student. It is not clear how well he did. A 'pass' was great – he did that at least. A 'credit' in six subjects was enough to allow one to apply for University two years later – admission in those days was by interview and fees had to be paid either out of own pocket or through scholarships. He didn't go to University, but given his athletics prowess, I suggest he would have been a shoo-in for Oxbridge but possibly cost may have been a problem."

By the time the 1931–2 winter cross-country season was looming, Sydney's thoughts had turned back to competitive running and in the December he and Stanley followed in the footsteps of older brother Alfred by becoming fully signed up members of Blackheath Harriers. The club's minute books reveal that the young brothers were proposed by Alfred at a committee meeting on a mild evening in central London on Monday 14 December 1931. They were accepted, along with three other new faces, during business conducted at the Devereux Hotel in Essex Street, off the Strand, an ancient tavern with an upstairs function room where the committee often met.

Nicknamed 'The Heathens', Blackheath was a lively club with 62 years of history, formed initially as 'Peckham Hare and Hounds', later 'Peckham Athletic Club' before taking the Blackheath name after settling at the Green Man hotel as their HQ in 1878. By now they were based in Hayes – around seven miles from Sydney's childhood home in Camberwell. They established this HQ in 1926 in Bourne Way at premises purchased for £850, which would become home for many decades to come. The club's strong links and long-standing friendly relationship with Sutton Valence School meant Sydney's recruitment was a natural fit.

Club members wore distinctive all-black shorts and singlet for competition and membership had risen to beyond 700 in the 1930s (more than 400 ordinary members and 300 lifers), including a talented raft of sprinters and middle-distance specialists. They had at least 10 men on the books who could run half-a-mile in under 2:02, which was a classy time for that era. Ahead of the 1932 season, Sydney's first with the club, the captain Harold Smith issued a determined rallying call, urging clubmates to build on the renaissance since the end of the 1914–18 war. Smith will have noted the potential of new recruit Sydney, but cannot have imagined just what a diamond they had unearthed, or that this skinny little beginner would one day be hailed 'The Greatest Heathen of Them All.'

3

One of the Dark Places

WITH the nearby QE2 Bridge barely visible in early morning haze, I slipped off the A206 skirting Dartford and headed down a scruffy pot-holed lane, past ugly piles of random fly-tipping, and down towards the southern banks of the River Thames.

It's a bleak and gloomy part of the world, a place that proves a lack of traffic and buildings doesn't always signify tranquility and a pleasant aspect. Referring to this area, novelist Joseph Conrad, a local resident, once wrote: "This has been one of the dark places of the earth."

But there was a welcome splash of colour across this grim landscape on a cloudy January day in 1932. Long lines of runners in the Kent Cross-country Championships headed down here from high on Temple Hill in the town – a spot near the main railway station – circuited the levels near the river and raced back up again, the course going past the huge riverside Joyce Green Hospital.

A recent outbreak of smallpox in the London area had seen an influx of patients at the hospital's isolation unit. It would be nice to think the poor souls suffering from the East End's worst contagions that winter would have had their day brightened by glimpsing the runners outside.

These semi-remote Dartford marshes were seen by the authorities as an ideal distance from London to house isolation wards and asylums; the perfect place for the treatment of madness and the pox. There was even a jetty for 'plague ships' to offload the latest victims. Likewise, the testing and varied open terrain was also perfect for cross-country racing.

This stop on my tour of Sydney Wooderson's race venues was, to put it delicately, rather an unprepossessing place, but a very significant location in the development of Sydney's career. It was effectively the place where his blossoming talent was seen for the first time by the great and good of the Kent running scene.

Sydney ran in the junior championship race that day, Saturday 9 January 1932, a tiny, skinny 17-year-old nervously tackling his first county-level event. Still at school, he'd only been on Blackheath Harriers' books a few weeks, and here on the edge of Dartford was keen to make a good impression on his new clubmates.

The racing took place mainly across the fields of Littlebrook Farm and there was a healthy increase in numbers compared to the previous year's races. Eleven senior teams fielded 116 runners while a further 43 youngsters lined up for Sydney's race. The headline act was the team representing the 2nd Battalion 'The Buffs' (East Kent Regiment) from Shorncliffe, who lifted the Kent title by turning the tables on holders Blackheath.

Slightly lower down the bill, Sydney provided an impressive spectacle for those spectators keeping an eye on the junior race. In his three-mile event he showed good judgement by keeping a watchful eye on runners just ahead as they trudged along under overcast skies and the relentless chilly wind coming off the Thames. He gathered himself as they went into the final circuit and headed back up towards the finish. The terrain was tricky, but Sydney smoothly maintained a pace below six-minutes-per-mile. He moved up strongly in the latter stages and once he'd grabbed the lead there was only one winner.

Crossing the line in 17:29 to take the county junior title was a significant milestone in Sydney's career. His only previous cross-country victories had been closed school events – never before had he won an open race against lads from other clubs and schools. Having now paraded his talent to county officials, today would represent one of the last occasions he could turn up for a race and enjoy the undisturbed anonymity of being unknown. Sydney was no longer merely a talented schoolboy, but an emerging force on a wider stage.

★★★

The Weald of Kent cross-country course used by his school – a scenic but tough five-and-a-half miles – was the venue for successive races in

February and March of 1932. In a match with Blackheath, it was decided Sydney should represent his school not his club, and he duly came second, 40 seconds behind Heathens captain Harold Smith, who won in 31:38. Significantly, he beat elder brother Alfred, representing Blackheath, by eight seconds, the latter tying with teammate Shee for third. A week later on Wednesday 27 February, the school welcomed Oxford Hare and Hounds and this time Sydney took second spot in 31:04, his fast time smashing his elder brother's school record for the familiar Weald route. There was a bit more brotherly love about his performance ten days later: he and younger sibling Stanley cruised across the line side by side to jointly win the annual school steeplechase with ease.

The going wasn't quite so straightforward on Putney Heath on the afternoon of Saturday 19 March, however. Sydney's chances in the Ranelagh Cup competition for public schools were badly hampered by a cut foot, sustained in a fall when he'd been well placed. He recovered to finish, but had to be content with sixth place and a time more than a minute slower than winner Etheridge (Hurstpierpoint College). Just over 100 runners took part and Hurstpierpoint triumphed comfortably in the 16-team contest, Sutton Valence down in eighth.

Sydney didn't neglect his academic work at this time and during 1932 passed his School Certificate at the second attempt and entered the sixth form at Sutton Valence. This meant becoming a boarder in Westminster House, whom he represented at rugby in addition to his running endeavours.

The annual school sports in late March proved slightly less successful than a year earlier for Sydney, but he still captured two titles, winning the 880 yards in 2:09 from George Nops and the mile in a relatively gentle 4:54 from brother Stanley. He was beaten by Fenton Nunn (11.0 secs) in the 100 yards and chose not to run the 440 this year.

Meanwhile, 1932 was proving an important one for athletics in general. The British Amateur Athletic Board (BAAB) was formed to replace the AAA as the British representation at the world governing body, the IAAF. Athletes were generally taking the sport more seriously than before; the end of the road was getting ever closer for those casual upper-class gentleman amateurs who found it distasteful to train hard or be seen to be making an effort. White City began staging the AAA champs and other key events, and as the 1930s marched on, international meetings were introduced as opposed to simple international matches. White City's brand new cinder track was in use by the start of the 1932 season and the revamped stadium also hosted QPR home matches, Rugby League and major British boxing events (90,000 would squeeze in to see Len Harvey fight Jack Petersen).

For Sydney, a first visit to the new home of athletics would have to wait, as his April 1932 date at the Public Schools championships was again fixed for Stamford Bridge. He returned there – stronger, faster and with more experience – to find the occasion once again marred by dreadful weather, the heavy rain dampening the natural enthusiasm of the hordes of young visitors both on the track and up in the stands.

In his mile heat on Friday 1 April, Sydney qualified for the final by coming second – his time unrecorded – to Sullivan of Shrewsbury (4:39.4) with a minimum of fuss. For the final the next day, Sydney appeared out of nowhere to produce his trademark finishing burst on the home straight, but narrowly failed to catch Sullivan again, this time missing out by barely 12 inches. He was travelling far faster than his rival as they crossed the line, but had mistimed that final sprint by less than half-a-second. Sullivan was given a time of 4:34.4 with Sydney two-tenths behind in the silver medal position and a personal best to boot.

It was a gallant effort, but gained him little media attention as most reporters chose to concentrate on the fact the championships were the first anywhere to try "an ingenious new invention" – a starting gate for sprint races. This device was designed to prevent false starts and involved a barrier of white tape designed to fly upwards and outwards when triggered simultaneously with the starter's pistol.

Its inventor, a Cambridge professor of engineering called Henry Rottenburg, had arrived an hour before the first race to set it up and it attracted huge attention. But, embarrassingly, the new equipment had to be hastily withdrawn for safety reasons after just two attempts to use it. Quarter-miler Elliott (Oundle School) got his neck tangled in tape and nearly throttled himself – so it was back to the drawing board for the professor.

Following those red faces at Stamford Bridge, it would be Sydney's turn to feel embarrassed when his next serious outing came along – the Kent track and field championships at Woolwich Stadium on Saturday 11 June 1932. His moment of calamity occurred at his very first competitive appearance in Blackheath club colours. The story goes that he was leading the junior mile race on this hot afternoon, but made a catastrophic miscalculation and thought he'd finished after only doing three laps, so stopped and stepped off the track, presuming he'd won. Officials disqualified him and a surprised Tommy Macoy (Aylesford Paper Mills) won the race, five yards clear of Blackheath's Derek Reynolds.

Clearly 17-year-old novice Sydney had a lot to learn about maintaining concentration during a track race, but it's reasonable to assume the other successes of the day by Blackheath ensured his personal disaster didn't live long in the collective memory. Not only did Blackheath win the team prize in Sydney's race anyway, they also had cause for celebration when sprinter Les Parkes was announced to have run 9.7 seconds in the 100 yards, thus equalling the ten-year-old British record set by Eric Liddell. It was subsequently not ratified for record purposes due to a following wind, but still underlined Parkes' supremacy, being one of five successive county title wins he achieved in the 1930s.

Having passed his 18th birthday in August 1932, Sydney's final year at school saw him serve as Honorary Secretary of the athletics section, in addition to winning the school's senior athletics cup jointly with sprinter Fenton Nunn. Added to this he'd also set new records for the Public School mile and Sutton Valence's mile and half-mile. He was awarded his athletics colours in 1933 along with two fellow school-leavers, his brother Stanley and R. D. McCorkindale.

Will Radford, Alumni Relations and Development Officer at Sutton Valence, says Sydney's seven-year stint at the school ended in April 1933, explaining that terms back then were far less structured than now, meaning it was quite common for pupils to start and finish at random times of the year. Shortly before his departure Sydney signed off his last cross-country season as a schoolboy with a brilliant series of four victories in just three weeks.

On Saturday 18 February he won the annual match between the school and a Blackheath team – covering the familiar 5.5-mile course in 33:25, some 15 seconds clear of all opposition. Five days later he showed he could cope with appalling conditions by winning a match with Wye College on the same Weald of Kent course, which was not only seriously muddy, but included patches of snow. Out again on Saturday 4 March for the annual school steeplechase, he claimed victory number three. The quartet of fine wins was in the bag seven days later at the annual inter-schools cross-country hosted by Blackheath over 3.5 miles in the Hayes Common area. They set off at 3.30pm with 23 teams battling it out in mild, bright conditions perfect for running. Burch of Haberdashers' Aske School gave Sydney a run for his money and led until the final run-in, where Sydney gathered himself and accelerated smoothly past, opening a gap of 30 yards by the line. He and Burch finished well clear and victory gained Sydney a large silver medal for his growing collection. The visiting schoolboys, numbering over 100, were then invited into the Bourne Way clubhouse where a bumper free tea was provided in two sittings.

And so an era came to an end when Sutton Valence's annual school sports were staged over two days at the end of March 1933, exactly a week prior to Sydney bidding his schooldays farewell. Sydney's predictable victories at 880 yards and the mile (2:11 and 4:42.8) were matched by a trio of wins for Fenton Nunn in the 100 yards, 440 yards and sprint hurdles, meaning the school decided the pair of them should share the cup for outstanding senior athlete.

The Wooderson brothers' departure from school in the spring signalled a move back into London for the immediate family, who were able to return to their former home at 7 Calais Street, Camberwell. Given his love of the countryside, Sydney must have been sad to leave Brookside in Chart Sutton, but this attractive property would stay in the family for a while longer with his half-sister Rhoda, her husband Christopher and their daughter Mary moving in and staying until late 1934 when it was sold on.

Although Sydney is recorded as officially leaving school on Monday 3 April 1933, his schooldays were effectively concluded later that month with his third and final appearance at the Public School championships, this time staged at the White City stadium. He banished memories of previous defeats by storming to victory in a world class mile time of 4:29.8, this personal best making him the first schoolboy on record to beat the 4:30 barrier. His late surge for the line climaxed an intense and absorbing battle with 15-year-old Denis Pell (Chatham House) which even featured a momentary stumble on the final lap. As Sydney broke the tape ten yards clear in first place he raised his hands to shoulder level – to avoid entanglement with the tape rather than a flamboyant victory gesture – and his head lolled back in exhaustion. Wearing No.27 and an all-white kit, Sydney was hoisted shoulder-high by jubilant schoolmates and it was clear that in this scrawny, bespectacled lad Britain had found a potential world champion.

Runner-up Pell also gained plenty of attention for his game showing that day, for at 15 he was younger and far less experienced than most, but clearly another miler of huge potential. As we shall see, this wouldn't be the last time Sydney enjoyed a battle royal with Pell.

Chaired shoulder-high after becoming first schoolboy on record to run a mile under 4:30.

4

Into the Big Wide World

WITH his 19th birthday a few months away, Sydney finally had to prepare himself for the big, wide outside world. It must have been quite a fearsome prospect for a shy young man. It was a world suffering at the height of the Great Depression, Hitler had just been appointed Chancellor of Germany and disturbing events were taking place under Nazi rule. The film King Kong made its debut in New York and the first sighting of a 'monster' had occurred beside Loch Ness.

Blessed with a respectable family and good educational background, Sydney was able to secure a job with prospects in the City of London. He began work at the offices of Keene, Marsland, Bryden and Besant, a well-established firm of solicitors based at 15 Seething Lane, EC3, a short walk from the Tower of London. He was taken on as an articled law clerk – effectively a five-year commitment as a trainee solicitor. It was a new direction for a Wooderson, as most of his immediate male relatives were in the family fruit and veg business.

For several centuries, being a solicitor had been a solid and respectable profession in its own right in which men worked in partnership with each other. It had become customary for new junior entrants like Sydney to work under them as articled clerks, learning the ropes and becoming formally qualified while contracted for a certain time. This career path steered them towards becoming a partner themselves. Many of the runners Sydney would be racing against around this time – particularly those from the north – would not have had such a settled and stable working life.

Under Ramsey Macdonald's premiership the country was bruised and battered by the worldwide economic depression and mass unemployment hit a shocking peak of 25 per cent exactly at the point Sydney left school in 1933.

After seven idyllic years, Sydney now had to swap the bucolic surrounds of school for a daily rail commute into the smoky financial heart of London. Like many other young men of the 1930s he would need to visit one of the growing chain of stores run by Burton or Horne Brothers, be measured up for a £3 suit, or maybe save time and a few shillings by going for one of the ready-to-wear off-the-peg numbers that were growing in popularity in London clothing shops. Accessories such as a bowler hat, brief case and umbrella would also be *de rigueur* in his new world.

It was a radical change of lifestyle and for much of 1933 athletics would have to take a back seat. In these early days as a working man, Sydney's world centred on Seething Lane, a busy little thoroughfare that had escaped the Great Fire of London by literally a few yards. Most of the medieval buildings in this street had survived deterioration into slum status thanks to renovations and modernisation. They were in the hands of agents, accountants, brokers and solicitors who serviced the new commercial aristocracy that was taking over from the old land-owning one.

As he settled into his new routine, Sydney's only recorded appearance in competitive athletics over a ten-month period would be his home debut in Blackheath colours, a club meet at the Catford Bridge track on Wednesday 12 July. On a fine evening, the club's under-19 members competed over 880 yards for the Howard Cup. In a dramatic finish Sydney couldn't quite overhaul R. H. Dark as they hurtled for the line, and lost out by a mere four-fifths of a second and no more than two feet. It was nevertheless an impressive track debut for the club and his time of 2:06 at age 19 showed massive potential.

These were exciting times for Blackheath Harriers. The big stars in The Heathens ranks, ahead of emerging talent like Sydney, included sprinters Charles Wiard, Les Parkes and Ernie Page, triple and long jumper Jack Butler, and 880 yards specialist John Poole. As the 1930s unfolded, Blackheath would become a very strong outfit at sprints and middle-distance – definitely one of the clubs to beat.

★★★

Up until this point, the world of amateur athletics had only produced two truly consummate milers – Englishman Walter George and Finland's Paavo Nurmi. But by the end of 1933 a new era was unfolding, the likes of Jack Lovelock, Luigi Beccali and Glenn Cunningham emerging as major mile talents. Was there anybody, a promising youngster perhaps, lurking in a backwater somewhere, who could soon be flying the flag at top level for Great Britain?

Sydney Wooderson, far too modest to acknowledge the fact, had shown enough raw talent already to suggest he might fit that bill. As the new year of 1934 got underway Sydney's life was dominated by other priorities, but nevertheless he must have been itching to do some serious running again. His last race had been six months earlier.

Making his way as the new boy in a busy solicitor's office, a greenhorn among the city slickers, will have been a stressful transitionary period. Running was a perfect antidote to all that and now that he was considered an adult member at Blackheath he could start to make a real name for himself. He'd already outshone most of the running achievements of talented elder brother Alfred and although all three Wooderson brothers were now on the club's books, Sydney looked the one with the most potential. Looking back at early adulthood he recalled: "At work I never got time off to train. I used to come home at six and train then. In the winter I ran round the streets in flannel trousers and a pullover."

He may have messed up on his cross-country debut for the club, but he was by now a little older and wiser and it was starting to look as if he could produce the goods outside the cloistered and less intimidating surroundings of school. Sydney's general demeanour and quiet nature did little to suggest confidence or a winning mentality, but people were beginning to take notice nonetheless.

Although Blackheath in the 1930s had no controlled policy or strategy for chasing success, the club did possess what its historians describe as many highly competent athletes "of the second and third rank". British athletics in general was said to be happily disorganised and very amateur around this time, but that didn't prevent Blackheath employing a part-time coach who made it his business to try and get the best out of young starlet Sydney.

This coach had been in place since the mid-1920s and was a man who had performed himself at the very highest level. Double Olympic champion Albert Hill was a London railwayman by trade, who won 800- and 1500-metres gold at the Antwerp games back in 1920 – a superb and largely under-appreciated achievement, particularly as he'd triumphed aged 31 when thought to be past his best.

Hill had turned to coaching in his mid-thirties, initially as assistant to Sam Mussabini, the famed senior coach at Polytechnic Harriers. Hill spent many hours at track sessions at Battersea Park and later Paddington and White City guiding the Poly runners – ace sprinter Jack London in particular – and with Blackheath using these same venues it had been only a matter of months before they too recruited Hill's services. Nobody seemed worried about a possible conflict of interests.

Eventually, though, Hill would part company with Poly – a stint not without the odd pay dispute – and began to concentrate on working with Blackheath who valued him highly. Hill's day job on London's sooty railways brought in barely £3 per week and he needed the coaching money to support his family. He was not a wealthy man, despite his status as a double Olympic champion. Indeed, Sydney later spoke of Hill taking night-shifts at W.H.Smith, sorting newspapers for distribution, to help make ends meet.

Hill was always a popular figure at Blackheath, taking an active interest in dozens of runners' progress and needs as membership soared past 600 in the 1930s. He contributed greatly to the development of talented sprinters like Page, Wiard and Parkes as well as devoting plenty of time to Sydney's emerging middle-distance talents.

According to his biographer Greg Moon, Hill had an ambivalent attitude to running style. Although he'd worked hard on improving his own style when competing, as a coach he opted to do very little to alter Sydney's natural action. He would occasionally point out that Sydney's high-swinging arms didn't do him any favours, but generally allowed natural style free rein.

Hill wisely chose not to hurry things along with Sydney, despite the early promise and obvious potential. He wanted the frail-looking lad to gain strength and experience at a steady rate in order for his natural talent to bear fruit. This patient outlook would, of course, subsequently work beautifully and Sydney began regarding Hill as something akin to a kindly uncle:

> "I think with other runners he was a bit more strict, but because I was rather slightly-built I think he was afraid of giving me too much hard training and was sort of feeling his way himself as to how much training I could take."

Over time Hill became recognised as Sydney's guide, philosopher and friend, and would be remembered by the runner as a very equable character, quite unflappable, never bad-tempered or aggressive. He would play a major role in selecting which races Sydney entered and how he approached them tactically. Sydney told journalist David Thurlow years later:

> "Without [Hill] at the start I would not have achieved what I did. In those early days I had no idea what to do and I owe him a great deal. He put me on the right lines and that is what a coach should do. You need a coach in the early days to instil into you what you should do and then you should be left on your own to carry out your training."

Hill, it seems, judged perfectly what Sydney did and didn't need from a coach. Consequently he didn't spend hours trying to improve Sydney's confidence or mental approach, never ranted and raved at him, nor bored or intimidated him with endless tales of his own triumphs either side of the 1914–18 War. The two men mostly met twice a week for training and a quiet chat, and rarely saw each other away from the track.

Training was usually on Monday and Thursday evenings at Battersea Park or Paddington tracks, doing workouts that seem light by today's standards and rarely involved modern staples like intervals and repetitions. A typical session would often involve a single set-piece of a timed 660 yards or three-quarter mile, and Sydney would rarely go home in a state of exhaustion, even though he'd done a full-day's work beforehand. Winter weeks would rarely exceed 20 miles despite the heavy demands of cross-country racing. Sydney reflected:

> "What training I did, I thought was more than most people did. But of course compared with the training of today it was very little and therefore I could combine my work and my racing and the training."

Sydney's quiet personality and his light training loads might have hinted at a lack of toughness, but this was clearly not the case at all – as evidenced by his gritty showings in cross-country contests throughout his career. His opening fixture of 1934 was his debut for Blackheath in a club match away from the track, and it was staged on a pig of day.

Temperatures plummeted well below freezing across the London region after nightfall on Friday February 2. Hayes Common and local pathways were still frozen solid by the time the race between Blackheath and the Dulwich public schoolboys from Alleyn's got underway the following morning. To make matters worse, fog descended on the region too – serious enough to halt ships on the Thames and planes coming into Croydon Aerodrome.

It proved a close and bone-chilling contest over the five-mile course. Although hosts Blackheath packed four men in the first five, the school team had more strength in depth and won the team event by ten points. Sydney and his clubmate Stan Bliss ran side by side at the head of the field for virtually the entire race, crossing the line five seconds ahead of Alleyn's leading runner Atkinson, to claim joint-first in 34:06.

At this point, still six months short of his 20th birthday, the bespectacled Sydney was barely five-and-a-half feet tall and weighed less than nine stones (1.68m/56kg), meaning he still looked deceptively frail. This perception was enhanced by the short-sightedness which forced him to wear glasses at all times, including when running. His appearance gave a false impression that would be remarked upon throughout his career. Typical were the words of famed sprinter, broadcaster and official Harold Abrahams, who called him: "A tiny figure… buffeted and almost apologising for occupying any space at all… the last person you would pick out as a king among milers."

Sydney may have looked delicate, but it was a ferocious frailness – as he proved again later in February when Blackheath visited his old school Sutton Valence for a five-mile match across the familiar scenic slopes south of Maidstone. There was mayhem at the finish, four runners including Sydney finishing together in a melee at the head of the race. A report in *The Times* gave the four men as equal-first, but others recorded Sydney and his younger brother Stanley with the same time (33:58), a single second behind their Blackheath colleagues Furness and Slater. The verdict didn't matter too much, for only pride was at stake as opposed to glittering prizes, and the nearest school opponent was 15 seconds adrift anyway. The finish-line drama underlined how Sydney certainly possessed the courage and spirit to mix it with bigger opponents when the occasion demanded.

There was plenty of severe weather during February 1934 and it wasn't only Sydney and his running mates clocking up the miles in snow, freezing fog and other extreme conditions. The misery inflicted by the worldwide depression was showing no signs of ending and thousands of poverty-stricken members of the National Unemployed Workers Movement spent most of the month marching from their home towns to converge on London's Hyde Park. A massive rise in unemployment had seen the work of the NUWM intensify and this was one of several 'hunger marches'. Sydney could be thankful his education and background had won him a secure-looking job, for more than three million Britons were out of work by now, and many lads of his age were struggling to make something of their lives.

5

Shock for Lovelock

TRACKS were dusty and sports fields scorched bone-dry by the time Sydney Wooderson returned to competitive action in summer 1934 wearing the all-black Blackheath kit. England was suffering its worst drought for at least 80 years but the heat and parched conditions on the afternoon of Saturday 9 June didn't prevent Sydney making the biggest breakthrough yet in his adult running career.

He'd already got himself noticed with various junior and schools titles, but this would be the day the athletics world really sat up and took notice of the little fellow in glasses from Camberwell.

It was certainly not the best of conditions for a gala athletics meeting in the grim heart of industrial Belvedere, beside the busy River Thames. Sydney was here to make his debut at the annual Kent AAA county championships and, two months short of his 20th birthday, would be up against the region's best men for the first time. His inexperience, the heat, pollution and generally unattractive surroundings didn't bode well – but our hero was undaunted and not only pulled out a personal best time to win the county mile title, he smashed the all-time Kent record by two seconds.

Hosting the big day was the sportsground that British Insulated Callender's Cables (BICC) had provided for its employees, adjacent to their huge riverside factory. Sydney emerged from the wooden pavilion that day still pretty much an unknown quantity. His appearance would certainly not have struck much fear into his opposition. But, less than five minutes later, a star had been born.

What was becoming his trademark late finishing burst won him the Kent mile crown in 4:27.8 by a three-yard margin, holding off the fierce challenge of Belgrave Harriers duo Jordan and Shaw. This pair could hardly believe they'd managed to break the seven-year-old Kent record set by R. D. Bell, yet had still been beaten by a young upstart weighing less than nine stones and wearing enormous baggy shorts.

Sydney's clubmates were jubilant, slapping him on the back and agreeing he'd been the star turn of the entire day's sport. Although the Thames was just a few yards away, the air on this hot day was thick and oppressive, making Sydney's run all the more noteworthy and because of his tender age it overshadowed six other county records set that afternoon.

It was Sydney's first senior title and signalled his readiness to start challenging for more honours in the world of men's athletics. Next up would be the even more prestigious Southern Championships, just three weeks hence in Guildford. As the new Kent champion and record-holder, Sydney would be expected to be there. He wasn't the type to jump impetuously to a level beyond his ability, but coach Hill was no fool and was happy for Sydney to run at Guildford, so that was all he needed to hear.

Blackheath were doing well as a club by this point, featuring prominently in league and regional meetings in many different disciplines. The terrier-like performances of young Sydney became a major feature of some memorable days out for the Heathens. Proudly they spoke of their boy having an outside chance of representing England soon, maybe even at the forthcoming Empire Games. It all seemed a tad over the top to begin with, but what unfolded on the track at Guildford on Saturday 30 June would validate all the optimism.

The Kent championships had been a stern test for a new boy, and Sydney hadn't been found wanting. His summer baptism would only get more fiery at Guildford three weeks later. The field contesting the Southern mile was large but strong in quality. British and recently-deposed world record holder, the popular New Zealander Jack Lovelock, was running and this guaranteed major media interest. A crowd of around 5,000 in their summer finery squeezed into the Woodbridge Road county cricket ground to watch proceedings.

Star attraction Lovelock was in his final year as a medical student at Oxford and currently working his way back to full fitness before the AAA championships and Empire Games, both to be held at White City later in the summer. Knee trouble had required an operation the previous winter and the charismatic Kiwi had recently lost his world record (4:07.6) to Glenn Cunningham of the USA, who swept to 4:06.7 at Princeton, New Jersey. But Lovelock still had the fastest mile on British soil to his name (4:12 in May 1932 at Iffley Road, Oxford), which was a massive 15 seconds quicker than Sydney's new personal best of three weeks earlier.

This was the 12th annual Southern Championships, open to amateurs from any of the 23 counties between Pembroke and Norfolk and Cornwall and Kent, being staged at Guildford for the first time with a record entry of athletes. Under a scorching sun, the milers gathered at the start to find of the 40 who had registered, 12 had already dropped out, including 27-year-old title-holder and Olympian Reg Thomas. The 28 starters nevertheless included the nation's top eight men, according to PB times, and officials had to organise them into three rows to get some sort of order. None of the big names were placed in the front rank and a slow, crowded race looked likely even though the grass track was in fine condition and there was no appreciable wind.

After the pistol fired, the serious contenders starting at the rear found themselves boxed in and buffeted. Lovelock later described it "a hell of a scrum." A disjointed first lap saw Tomlin the only well-known runner able to get near the lead. First place at that point was held by Pearce with young Aubrey Reeve on his heels. A worried Lovelock was down in 12th. When Britain's 1932 Olympic 1500 metres medallist Jerry Cornes passed Lovelock, the Kiwi latched on and they made their way through the pack. Sydney was hidden by bigger men and ran most of the race unnoticed. Only by the halfway point had Pearce, Lovelock, and Horace Craske taken some sort of charge, hitting 880 yards in 2:07.4. As the third lap unfolded, Lovelock was relieved to establish a position on the inside lane without interference.

At the bell (3:14), Cornes seized the lead, with Lovelock on his heels and Reeve moving into third. However, the unrelenting sun and tiredness caught up with civil servant Cornes, who was well short of peak fitness having only recently arrived back in Britain from his Nigerian workplace. He simply ran out of steam with 220 yards to go. Reeve shot past him but Lovelock hesitated, expecting Cornes to recover and make a late burst which he could follow. Sydney was further back but most observers only had eyes on the front three. Reeve found he had a 12-yard lead going into the straight and only now did Lovelock realise his mistake and jerk himself into life, swinging past the flagging Cornes and giving chase.

Lovelock gained ground but had kicked too late and as he began to tire in the final few yards, Sydney suddenly appeared as if from nowhere and caught him inches from the line. Reeve had won by two yards but Sydney was runner-up by the width of his black vest from Lovelock. The trio crossed the line in a blur – less than half a second between the three of them – as the Guildford crowd roared its delight. Sydney and Lovelock were given the same time of 4:15.2, just four-tenths of a second behind Reeve. Astonishingly, two young Englishmen had beaten the great Lovelock!

Reeve's winning time of 4:14.8 had beaten Cornes' Southern record by more than two seconds and he and Wooderson had certainly conjured up the race of their young lives; 22-year-old Londoner Reeve had never gone under 4.20 before, whereas Sydney had slashed an incredible 12.2 seconds off his PB. It was a clocking that rocketed him into the all-time top ten British-born milers. The papers marvelled at all this and one reported: "[These two are] persevering lads, both will show further improvement yet, and they are coming along at the time when England needs milers of promise most."

Sydney had, for the first time, demonstrated his trademark fast finish on a national stage: "I was delighted to find I had enough speed in the home straight to snatch the verdict for second place from Lovelock," he told *World Sports* magazine. He was still only 19 and many years later would call this one of the best races of his life. He would reveal that the up-and-coming Reeve shared his own tendency towards bad nerves before big races:

> "Aubrey Reeve was a very nervous runner. He vomited before every race. In the tunnel leading from the dressing rooms to the track at White City there was a basin and he was always being sick in that before a race."

Events at Guildford created an interesting situation as regards British athletics fans' obvious affection for Lovelock. Although born and raised in New Zealand, he competed primarily as an Oxford student and as a champion miler was a product of English coaching methods. But would his popularity begin to wane now that the Brits had two young stars of their own in Wooderson and Reeve?

For his part, Lovelock was stunned, although not especially unhappy, over what had occurred. Given his fragile knee and the fact he'd only finished exams the day before the race, he'd expected a time of 4:19 would be enough to win at Guildford. He'd been delighted to run 4:15.2 in the circumstances – easily his fastest mile since coming back from surgery – but was also shocked this hadn't been enough to get him in the first two. He had felt "all in" after crossing the line and was violently sick, but pleased to find his knee hadn't become swollen or sore. In his journal he recalled:

> "This was a very, very hard race… it was the largest field I had ever been in and there seemed to be a jolly sight more than the 28 which the papers announced… there was a hell of a scrum at the start."

Naturally the mile proved the highlight of the day and, having been early in the timetable, led to many more noteworthy track and field performances feeling rather anti-climactic. Sydney's usual restrained and inscrutable demeanour after the race will have contrasted with that of his thrilled Blackheath colleagues and no doubt coach Hill was already mulling over how to best advise Sydney in advance of the even bigger test that loomed a fortnight hence – the 51st AAA championships at the White City.

It's fair to say that in the early 1930s the AAA's big day was, and had been for years, Europe's most prestigious athletics meeting. And here was the teenage Sydney Wooderson running its 'blue riband' mile in only his third appearance on a track since leaving school. It was a daunting scenario for one so raw and inexperienced.

As it turned out there would be plenty of tension and anticipation, but sadly precious little drama for the big crowd that gathered in west London. Just as the Southern thriller at Guildford had exceeded expectations, so the White City contest went the other way, a slow, tactical race lacking excitement and proving a drab anti-climax.

Sydney had run at White City some 15 months earlier at the Public Schools' event, but the AAA's weekend of July 13 and 14 was a totally different experience; the size of the crowd and sense of occasion this time made it feel like a different world. On the Friday evening the weather was pleasant and things went smoothly for the big names in the heats of the mile. Sydney's heat was first up, and he cruised to victory without problems, narrowly beating Frenchman Roger Normand and Londoner

Bernard Eeles. The lack of incident and fairly modest time of 4:21.4 was an ideal way to secure a place in the following day's final without undue exertion. Likewise for Lovelock, who quietly qualified in a later heat in an even slower time.

The day of the final dawned with ideal weather conditions and the papers were full of excited chatter about world record holder Lovelock and the challenge he was to face from Sydney, the up-and-coming British underdog. It was the first time such widespread pressure had been exerted on Sydney before a race. Only he would know what he was feeling inside, but to onlookers he seemed to be coping admirably.

Although Lovelock and Sydney would be able to hold their heads high after the race, there is no doubt the mile turned into the most disappointing event of the day. On paper the nine-man field had looked good enough to provide real fireworks, featuring the likes of Jerry Cornes, Aubrey Reeve and Hungary's Miklos Szabo. Sadly it became a real dawdle, a tactical battle that may have intrigued aficianados of miling but did nothing to excite the crowd. Once they had sorted themselves out in the first 50 yards or so, the runners almost came to a dead stop as all nine waited for someone else to take the initiative.

Cornes reluctantly made the pace in what one report called "a somewhat perfunctory manner" and stayed there untroubled until 150 yards to go. It was an uneventful procession and the only interest centred on who might suddenly make a break and spurt for home. The answer didn't come until the final stages when Lovelock hit the throttle just before the home straight and Cornes was unable to respond. Only Sydney made a genuine attempt to catch him and although it proved a close finish the Kiwi was always in control. His winning time of 4:26.6 was the event's slowest for 12 years and was only marginally quicker than the opening mile in that day's three-mile race!

Sydney finished 1.2 seconds behind in second, his overall time also undistinguished even as a relative beginner: "Lovelock produced a last lap of 58.5 seconds which, I am afraid to say, left me eight yards behind, recording a miserable 4:27.8," he told a reporter.

The *Sporting Chronicle* called it "a festival lacking in thrills" but Lovelock was privately delighted and wrote in his journal: "I had scarcely dreamed that the whole field would play into my hands so easily." He'd been sorely tempted to step up the pace and take the lead in response to the taunts of the crowd, but decided not to risk throwing away certain victory merely to amuse spectators. Cornes had indulged in some 'sledging' beforehand so beating him had been sweet for Lovelock, and, to a lesser extent, revenge over Sydney had also been pleasing. For Sydney it was presumably a lesson learned.

Experienced *News of the World* athletics reporter Joe Binks used the race to get his first close look at rising star Sydney, and candidly admitted he wasn't particularly impressed: "The mile was nothing but a crawl throughout," he wrote. "What was in the minds of such as Reeve and young Wooderson I do not pretend to know, but nobody made any effort to raise paces worthy of the event."

Once the dust had settled, focus switched to the second staging of the British Empire Games, taking place in the same stadium less than four weeks later. Here the main players would all meet again. Most of the English track and field stars warmed up for the Games by taking part in a match with France at Colombes at the end of July, but Sydney played things low-key and chose the City of London Police Sports at White City instead. This enabled his first taste of mile handicap racing, which had become something of a cornerstone of British athletics in the 1920s and 1930s.

The idea was for the slower runners to start at various points ahead of the top men, according to ability and form, meaning the final lap was likely to produce an exciting finish for the crowd. It meant runners would be dotted around the track at the start, with the star performers like Sydney on or near the 'scratch mark' and facing a real challenge. Handicapping would go out of fashion after the Second World War and be all but extinct by the late sixties, when British athletics went 'metric'. But at these Police Sports it was something new for Sydney and an intriguing challenge. The handicapper placed him 30 yards ahead of the scratch mark and ultimately he came in fourth, the three men ahead benefitting from starts of well over 100 yards.

6

Silver for England

THE inaugural Empire Games in 1930 in Hamilton, Ontario met with little enthusiasm from the British, but once London was announced as the 1934 venue that all changed. Originally Johannesburg had been chosen, but delegates who met at the 1932 Olympics switched it to London due to worries over South Africa's stance towards ethnic minority athletes.

England pulled out of the 1934 European Championships to concentrate on putting up a good show at the Empire Games at White City, and named 87 athletes in their team, calling up Sydney for the mile alongside the more experienced Cornes and Reeve. Team manager Arthur Turk appointed Jack Crump as his assistant and instructed him to look after a mini-squad of eight youngsters, including Sydney, who were tasting big-time athletics for the first time.

As London officials put the final touches to Games preparations in the early days of August 1934, news broke that Paul von Hindenburg, president of the Weimar Republic of Germany, had died. It opened the door for the tyranny of Adolf Hitler, appointed chancellor 18 months earlier. Hitler decided he should succeed Hindenburg, not as president but as Führer (supreme leader) of the German people.

Meanwhile, with the Games due to commence on Saturday 4 August, the 500 or so athletes from 16 countries assembled in London a few days beforehand, some 350 of them heading for St James' Palace where Edward, Prince of Wales, dutifully shook every single one by the hand.

Shot putter Robert 'Bonzo' Howland from Cambridge University was named England captain and had the task of taking the Oath of Allegiance and carrying the union flag during the opening ceremony. Swimmer Reg Sutton carried the flag bearing the cross of St. George and 400-metre man Godfrey Rampling carried a large silver shield bearing the name 'England'. Howland dutifully grasped a corner of the Union Jack and announced:

> "We declare that we are loyal subjects of His Majesty the King, Emperor, and will take part in the British Empire Games in the spirit of true sportsmanship, recognising the rules which govern them and desirous of participating in them for the honour of our Empire and the Glory of Sport."

The pomp and ceremony delighted a 50,000 crowd – not quite White City's capacity – and the procession of 500 competitors was headed by the Brigade of Guards, with Sydney and the rest of the England team bringing up the rear, smartly dressed in dark blazers and white trousers and skirts. The Oath and other speeches were marred by an annoying echoing on the loudspeaker system, but overall it was an impressive spectacle in the August sunshine.

There would be six sports over the four days – athletics, boxing, cycling, lawn bowls, swimming and diving and wrestling. Something of a breakthrough was the fact that women were permitted to take part in athletics events – as long as they were in races considered 'not too exhaustive'.

The Empire's best athletes moved into action on Monday 6 August, a day on which much of Europe's attention was focussed on Berlin where Germany's new dictator was addressing the Reichstag. The previous day's *News of the World* suggested: "Hitler faces problems that would daunt a Mussolini, a Roosevelt and a Napoleon all rolled into one."

Bank Holiday Monday was hot and muggy and the White City track looked uneven and heavy. Sydney was drawn in the second and toughest of two heats in the mile, having to compete against big guns Lovelock and Reeve for a place in Tuesday's final. But he knew four of the seven starters would qualify and that only an unforeseen disaster would see him miss out. Any lingering nerves might have been eased had he known Lovelock was privately anxious about his ongoing left knee problem and desperately keen for an easy ride.

The start was brisk, but star turn Lovelock allowed himself to hang back and by halfway was still 10 yards behind the field. Sydney and the rest then slowed noticeably on the penultimate lap, which allowed Lovelock to maintain his steady pace and still start passing them. Sydney stayed with Reeve at the front and with a minimum of fuss qualified in second place. Lovelock, apparently chatting to Canada's Les Wade, slipped easily into third and the first three came home close together but without ever racing hard. Reeve was first in 4:24.0, Sydney less than a second behind.

The final day promised much with 12 track and field finals plus the marathon, but as it was a Tuesday the crowd barely reached 10,000, meaning large areas of the stadium were unoccupied. It rained heavily in the morning and was overcast, windless and muggy by the time the action started. The mile final was first on track at 2.45, meaning the surface was in reasonable condition considering the recent rain, and all the talk was of the four English finalists working as a team to foil Kiwi favourite Lovelock.

This looked to be the case once things got under way, with Horace Craske leading them round the first lap in under 60 seconds, stretching the field and ensuring this wouldn't be a repeat of the pedestrian heats. Craske stayed ahead as they hit halfway in 2:06 but was beginning to show the strain and Cornes took over, closely marshalled by Lovelock. Little changed until the bell, suggesting the English strategy had come undone. Wearing a large No.10 on his white England vest, Sydney had stayed in touch and suddenly surged into the lead with 440 yards left. However, he couldn't sustain his speed and was soon re-passed by Cornes at the top of the back straight, and then by Lovelock. It looked like he'd blundered by kicking too early.

Capricious or not, Sydney was nevertheless able to gather himself again and pushed hard for home with 220 yards left. He had plenty to do and Lovelock looked ominously comfortable. The Kiwi powered into another gear just before the last bend and was clearly out of reach, breaking the tape in an excellent 4:12.8 and looking immensely strong. Sydney's late burst took him past the taller Cornes to come home six yards behind Lovelock in 4:13.4. Not only was this a big PB, it meant Sydney was now joint-second in the list of all-time fastest British-born milers. He shared this accolade with Reg Thomas whose 4:13.4 came three years earlier at Stamford Bridge, leaving the pair of them less than a second adrift of the No.1 spot, occupied by Walter George since 1886.

What a summer it had been! In less than nine weeks, 19-year-old Sydney had become Kent mile champion, then southern region champion, runner-up at the national championship and now an Empire Games silver medallist. His emergence had certainly impressed Lovelock, who wrote in his private journal:

> "Wooderson is going to be a great danger in a year or two, when he gains more strength, for he is so cool, clever and fast. By 1936 he will be worth watching very carefully... just before we entered the home straight I felt Wooderson was going to come by, so I stepped out past Jerry Cornes and jumped them both about 60 yards from the tape. From then on, it was an easy run-in, and I finished scarcely puffed."

Sydney was no longer an unknown quantity, *The Times* the following day calling his effort "heroic". Many athletics fans had become enchanted by the serious-faced little fellow in glasses and flapping kit. Despite not quite taking gold he'd emerged as a real star of these Empire Games and it appeared all he lacked was a degree of strength and tactical nous that would surely come later with age and experience.

It had proved a summer never to be forgotten for a young man still just shy of his 20th birthday and for whom his debut season in men's athletics had been a real baptism of fire. Two big titles, a finish ahead of Lovelock, plus a huge PB and an Empire silver medal was a stunning return for his efforts. If he'd been overawed at any point by the bewildering turn of events, and all the associated attention, it certainly wasn't showing.

It was time for a breather for Sydney, and four months without any racing followed the Empire Games. Club life continued of course, but it was a period in which Sydney kept his training fairly low-key. He was happy to go along with coach Albert Hill's view that he ought to take things steadily and be sure to avoid burn-out in these early days. Running took a back seat until Sydney stepped things up at the very end of 1934 when cross-country got properly underway.

Ten days before Christmas Sydney finished two minutes adrift of the leaders in 37th place when Blackheath's annual mob match with Ranelagh Harriers was staged from The Green Man on Putney Heath in relentlessly miserable weather. Runners trailed into the finish, the sodden

Sydney's vest and silver medal from the 1934 Empire Games.

linen numbers on their vests curled and unreadable thanks to flying mud. Conditions were awful, but most were undaunted and glad to be back in the swing of things. On Boxing Day Sydney stretched his legs again, this time setting off early on a damp day as one of the 'hounds' in a festive Blackheath hare and hounds event from Hayes.

7

Running With the Mob

AN ELDERLY runner chugged slowly but surely across blustery Chingford Plain in splendid isolation on a bright but chilly afternoon in late 2016. From where I watched on a muddy, neighbouring slope, it looked for all the world like the ghost of Sydney Wooderson. Was I hallucinating? Was this a result of getting a bit too obsessive about my 'tour' of Wooderson race venues?

I did a double take. From 100 yards away it certainly looked like Sydney. Perhaps the spooky apparition really was him, reliving past glories here on the edge of Epping Forest, recalling colourful camaraderie and muddy battles of his running youth? Or maybe just a local veteran who happened to resemble Sydney.

Whatever, our hero did race here at the home of Orion Harriers AC four times in his career. Races into Epping Forest took place adjacent to Orion's splendid and imposing HQ, the Royal Forest Hotel (still open today) and its neighbouring royal hunting lodge. Saturday 19 January 1935 was the first of these occasions, Blackheath versus Orion, one of the three annual 'mob matches' that Blackheath officials were desperate to win in order to make 1934–5 a cross-country season to remember. Mob matches involving Blackheath, Orion, South London Harriers and Ranelagh Harriers had taken place since the 19th century and generated passionate entreaties in Blackheath's *Gazette* newsletter, reminding members it was their duty to support the club at these events. This was never a problem for Sydney, who loved the camaraderie and shared experiences of a team effort, and would always turn up if he possibly could.

Pride was at stake in these mob matches and the rivalry highly potent. The turnout would vary from match to match but was usually high, and several contests in the 1930s featured fields of more than 200. Outcomes were often tense and close affairs. Whoever was Club President for any particular year would be desperate to chalk up wins during his tenure.

Sydney's run here at Chingford in January 1935 would be affected by a strong wind in the non-forested sections with much of the going very sticky following recent heavy rain. Knowing many of their men wouldn't be present due to illness or work commitments, anxious Blackheath club officials waited with bated breath to see who would turn up fit to run. Thirty minutes before the start they only had 30, with 15 minutes to go it was still below 40. But then nearly four dozen arrived with just minutes to spare: "Eighty five of our dusky brethren lined up" reported the delighted *Gazette* correspondent. Despite the late influx, the starter was determined not to hang around and the field was sent on its way with several runners still sauntering over to the start!

By the time the leaders reached Green Drive, the field had spread out. Heathens captain Richard Walker led after a mile and was never passed, with Vines of Orion pipping Sydney for second place around 30 seconds down on the winner. Sydney's stamina as a scrawny 20-year-old surprised his colleagues. He'd also impressed a fortnight earlier, winning outright a club cross-country for the first time, at the Blackheath-Lloyd's Bank match at Hayes over five miles, seconds ahead of teammates Poole and Beard. Here at Chingford Sydney's fast finish for third was crucial in Blackheath's victory. The singing and merriment continued into the changing rooms where the jubilant visitors enjoyed "first class bathing accommodation."

Sydney loved cross-country, where the pleasures of running free across open land was allied to a cheerful team spirit rarely experienced at track events. It was as if the shackles of his shyness and of the tough working week had been released. He will also have been quietly pleased to be proving himself among the old hands in the club and helping the Blackheath team effort into the bargain. His efforts certainly didn't go unnoticed and the club seniors were thrilled a young man making a name for himself nationally would be so determined to put his club first in this way.

Club historians Saunders and Weeks-Pearson would reflect how the size and scope of Sydney's contribution to the club cause was remarkable for someone constantly subjected to the stresses of publicity and other demands that didn't affect ordinary club runners:

> "From his earliest years in the club he received praise for his scrupulous support of fixtures and it is a fact that even, for example, during the period 1935-46 when he was defeated in a handful only of serious contests, there was remarkable intermingling of humbler races with these demanding competitions."

Two weeks after hammering Orion, Blackheath took on Oxford University on their renowned and fearsome Shotover Hill course starting from OUAC's Iffley Road base. This would be the first of three occasions when Sydney tested himself on this course on the edge of the city.

On a grey and rainy day in 2016, armed as usual with running shoes, notebook and camera I ventured here to check out the 'psychogeography' of the place. Apart from regular visits from runners, Shotover has seen plenty of excitement over the years. It was once part of a Royal Forest providing a hunting ground for noblemen, fuel and grazing for local people and timber for Oxford's historic buildings. After it became open farmland the main road to London passed across Shotover Plain and here travellers were often mugged by highwaymen.

Around the time Sydney ran here for the first time, the City Council began managing Shotover as a public park. During the war Slade Camp was set up here to provide a temporary home for soldiers taking part in the D-Day landings and on the slopes of Shotover Hill military training took place and tanks were tested. Runners of various sorts still frequent the area in modern times in high numbers, slogging up the tricky slopes in kit rather more brightly coloured than when Sydney and cronies ran the University mob matches of yesteryear. The weather was miserable for the duration of my visit – but I was assured the place is normally a riot of nature's finest colours and aromas.

The students team pipped Sydney's team of Heathens here in February 1935 by a mere three points thanks to McIntyre and Edwards finishing together in joint-first in 44.50, with Richard Walker and Sydney storming home 15 seconds later side by side for equal third. Sydney caught his captain near the end after passing Arthur Robertson of Bailliol College, another talented youngster with a big future in the sport.

A fortnight later Sydney enjoyed a fairly comfortable victory when Blackheath welcomed South London school teams Emanuel (Battersea) and Brockley County to Hayes for a three-cornered contest across the Common. He and brother Stanley always looked in charge and Sydney cruised home in 28.03, four seconds ahead of his sibling. Members of the club committee had been extra keen for this race to pass without incident and not inconvenience any local non-runners: They had recently been in hot water after a letter appeared in the *Kentish Times* complaining about trails of paper scattered on the Common, laid during their 'hare and hounds' outings. Subsequently the committee offered to use flags instead of paper in future in a bid to keep everybody happy.

The race against the school teams was a prelude to a much tougher task on Saturday 23 February when the best runners of the Southern Counties gathered at Hassocks, a large village at the foot of Sussex's South Downs, for the annual regional cross-country champs. Being under 21 meant Sydney was in the junior race and in such youthful company found himself one of the more experienced competitors. With coach Hill looking on, he set off with the lead pack on a long uphill start. He was never far from the front throughout but was beaten in a stirring finish by teenager Denis Pell of Herne Hill Harriers, whose storming last half-mile was enough to create a 10-yard gap between them. Among the applauding spectators, leaning on his walking stick, was Walter George, now aged 76 but still the last Briton to record a world's best time for the mile. Walter's health had begun to fail him recently and he was soon to retire as part-time groundsman/coach at Mitcham AC, but still ventured out when he could to watch races such as this.

Afterwards a group of about 50 from Blackheath and Ranelagh Harriers got together and went for a meal at nearby Hassocks Hotel, a rather austere and poorly-heated venue, where the hungry runners enlivened the bleak surroundings with some noisy refuelling.

As the 1935 summer season approached, Sydney's plans were turned upside down by a foot injury. Oblivious to this, the sporting press licked their lips about the prospect of another showdown between Britain's young pretender and the great Jack Lovelock at the White City on Saturday May 25. But when this Polytechnic Harriers' Kinnaird Trophy meeting came around it was wet and windy and Sydney decided he was not fit enough to run. Lovelock, probably relieved fast-finishing Sydney was out of the picture, had aimed at 4:10, but conditions meant he was happy with his 4:13.8 event record. His main 'home' opposition, which fizzled out towards the end, came from Aubrey Reeve rather than Sydney, as many of the big crowd had hoped.

For Sydney it was a period of frustration. He tested his injured foot in low-key fashion in a handicap mile in early June, but didn't push things too hard and hoped all would be well for a return to serious competition at Plymouth ten days later. He was keen to make an impact this summer as the Olympic Games in Germany were only a year away and he needed to build momentum before then. He was considered one of seven or eight decent British prospects for a medal in Berlin, but their chances – according to Joe Binks of the *News of the World* – were being hampered by a lack of assistance and investment from the British athletics authorities. Binks wrote:

> "It is appalling to think that England, the acknowledged mother of sport, cannot supply a few pounds, or a stadium, so that her athletes can be coached to meet the world's best every four years... every nation, excepting England, seems to view the Olympic Games as a national event and considers the expense worthwhile."

It certainly wasn't just athletes and their coaches whose thoughts had by now turned to Germany. Serious concern was mounting across Europe following the recent news that Adolf Hitler was ignoring the Versailles Treaty and had ordered Germany to re-arm, reintroducing military conscription.

8

High Jinks at Plymouth

SUNDAY 16 June 1935. A Great Western Railway passenger train stands beside a platform at Plymouth station ready to depart for London Paddington. Inside, a large troupe of glamorous girls from a touring theatre company sit quietly while a group of male athletes on the train start showing off. They perform what they described as 'a series of rockets'. The girls were a well-travelled bunch, but this form of entertainment was new to them; their stunned reaction was possibly because they were spellbound, but more likely due to sheer bewilderment.

They were professional dancers, not easily impressed, but the lads' antics went down a storm. Unfortunately exhaustive research on this author's part has failed to uncover precisely what 'rockets' actually involved. Was it gymnastics? Indoor fireworks? Were parcel shelves or luggage trolleys involved? Or was it a now long-forgotten 1930s parlour game? Whatever, we must assume it was high jinks of a relatively harmless nature – although the editor of the Blackheath Harriers' *Gazette* did confess he had to 'modify' a report of the day's events to protect the guilty!

The providers of the impromptu show that morning were well-known runners from London and Oxbridge athletics clubs, including a quartet from Blackheath who had won the prestigious Travers Stubbs inter-club trophy at Home Park in Plymouth the previous day. Intriguingly, the normally reticent and well-behaved Sydney Wooderson was present, although it is hard to imagine he was among those horsing around! According to the *Gazette*:

> "Leaving the trophy in capable hands, we set out for the station. We thought we would sleep all the way [back to London], but a treat was in store for us. Ernie Lotinga's Theatre Company, bound for London, were with us, including a whole coach load of young ladies. Led by sprinter Tremeer of London AC, we entertained these 'beautifuls' to a series of 'rockets'. This went down well, they had not seen it before. Then we loaded up a luggage truck with them and pushed them up and down the platform, Mr.Wiard and Mr. Evan Hunter on board to see that they came to no harm. Blackheath's Ernie Page came down to see what it was all about, but then had to sprint back to his compartment to avoid being deprived of his braces. The Station Master was relieved to see us go – he seemed quite annoyed at our yelling 'All change!' when a local train full of day trippers pulled in, causing the platform to become a struggling mass of mums, dads and kids, the latter armed with lollipops and luggage, all yelling 'Porter! Porter!'"

Noisy young people behaving badly on trains is clearly not a phenomenon confined to modern times. But of course Blackheath's boys had good cause to be in celebratory mood, having won the Travers Stubbs Trophy by a mere two points from Achilles, with London AC back in third place.

It had been the fifth annual athletics meeting at Home Park, Blackheath sending a four-man team of Ernie Page, Charles Wiard, John Poole and Sydney. The morning of the event saw the Blackheath boys sampling the slot-machines and other attractions of the sea front. Throughout these adventures the rain bucketed down, meaning the track at Home Park was wet and heavy for Saturday afternoon's serious business.

Six clubs (Stade Francais, Milocarian AC, Achilles AC, London AC, Devonport YMCA and Blackheath) were in competition over five events for the main trophy – the mile, half-mile, quarter-mile, 100 yards and mile relay. As well as the glory of victory, Plymouth was known to offer an interesting prize-list: a portable gramophone, wrist watches, pen and geometry sets, and dressing gowns for winning relay runners.

In the tricky conditions Sydney grabbed the lead on the final bend to win the mile in a slow 4:47. With little time to recover he then ploughed through the heavy going for another two laps to help Blackheath pip a crack Achilles outfit in the mile relay, the team's total time given as 3:52.5.

It had been a memorable and sociable weekend in Devon, but a week later Sydney faced up to the sterner test provided by the 13th annual Southern Counties AAA championships at Portsmouth, where he was in with a great chance of a major title. With Lovelock away in the USA, Sydney's task was to avenge the narrow defeat in last year's thriller at Guildford by Aubrey Reeve; he and the Poly man were the two outstanding favourites, with Bernard Eeles of Southgate a good each-way bet. A special train was laid on to take London-based officials and athletes to the venue at the Royal Naval Sports Ground in Portsmouth's Pitt Street district. In direct contrast to a week earlier, the weather was magnificent – the first really sunny Saturday of the summer so far.

Watched intently by the Lord Mayor and a big crowd, 13 men assembled on the cinders for the 13th annual Southern mile. It turned into an enthralling contest that one paper described as "simply wonderful". Bretherick (RAMC) led after the first lap in 61.8, just ahead of Reeve but by halfway (2:09.8), Blackheath skipper Harold Smith had eased ahead with Reeve lurking on his shoulder. By the bell in 3:17.4 Reeve had regained a small lead and looked ready to hit the gas at any moment as he hugged the inside lane. But around the top bend things began to happen, Sydney accelerating to join him, followed by Eeles who decided to try and hit the front only for Reeve to hold him off as they came into the home straight. Suddenly Sydney made his burst, but Reeve was ready for it and put up a tremendous fight to stay in contention. Sydney was simply too quick however, and held him off at the post, winning in 4:18.6 as the crowd roared its approval. It was a real thriller and Reeve and Eeles finished within six-tenths of a second behind him.

Naturally Blackheath were delighted to see their man emphasise his regional superiority, and Sydney was lauded in the *Gazette*, the writer even inspired to paraphrase Milton's *Paradise Lost* at one point:

> "Mile records are [currently] falling like leaves in Vallombrosa and some of the finest milers the country has ever produced are running to gladden our hearts. The first-class miler today must have the speed of the sprinter, the endurance of Pheidippides and the heart of a lion. In Wooderson we have an athlete that combines these qualities in the highest degree."

Sydney was hitting top form at just the right time. Portsmouth would be followed within a month by the AAA championships and then a GB-France match, both at White City. Most of his important training was currently at the Battersea Park track on Tuesday evenings under the watchful eye of Albert Hill, although the White City track had become available for club runners to train on too. If they preferred a more homely club atmosphere Sydney and colleagues could roll up on a Wednesday evening at the Blackheath clubhouse in Hayes and after running enjoy a cold supper for just two shillings.

To hone his sharpness for the massive July meetings at White City, Sydney ran the Southern League mile team race at the Civil Service AAA meet in SE London, where he produced an irresistible late burst to win in a relatively modest 4:25. This was his first appearance at Herne Hill Stadium on the cinder track created more than 40 years earlier inside a concrete cycling track. Home club Herne Hill Harriers would soon be moving out to settle at Tooting Bec, although the stadium would go on to host cycling events for the 1948 Olympics, and the running track survived until being grassed over in 1980.

In early July Sydney grabbed the perfect opportunity to test his raw speed by running two 880-yard legs for Blackheath – one a four-man event covering two miles, the other the medley relay for the Kent relay championship title. Blackheath won both at a sunny Lee Green in SE London by large margins, retaining their medley title for an eighth successive year. Sydney's explosive 1:54.8 helped them smash their own event record by around five seconds – their 3:29.8 bringing them in 50 yards clear. Sydney hadn't run too many serious half-miles at this point, and his effort was a personal best by a considerable margin.

In contrast to the relaxed family atmosphere at Lee Green, a far more nerve-wracking occasion awaited Sydney the following weekend: the AAA championships and a fifth tussle with the great Jack Lovelock in just over 12 months. The Kiwi had just returned from winning the so-called 'Mile of the Century' at Princeton University, New Jersey, and was of course favourite to retain his AAA title, but Sydney was quietly confident he could give him a run for his money. In the pair's previous four clashes, Lovelock had triumphed in two finals at White City while Sydney beat him at Guildford and in a White City semi-final. Athletics followers who paid close attention to recent form knew this had the potential to be a real thriller and were licking their lips in anticipation. But in the *News of the World*, Joe Binks was apparently yet to be convinced about Sydney – he reckoned it would be "a sensation" if Lovelock didn't win the mile.

Sydney's fastest mile so far was his 4:13.4 at the Empire Games, well short of Lovelock's two-year-old PB of 4:07.6 – and a fair chunk slower than Lovelock's recent 4:11.2 in beating world record holders Cunningham and Bonthron in the USA. But the interesting question was whether or not Lovelock had already peaked this summer and might feel flat after his American adventure and a busy year of work and study at his London hospital – not forgetting all the dances and parties he mentions in his journals. Sydney's life had been far more settled and well ordered in comparison and his running was most definitely on an upward curve.

His coach, the unflappable Hill, knew what it took to win the AAA mile, having done so twice himself, and didn't want to pressurise his 20-year-old charge too much. He was more than happy for Sydney to go to White City as underdog. Hill will have noted how the press was starting to talk of Sydney as a medal prospect for the 1936 Berlin Olympics, although there had been a cautionary message from correspondent W. Capel-Kirby in the *Sporting Chronicle* warning that many potential GB Olympians were undertaking too much strenuous and ill-scheduled training during that summer of 1935, against the advice of their coaches, and were getting injured as a result.

The heats of the AAA mile started around 6.40pm on Friday 12 July in perfect weather, but on a somewhat rough-looking track. Title-holder Lovelock looked unhappy qualifying for the following day's final in the first heat, annoyed about an uncomfortable first lap and then needing to strain at the end to win in 4:23.8. Afterwards he pulled on a white sweater and sat on the in field, applying ice to his right knee and chatting with USA pole vaulter Keith Brown. He wrote in his diary later: "Feeling very dead and heavy, spiritless and listless." It further underlined how he'd gone into these championships in a poor state of mind.

On the other hand, Sydney, wearing No.35 in the third and final heat, was able to qualify with ease behind Bernard Eeles in a slow race where serious exertion wasn't needed. If the next day's final was to be the two-horse race everyone expected, there was little doubt over which runner would be starting in the better frame of mind.

9

'Inside I Was Boiling'

FINALS day of the 52nd annual AAA championships at White City dawned bright and breezy and the temperature had risen sharply by the time a crowd of over 30,000 took their places in the stadium. They had come to see the biggest field of foreign athletes ever assembled at a national championship, and a memorable day's sport in the sun was in prospect.

The track looked in poor condition even before the hectic roster of events began at 11 that Saturday morning. By the time the nine finalists for the mile were called to the start at around 4.40pm the soaring temperatures were being tempered by a stiff breeze. Records looked unlikely in such conditions but an intriguing race was certain.

With hindsight this contest would come to be regarded as the first great clash between two master milers Lovelock and Wooderson. And we now know from his journals how anxious title-holder Lovelock was when going to the line that day – even though Olympic sprinter and journalist Guy Butler wrote that Lovelock "had little reckoning of the rod in pickle" that Sydney was waiting to serve him!

Butler, writing in the *Morning Post*, called the scenes "sensational" as Sydney demonstrated he had the courage and cleverness to take on the Kiwi at his own waiting game. Sydney kidded the champ he was playing into his hands by taking the lead at the bell, and not only got away with this move, but decisively proved Lovelock's domination was at an end. The *News of the World*'s old-hand Joe Binks marvelled at scenes of "indescribable excitement" created in the closing stages.

Peter Ward of Achilles had shot into the lead at the start, with the rest settling back, Ward recording a 61.2 first lap at least 20 yards ahead. The pack was headed by Lovelock who suddenly decided Ward was moving away too fast and with the other seven clinging behind him, took off and hauled Ward in. They passed halfway in 2:06.8 and then followed a slow third lap with Lovelock tucked in behind Ward, apparently grateful for a breather. But when the bell sounded at 3:15.4 it all kicked off. Lovelock immediately jumped ahead, only for Sydney to react a split second later and slide smoothly into the lead. Frenchman Roger Normand took Sydney's place at Lovelock's elbow.

Normally Sydney's bold move would have delighted Lovelock ("Ordinarily, over the last 80 yards I would have massacred him") but when the Kiwi tried to kick for home on this hot afternoon his power simply deserted him. After an attempt to pass Sydney 20 yards short of the home straight, the smaller man went away and the biggest name in miling could do absolutely nothing about it. The crowd let loose an almighty roar. Lovelock began to ease up, realising he was well beaten. Bizarrely he was grinning broadly as he crossed the line several yards adrift: He would explain this laughter later. Sydney had produced a 61.2 last lap for 4:17.2, winning by 1.2 seconds. Eeles clung on for third, just ahead of French pair Normand and Chermat.

The record crowd was delirious, among them Sydney's proud mum Nettie and coach Hill, whose own time of 4:13.8 some 14 years earlier survived as championship record. Despite the general mayhem after the finish, there would be no show-boating or bombastic interviews from the victor himself. That was true to form, of course, and partly why the public were becoming so fond of him: he was an Englishman, modest, unassuming and did his talking on the track. Lovelock, on the other hand, was a very different case and had plenty to say. Although he acknowledged Sydney's ability and promise, he made great play of his own shortcomings on the day, blaming the result almost entirely on his own failings rather than Sydney's brilliant tactics.

Lovelock reckoned the race ranked alongside the Los Angeles Olympic final of 1932 as one of the big fiascos of his career:

> "I appeared to be in a stupid daze, mentally and physically dead tired and completely disinterested, and semi-detached most of the

> way. I ran an appallingly bad race... I was laughing heartily as I came up the straight, for something about the whole business appealed to my odd sense of humour – my pathetic inability to cope with the situation, the absolute grim determination of my little opponent, the astonished gasp of the crowd and perhaps the thought of what the press would say later... [I was] dead stale, worn out mentally and physically with too much hard and exciting racing with work and late hours at the hospital and on parties".

Sydney's club was naturally over the moon at their young colleague rising to the rank of national champion. One official said Sydney had run to a pre-arranged plan in which he gave an unsurpassed example of great tactical running. Peter Lovesey's *Official Centenary History of the AAA* would record: "They came home in the second lane, the small pale man in spectacles going at full steam like a goods train passing an express."

Billboards in London streets screamed afterwards: 'Lovelock meets his match' and 'GB has new mile king'. Thanks largely to Sydney and some records which fell in field events, 1935 would long be remembered as the year the annual championships provided sport of a quality unequalled for a very long time, said one report. Among the well-known onlookers was Harold Abrahams, former Olympic sprint champion now a journalist and broadcaster, who jotted down his thoughts in his copy of the AAA programme for that day: "The winner [Wooderson] is a good sound miler beyond dispute, but Lovelock lost the race through a big swelled head. It is as well not to despise a field of finalists in the AAA after all!"

Sydney appeared to take the fuss in his stride, but his controlled demeanour belied turmoil beneath. He would recall how someone on this day complimented him on being so calm before and after races: "But I wasn't calm. Inside I was boiling." He did suffer from nerves, he admitted, and many times had to slip away after races to be sick, a problem that would only diminish after he discovered that taking glucose 30 minutes before a race helped him.

If Sydney doubted that he'd now become a big star, he wouldn't have long to wait for confirmation. His name appeared shortly afterwards on every menu card at all the Lyons tea shops across London and the provinces. This was no trifling matter, for there were well over 200 of such premises. The menus advertised the fact that Sydney had been awarded a complimentary cake by the editor of *Lyons Sports Sheet*, in recognition of his superb running at the AAAs. Naturally his club colleagues thought this hilarious and the gentle ribbing began; one of them suggested in the club *Gazette* he ought to get a menu engraved as a souvenir.

To maintain sharpness for two more big summer races, Sydney committed to a couple of midweek club fixtures in mid-July. On a warm evening at the Catford Bridge track on Wednesday 17 July he had a run-out in the mile. He took command after the bell, having previously cruised for three laps some 10 yards behind the field, and came home first in 4:25.4. Two nights later, in muggy and greyer conditions, he led Blackheath to victory in a mile invitation relay, part of an Army meet at Aldershot Garrison. His effort over 880 yards saw the Blackheath quartet (Les Cornish, John Poole and Frank Whittingham and Sydney) clock 3:36.0, showing a clean pair of heels to nearest challengers Surrey AC and Thames Valley Harriers.

By the last week of July, Sydney was feeling in great shape and more than ready for two more key events to end his season. His GB debut at a match with France at White City on July 27 would be followed a week later by a special mile handicap at Glasgow Rangers' annual sports at Ibrox Park, where he would again be pitted against Lovelock. In mid-July Sydney had accepted the invitation to Ibrox – by far the furthest he would have travelled so far to perform. It was an exciting but nerve-wracking prospect for a 20-year-old, as this was the biggest event of its sort in Britain, an annual gala involving five-a-side football between Scotland's top clubs, with running and cycling races during the breaks between the football, all played out before a huge crowd.

The Saturday afternoon sun was blazing again when a French squad pitched up at White City for the 12th annual match with Britain. A slightly disappointing crowd of around 10,000 paid to see the opening parade and 14 events, GB winning eight of the nine track races, the visitors restoring a little Gallic pride by taking all five field events. It was another proud day for the Wooderson family – for having represented England at the Empire Games in 1934, today marked Sydney's first appearance in the colours of Great Britain. As widely expected he won the mile, featuring two runners from each team, in a time of 4:19. He held off French champ Roger Normand by 1.2 seconds (six yards or so) after the French pair had slowed things down in the second and third laps, which played into Sydney's hands. He simply waited for the bell, lengthened his stride and reeled off a 60.6 lap which Normand couldn't match.

Sydney polishes some of the trophies won during his early years as a senior athlete.

It had been an eventful, pivotal summer in Sydney's blossoming career and now he had just one race left before it was time to direct all available energies into work and law studies. It was a period in which he had to get used to press attention; as he set off for Glasgow, a photographer from a London daily asked him to pose on the platform at Euston. The result was a photo of Sydney smiling broadly and leaning out of the window of the train taking him north for a first race on 'foreign' soil.

The Rangers Sports was the highlight of the Scottish athletics season, staged every year on the first Saturday in August. A bumper crowd of around 50,000 turned out on a mild but windy day – a number boosted by the pre-event hype that Jack Lovelock would be attempting a mile record. Dark rumours that the Kiwi might have to pull out due to tiredness proved unfounded. There were to be five starters in the eagerly anticipated mile handicap, with Sydney and Lovelock both on 'scratch' and conceding a generous 25 yards to Aubrey Reeve, 35 yards to the 30-year-old Scots champion Tommy Riddell and 70 yards to Reg Thomas.

This handicapping was ostensibly designed to provide a close finish and some thrills for the big crowd, but it appears Lovelock himself had a major say in setting the handicaps. According to Norman Harris in his 1964 book '*The Legend of Lovelock*', the Oxford-based champion had written to the senior official at Ibrox, the Rangers manager Bill Struth, and given him his ideal handicaps for the race. Being the star of the show, the Rangers people were seemingly quite happy to set things up just as Lovelock wanted.

There would be plenty happening throughout the day, but it was the Invitation Mile that got the big build-up, with the papers promising a record attempt that would see Lovelock and Sydney bidding to run each lap in 62 seconds, with Reeve and Riddell and then Thomas giving them pacing targets in turn as it progressed. Instead of dwelling on his own anxieties, Lovelock chose to sing Sydney's praises in his *London Evening News* column the day before the race. It was an article he'd pondered long and hard over before dictating it by phone to London from Glasgow, writing candidly and generously that great things were expected of young Sydney.

The duel was certainly an intriguing prospect: Many thought Sydney surely couldn't possibly humiliate Lovelock again, but *The Times* talked up his chances:

"The bespectacled, but none-the-less watchful Wooderson, smaller and more lightly-built even than Lovelock, not so obviously the complete miler, but indisputably a rare blend of whipcord, nimble stride, pluck, and stamina. The kind of little fellow who would worry 'Springheel Jack' himself out of a race."

With the Scots crowd naturally disinclined to support an Englishman, they got behind Lovelock with a vengeance, and even the stadium announcer only gave Lovelock's lap times as the race progressed. The start looked fast and Lovelock, in his Achilles AC white kit wearing No.1, forced the pace, closely followed by his black-clad shadow wearing No.2 as they set about chasing down those with a lead. Lovelock would admit later he misjudged the early pace and went too fast on the first quarter and then too slow on the second. The handicaps proved "useless" in terms of providing something for them to chase, he would admit.

At the half-mile, Lovelock was clocked at 2:07.1, Sydney less than a second behind. The pair then completed a lap together in just under 65 seconds. Soon after the bell sounded it looked highly unlikely Riddell and Reeve would be caught, but all eyes were focussed further down the track on the duel between Sydney and Lovelock. Around 250 yards from the tape, having clung to his opponent's heels for so long, Sydney now went past in a gloriously judged effort. Although Lovelock just about held his ground for 100 yards, Sydney surged again and outpaced his man in a tremendous finish.

Reeve had by now crossed the line first, some 10 yards ahead of the fast-finishing Riddell, in a time of 4:10.5 (equivalent to a mile of sub 4.14), but as Sydney was only five yards down on popular Scot Riddell he had clearly achieved the fastest time of the day. As at White City, Lovelock raised his head and eased up when he saw the task was beyond him and came in grinning, 12 yards further back in 4:15.6, Thomas having tailed right off.

Sydney's time of 4:12.7 was not only a personal best, it scythed a massive 7.7 seconds off the Scottish allcomers record set by Lovelock here two years earlier. Sydney's lap splits were 61.6, 65.8, 64.4 and 60.9. It was a world class performance, less than six seconds outside the world record set the previous summer by Glenn Cunningham in his native USA.

Sydney had run the fastest mile ever by a British-born runner, but it would only be years later that it would go in the books under the description 'UK record'. At this point in athletics history the authorities only recognised 'allcomers records', meaning a run of 4:12.0 at Iffley Road, Oxford in May 1932 by New Zealand-born Lovelock was regarded as the 'British Record.'

I consulted former *Athletics Weekly* editor Mel Watman and historian Andy Milroy over this apparent anomaly. Watman explained:

> "My understanding is that there was no such animal as a specific UK record in Sydney Wooderson's day, and the reason why his 4:12.7 was not referred to as a British record is because that was officially the property of [New Zealander] Lovelock with his 4:12.0 at Oxford! Sydney's time wasn't even an English native record as it was made in Scotland."

And Milroy added:

> "A Briton could set a world record abroad in the Olympics, for example, which would be ratified by the IAAF but it still would not be recognised as a British record by the AAA, or even an English record, because the British record would be the best time set in Britain irrespective of nationality."

The race had the London-based athletics correspondents in a tizz. Joe Binks commented:

> "Personally I thought Wooderson held Lovelock quite easily in every part of the race, and what he can really do is still something of a puzzle... Albert Hill, the famous Olympic champion, believes his charge can beat anybody in the world over a mile. I thought Lovelock did not look very well at the finish. He is certainly not the man we saw on the tracks last year."

It had been a marvellous way for Sydney to bring his deliberately truncated season to a close, in stark contrast to the misery of Lovelock. The New Zealander was unwell at the end and was later sick. He wrote in his journal that his mind was now made up – he must beat Sydney during the following year of 1936 or die! He knew it wouldn't be easy though, and castigated himself for twice failing to fight back when Sydney tested him on those final laps at White City and then Glasgow. It was clear to all that Sydney had come up against a somewhat under-par Lovelock, and the general feeling was that a head-to-head when Lovelock was in his best shape would be worth going many miles to see. Immediately after the Glasgow defeat, Lovelock's coach Bill Thomas and Sydney's adviser Hill both urged him to cut his losses immediately and take a much-needed rest.

Despite their vocal support for the man beaten by sassenach Sydney, the crowd thoroughly enjoyed the race and treated it as the high point of a day that included a five-a-side football tournament in which host club Rangers beat Celtic 2-1 in a predictably feisty final.

Sydney left Scotland with his reputation enhanced and his rivalry with Lovelock fast becoming an obsession with the sporting press and athletics fans. According to author Norman Harris, such was the interest in the duo's ongoing battle for supremacy, people were now talking about it as far away as the Middle East: Harris wrote that marathon runner Sam Ferris had recently been on holiday to Baghdad where he was stopped in a back street by an elderly Arab who asked who Ferris thought would win the next confrontation between Sydney and Lovelock. The Arab told Ferris he endorsed the view that Lovelock had so far been over-confident against Sydney and would eventually bounce back and win a harder-run race between them!

The Ibrox fun and games brought Sydney's 1935 summer season to an end as planned, for he now had to give priority to work and concentrate fully on studying for his law exams. He duly excused himself from events such as the GB-Germany match scheduled for August 11. Normally he would have supported his club's endeavours over the forthcoming winter season (1935–6), but they understood that he must now quietly back off from training and racing to put his career first. At its annual general meeting the club paid tribute to him for supporting events whenever he could, even though nowadays he was 'public property.'

Sydney's one concession during his autumn and winter hiatus would be to turn out for the first of the club's annual 'big three' cross-country mob matches that meant so much to the participants. This involved a trip to Coulsdon on Saturday 16 November to lock horns with the old enemy South London Harriers, with the spoils of victory being the Nicholls Cup. Blackheath President W. D. Whiter, like Presidents before and after him, was aware of the kudos hanging on these matches and was desperate to win. Perhaps it was he who talked Sydney into abandoning his studies that Saturday? Underlining the importance of the match, the front page of the *Gazette* was taken up by an announcement in bold type, complete with many exclamation marks, imploring:

> "Every able-bodied Heathen must turn out on November 16 ready to run as he has never run before... this year the Coulsdon bogey must be laid for ever!"

Cometh the hour, cometh the men in black! They did it – finally laying that bogey and thumping SLH at Coulsdon by a considerable points margin. From a field of 169 runners – 99 from Blackheath, 70 in home colours – the ruling was that 67 from each side would score. After the usual fast start on Farthing Downs, they ploughed over a 7.5-mile course that was wet and slippery under forbidding skies. Leading the way was Laurie Wetherill of SLH, a runner well known for his grey gloves and stop-watch. Although Wetherill and three teammates came in joint-first, the day would turn into a great triumph for the Heathens. Sydney's contribution was barely noticed – his first outing of any sort in more than three months saw him come in joint-42nd with teammate Dew, around five minutes after the winners. After the first 60 or so men had crossed the line the result remained in the balance, but Blackheath had more strength in depth and packed their middle ranks to win comfortably by more than 700 points. Their big smiles at the end defied the miserable weather and set the scene for some lively celebrations. At the Coulsdon Hall race HQ, the two clubs staged a darts match which Blackheath also won, and then runners and officials assembled at the Railway Inn in nearby Purley for "an excellent supper and smoker", during which the Nicholls Cup was handed over amid joyous scenes and the raucous sound of the traditional club 'cry'.

The year of 1935 had been a remarkable one for Sydney Wooderson and would be rounded off nicely shortly before Christmas when he was named in a GB squad of 'potential' candidates for the following year's Berlin Olympics, along with clubmate Frank Whittingham. Although his selection for this list had been a mere formality, it was another signal that he and Albert Hill could carry on planning for 1936, their intention being to focus solely on the build-up to Berlin once Sydney's exams were out of the way in the spring.

10

Freak Accident in a Rabbit-Hole

MANY a ghost flits around Broomfield Park in Palmers Green. It's a tranquil North London haven where at almost every turn another reminder of the past reveals itself.

The ancient and previously splendid Broomfield House, for example, has survived major fires but now stands forlornly derelict, encased in scaffolding. A short walk away, the site of the park's former running track is easy to make out: The big clue is the concrete terracing which used to hold spectators and is still largely intact, although the sports pavilion at the top is long gone.

Sydney Wooderson raced only once on this track, and it took place 80 summers prior to my visit. Blackheath Harriers gathered here on a cloudy Wednesday evening in May 1936 and in an eight-lap relay, Sydney helped them trounce home side Southgate Harriers by seven seconds.

The sunken area where the track stood was a former gravel pit that had provided road building material, which by 1905 had been levelled and grassed. The first running track to be created here had square corners, but this was modernised and became the home of Southgate Harriers after a grand opening ceremony in 1933. It soon became clear the home straight went slightly downhill, meaning unusually fast finishes to races were often witnessed. The action would be halted during the 1939–45 war when it was temporarily ploughed up to grow potatoes. Eventually the track's varied life ended when Southgate changed its name to Haringey & Southgate AC in 1974 and moved to pastures new. Nowadays it is grassed over but from subtle changes in grass texture you can still see it had six lanes and a long-jump run-up.

Sydney Wooderson would remember this track as the place where he began producing convincing evidence he could become a world class half-miler as well as maintain his status as Britain's fastest-ever miler. His remarkable debut at 880 yards at Lee Green in 1935 (1:54 in a relay) had been followed by a straight half-mile at Catford Bridge in mid-May 1936 (1:56.8) and a fortnight later came this 4 x 880 yards relay in Broomfield Park. Sydney went off third for Blackheath, repeating the Catford time of 1:56.8 and Blackheath's aggregate clocking was 8:22.6 (Len King, Derek Reynolds, Sydney and John Poole).

Sydney was star of the show that afternoon and it was another run of tremendous potential, coming at a time when the world record stood at 1:49.8 (Ben Eastman, USA). For now, he was not getting carried away, but will have been quietly pleased to be showing signs of form as the momentous Berlin Olympic summer of 1936 got underway.

It had hardly been an ideal winter's preparation for a young athlete of whom so much was expected at Berlin. Far from spending the colder months improving and maintaining basic strength and stamina in cross-country, Sydney had abandoned all winter racing to prepare properly for his Law Society exams.

It was an important time for Sydney and a period of great historical significance generally: Edward VIII had succeeded his father George V on the throne after the latter died aged 70 at Sandringham. This sparked a developing constitutional crisis, for it wouldn't be long before the new king announced his intention to marry American divorcee Wallis Simpson. It caused a sensation and would lead to abdication before the end of the year. Once it leaked out, news of royal romance and its implications held the nation spellbound, but for Sydney other things were at the forefront of his mind. To be back in the fresh air and flying around running tracks in May, for example, must have been a huge physical and psychological relief for him, following those endless days penned indoors poring over law books.

Sydney continued to enjoy his long Sunday walks into the countryside as a release from the drudgery of the working week, but had done little in the way of serious running for nine months until May arrived. All his painstaking study led to a positive outcome, anyway, the pages of *The Times* in early April listing the names of those who had passed the 'Trust accounts and bookkeeping' portion of their Intermediate exam. Sydney's name was one of 362 passes out of nearly 500 who sat the tests.

★ ★ ★

The 1936 summer season would prove another hugely eventful and largely successful one for 21-year-old Sydney, but for all the fabulous performances he put in, there was always a shadow looming in the background. This was created by a nagging injury to his left ankle which, at first, seemed relatively minor and had little impact on his running for a number of weeks, certainly as far as racing went. However, the fact that he never allowed it to heal fully must have aggravated the problem, for it would worsen and ultimately play a major role in defining his season.

It remains unclear all these years later exactly when the ankle trouble began. Some reports suggested it was a sprain that occurred in mid-May, others – including a quote attributed to Sydney himself, plus a passage in Chris Brasher's 1960 book *Road to Rome* – talk of the incident occurring during a Sunday morning walk in the countryside near Sevenoaks during June. It could be the confusion stems from either or both these incidents actually being aggravations of a problem that first occurred much earlier. There is evidence Sydney told one reporter the problem dated right back to late 1934, to an occasion he stubbed the ground when attempting to kick a football.

He told another interviewer: "Every Sunday brother Stanley and I would go for these long walks, 15 miles or so, the longest being 30 miles. We'd leave after breakfast at 9 and be out all day. Sometimes taking the train to Wimbledon, we'd walk over the Common, or to Guildford, Dorking or Sevenoaks. It was near Sevenoaks I stepped in a rabbit hole and twisted my ankle, but I didn't know [how serious this was] at the time. We would take the train to Surrey sometimes, near the Pilgrim's Way, pick up the Way and walk along it, crossing into Kent and going on till we felt like coming back, walking roads and tracks over the open country, sandwiches and a thermos in our pockets."

Whatever the true injury timeline, Sydney's opening run of the season in mid-May saw him looking in fine shape as he won a Blackheath club half-mile in a classy 1:56.8. With 200 yards to go he'd pulled clear of John Poole to win well in good weather on a fast Catford Bridge track. A week later, on the evening of Wednesday 20 May, he won the mile in a club match against Cambridge Harriers at Charlton Park in SE London. He recorded a modest 4:44.6, not being stretched by the opposition, beating the home team's Hugo Young by four seconds, and his brother Stanley coming third. A week further on came the Palmers Green track meet mentioned earlier, when he replicated his 1:56.8, thus proving the time had not been a flash in the pan.

The first important fixture of the summer was the British Games at White City on Whitsun Bank Holiday Monday – into which the Inter-Counties championships had been incorporated for the first time, as part of an all-day programme. Twenty counties were represented and most of the top athletes in contention for Berlin turned up on a bright, chilly afternoon. Sydney's mile rival Jerry Cornes was among them.

Cornes showed his commitment to the British cause by taking a nine-month sabbatical from his Colonial Office job in South Africa specifically to prepare for the Olympics. He threatened for much of the mile race at White City only to finish fourth, unable to cope with a storming last lap. Sydney was in irresistible form and in the colours of Kent set up a new inter-counties record of 4:16.4, holding Bernard Eeles off in controlled fashion.

Sydney's timing and judgement had again looked impeccable as he showed them all a clean pair of heels and the *Sporting Chronicle* was highly impressed: "In Wooderson we definitely have a potential 1500m Olympic champion." Joe Binks was even more bullish:

> "I feel confident that, excepting accidents, Wooderson will defeat the world in the 1500 metres in Berlin, just as his adviser Albert Hill did at Antwerp in 1920. From where does 8st 2lb Wooderson obtain that tremendous power? It requires great strength to take the lead at the bell in front of class runners, then ward off the opposition and sprint away at the finish, yet Wooderson does it with apparent ease. I could see by his action all around the last lap that Wooderson was running with plenty of reserve."

The sporting public of the Medway towns were clearly impressed by Sydney's growing reputation and five days later, on Saturday 6 June, came out in force for his first appearance in their district, at the Kent county championships. The track at the United Services Ground in Gillingham was in fine condition and although the weather improved after a week of cold winds, it was hardly flaming June as the county titles went up for grabs. Sydney had opted to come here and regain the county title rather than honour his selection for the AAA team in a midweek contest with Cambridge University AC at Fenners.

For much of the mile race at Gillingham he loitered behind the main pack, running alongside brother Stanley, but was galvanised into action by the bell, whereupon he lengthened his stride to win comfortably by five yards or so from Hugo Young of Cambridge Harriers. It was a relatively slow 4:27.4 but still a new Kent record, prompting onlookers to ponder whether any county record had ever been made with such consummate ease. Had he been pushed, Sydney could have achieved a much faster time, but wasn't in pursuit of records, his motivation clearly a slow and steady climb towards a bigger goal later. He was pleased to regain his county title, having missed the meeting in 1935, and glad to be a part of a highly successful day overall for Blackheath.

The poor weather plaguing the start of the English summer continued into the following weekend, but heavy rain failed to dampen the spirits of crowd and competitors alike at the Kinnaird Trophy meeting at White City, an annual inter-club contest established before the Great War. The past and present Oxbridge men of the Achilles club finished top of the pile for the umpteenth time, with Blackheath fourth, and many of Britain's Olympic hopefuls shone brightly during the day.

Thirty-seven-year-old Arthur Norris won the Poly Marathon in 2:35.20 to retain his title and the meeting included an astonishing debut performance at three miles by Jack Lovelock, who smashed the meeting record with 14:20.2. Sydney had no interest in longer races at this stage and stuck to the mile, where he again sprinted away in characteristic style late on to win by 10 yards in 4:20.2, Jerry Cornes never looking like catching him. A slow second lap played into his hands allowing him to smoothly move into position on the penultimate circuit, before hitting the front just after the bell. He was cheered heartily to the tape by a good number of Blackheath men among the 5,000 crowd, including his brothers Alfred and Stanley. The control and ease with which Sydney was handling these big mile races suggested he was confident and building nicely towards a peak at Berlin.

11

Like an Arrow from a Bow

ONE thing always bugged me during the years I lived in Chelmsford. There was a stretch of the A1060 just around the corner from where I lived, known locally as Bundick's Hill. The detail of Bundick's identity seems to have disappeared in the mists of time, and I became convinced it would be far more appropriate to re-name this location 'Wooderson Hill'.

For this undulating section of road swoops past Admiral's Park and Tower Gardens to the west of the city, passing the spot where Sydney smashed the British mile record on a summer's afternoon in 1936 with a stunning performance – and he did it on a makeshift and misshapen grass track too!

Sydney's historic run of 4:10.8 sent shock-waves through the sporting world, and enthralled 5,000 locals on the afternoon of Saturday 20 June. It plucked the record from the grasp of Jack Lovelock who was in attendance, watching smilingly in the sunshine, having opted to run the half-mile instead of doing battle with Sydney again. Lovelock's non-participation no doubt encouraged Sydney to go for the record as it meant their ongoing duel would not be a distraction. It was reported that coach Hill had suggested Sydney use Chelmsford as a time-trial with the aim of running an unprecedented four equal laps of 62 seconds.

Exactly when Sydney decided on a record attempt is unclear, but it can be safely assumed his preparations for Chelmsford were considerably more circumspect than those of playboy Lovelock. The Kiwi apparently spent the previous day indulging in some nude swimming and sunbathing, before going dancing in the evening. The first two of those activities were at a notorious spot known as Parson's Pleasure, beside the River Cherwell in Oxford's University Parks. It was strictly a men-only facility, with a women and children's equivalent, known as Dame's Delight, apparently positioned on the opposite bank. Lovelock's dancing – fully clothed presumably – then took place on the Friday evening at Rhodes House, a remarkable mansion in Oxford built less than ten years earlier as a meeting place for Rhodes scholars. It was an interesting, if unconventional, way to prepare for the 14th annual Southern Counties AAA championships in Chelmsford the following day.

These 'Southerns' were being hosted with great enthusiasm for the first time by Chelmsford AC and friends, despite the fact they had no proper cinder running track to offer the elite athletes in attendance. Massive local interest and good weather saw programmes sell out completely, and the record crowd tightly packed under the parkland trees enjoyed plenty of drama – including pole vaulter Vanall coming a real cropper when his pole spectacularly snapped in two.

Earlier, journalists and athletics' officials – including a number of the British Olympic selectors – had strolled up Rainsford Road to the ground from the railway station, their conversation centred on rumours in the London papers that Sydney was to attempt the GB record. His alleged intentions had been leaked to the Fleet Street correspondents who, almost to a man, decided Sydney had little or no chance of running under 4:12 on this imperfect track, despite his good form of late. 'Ubiquitous' of the *Sporting Chronicle* would eat humble pie afterwards, admitting Sydney had proved him wrong in the most surprising race he'd ever witnessed.

On this warm afternoon, the 3pm scheduled start of the mile was delayed in comedy fashion when latecomer Hodges (Southgate) suddenly hove into view and pleaded loudly to be allowed to get changed and compete. This was granted and eventually 21 men were sent on their way by the pistol, one quitting very early with a nasty calf wound after being spiked. Uncharacteristically, Sydney shot off quickest, but gave way after roughly 200 yards to Henderson (Polytechnic Harriers), who clearly had the job of pacemaker.

A gap soon opened as Henderson completed the first lap in a swift 60.2, closely pursued by Sydney, and then slowed a little to reach halfway in 2:04.4, within GB record schedule. At this point Sydney was left in front alone as his pacemaker dropped back. It would be a solo effort, no waiting games today, and crystal clear to any doubters that this really was a record attempt. He maintained form and the rest couldn't live with him, the lead slowly increasing to some 30 yards by the start of the last lap (3:08.8). The noise levels rose, but Sydney looked smooth and untroubled.

A rather colourful radio report described him as shooting clear at the start of the third lap like "an arrow from a bow" but this was pure hyperbole, for he was perfectly on course for the record by now and had no need to surge. There was perhaps a slight slowing just before the bell – possibly due to the slope, possibly a sign of mental strain – but with nothing to chase except the clock on that final circuit Sydney clocked 62 seconds and a fabulous new record was his. It was a thrilling sight as the sun blazed down on 5,000 roaring spectators, talented men trailing helplessly in his wake as he won by 45 yards, nearly eight seconds clear of the RAF's Reg Thomas.

It was a new British record, 1.2 seconds inside the 4:12 set by Lovelock in Oxford four years earlier. To knowledgeable onlookers it was not only a big surprise on this unfavourable track, but remarkable in that he'd managed it with such ease and confidence. Sydney's 1935 run in Glasgow had made him the fastest British-born miler of all time, but this elevated him to the fastest ever on British soil. With the Olympics less than seven weeks away it was a huge morale boost. Even level-headed coach Albert Hill looked jubilant. What made the new record so notable was the nature of the Rainsford Road track: This was no springy, sheltered, perfectly flat neoprene running track like the ones we enjoy in the 21st century. Sydney was basically running four laps of a cricket field, complete with misshapen, almost rectangular corners, slopes and dips. He had to travel outside the boundary ropes, meaning he was on grass used by spectators and not the cricket field itself.

One correspondent wrote in awe of what he'd seen:

> "The graceful ease with which this marvellous run was accomplished; the utter absence of any symptom of distress – during its performance or subsequently – and the manner in which Wooderson sailed away from such magnificent previous champions, left an ineffaceable memory."

For Blackheath it was a case of "we told you so". One club official wrote:

> "Most of us have known for two years what our miler could and

would do, but people have been sceptical. During the Counties' mile at the [White City] Stadium on Whit Monday I said to the athletics correspondent of our most important daily: 'My club believe our boy Sydney has 4:10 in this pocket when he wants to produce it.' He thought it was a leg pull."

Lovelock, whose half-mile race was much later in the afternoon, was pictured in the next day's papers offering congratulations to Sydney, looking the height of Oxbridge cool in his Oxford bags and sports jacket. Both men were smiling broadly and the handshakes looked sincere despite their fierce rivalry. Also in one of the Sunday editions was a cartoon by Mercer, who joked about Sydney running faster than a LNER train, so fast that even his own shadow couldn't keep up, and would still have won if he'd run in top hat, tails and sea boots!

In a more serious vein, the *Sunday Times*' Harold Abrahams said Sydney had become the most talked-of miler in the world, his winning time only ever bettered twice in history throughout Europe. Abrahams even suggested a world record might be on the cards at the Olympics.

★★★

A week later Sydney was on his travels again, this time by train to Devon. Albert Hill had expressed a wish to put him up against different competitors, at different types of venue, in order to further his development – and Home Park in Plymouth, 250 miles from home, was indeed a different sort of challenge. Sydney once again ran well inside the Olympic qualifying time of 4:32 – as he won the inter-club mile race for the Travers Stubbs Trophy in a relatively steady 4:24.2. The quartet of Sydney plus Poole, Page and Wiard again travelled westwards to defend the trophy they'd won a year earlier. A good crowd of around 7,000 saw Peter Ward (Achilles) lead for much of the race while Sydney stayed handily placed and pounced decisively 250 yards from home to win by a good ten yards or so. His other duty of the day was to run a half-mile leg in the mile relay, which he completed in one second over two minutes.

Blackheath tied for the overall club prize with Achilles and an enjoyable weekend away for their quartet was capped on the Saturday evening by a dinner hosted by the Lord Mayor of Plymouth. To his relief, Sydney wasn't expected to join the list of speech-makers, but did find his new status as British record holder won him more attention from well-wishers and admirers than he was used to.

June 1936 had seen Sydney race over a mile at a consistently high standard in widely differing surroundings. He'd won all five races in an average time of just under 4:20, i.e. more than 12 seconds inside the qualifying standard for the Olympic mile. The only worry in the back of his mind remained the health of his left ankle. He'd certainly put it to the test recently, but was it steadily healing or was he impeding his own recovery? Clearly he needed to build up properly to the Olympics, but putting too much stress on the ankle might be disastrous. Getting things right over this crucial period presented a huge dilemma: Sydney was able to run and run hard, so he ignored the discomfort, but it did become evident during the month of June that after races he was showing signs of a definite limp.

Towards the end of the month the limp had become more acute and it must have been clear the remedial treatment he was having was not overcoming the damage being done by continuing to race. The injury, publicly at least, was diagnosed as bruising of soft tissue and a slight, but persistent strain. With hindsight we can see he managed to race at least once a week between early May and mid-July with no serious setbacks. But it became a bigger talking point in early July, a month before Berlin, when he walked out for the AAA championships with the ankle heavy strapped.

His last outing before the AAAs was the Kent inter-club mile relay at the annual Ravensbourne Sports at Lee Green. As Sydney was still living at the family home in Camberwell at this point, reaching this fine venue only involved a short hop of barely five miles on the cloudy, rather humid afternoon of Saturday 4 July. The annual Ravensbourne gala, with its leisurely programme lasting all afternoon and well into the evening, was sometimes referred to as SE London's answer to Ascot. One regular Blackheath visitor reflected fondly how it had become one of the few remaining 'flower show' sports meetings:

> "Although [the programme of sport] was five hours long, there was always something to watch in what the long summer of memory recalls as fine weather, accompanied by tents, bands and a garden party atmosphere that did not seem at all unfamiliar to the main surviving 19th century member of our club."

Sydney was part of a four-man Blackheath 'A' team which won the mile medley relay title for a ninth successive year. The time for his 880-yard leg was a swift 1:58.2, prompting gossip in the press that he might be thinking of 'doubling up' at 800 and 1500 metres at the Olympics. His run contributed to a mile time of 3:33.4 by Blackheath's quartet, which blew away all opposition. The occasion was rounded off nicely when an AAA official presented Sydney with an engraved plaque to commemorate his mile record at Chelmsford.

Less than a month before the Olympics were due to start, the AAA championships at White City attracted arguably the strongest field of milers ever seen on British soil. It all helped focus yet more attention on Britain's prospects for Berlin and in particular those of Sydney, the young pretender to Lovelock's crown as King of the Mile. These two were set to go head-to-head again this weekend over the classic four-lap distance for the first time in 11 months, but first had to deal with qualifying heats on the cold, damp and windy Friday evening of July 10.

After his heroics over three miles on June 13, Lovelock was by now sharpening his speed and a few days earlier ran a 660-yard time-trial in 1:20.2, his fastest ever, at Herne Hill. If this put the wind up his opponents, there were no celebrations from Lovelock himself, for he remained unhappy with his general fitness – and after his AAAs heat spoke about his prospects in the final: "[There is] no great kick there yet, and I may not be able to summon up enough of the will to win. But we shall see tomorrow afternoon." He had qualified by coming third in 4:22 in his heat, while Sydney enjoyed a slower but less anxiety-ridden ride to qualify in second place in a separate heat in 4:25.4. Sydney's ankle bandage, however, showed he too was less than 100 per cent happy about his fitness.

By wearing strapping and bandages quite openly, it seems Sydney prompted the Lovelock camp to believe the injury was just a minor issue otherwise he would have been much more 'secretive' about it. They were probably wide of the mark with that assumption, for kidology wasn't normally part of Sydney's armoury.

Saturday's final of nine men featured a real star-studded galaxy of milers, Sydney and Lovelock alongside the likes of Scot Bobby Graham, Jerry Cornes, Bernard Eeles and Denis Pell. Guy Butler of the *Morning Post* had followed and analysed the careers of Sydney and Lovelock more closely than anyone else, and he told his readers the mile was the most dramatic race of the championships and roused a big crowd to a great pitch of excitement. He wrote:

> "I formed the opinion from heats that Graham's only chance would be in a really hard race. He did the make the pace [in the final] but it was not nearly hot enough to extend Wooderson and Lovelock, both of whom kept with him, moving with almost nonchalant ease. His 2:09 for halfway was probably six seconds too easy for the world beaters."

Lovelock wanted to test his finish against Sydney's, to discover just where he stood with a view to the Olympic 1500 title. He wouldn't have enjoyed the start of this race, at which point the day's bad weather was at its worst – the rain pelting down heavily. The Kiwi was badly buffeted in the helter-skelter of a fast start. He tucked in behind Cornes who led at halfway and then did the same behind Sydney who hit the front at the bell. Lovelock exerted pressure with 250 yards to go but Sydney responded well to this rather half-hearted effort and Lovelock simply dropped back instead of kicking again. They seemed to cruise around the final bend before he made a second effort with 60 yards left, but everything he was doing was being covered with ease by Sydney.

The big smile returned to Lovelock's face – even during a final fruitless push in the last ten yards. Sydney came in full of running, having covered the final furlong of 220 yards in 30 seconds dead. Given the appalling conditions, his winning time of 4:15 was excellent running. It was another boost for home fans to see him beating Lovelock again, although it was fairly clear the latter was only interested in peaking in Berlin and wouldn't be overly worried at finishing second. Indeed, he intimated after the race he knew he could get better and suggested Sydney might have hit peak form too soon. "We shall see in Berlin!" he added.

The British press was going Wooderson crazy by now though, tipping Sydney for Olympic glory despite the ongoing ankle trouble. He was again seen to be limping after this race, but *The Times* called him "a consistent master of his craft" who had conquered gruelling conditions as well as top opposition. The British team for Berlin was announced immediately after the AAAs event and, predictably, Sydney, Cornes and Graham were named as our men in the 1500 metres. Lingering speculation that Sydney might also attempt the 800 metres proved wide of the mark.

Britain's medal hopes for Berlin –
Godfrey Brown, Donald Finlay and Sydney Wooderson.

Sydney had worked hard with coach Hill lately to sharpen his speed – including those outings at 880 yards – and it appeared to be paying dividends. He was proving almost impossible to pass once he kicked for home in races. But, typically, he was keeping quiet about his prospects, and must have been praying the ankle problem wouldn't worsen.

A week after winning in the pouring rain at White City, Sydney decided not to join Blackheath teammates competing in a colossal programme of events in Durants Park at the Ponders End meeting in North London. This wasn't entirely a case of wrapping himself in the proverbial cotton wool, for he turned out for the club in another 'sharpener' – a 4 x 880 yards relay at a southern league meeting in Deptford Park on the evening of Wednesday 22 July – exactly a fortnight before he was due to take the track in Berlin. Here he helped Blackheath into second place behind Polytechnic Harriers, running the anchor leg. He ran well but the ankle was worryingly sore afterwards.

Most British competitors completed their public preparations on Saturday 25 July, exactly a week before the Olympics' scheduled start. A good number performed at the Waddilove Trophy inter-club contest at the Birchfield Harriers Sports in Perry Barr, Birmingham, in front of a bumper crowd of 8,000. Sydney didn't join them, but was no doubt interested to hear that Lovelock (9:03.4) knocked a tenth of a second off the British two-mile record held by Alf Shrubb for 32 years.

12

Crunch Time in Berlin

A WEEK or so before the British team were to leave for Berlin, Sydney judiciously sought expert advice before making the final decision whether to travel or pull out. His ankle was X-rayed at Charing Cross Hospital, and after nothing serious could be seen, got the all-clear to continue running – even though he was scarcely able to limp around a training track at this point.

The injury had definitely felt worse over the last fortnight, but he now had two weeks for it to recover and the decision was taken to give Berlin a shot. It was clearly a risky business, but this was the Olympics after all. He spoke at length with Albert Hill and they quietly went ahead with their plans and everyone hoped for the best.

Blackheath officials were paying for Hill to travel to Berlin, and in addition to his valuable presence, Sydney knew he'd be able to get treatment from masseur Mick Mays. Mays was not part of official GB team management, which was a pitifully small group, but part of a travelling party organised by Surrey official Jack Crump. Crump was helping GB on an unofficial basis and promised Sydney that Mays would help him. Over time, Sydney would develop immense faith and trust in the ability of the hard-working Mays, whose background was service with the St John Ambulance Brigade, the Royal Army Medical Corps and at Tooting & Mitcham Football Club. Sydney's mother Nettie and brother Stanley would also be in Berlin, to lift morale if needed, although travelling independently and staying elsewhere in the city.

Observing Sydney's condition at close quarters en route, and later in Berlin, Mays became very unhappy about his participation in the Games. Although there is no record of Mays urging Sydney not to run, he did confide his disapproval to Crump after becoming convinced the injury was of a quite serious nature.

The German and Italian athletes were among those benefitting from full financial backing from their governments, but for the likes of Britain, funds were limited as regards travel and the 'backroom' team. GB was relying heavily on a public appeal to boost interest among the public – and thus increase donations – and accordingly our medal hopes were 'talked up' in confident style. Officials didn't want to play down Sydney's chances because of his ankle, although of course the speculation did begin in the media.

In quiet moments Sydney must have pondered on how things would pan out if his ankle didn't heal in time. If he dropped out, would he be letting everybody down? His family? His coach and his club? Would he ever get another chance to be an Olympian? If so, where would that be? Maybe in London in 1940 when he would be 26 and at his peak as a runner?

Future Olympic venues were a big talking point that week, and just as athletes and officials began arriving in Berlin from all over the globe, news broke that Britain had withdrawn its bid to stage the 1940 Olympiad. This left the way clear for a straight fight between Finland and Japan and within a few days the latter was declared winner by the IOC by 36 votes to 27.

Japanese competitors were among the first arrivals in Berlin, having travelled for 12 days along the trans-Siberian route. Spain were absent altogether due to the civil war by now raging in that country, while Brazil, bizarrely, sent two teams as their sport was administered by two separate national federations. The early arrivals were keen to get a lengthy period of acclimatisation, including the Australians who had endured a six-week journey.

The British men's squad didn't set off until late on Wednesday 29 July, catching a mid-evening train from Liverpool Street bound for the Harwich ferry to the Hook of Holland, where they would continue by train to Berlin. Every individual was given a return ticket from London to Berlin by the London and North Eastern Railway Company, plus good quality meals and a reserved sleeping berth on the overnight ferry. It was a 20-hour journey in all, and the North Sea crossing proved very rough; it was reported several athletes chose to spend much of the night out on deck because of seasickness – among those looking particularly unwell were Sydney and Godfrey Rampling.

On arrival, however, Sydney managed to summon up a cheery demeanour for the cameras, although he couldn't hide his limp. His smile no doubt masked his concerns, especially when told that rival Lovelock had travelled 48 hours earlier than him, and by now had already done some work on the Olympic village training track, where he'd been seen chatting with the legendary Paavo Nurmi.

The British men were welcomed to Berlin by remarkable scenes, thousands greeting them on the platform and in the station square, hands upraised in a Nazi salute as a brass band blared out the British national anthem. The *Sporting Chronicle* was touched to hear 'God Save the King' in this setting, and called the whole scene "almost overwhelming". The city was alive with noise and a carnival atmosphere, decked out with swastikas and flags everywhere.

No Olympics had ever looked or sounded like this before, and the grandiosity would set a precedent for future Games. The Brits were given an official reception at the main civic hall but were no doubt relieved when the time finally came to head for their quarters in the Olympic village. It had been built in the countryside a short distance to the west of the city; the rooms were small but adequately equipped, the food was good and the organisation generally superb. The British were wide-eyed as they gazed at the roadsides en route to the village, for they were packed ten deep with Berliners. Sydney wasn't the only one who had never seen anything quite like it.

The following day the British women arrived at breakfast time, tired and weary after missing a rail connection at Aachen. They'd been kept well away from their male counterparts, having taken a train from London to Dover and then put on the Ostend ferry. There was no official reception as for the men, and much less fuss. They were told in no uncertain terms they had to be in bed by 10.30pm, and earlier on nights preceding competition. As they settled into their separate quarters, not in the Village but close to the stadium itself, on the Friday morning, Sydney was seen out in the sunshine with other runners, none of whom appeared to be training hard at this stage. He was still limping slightly, the reporters noted, but told them his ankle felt much better and he thought it wouldn't affect him in the races.

Other nations seemed to believe the British had arrived far too late to allow proper acclimatisation. Particularly outspoken on this topic was USA coach Lawson Robertson, who said the GB timetable hampered its own athletes – althought he firmly believed Sydney would win the 1500 gold medal ("He can beat Lovelock as he likes – he must be some boy!"). Of course the Americans had their own unique problems to deal with – various antics on the ocean liner bringing them to Europe had caused controversy before they even reached German soil: Nightly cocktail parties were reportedly lengthy and lively, and on one occasion officials entertained athletes by performing a mock marriage and mock trial said to have descended into 'X-rated' behaviour, prompting some onlookers to walk out. Among the shocked audience was swimmer Eleanor Holm Jarrett, who ended up being axed from the USA squad for allegedly drinking too much.

It was all grist to the Berlin rumour mill, but when thoughts turned to the Games themselves, the major gossip in the GB camp centred around three big questions: Firstly, which teams would give the Nazi salute during the opening ceremony and which would refuse; secondly, would Lovelock opt for a 1500-and 5000-metres double at these Games; thirdly, was Sydney Wooderson fully fit and flying?

The fact he had doubts so late in the day is further evidence how Lovelock, for all his talent, struggled with anxiety throughout his career despite an almost arrogant exterior. Sydney, quiet by nature and further inhibited by the injury worries, predictably kept a low profile and only shared his hopes and fears with coach Hill.

The British team was hardly an ideal example of unified team spirit: Jack Crump reflected later in his memoirs *Running Round the World* that they were split into two camps – the 'ordinary' Brits and the Oxbridge set. Broadly speaking, this was also the case among British athletics fans too: fans of Sydney – the people's hero – knew their man lacked Lovelock's experience and know-how but were banking on his proven ability to hang on and use his superior finishing speed; on the other hand supporters of Oxford man Lovelock were convinced he'd been building towards the 1500 metres all along, and that was all that mattered to him. Sydney must have sensed how desperate the nation was for him to succeed – meaning his injury dilemma will have tormented him all the more. He hated letting people down.

The opening ceremony and parade of athletes was staged with unprecedented pomp and circumstance on the afternoon of Saturday 1 August. Athletes with events the following day had dispensation not to attend, but 100,000 stadium seats were still occupied. The roars of 'Sieg Heil' as Hitler arrived drowned out the booming loudspeakers and the orchestra playing Wagner. One athlete recalled an atmosphere of near hysteria invading the arena. Sticking to tradition, the Greeks led the parade past the balcony where Hitler and cohorts stood. Then followed around 50 other nations in alphabetical order with the 400-strong German team bringing up the rear. The British contingent lined up behind their flag-bearer, the rower Jack Beresford, who was at his fifth Olympiad. Despite the financial constraints, the Brits looked smart in dark blue blazers and white flannels and skirts.

With no specific orders how to react when passing the VIPs, some nations gave the Nazi salute (e.g the French, winning themselves a huge ovation in the process), some gave the Olympic salute (not dissimilar anyway), and others, including the British, merely performed a military-style 'eyes right'. This had been advised by GB management, one athlete confirmed later. The *Daily Express* condemned this, suggesting GB should have followed "the unexpected example of France" and won the approval of the crowd instead of provoking the embarrassing near-silence that greeted them. When it came to lowering flags at the point of passing the dignitaries, every nation followed protocol – except the USA. The Swiss team added a spot of show-boating, their lead athlete repeatedly twirling his flag skywards and catching it again.

Presumably diplomacy, politically-motivated posturing and the worrying rise of Nazism didn't occupy the mind of Sydney Wooderson for too long. He had to get back to the Village to have more treatment and rest his ankle to have any chance of running on this same track four days later. But of course he couldn't fail to be fascinated by the amazing scenes, and at some stage managed to point his camera and snap a picture of the Führer. It survives to this day in the possession of his son Philip.

The first three days of competition at this 11th Olympiad proved unproductive for Britain, which only intensified the hopes pinned on Sydney back home. Those with radio sets would struggle to get immediate news of his qualifying heat on Wednesday 5 August, but could look forward

Sydney's own snapshot of Hitler (circled) in the Berlin Olympiastadion.

to a live broadcast the following day of the 1500 metres final. It would be on the BBC's National Programme (appropriately broadcasting on the 1500 metres wavelength!) and would be heard at 4.10 in the afternoon. It would be a 20-minute slot, shoe-horned between a talk by literary critic Eric Gillett, and music from the Cellini Trio and Tommy Finnigan and his Band. That day's schedule also featured programmes on farming, dentistry and the Eisteddfod of Wales. The BBC was nothing if not eclectic in 1936.

And so, after nearly a week in Germany nursing his ankle along, closely monitored by Albert Hill and Mick Mays, the fifth day of the Games arrived. Sydney was putting a brave face on things but had found the tree-lined training track in the village much too firm for his liking. Nevertheless, he'd got on with his schedule of light training and despite all the worries was going to give it a go. He could still run fast on the damaged ankle, and with luck it would tolerate the two tests in two days at the *Olympiastadion*. Breaking down on the track was a horrendous prospect, but dropping out beforehand seemed just as unthinkable at this late stage.

The day of reckoning dawned and the weather in Berlin was cloudy, cool and showery. The four heats of the 1500 metres were scheduled to take place between 5 and 6pm that Thursday, meaning Sydney faced a long and nervous day of hanging around before the moment of truth. The line-up of 11 men in his heat, on paper at least, did not look especially strong however. If he ran anywhere near his best he would surely make the final with ease. The only cloud on the horizon was the bandaged ankle – and it was a big cloud. Everybody outside his inner circle had been told he'd be fine and didn't expect it to unduly trouble him. This, of course, was piffle. In a club colleague's words, he went into this race "hoping against hope."

During that chilly Thursday afternoon Herr Hitler and General Goering and cohorts made their fifth successive daily visit to the stadium, settling into their seats just in time for a heat of the women's 80 metres hurdles. They witnessed the comical sight of a nervous German competitor losing her balance and falling over during the wait for the starter's pistol. This gave a Dutch girl beside her a fit of the giggles and the start had to be delayed – even Hitler and Goering raised a smile. Once they got away the race was won by Londoner Violet Webb in close to record time.

Most onlookers' minds were focussed on the day's big finale when Jesse Owens would bid to add the 200 metres title to the 100 and long jump golds he'd already won. But before then the four heats of the men's

1500 would begin around 6pm in windy and chilly conditions. The first three in each heat would make the following day's final. Jack Lovelock and Britain's Jerry Cornes eased through in a slow-run second heat, and in the third Scotsman Bob Graham put up a magnificent fight but missed third place by less than half a second.

Sydney was drawn in the fourth and final heat. He must have reflected on the bizarre fact that this Olympic debut was also his very first race over the so-called 'metric mile' of 1500 metres – a run 109 metres shorter than the imperial mile he was used to. He expected his most dangerous opponent to be USA's Archie San Romani, in many eyes a dark horse for a medal at these Games. Pat Boot of New Zealand had withdrawn to concentrate on the 800 metres, suffering like Sydney with a lower leg problem. It meant a place in the top three looked, on paper at least, a formality for someone of Sydney's talent.

If the early stages weren't too demanding and it turned into a slow race like Lovelock had enjoyed, then Sydney could cruise round and, if necessary, unleash his fast finish without stressing his injury too much. The weather was still miserable, the atmosphere rather gloomy and what Sydney didn't need was a fast and uneven tempo early on. But that was exactly what he got.

Wearing the GB kit of all-white with a red and a blue hoop around the vest, a large No.258 pinned to his chest and a heavily strapped left ankle, Sydney, as usual, looked the smallest man in a field of 11. Reporters noted that the limp they'd all seen during his preparations was still discernible as he passed on the first lap. It was clear the problem hadn't worn off in recent days as the British camp had hoped. Nevertheless Sydney could still travel at a decent clip and seemed to have the measure of those ahead of him. San Romani led at 400 metres in 59.8, and halfway was reached in 2:08.4, by which time Sydney had moved up from sixth to fourth. At the bell he slipped back a little, but along the final back straight pushed on into second place, although his usual smooth and springy stride was not evident. He couldn't build on this and faded back again to fourth before another plucky push saw him haul in the leaders again and, for a second or two, victory looked on the cards.

Then, just as it seemed he might overhaul Fritz Schaumburg of Germany he suddenly jerked and slowed badly. "It was as if his progress had been checked by an invisible strand of wire," reported the *Sporting Chronicle*.

Sydney reeled as if in pain or shock, possibly both, but for a few seconds seemed desperate not to quit. With less than 50 yards to go, he seemed to hop awkwardly on the damaged foot before limping wearily at walking pace looking battered and downcast. He had practically stopped by the time he was 20 yards from the tape and the others all flew past him. Onlookers were stunned, Britain's great golden hope in these Games was done for at the first hurdle. Amid the confusion it remained unclear whether he even finished the race. Some reports said he came 11th and last, some records have him down as not finishing, while Reuters reported he was 8th. Frenchman Robert Goix won in 3:54, San Romani was exactly a second behind, and Schaumburg took the final qualifying spot with 3:55.2. These were, of course, 1500 times comfortably within a fully-fit Sydney's capability.

W. Capel-Kirby wrote in the *Chronicle*:

> "It was pathetic for those of us who saw him beat Lovelock at the AAAs a month ago and also witnessed his British record run at Cheltenham [sic] this year. We could scarcely believe our eyes. I had feared the worst and hoped for the best since the team's arrival last Thursday. It will be remembered that I stated all was not well with Wooderson and other members of the British party. Efforts were made to cloak the true state of affairs. After all, seeing is believing, so within a couple of minutes of this tragedy I paid a visit to the GB dressing room area and was nearly bowled over by Lord Burghley who was doing 'evens' along the passage after a visit to see how Wooderson was. I do not know whether anything was said to Wooderson about making excuses, but he was unusually secretive when I asked him what had gone wrong: 'It was nothing,' he said. 'Did your ankle let you down?' I enquired. 'No I don't think so. I was just whacked,' came the reply. Then, under pressure, Wooderson did admit that it hurt him a little when he started his sprint for home, and I left him limping painfully to the bathroom. It was good to see him take the reverse in the best sporting spirit."

Jack Lovelock was among the first to commiserate and shake Sydney's hand, offering sincere words of regret over what had happened. The next day's *Times* said Lovelock now carried the weight of GB hopes into the final, reflecting the fact that a win for the New Zealander would be considered a win for the British Empire.

It had been a day of triumph and tragedy screamed the British sports pages the following day, referring to motor mechanic Harold Whitlock's great win in the 50-kilometre walk and Sydney's disaster on the track. Unfortunately for Whitlock, the British contingent were so deflated by Sydney's fate that the cheers he received shortly afterwards seemed a little subdued.

Jack Crump was among those feeling devastated although not really surprised:

> "In view of Mick Mays' anxious doubts about Wooderson's fitness I was not surprised… [He] looked likely to qualify at one stage of the race, but just couldn't speed up for anything like his normal finish, and finished a bewildered, lonely little figure, limping off the track in almost a dead silence. It transpired afterwards that he had a hair-line or stress fracture of the ankle which had not shown on the x-ray plate and that he should never have competed. Indeed, to train on and compete in such a condition constituted a feat of no mean courage."

How a fully fit Sydney would have fared in the all-star final we will never know. For British fans his absence was a crying shame, but for the Games in general it was soon forgotten as the race turned into a truly memorable contest. Lovelock, relieved of his worries about Sydney snapping at his heels, ran a masterful race, setting a new world record of 3:47.8, beating the all-American hero Cunningham more comprehensively than the margin of 0.6 of a second suggests. Beccali of Italy took the bronze, while Britain's Jerry Cornes ran well for 3:51.4 but could only manage sixth in a great race. As Lovelock was such a big name in England, thousands still tuned into the BBC radio broadcast despite Sydney's absence – and the sound of Harold Abrahams' almost hysterical commentary spread excitement throughout the land ("Come on Jack, 100 yards to go, come on Jack! My God he's done it! Jack, come on, Lovelock wins!")

Lovelock ran the fastest third lap of his life and kicked for home earlier than usual. Around 60 yards out – exactly where Sydney's world had collapsed the day before – he glanced around to size things up before powering on to stay clear of Cunningham. The German crowd reaction was remarkable, largely because they wanted to see the American beaten, it seems. "It was undoubtedly the most beautifully executed race of my career, a true climax to eight years of steady work, an artistic creation," wrote Lovelock later. When he was awarded his gold medal, 'God Save the King' rang out, in recognition of New Zealand's place in the British Empire. The sound of the national anthem was at least some compensation, one supposes, for the thousands back home who had pinned their hopes on Sydney.

Sydney's thoughts will have quickly turned to getting home where he could reflect quietly on the biggest disappointment of his sporting life so far, and get his injury examined and treated properly. His popularity among the public, his peers and the press would be reflected by a flood of sympathy. Columnist 'Ubiquitous' wrote:

> "I had hoped after the assurance given me by Wooderson and his father, that I had taken too pessimistic view and that the English champion's injury was less serious than I believed. Candidly, I wish I had been wrong. We are all sorry for Wooderson, who failed when he had the mind to do his best. He lives to try again, I hope, but I am afraid he will find a rest to his advantage. We have not seen the best of him. If Wooderson reserves that for another season all will be glad."

In the subsequent British Olympic Association Official Report, criticism was made of Sydney being allowed to run without a medical expert's permission, given that he'd been widely seen to be limping beforehand. The report conceded that although the ankle caused trouble in the latter stages of his heat, earlier on he had seemed to be hit by 'mental depression' that amounted to more than just stage fright or his own concern about the injury. His running had 'lacked life' as a result and during the race he'd obviously been at sixes and sevens over what course to pursue. The report highlighted the fact that event winner Lovelock's one regret had been the absence of Sydney Wooderson, but [the writer] believed no man in the world could have beaten Lovelock that day.

The BOA report's inference that Sydney flopped because the occasion was all too much for him seems rather harsh and simplistic with the benefit of hindsight. More likely it was a combination of several factors – including tiredness, the injury itself, the huge pressure of the occasion added to the anxiety over the injury. Sydney's refusal afterwards to use the injury as his main excuse seems a little strange – but begs the question had Lord Burghley rushed to the dressing rooms to advise him not to make too much of the injury. Clearly British officials wouldn't want to stand accused of pressurising an injured man to run. This is, of course, pure speculation, but might explain why Sydney's responses to journalists were so vague and bland when they asked what had gone wrong. The way he had stopped short of the finish-line was out of character and completely unprecedented.

Joe Binks, a respected and experienced observer, was certainly prepared to accept the theory that Sydney had simply blown up due to exhaustion, probably caused by over-training. A few days after the event, he wrote:

> "Watching Wooderson closely, I say nothing to cause alarm. He had a good position and the limp was no more pronounced than in previous races. Running strongly, to all appearances, he had just reached the third man, 20 yards out, when suddenly he stopped and walked to the winning post, rubbing his head as if puzzled at the happening. I spoke to Wooderson later and he seemed quite unperturbed. He said he could not find the speed to beat the third man, to qualify for the final, and therefore stopped. I think Wooderson had just gone over the line in his training and needs a rest."

Forlorn and desperate to get home again, Sydney would find himself pondering the state of mind of the champion Lovelock as the athletes made their way out of Berlin. As members of the British team waited on the platform at Friedrichstrasse station, he noticed Lovelock sitting alone, perched on his luggage, not mixing or talking with anyone, and seemingly oblivious to all around him. Papers held in the Alexander Turnbull Library in New Zealand show that many years later Sydney would reveal his thoughts of that day to interviewer James McNeish:

> "I wondered if [Lovelock] was on drugs. Lord Aberdare went over to him, asked if he was all right, but Lovelock just brushed him off."

Admitting to a long-standing fascination with Lovelock, Sydney continued:

> "I used to look up to Lovelock. He was my hero. I went to see him run in North London… he seemed to be in command, knew

exactly what he was doing. I was impressed. But when I began to beat him, it [became] a duel... he was a bit toffee-nosed, they seemed conceited these Oxford chaps. The spectators would shout [to me]: Come on 'Syd', not 'Sydney' [because, unlike Lovelock] I was an ordinary chap to them. I always wondered how Lovelock managed not to get himself boxed in [during races]... it happened a lot to me, as I was too small and had poor eyesight."

In the same interview an unusually talkative Sydney recounted the tale of British 10,000-metres runner Alec Burns returning to the Olympic village having been shown one of the Nazi's so-called 'baby farms': "[Burns] was very impressed. It was purely for breeding. He said they'd invited him to participate!" Sydney had been fascinated by the sights of Berlin, but couldn't keep pace with the likes of Burns, who not only visited the 'baby farm' but reportedly had lunch with Jesse Owens and met Hitler and Goering.

With a degree of shell-shock added to his normal reticence in the immediate weeks after Berlin, Sydney predictably had little to say about his disaster. Any quotes he gave over this period were the usual unrevealing mixture of politeness and brevity, but years later we would learn more. He summed things up to McNeish:

"Berlin was terrible. I was over-awed. I was very young and nervous and didn't talk to anyone much. I remember those big American athletes like Jesse Owens, they were all so tall and fit. I felt very inferior."

This echoed his admissions to Chris Brasher for the latter's 1960 book *Road to Rome*:

"Probably the mental effects [of the injury] were far more damaging than the physical. All the time I was worried about breaking down and it was in this state of mind that I went to Berlin. Albert Hill did all he could to restore my confidence but with little effect. When I went to the starting line for the heat of the 1500 I was in a limp and lethargic condition. I finished halfway down the field an exhausted, disappointed and dejected young man."

Speaking to Chris Tobin, another New Zealand writer, Sydney would admit that after reflecting fully on Berlin he doubted whether he would have beaten Lovelock in the final even if fully fit. He said he'd been too inexperienced at international level then, and didn't rule out the possibility that when travelling and racing away from his beloved England he was never able to perform at his very best. During this interview he admitted he'd never really got to know Lovelock and hinted they were never likely to have become friends as they were poles apart in almost every way. They'd raced each other a total of six times in two years, Sydney winning four, but their relationship was strictly that of two well-matched competitors and nothing more. Tobin points out that Sydney, not being part of the Oxbridge set, was never associated with the so-called glamour that always surrounded Lovelock:

> "Perhaps Lovelock was a bit condescending in his attitude [to Sydney] – he did become a bit of a social snob even though he came from quite humble origins in New Zealand."

* * *

During the latter stages of the Berlin Games Sydney was rather optimistically named by the GB selectors for the relay squad for a forthcoming match in London between the British Empire and USA. By then Sydney was already back home, having his foot examined. He declared himself unfit for the USA match, revealing that immediate surgery was required. An eminent orthopaedic surgeon called Paton carried out the X-rays and the damage to Sydney's ankle and lower leg was confirmed and he was hospitalised on Tuesday 18 August. The operation was hailed a success and described as a straightforward procedure to correct muscle displacement that had been due to a splintered fibula.

With his recuperation underway, Sydney fired off a letter to the editor of the Blackheath club *Gazette* to update members and thank them for supporting his Berlin adventure. Being a polite chap who wouldn't have wanted to make a fuss face-to-face with his colleagues, this was a predictable move – but what was slightly surprising was his use of this letter to have a little dig at the athletics authorities:

> "Dear Sir – I should like to thank the Club and certain prominent members for sending Albert Hill with me to Berlin. I was all the more thankful that he was able to stay in the Village, because of my injured leg. Hill certainly did all he could to get me fit, and the fact that I failed was no fault of his. Actually, he was a great help to a good many of the British team, and the Club, by sending him over, showed up a bad oversight of the AAA. The track in the Village was terribly hard, and I think this brought my foot trouble to a head. I am certain that the tracks had a lot to do with several failures of our team, as is borne out by their doing much faster times in the [August 15] match against USA. I am grateful to Mr Sercombe and Mr McIvor, who have supported me through the season and especially in the latter part, when they gave up much of their time to come to Battersea and even to the White City on training nights to inquire about my injury and to offer what help they could. As events have turned out, nothing could have put me right in time. Nevertheless, the trip to Germany was a wonderful experience and one which I shall always remember. Yours Heathenly, S. C. Wooderson."

Gordon McIvor, club secretary, said the findings of the orthopaedic surgeon and the subsequent surgery Sydney required was an emphatic answer to those press reports which suggested Sydney's defeat in Berlin was down to "staleness, injudicious training, nerves, being overawed by the occasion and many other theories". These remarks were surely partly directed at the British Olympic Association's Official Report of the Games, which suggested Sydney had suffered 'mental depression' in Berlin.

McIvor added: "Fate decreed that Wooderson should be denied his first Olympic final, and no-one deplored his absence more than Lovelock himself." By now it was looking as if Lovelock might soon retire from top-level athletics, and although Sydney had achieved the ambition of beating him already, the likelihood of the pair meeting on a track when both were fully fit now looked doubtful.

13

Out of the Limelight

BACK home in SE London, Sydney allowed himself to recover slowly and without fuss from the surgery and the stressful summer. His weekend walks in the countryside kept him active and helped strengthen his damaged body in the weeks before he resumed proper running again. He went along to his club's annual dinner later in the year, but opted not to run any cross-country throughout the winter of 1936–37.

Apart from brief publicity when the AAA formally ratified his English native mile record at Chelmsford (4:10.8), Sydney's name slipped out of the spotlight for months. It was a period when the nation would face a constitutional crisis, and once the full implications became clear, little attention was paid to much else in the news.

In mid-November the King informed Prime Minister Stanley Baldwin of his intention to marry divorcee Wallis Simpson. On being told the British public would never accept a twice-divorced American as their Queen, Edward caused an even bigger sensation stating he'd be prepared to abdicate if the government opposed the marriage. He duly signed an instrument of abdication on December 10, made his famous broadcast to the nation and headed off to Austria. His brother the Duke of York would succeed him as the new monarch, George VI.

Sydney's long absence from competition following the Olympic debacle lasted more than nine months. He didn't place a toe on a single start-line between August 1936 and May 1937. He resumed training during the winter once the ankle problem had healed, but it was never a

Back in the old routine after the Berlin fiasco.

particularly heavy workload, just enough to maintain good general fitness with steady 'sharpening' as the summer of 1937 approached.

At this point he was still living in the family home in Calais Street SE5 – and although he absented himself from an entire cross-country season, he didn't become a complete running hermit. The occasional letter begging his attendance at a function would still turn up – one such request was to present prizes at a sports meeting on May 14, which elicited a polite reply and acceptance from Sydney on bright blue writing paper. This document would appear on eBay in 2015, an American dealer asking £800 for it!

He was in no hurry to rush back into action, a fact underlined when he was unable to join an AAA team in Belfast in May, due to what was described as a 'minor disposition.' This came the same week as the coronation of George VI and Queen Elizabeth at Westminster Abbey on Wednesday 12 May, an event chosen to be the BBC's very first outside broadcast. Sydney's invitation to Belfast had come too soon, for he preferred his comeback, in this fourth summer as a senior athlete, to involve low-key events closer to home.

A week after the nation celebrated the coronation, Catford Bridge staged the traditional Blackheath evening meeting to open the summer season proper. Ronald Philo was newly installed as club captain and, as ever, bags of optimism and enthusiasm greeted the lighter evenings and lighter running kit. However, the weather was rather gloomy beside the railway tracks of Catford Bridge and an already soft track was made very heavy and the grass cut up badly. Blackheath's 'hardy annuals' turned out for this meet, although Sydney had only one opponent – half-mile specialist John Poole – in the 880 yards club championship race. Poole took an early lead and ran the first lap in 61 seconds, closely trailed by Sydney, who looked easier as the race went on, his strides gradually lengthening. In the final furlong he quickened up and his 2:03.4 won him the Barclay-Essen Challenge Cup.

This was widely regarded as his first proper race in the 41 weeks since Berlin, although records show he did run a 440 yards handicap at a club gathering on the Charlton Park cinder track on the cloudy, chilly Sunday evening of May 9. Here he was narrowly beaten into second place by John Furniss after clocking 51.9 off a 17 yards start. Earlier that night Sydney had won his 440-yard heat in an impressive 51.0 seconds.

Friday 28 May 1937 was a red letter day for the nation, with 68-year-old

Neville Chamberlain succeeding the retiring Stanley Baldwin as Britain's Prime Minister. But Sydney's mind that day will have been occupied largely by his return to big-time athletics the following day, for he was down to run the mile in the annual Kinnaird Trophy meeting at White City. The word among Sydney's friends was that he'd wintered well, and his ankle was well healed, reported *The Times*.

His showing at White City, particularly on a final lap of 57.5 seconds, would prove he was back to form and on course to retain his national mile crown. Wearing No.7, Sydney was in a big field of 24 as this annual Polytechnic Harriers event pulled in a big crowd in delightful conditions. It was no surprise when, for the 14th time, Achilles won comfortably via their strong team of Oxford and Cambridge athletes past and present, against 11 other squads. They amassed 79 points, and next best – thus making club history, although a long way behind – were Blackheath with 28. The mile was highlight of the day, with much interest in Sydney after his lay-off.

On a crowded track, at the end of the first lap Jack Emery (Achilles) led in 63.6 and was still in front at halfway in 2:12, but by the bell Franks (London AC) had taken over in 3:19.3. Over the first two laps in particular there was plenty of jostling and protruding elbows, causing anxiety among Sydney's clubmates and fans, but he stayed on his feet and escaped being spiked to steer clear of trouble. Ever-watchful, he decided to go for the relatively inexperienced Franks in the back straight on the last lap and passed without trouble. Frank Close, a cross-country specialist, displayed unexpected prowess at the shorter distance and challenged Sydney with great spirit, almost catching him at the top of the home straight.

The big Scotsman, Hamish Stothard of Achilles, was also not giving up yet, but Sydney was able to kick again creating an audible gasp from the bewitched crowd. His sprint took him well clear to win in 4:17.1, the second best time recorded in this annual mile. He'd won by around 12 yards and looked fresh at the end, even after a last lap of under 58 seconds. The rest staggered home in the oppressive heat in varying degrees of distress. Close, Franks and Stothard had at least given Sydney a run for his money, but the better-known Eeles and Reeve put in disappointing displays. The *Gazette* commented later:

> "We know it is difficult with 24 competitors in a class field such as we had, but we do not think that all the shoving is essential. One of

> these days someone will get badly spiked in these big fields when everyone is waiting for the other man to take the lead."

Sydney's successful return was big news in the sports columns, but the front pages of the time were awash with scandal after the Duke of Windsor married divorcee Wallis Simpson at a château loaned by a French millionaire. No member of the Royal family attended the former monarch's nuptials and soon afterwards, when the happy couple visited Hitler in Germany, gossip columns pondered suggestions he was a Nazi sympathiser and she a German spy! The scandal and outrage was immense.

The warm weather continued into June and, a week after White City, Sydney headed for Gillingham's United Services Sports ground, positioned a short walk from the historic Chatham dockyard on the River Medway. He successfully defended his Kent county mile title in hot sunshine on a badly disintegrating cinder track. A relatively modest time of 4:30.8 was all it took to lift the crown, and his well-known electric burst of speed was only required for a brief surge in the second lap in order to establish a good position.

Despite the 4:17 a week earlier, some quarters of the press seemed disappointed Sydney only managed 4:30.8 at Gillingham. If he was miffed by such criticism, he characteristically didn't display it publicly, and it was left to the editor of the club's *Gazette* to castigate the moaners. The writer was jubilant at Blackheath's showing:

> "I don't think the club has ever shone more resplendently than on this occasion. Sprinters Parkes and Wiard, middle distance men Poole and King and distance man Reynolds all performed with style and headline act Sydney capped all this with a comfortable win in the mile."

★★★

Although still well short of Glenn Cunningham's world mark and Tommy Hampson's British record, Sydney was showing considerable promise as a half-miler. He'd had little difficulty so far in dipping under two minutes for the two-lap discipline. The half-mile was a useful sharpener ahead of important mile races, and if Sydney was ever unsure of pitting himself against others over two laps, he couldn't have been better positioned than to have Albert Hill as adviser – a man who'd managed a time of 1:53.04 himself nearly 20 years earlier, and had regularly performed at elite level at both 800m/880y and the mile.

Albert and Sydney were certainly happy to mix it up at this stage of his career and, following the rather gentle Kent mile win, Sydney put his head above the parapet and ran two half-miles in a busy 48-hour period that also included plenty of travel. The first, on a unseasonably cool Thursday evening in London, saw Blackheath again beaten by Achilles in a London Territorial Inter-Battalion meeting; the Oxbridge men took the mile medley relay in 3:36.0, a mere eight-tenths of a second ahead of the Heathens, for whom Sydney had set off first, clocking 1:57 for his half-mile, the baton then passing on to John Poole, Neville Cullen and Les Cornish.

A train journey to Plymouth the following day resulted in another defeat by Achilles, but for Sydney the winning feeling returned when he won the half-mile at the city's Hospital Sports in fine style. The occasion, on Saturday 19 June, was the annual contest for the Travers-Stubbs Trophy, normally a happy hunting ground for Blackheath. This time, however, the club was seriously weakened by the absence of injured Ernie Page, plus serious concerns over Charles Wiard who was nursing a leg problem. When Wiard did ultimately break down in the sprints the club's hopes were dashed and they eventually finished third overall, Achilles pipping London AC for the main prize.

On the Home Park grass track, Sydney was, as usual, centre of attention in his half-mile. Brian McCabe (London AC) led until 220 yards from home, at which point Sydney accelerated and passed with great assurance, looking well in control as he won in 1:59.6 by a good three yards or so. In the medley relay, at the suggestion of a fair-minded opponent, Blackheath sought to replace the injured Wiard with Sydney's brother Stanley. However, the referee was having none of it, and quoted a regulation stating that only runners named in the programme could appear, unless a clerical or printer's error had been made. So a limping Wiard had little choice but to take his place for the final leg of 440 yards.

Sydney took the opening half-mile leg and passed Barry Hudson of Achilles (later a distinguished QC) and opened up a decent lead before handing over the baton. Despite a game effort by the other Blackheath men, Wiard's handicap slowed him down and Achilles pipped them at the close by 1.2 seconds with 3:38.6. Sydney chose not to run in either the mile or the open handicap mile, and the limelight in the latter was taken by brother Stanley who had a 120 yards start and showed impeccable judgement to win in 4:11.

14

Looking Regal in Regency Brighton

AND so to Preston Park, a substantial 63-acre chunk of recreational space on the edge of trendy Brighton. I headed here to the verdant spot that nowadays hosts the hugely popular Brighton Marathon, but in past decades witnessed the exploits of the most famous track runners and cyclists in the land. A cinder running track was first laid here before the first world war, sitting rather uncomfortably inside the banked velodrome track which is still there today.

Sydney Wooderson's visit in the summer of 1937 would be his only race here – and he would put on a memorable and powerful display that belied his tender years and lightweight frame. The 3pm mile race within the Southern AAA championships on Saturday 26 June roused the greatest excitement of the day from a good-sized crowd. They looked on admiringly as Sydney won as he pleased, to coin a phrase of the day. Only a royal wave could have made his progress around the picturesque Preston Park grass track any more regal.

Looking as if he wasn't even breaking sweat, he had the race in his pocket from the start, clocking laps of 64.5, 64.5 and 65 seconds, tucked in behind the labouring leaders. Peter Ward made the pace, leading in 63.8 after a lap, at halfway in 2:08.8 and still there at the bell in 3:14. But Sydney gathered himself without fuss and with about 300 yards left produced that famous kick and surged clear apparently effortlessly, putting in a final lap of 60.6 to win by 12-yards in 4:14.6.

It was ideal weather for athletics although it was noted there were a number of occasions where the organisation fell short of what was expected at a regional championship. Blackheath official Sercombe, who had seen more Sydney victories at this point than virtually anyone, reckoned none had seemed as convincing as this one. It was the fastest mile by a Brit since Sydney's own native record at Chelmsford a year earlier (4:10.8) and would surely have been quicker on a firmer cinder track. The experts reckoned it was only a matter of time before Sydney would set a world mile record – something no British-born runner had done since Walter George 50 years earlier, back when Victoria was on the throne.

George's achievement might well have been in Sydney's sights around now, but the old runner's image as a playboy is unlikely to have caught his imagination. George was a lively character back in his heyday, confessing to a weakness for "a cigar, a drink and a spree" between training runs. Walter and Sydney were both great milers, but there the similarity ended. In physical and personality terms they were poles apart: WG was a tall, handsome fellow who loved his celebrity status and occasionally strayed into the type of trouble that didn't befit an athlete of international status. One typical episode involved a drunken midnight foot-race along Regent Street in Central London with some pals. Ignoring a policeman's advice to go home to bed, Walter then trekked through the night to meet a lady-friend in another part of London. This was followed by a hectic morning's shopping and a lavish lunch in the West End before our hero then bowled merrily into the Lillie Bridge stadium to casually smash another record. It would be fair to say Sydney's build-up to big races tended to be a little more circumspect than this.

Apropos of Sydney's good form and his display at Brighton in particular, 'Tempus' of the *Sporting Chronicle,* was in outspoken mood in advance of the 1937 AAA championships, set for three weeks later. He simply couldn't fathom the reason behind recent press doubts cast on Sydney's current capabilities and short-term prospects:

> "The Wooderson rumours strike me as utter nonsense. He has carefully nursed his [1936] leg injury, which is more than other notables have done. He has run fast at all the intermediate distances up to and including the mile, his pluck and judgement are undeniable and he can turn on the speed tap with such an astonishing facility

> as to make even Lovelock marvel. And this is the man that some of our experts said is not good enough. There may be better milers, but they are not in this country and I am not sure they are in any other. Wooderson fit and well is good enough for me."

In terms of peaking for the most important events, Sydney's summer was warming up nicely by early July – both metaphorically and literally. There was glorious weather for the 66th annual sports and garden party hosted by the Ravensbourne Club at Lee Green – and a record crowd turned out for the occasion. Fortunately a cooling breeze helped make things tolerable as temperatures soared. There was a quintessentially English summer atmosphere at this popular and well-established event, with marquees and tents housing refreshments, lunches and an Old English Fair, the soundtrack provided by the Band of the Life Guards. There was a huge schedule of sporting contests to entertain the bumper 12,000 crowd, amounting to 36 foot and cycle races on the track, including a sprinkling of events for women. It all began at 2pm and drew to a weary close some five hours later.

Blackheath turned out in force for this local fixture, many members there to relax and support clubmates rather than compete. The temperature was not far short of 90F at 3.50pm for the open scratch mile in which all eyes were, of course, once again on Sydney. He ran a characteristic race, winning with ease to the crowd's approval in 4:20.6 after striding side by side with Sussex champion Grosse (Horsham Blue Star) for a spell before taking off with half a lap to go. Crouching beside the track on the infield throughout the race had been brother Stanley, shouting the all-important split times for each lap as the main man flew past.

Around 90 minutes later Sydney had to get ready for the medley mile relay championship of Kent, in which Blackheath successfully defended the Camden Cup it had held since 1928; the time for Sydney's opening half-mile leg is unknown but he got the men of Kent off to a great start. In the Ravensbourne club's magazine, Stanley Halsey would later express astonishment at Sydney's display, suggesting he'd given his team such a powerful start it would have been near impossible for them to lose after he handed over, even with two laps still to run. Blackheath's final runner John Poole looked distinctly tired after his earlier exertions, and the winning time of 3:38.0 was almost nine seconds outside their own event record of

1935. Only Cambridge Harriers provided any semblance of opposition but Poole was always well clear and never in real trouble. Tradition had been maintained for another year.

All the action took place on the well-maintained sports fields beside Weigall Road and the Quaggy River. Eighty years later I took a look at the site, and found it hasn't changed immensely, and is still dominated by the imposing building on the north side of Eltham Road where the Ravensbourne clubhouse was created in 1912. It was built for the many employees of Cook, Son and Co (St. Pauls) Ltd., a huge wholesale clothing company. This handsome four-storey edifice was refurbished in 2007 and retains its U-shape around a quadrangle at the rear, where there used to stand the employees' swimming pool and running track. Athletics historian Kevin Kelly showed me a copy of the official 48-page programme for the 1937 meeting and said at 48 pages it was a pretty posh effort for a sports event of that era. One scribe of the day described Ravensbourne's gala day as SE London's answer to Ascot; Kelly confirms it was a high-class meeting of athletics and cycling which always attracted top performers for its open events and was also used by Kent and the Southern Counties to decide some of their relay championships:

> "Cook's described their meeting as a garden party, which would have prompted the ladies to don their best frocks just like Ascot does. A 'sports' followed by a 'dance' format, combined with a 'fete' was fairly common at company sports events, probably to attract women and children."

Meanwhile, occasional suggestions in the press that Sydney was below his best following his 1936 injury and inactive winter were beginning to look wide of the mark. With the AAA champs and some international action on the horizon, Sydney would surely be peaking at exactly the right time. Perhaps his relay running was helping the fine tuning of his leg speed and tactical judgement. Relays exert a whole new pressure on a runner due to the inescapable fact that your mates are depending on you, especially when you are British mile champion – but in Sydney's case, this pressure seemed to be adding an extra zip to his running.

A week before the main AAAs programme, Sydney picked up the

baton once again for Blackheath in the Victory Trophy 4 x 1-mile team relay championship. The event was hosted by London AC at White City, alongside the AAA junior championships on Saturday 10 July and contested by eight clubs. Sydney took the anchor leg with brother Stanley opening for the Heathens. With a fierce wind battering runners on the back straight, Sydney's teammates were unable to produce their best form, Stanley's opening leg of 4:35 being workmanlike but below his best, and meaning the first changeover left Blackheath in last place. Derek Reynolds took over and carved a chunk out of the deficit by recording 4:28 and handing to vice-captain John Poole in third place. Poole kept Blackheath third, but his 4:38 was a disappointment and left Sydney with much to do on the final stage.

At the point he grabbed the baton, Sydney was around 70 yards behind Peter Ward of Achilles, and his task looked impossible. Ward's speciality was three miles rather than one, but his lead nevertheless looked impregnable. Sydney was prepared to give it his best shot, however, and completed an opening lap of 60 seconds, passed halfway in 2:07 and the three-quarter point in 3:12.4. With 440 yards left he had reduced the gap to only eight yards. He sped up on the final lap, inching ever closer to Ward in dramatic fashion. There was just a couple of strides between them as they rounded the final bend. But the task proved just too much, Sydney's final lap of 61.2 seconds representing a glorious failure as he hit the line less than a second behind a distinctly relieved Ward. Southgate Harriers were a long way back in third. Blackheath's disappointment at not quite managing a wonderful victory was tempered by the fact Sydney was clearly in top form; the AAA mile was only a week away and a championship record was surely on the cards.

On the weekend that marked the first anniversary of the start of the Spanish civil war, rather more good natured hostilities broke out at White City on the occasion of the AAA championships, Europe's most prestigious athletics event. Various qualifying heats were held on the evening of Friday 16 July, including the appearance of Sydney, wearing No.1 as reigning champion, who qualified for the next day's mile final with ease: Just before 7pm he crossed the line in unhurried fashion in third place in the first of the three heats, in a time estimated at 4:21. In beautiful weather, Denis Pell of Herne Hill Harriers won the heat with Bernie Wright of Southend & County second.

Next day, the main programme ran from noon till the anticipated arrival of the first marathon runner at 5.30. Although the best Oxbridge men were away in the USA, the mile featured a strong field of 32 and was scheduled for 4.40. Speculation was rife that holder Sydney was interested in smashing Albert Hill's championship record. In addition to worrying about records, Sydney and his coach had noticed young rival Denis Pell was in the form of his life and bound to pose a big threat.

Pell, a civil servant at New Scotland Yard, was gaining a reputation as a maverick, due to his relaxed attitude to training and occasional poor time-keeping. Historian Kevin Kelly told me:

> "Pell had a habit of arriving very late for races and I believe they even delayed the start for him at one event, as he was still struggling into his kit and spikes. I think the usual rush from his motorbike [to the start-line] became his warm-up! He would be a very sad loss to the sport later on when killed in a flying accident during the war".

The mile final had the present and two former GB record holders in the strong field, but it was the German Friedrich Schaumburg who raced into an early lead followed closely by Bernard Eeles. They completed a lap of 63 seconds with Sydney lying well back. Bob Graham then slipped into the lead, closely monitored by Pell, who eased ahead by halfway at 2:07. Sydney studied what was happening and accelerated into third place as the bell sounded at 3:11.6 with Pell in front. Within a couple of seconds Sydney had snatched the lead and as they entered the back straight for the final time, Graham was clearly a beaten man but Pell would not be shaken off. Sydney accelerated again but Pell looked determined to hang on as the crowd roared them on. With around 250 yards to go, Pell dramatically moved up to Sydney's shoulder, staying with him as he accelerated. Twice Sydney glanced behind to see how his relatively unknown challenger was doing, finding Pell was showing no sign of weakening yet. Then, 90 yards from the finish Sydney kicked again and at last began to move away.

Albert Hill was seen dancing with excitement at trackside, knowing his 1921 mile record – achieved in a great race with Henry Stallard – was surely about to be smashed. To keep Pell at bay, Sydney was flying and swept through the worsted yarn in 4:12.2, beating Hill's championship and former GB mark by 2.6 seconds. It was Sydney's third successive AAA mile crown – a marvellous hat-trick. Brave Pell had run the race of his life and ended up 3.2 seconds down and only half-a-second clear of Graham, but won high praise for making it such a great spectacle. Schaumburg broke the German mile record, but was only fourth.

"Wooderson makes one wonder how so much vitality can be packed into so small a space," marvelled Tempus of the *Sporting Chronicle*. For taking his third successive AAA mile title Sydney was presented with the challenge cup put up by Sir Charles Bennet Lawes-Wittewrong, an accomplished sculptor, rower and runner. At the formal dinner accompanying the event, Sydney was a model of modesty when he stood up and expressed surprise he'd been called upon to speak, when there were other athletes around like Finlay, Cooper and Robertson who had won more successive championship titles than he.

Having underlined his credentials as Britain's top dog, Sydney now had to shoulder the responsibility of being the star turn in the national team, as Britain prepared to take on the big names from abroad. His return to top form was seen as particularly significant because the young-looking GB side named for the annual match with France was missing several top names. Jack Crump had been given the job of GB team manager for the first time at a senior international and eagerly took his team of 30 athletes into battle at the Yves-du-Manoir (Colombes) stadium in the Paris suburbs on Saturday 24 July.

Crump's confidence was vindicated by a superb victory. Britain dominated on the track and did unexpectedly well in the field to triumph by a big margin. The track was fast with long straights and in good condition despite heavy rain which reduced the size of the crowd. Sydney forged a big lead in the 1500 metres amid rapturous cheers from the home crowd – who may have thought a record was on the cards – even though he outclassed their own Roger Normand and Robert Goix. Sydney hit the tape on 3:51.0, at least 30 yards and five seconds clear of teammate Reg Thomas. Although he won with ease, the time represented his fastest over a metric mile and would have been good enough to win Olympic gold before 1936. With five points for first places, three for second and one for third, Britain romped to a 66-54 triumph.

15

Tasting International Supremacy

INTERNATIONAL athletics of high calibre lit up the White City on August Bank Holiday 1937 in a showpiece that was hailed the greatest gathering of athletes in London since the 1908 Olympics.

This first international gathering of its sort generated huge excitement, the stadium gates having to be closed early; although reported crowd figures varied wildly, a fairly conservative estimate suggested at least 50,000 made it inside. Sixteen countries were represented, including a particularly strong contingent from the USA, and around 50 of the athletes had appeared at the Berlin Olympics less than a year earlier. *The Times* recorded that the meeting had only been possible thanks to a change of AAA policy, allowing the travel expenses of competitors to be guaranteed by the White City Stadium Ltd. Hitherto such financial support had only been granted to those arriving for international matches between GB and a single invited nation. This development was generally welcomed with caution, although *The Times* warned: "It is for the AAA to see that the more serious dangers to amateurism are held in check."

The showdown between Sydney and the talented American Archie San Romani was the major talking point of the day. The man from Kansas was reportedly planning to combine the athletics at White City with a honeymoon trip, having just married Miss Lena Plumley. He would disembark the Queen Mary at Plymouth and then fly to London, it was announced, although other reports suggested he was unlikely to appear at all. Confused fans were put out of their misery by an announcement early in the meeting that San Romani had made it to London and would be running. The cheerful Bank Holiday crowd let loose great cheers and waves of applause at this news. It transpired he'd arrived in the capital just two hours before the event, so expecting him to be at his sharpest was a little unrealistic. Indeed, at least one reporter observed that he looked very unfit when emerging to limber up.

San Romani's appearance sparked much discussion about how money was becoming an increasing factor in the staging of major, supposedly amateur, athletics meetings. In an unsigned editorial in Blackheath's *Gazette*, one club official complained Sydney was being put up against an opponent who had been produced like a rabbit out of a hat, or a clown out of a big drum at the circus:

> "A fit San Romani would certainly have found our man [Sydney] straining at the leash, but… at best his appearance may provide some excitement but nevertheless it will remain something of a circus turn [to] add substantially to the gate… Britain's amateur athletes have been invited and persuaded to provide entertainment for a gate-paying Bank Holiday crowd under the pretext that more international competition is a necessity. It is difficult to see where the international competition comes in this afternoon. Is San Romani fit enough to accept an invitation to run for USA? I am afraid that it is the money-bags rattling."

He went on to condemn the widely held opinion that San Romani had been very sporting to agree to run while on honeymoon ("this sob-stuff is nonsense") and issued a warning that the sport was now facing some big issues and was at a crossroads: "The right turning is not always the obvious one. A smooth concrete road with gilded lamp posts can soon lead into a dark, muddy, sticky lane full of potholes," he warned ominously.

Wearing his all-white GB kit with a No.6 on the chest, all eyes were on Sydney in the race billed as the highlight of the day. However, despite another fine victory, the contest didn't live up to the hype. Sydney had, unusually, seized the lead early, taking fellow Brits Reg Thomas and Frank Close with him; they appeared to be running as a team and Close opened up a lead of 15 yards and worked tirelessly as if on pacemaking duty (440 in 61.8). At halfway it was all much closer at the front (2:08); Thomas followed by Miklos Szabo (Hungary) hit the front on the third lap (3:14.8) but Sydney remained in the picture as usual and on the final quarter cruised past them to be chased home by Szabo. He accelerated on the final bend and won in 4:15.8 by about three yards with Szabo on 4:16.2. Thomas took third and San Romani an unimpressive fifth.

It was a hectic period and Sydney had little chance to rest before taking a train north to Glasgow. The following Saturday, 7 August, saw the 51st annual Rangers Sports at Ibrox Park, the second of Sydney's five visits to this highly popular gala. On this day London recorded temperatures of 83F in the shade but in Glasgow there was 13 hours of continuous rain and a high wind! A crowd of over 40,000 packed into Ibrox nevertheless, looking forward to the handicap three-quarter mile race in which Sydney was expected to go for Frenchman Jules Ladoumegue's world record. Expert onlookers reckoned the strong wind was a hazard worth at least one second per lap, so it was a tall order.

Welcomed by Rangers manager Bill Struth, Sydney roared round to break the British three-quarter mile record in 3:00.9, chopping 1.3 seconds off Jack Lovelock's old mark but missed the world mark by a whisker. From the start it was clear the handicappers did not know Sydney's capabilities well. "The handicapping was ludicrous," said one Blackheath official, indicating it hadn't assisted Sydney's chase for the world record. Bob Graham and Sydney were on scratch, Reg Thomas 10 yards, Bernard Eeles 12, Frank Close 18, and Ernie Lansdale 21 yards. Sydney did the first 220 in 28.5 secs and hit 440 in 58.2, by which time he'd caught half the field; 660 yards were done in 1:28 and he was up with the leaders; at 880 he had the lead and clocked 1:59. He was still inside world record schedule for the three-quarter mile in 2:29 and then had to head into the teeth of a gale.

The Ibrox crowd was bewitched by this sassenach and roared him across the line just three-tenths outside Ladoumegue's record, but a Scottish allcomers, British and English native record was made. Thomas came in almost 40 yards adrift and Eeles a further 30 yards down, the rest nowhere. Clearly the wind had an effect, but the crowd had done their bit to help and if Sydney had imagined the partisan Scots might not take to a runner from south of the border he was much mistaken. The reaction had been warm and he would gladly return in future years. On the in field, the five-a-side football tournament was won by Celtic, with homesters Rangers surprisingly ousted in the first round.

★★★

Out of necessity rather than design, Sydney's training programme – never high mileage at the best of times – would remain low-key throughout August 1937. His next race, back at White City, would be his fifth major outing in front of a big crowd in less than a month. A crack, full-strength German squad was in town to take on GB on Saturday 14 August. Sydney and Denis Pell were both down to run the mile, meaning here was an event where team manager Crump could count on maximum points for Britain in the four-man race. However, he later revealed:

> "Sydney came to me some time before the race and asked if there was any way in which he could run to help Denis [in order to] ensure maximum points. Denis, a great but not dedicated athlete, told me, when I approached him on the tactics to be employed, that Sydney should go it alone, since he [Denis] had only that day returned from holiday and had not had a track shoe on for a fortnight. It was too late to do anything then, and Sydney won but Denis was fourth and instead of gaining a five-point advantage from this one race we gained only one."

The track had been saturated by rain the previous day and took another drenching before the start, partly flooding the bends. A humid atmosphere and more rain meant performances in the 13 events were hampered. To Crump's dismay, Pell couldn't reproduce his AAAs form and Schaumburg proved Sydney's main rival on the day, but "eschewing all fireworks" Sydney controlled the race beautifully and won in 4:19.0, 1.4 secs in front of the German, who had teammate Edmund Stadler on his heels at 4.21.2. Pell came in last in 4:23.4.

Going into the final race on this damp but tense day – the mile medley relay – Godfrey Brown was exhausted after his individual half-mile but agreed to take on the great Rudolf Harbig. He ran brilliantly, grabbing the baton with a 10-yard lead, setting off and running a heroic 52 seconds lap. Despite a brief wobble near the end, he came in first to win the match for GB, and while teammates danced in delight poor Brown collapsed on the fence to be violently sick. Crump was then told he had put GB in peril of disqualification by screaming advice at Brown from trackside – and it needed humble apologies before victory was confirmed.

Crump's misdemeanour notwithstanding, Britain's sporting reputation was further enhanced by this first-ever win over a German squad regarded as joint-best in the world alongside Finland. The margin of victory was a mere two points, each nation having six individual winners. Thanks chiefly to points amassed in the various track events, Britain had inflicted only Germany's second defeat in an international match in a period of 17 years. The underdog had triumphed and the crowd, lower than hoped because of the weather, went home happy.

Shortly afterwards, the French Athletic Federation invited Britain's 'big five' (Sydney, Godfrey Brown, Cyril Holmes, Peter Ward and Don Finlay) to take part in an international meeting connected to the Paris Exposition, scheduled for Sunday 22 August. Sydney's name was also down to run a relay for Blackheath in the 35th annual meeting of the London Fire Brigade Athletic Association at Herne Hill.

Before long however, Sydney made it known he was withdrawing from both these commitments for he had other plans for rounding off the summer season of 1937. A world record on a picturesque track close to home was in his sights.

16

Magnificent Motspur Park

SPANNING a period of ten years, Sydney Wooderson would race three times at the attractive University of London Athletic Ground in the leafy residential suburb of Motspur Park. He would make athletics history on all three occasions.

The excitement and noise levels on those occasions were a far cry from the day of my Motspur Park visit decades later. As I went in search of the exact spot where Sydney made world headlines in 1937, 1938 and 1946, I found the very same field was hosting another sporting occasion. Peering into what was now highly secure and carefully-screened premises, Fulham FC's under-18s were beating visitors Reading 3-2 on what was once the infield of the famous Motspur Park track. It was a contest that barely warranted a line in the sporting press, unlike the massive headlines Sydney garnered for his heroics here either side of the 1939-45 War.

The cinder 440-yard track created here in New Malden in 1928 had six lanes, with 11 lanes on the straight, built on a chunk of open countryside acquired for the University of London for the princely sum of £18,000. It would grow into one of London's most important athletics venues over the next 40 years or so. The track would eventually be grassed over in 1995 having not been used for athletics for five years and the entire ground would be sold in 1999 as a training base for Second Division champions Fulham FC, owned then by Harrod's boss Mohammed Fayed and managed by Kevin Keegan.

The covered grandstand that overlooked the old running track would be spared the wrecking ball and remains in place today, now painted in Fulham's black-and-white livery. Sydney's exploits made Motspur Park a famous sporting landmark, and the track was also used in three feature films, most notably the Oscar-winning *Chariots of Fire*. Although the cinders are long gone, the track's curved sweep remains a feature of the present Arena field, as does a home straight that accounts for the large divide between pitch touchline and stand. The calibre of the facilities has meant international football teams often base themselves here, visitors including Brazil, Colombia, England, South Korea and Sweden.

Sydney's 1937 plan to break the world mile record at Motspur Park was certainly no secret, covered widely in the press and given prominent billing on leaflets and posters. There is no record of him making any special preparations for the attempt – and it's probably safe to assume he wouldn't have copied the regime of his coach Albert Hill, who prepared for his own record attempts many years earlier via long walks across the South Downs, demolishing bags of jam-puffs along the way!

In this era before record attempts using 'artificial' pacing were frowned upon, Sydney knew exactly what he was up against on the highly-charged afternoon of Saturday 28 August 1937. He would be running from scratch in an invitation mile handicap race at the Team and Relay meeting between Blackheath, London AC, Met Police AC and Polytechnic Harriers. Public interest was huge and admission to the ground was set at one shilling, with some limited seating space in the main stand costing half a crown. Officials and helpers prepared themselves for a hectic day.

Blackheath representatives started arriving at an overcast Motspur Park more than an hour before the scheduled 3pm start, and there was immediately an acknowledgement there was a whiff of something special in the air that day. The track, prepared by groundsman Mr Sterry and colleagues, looked in superb condition. The weather was near-perfect – no scorching sun and scarcely any breeze. The setting was a picture, the trees surrounding ground gently glistening with the centrepiece the impressive 500-seater grandstand with its roof of ten prominent roof vents servicing the changing rooms at the rear.

The crowd began to fill the ground around 2pm, the earliest arrivals without tickets for a seat gathering either side of the stand for the best view. Blackheath people by the dozen began to gather and chat. The Wooderson party arrived, Sydney, brother Stanley and their parents accompanied by coach Hill, who stepped forward protectively and politely reassured everyone within earshot that his man was well and confident. The huge frame of Tom Crafter, more than 50 years with Blackheath, bustled over and shook hands with the much smaller figure of Sydney and people craned their necks to listen as he gave a friendly little speech of encouragement, assuring Sydney his achievements of late had thrilled the older members, and he was a credit to his club.

The stand was full by 2.45 and the crowd had filled just about every space around the track, with hundreds still queuing outside. Such a gathering had never been seen here and the atmosphere crackled. Proceedings began with the long jump, which felt like an anti-climax until cheering broke out when the announcer stated the second event would be the mile.

The crowd knew Sydney would provide an entertaining spectacle regardless, but what they really wanted was to witness a record. They wanted to be able to return home, and then work, and tell everybody they'd witnessed something never before seen in the world of sport.

Reports suggested Sydney's training, mostly at Battersea Park track, had been going superbly well and there was every chance of success here today. No Englishman had held the world mile record since Walter Goodall George ran 4:12.75 more than half a century earlier in West London. George was here today, wearing a slightly shabby brown suit and propped up by a walking stick, just 12 days short of his 80th birthday. He'd been helped to the ground today from his home four miles away in Mitcham to see if athletics history was to be made.

The more knowledgeable in the crowd were aware of the times to look out for – Sydney's own British record stood at 4:10.8 (a year old and ripe for beating) and Glenn Cunningham's world record stood at 4:06.8 (three years old and seen by some as impregnable). There were four AAA timekeepers at the ground and they were not taking any chances, having had the track measured in advance. It was found to be between eight and ten inches short of a mile over four laps and when Sydney was informed of this, it was agreed he'd start a foot or so behind the normal start-line.

The eight runners loosened up and waited for the call, starting from different positions around the track in a formation designed to ensure Sydney had somebody to chase at all times and therefore the best possible chance of blowing Cunningham's record out of the water. Sydney, in all-black kit with a small and rather tatty No.1 pinned to his chest, was on the scratch mark. Reg Thomas (RAF) had a ten yards start, Bernard Wright (Southend & County) had 60 yards, Bernard Eeles (Southgate) 65, Ernest Hengle (Met Police) 92, Jack Powell (London AC) 100, Derek Reynolds (Blackheath) 120 and brother Stanley 140 yards. If Sydney was nervous he wasn't showing it. He was an oasis of calm, there were no histrionics, his warming-up was kept to a minimum and as far as possible he kept himself to himself.

They were called to attention by the starter and instantly the buzz of the excited crowd dropped to complete silence. The pregnant pause seemed to last an age and throughout you could hear a pin drop… it was a spine-tingling moment, nicely summed up by a Blackheath man who later wrote:

> "The impressive silence emphasised the fact that one of the supreme moments of athletic history had arrived."

Percy Gilby, the starter from Essex, fired his pistol and Sydney, with Thomas up ahead, flew off to a thrilling fast start. Motoring along smoothly, Sydney inched his way closer to the RAF man and his quarter-mile time was announced as 58.6 seconds. Was this a shade too fast? On the second lap, Sydney got closer still and with Thomas still narrowly ahead he hit the halfway point at 2:02.6. At this news, once again the more knowledgeable onlookers would worry he'd possibly set off too quickly.

Into the third lap they went and Thomas' job was done after 1,000 yards; he unobtrusively stepped off the track to let Sydney go through and give chase to the other key pacemaker Jack Powell, a former AAA half-mile champion. If Powell did his job as perfectly as Thomas had, and Sydney maintained form, the record was surely there for the taking. The track had been so beautifully and smoothly prepared that the eight runners' own footsteps were the only marks on it – and more than one observer noted that Sydney was actually running so consistently that with every stride he was hitting his own footsteps from the earlier laps. Crucially, he was able to stay in the inside lane for the entire trip.

The crowd was noisy and excited as the announcer barked out 3:07.2 with one lap left – but those calm enough to make hurried calculations in their head would have realised he now needed to accelerate hard and finish with a sub-60 circuit to achieve the world record. Any Doubting Thomases immediately had their spirits lifted when the sound of the bell prompted a surge from Sydney, immediately closing the 50 yards behind the leaders, and just 20 yards behind Powell. Sydney then passed the 1500 metres mark in 3:50.3, making him the fastest Briton in history over the 'metric mile'.

This last lap would be described in the next day's papers as thrilling as any race ever run in this country. Powell obediently set a terrific pace for the final stages and before the furlong mark he caught the leaders with Sydney almost on his heels. For the most part the others helpfully moved aside to let this pair through, although one report suggests there was a moment where Sydney found himself very briefly boxed in. If true, this problem didn't last long, Sydney's long stride seeing him draw alongside and then flash past Powell, the crowd noise reaching a crescendo as he sprinted for the tape. Powell, an elegant runner who worked as a local newspaper reporter and later a poultry farmer, had run brilliantly for Sydney's cause. He'd given him something to chase in those energy-sapping final stages and Sydney passed him close to the finish, breasting the tape with Powell less than two yards behind. Third home was Bernard Wright who, inspired by the atmosphere, ran the race of his life, but hardly anyone noticed.

Four minutes of persistent cheering had risen to become simply deafening at the climax. Sydney had kept his form and posture brilliantly on that last lap, crossing the line with little sign of flailing arms or lolling head. He came to a steady controlled stop, rocking a little as he braked but without signs of distress. The hunched timekeepers studied their watches, went into a lengthy huddle and then called for the bank manager E. J. 'Billy' Holt, who was referee for the day. More discussions, leaving the crowd desperate for news. The wait was unbearable. Had he done it? Was that the fastest mile ever run?

Finally the agony was soon over and all hell was let loose. Although the actual announcement of a world record evidently lacked the drama of Norris McWhirter's famous performance at Iffley Road a few years later, this one nevertheless sparked great scenes of jubilation all around the ground, and particularly down at trackside. Sydney disappeared from view in a frenzy of back-slapping and hand-shaking. Proud coach Albert Hill wandered around sweating profusely, a big smile across his features.

He'd run a world record. There was sheer pandemonium as everybody, including those in the race, cheered in unrestrained fashion, delighted to have been here to see, or be involved in, history in the making. Sydney had run 4:06.6, a spectacular time that would three days later be reduced further to 4:06.4.

A new world record: Hitting the line at Motspur Park.

It transpired the four timekeepers on duty had returned a 'split verdict' with two of them showing 4:06.4 and the others recording 4:06.6. The referee, in accordance with general practice, announced the slower time after the race, but it later emerged one of the watches had not been certified, and the rules only stipulated three watches needed to be used anyway. Therefore with the elimination of the uncertified timepiece, the verdict of the two watches agreeing upon 4:06.4 was accepted. During the proceedings referee Holt had been shown a surveyor's certificate regarding the track, which he noted was at least a month old. He decided that he and London AC President Jack Densham needed to re-measure the track to ensure Sydney's record couldn't be disputed. Instead of the steel measuring tape provided by groundstaff, they managed to find a new, more efficient device to use. After their careful deliberations, the news was good: The track was 22 inches longer than one mile.

Sydney's run beat Glenn Cunningham's three-year-old world record set at Princeton, New Jersey, by 0.4 of a second. Cunningham had actually been recorded as 4:06.6, but the IAAF didn't recognise fractions less than one-fifth of a second so it had been rounded up to 4:06.7. Cunningham had run the first lap of his record more than three seconds slower than Sydney, but the third lap around three seconds quicker. Looking at the lap splits of the previous four world record miles (two run by Lovelock, one each by Ladoumegue and Cunningham), we see that Sydney's was less even-paced than Ladoumegue and Cunningham, but more so than the Lovelock efforts.

By beating the personal best he'd recorded at Chelmsford by a massive 4.4 seconds, Sydney had set a world mark that would stand proudly unsurpassed for five whole years. He looked a little stunned on the Motspur Park in field as realisation set in of what he'd achieved two days short of his 23rd birthday. He certainly wasn't jumping around in delight – and it even took considerable persuasion before he set off on a rather restrained lap of honour. Nevertheless, behind that modest façade there was considerable turmoil and bewilderment, as he would admit many years later to writer David Thurlow:

> "I was quite amazed, and couldn't sleep undisturbed for some days after."

He was now officially quicker than Jack Lovelock, faster even than the great Paavo Nurmi. It was a huge thing to absorb. Runners and clubmates hoisted Sydney on their shoulders for the photographers as the Motspur Park announcer read out a list of thanks to all those who contributed – Thomas and Powell were mentioned for their pacemaking and the groundstaff for preparing such perfect conditions underfoot. Long-time professional record-holder Walter George was brought forward and warmly congratulated Sydney with Albert Hill and Reg Thomas also in shot as the flashbulbs exploded. Blackheath secretary Gordon McIvor ran around taking pictures galore to preserve this historic moment for the club, and was particularly delighted to locate Sydney's proud mum among the joyous faces and snapped her too.

Up in the main stand with the VIPs, the 18-stone, white-haired figure of Blackheath stalwart Tom Crafter rose to his feet with the remark: "Gentleman I think this is an occasion!" and then led the surrounding Blackheath members in a lusty rendition of the traditional club cry: "Black – lack, lack, lack, Black – lack, lack, lack, Black – HEATH!" The 'cry' always made an almighty racket – it was said to have once shattered a glass globe at the club's HQ in 1909 – although this time round it merely added to the general mayhem created by Sydney's once-in-a-lifetime performance. Crafter, along with club colleague Esse, were thought to be the only men on the ground on this day who had also witnessed Walter George's record-breaking mile of 51 years earlier in August 1886. For his part, a smiling George gazed around at the colourful scene and praised Sydney for: "The grandest and greatest mile ever run, so far."

The back-slapping and congratulatory hand-shaking showed little sign of abating until Sydney caved in and agreed to jog a lap of honour. It would take a good 30 minutes for the fuss to die down and allow the rest of the meeting to progress unhindered. Inspired by Sydney's triumph and the charged atmosphere, the Blackheath men in the sprint relays and the mile team race ran superbly to victory.

The next day's *Times* called this the most inspired effort yet by the British champion. Guy Butler, *Morning Post* correspondent and a committed Wooderson fan, called it:

> "As great a bit of running as I have ever seen… nothing this young runner can do will surprise me, he is a wonder."

Amid all the praise there was the odd cautionary note from observers who felt that records set in these specially-prepared handicap events amounted to 'unfair assistance' and had less merit than records achieved in a straight race. New Zealand writer Wally Ingram pointed out:

> "Wooderson is a great athlete, of that there is no doubt... but assisted racing does not necessarily produce the greatest asset of all – racing brains!"

Coach and author Frederick (F.A.M.) Webster spoke on similar lines:

> "If Wooderson has a fault it is that of being too easily persuaded to seek records through the medium of handicaps at which the starts are arranged to draw him out."

And Harold Abrahams chimed in:

> "Wooderson is singularly devoid of tactical skill on the track. He almost invariably involves himself in difficulties, bad positions from which only his superb reserve power can extricate him. Wooderson has yet to prove himself a world-beater among a really class field. When he has done that, I think even Lovelock's most ardent admirers will award Wooderson pride of place."

Perhaps the last word should go to the joyful elder statesmen attached to Sydney's club, whose spokesman summed up the Motspur Park afternoon thus:

> "Those who beheld the marvellous feat were stirred to their innermost depths, and never has the spirit of pure sportsmanship been more eloquently demonstrated than by those who accompanied the champion, who openly expressed their joy in having been privileged to do so."

He added that if you discounted Sydney's "Berlin tragedy", he had now remained unbeaten on level terms in the course of 43 races, including 16 one-miles in times ranging from 4:06 to 4:19.

Sydney decided his historic mile should mark the end of his season and declined an invitation to run for Britain on a September tour to Scandinavia. He planned an autumn of recovery followed by some cross-country in the winter at carefully chosen club races. Meanwhile, the AAA ratified the run as an English native record in October at a general committee meeting in Birmingham, and approved it to be submitted to the IAAF for their ratification as a world record.

Soon followed a grand club dinner honouring Sydney's achievements in formal and glamourous surroundings at The Waldorf Hotel in central London. Among the guests were Mr Paton, the surgeon who fixed Sydney's ankle in 1936, 80-year-old Walter George, plus the referee, starter and two of the Motspur Park timekeepers. Charged with reporting events at this special occasion was schoolmaster Joseph Cort McPhail, an enthusiastic Blackheath man who would later officiate at the 1948 Olympic Games among other events. A feature of McPhail's write-up was Sydney's famous modesty and restraint:

> "We were waiting… wondering what Sydney would say [in his speech]. I was willing to gamble that he would not talk for 4 mins 06.4 seconds! Since 1934 I had always sat next to or near him at the Championships Dinner, and I knew that he had never sought the publicity of speech. But this was his night and he did not shirk his part by fobbing us off with a perfunctory acknowledgement. He thanked the club for the reception and for their help in connection with the record attempt… but the one who had helped him most was the club trainer. When he joined the club he had been told to listen to everyone – but to follow Albert Hill. He urged other members to make more use of Hill's advice. The speech, in its tone, content and diction was an example of the spirit that the proposer had underlined. Sydney was an athlete who revelled in competition, for three years had lived in a blaze of publicity, but nature had made him imperturbable, and he had remained his natural self. Blackheath liked him, admired him, and was proud of him as an example of an English gentleman."

In his speech, Sydney singled out two Blackheath men in particular for their key part in his development as a runner – Gordon McIvor and H. W.

E. Sercombe. The latter, a club official since 1898, had been particularly supportive during Sydney's early years on Blackheath's books when his worth and potential had, with hindsight, been undervalued by the club in general. Sercombe wore glasses and had the appearance of a clergyman, and had a reputation for popping up on cross-country courses in all weathers to shout encouragement – usually finding a spot where runners were beginning to feel bad and needed a lift. He would surprise even the most humble member by knowing their names and this would lift spirits and performance at just the right moment.

Sydney also, of course, had praise for coach Hill, who was presented with a cheque by the club in payment for his efforts. Responding, Hill admitted Motspur Park had been the first time he'd seen Sydney really seriously extended, and he'd done a phenomenal job. However, he felt the little man's best performance of all thus far had been his Ibrox Park effort of three weeks earlier, because of the dreadful conditions totally unsuited to record breaking. Hill added that in coaching a runner had to choose a man and stick with him: "I am glad Sydney has stuck to me and ignored other people." He added there was no reason why Sydney could not extend his talents to a serious crack at cross-country racing if and when he chose – so far in his career he'd only really dabbled in that area.

Walter George got to his feet and urged caution over Hill's latter point – urging Sydney not to race flat out where cross-country was concerned: "Learn to run well slowly. Run fast during part of a race and go out over your distance at the end." He believed Wooderson could run a mile in four minutes one day, but not if he "tore himself to bits" on the country.

No doubt Sydney was pleased to accept all this advice, pleased that the nerve-wracking public speaking was over with, and pleased to be able to sit back and enjoy the entertainment offered up. This included a jolly little number by Blackheath runner Brian Lymbery, in which he sang:

"Don't let them give away the Empire,
Don't give the colonies away,
Give away Mosley's blouses,
Give away the nudists trousers,
But don't, don't, don't give the colonies away!"

Commemorative medal for the mile world record.

During the autumn Sydney had to say 'no' to Sydney… he was one of a number of top athletes who indicated they would be unavailable for selection for the 1938 Empire Games in Sydney, Australia, taking place the following February. With the team travelling by sea, participants would need to leave in December and not return until March – an absence of almost four months for just one competition. A typical passenger liner trip between London to Sydney in the 1930s could take between 30 and 40 days each way.

Sydney dropped out with great reluctance, it seems. He had no wife and family to support like many of his fellow athletes, and his withdrawal was purely due to work commitments: he had many weeks of vital 'cramming' to complete before his final Law Society exams. Back in 1934, when the Empire Games were staged in London, he had been one of 87 athletes proudly making up the England team, but this time round, the huge implications of a winter trip 'down under' reduced the size of that team to just 25. Amateur athletes in the 1930s were generally working people who simply couldn't afford lengthy periods off work for sport, however famous they were.

17

No Sleep till Felsted

ESSEX public school Felsted was probably the only educational establishment in the country in the 1930s where the daily timetable demanded pupils go to bed at lunchtime for a 30-minute nap!

This was the case for a number of years while the school was being run by charismatic and controversial headmaster Julian Bickersteth. Designed to improve boys' health and well-being, the Felsted 'siesta' must have meant their cross-country team was well rested when they faced afternoon races against the might of Sydney Wooderson and Blackheath Harriers either side of the second world war.

This fixture was always a lively affair, generating loud enthusiasm from boys in the school grounds in this normally quiet and refined corner of mid-Essex. When I visited and ran part of the course in 2016, the quietude was punctuated only by the odd passing car or cheery person on a bicycle. Visually, as far as I could tell, this would prove one of the least-changed of Sydney's race locations.

His debut at Felsted in November 1937 certainly generated high excitement among pupils, well aware he had only recently created a world mile record in London. A somewhat high-pitched hero's welcome to Essex was guaranteed. Sydney duly won the 5.25-mile cross-country contest in 31:30, comfortably ahead of teammate and brother Stanley, the nearest challenger. It helped seal a comfortable 49-29 points victory.

The leading boys couldn't match the class of the Heathens despite the recent experimentations of headmaster Bickersteth, who, in a speech in Bury St Edmunds that same month, had revealed:

> "It's awfully jolly to go fast in order to get over the ground as quickly as possible, but do let us try and cultivate while we are young a real joy in leisure. Everyone of my boys at Felsted goes to bed in the middle of the day for half an hour. The health of the school and the work of the school have gone up ever since the system began."

Felsted provided evidence that Sydney was back in the groove following ten weeks away from competition after the Motspur Park world record. Rested and refreshed, his first race back had been a week earlier in starkly different circumstances to the world record run: On a dry day with a touch of frost in the air, the annual mob match over 7.5 miles of Coulsdon hills, mud and grass had seen the Blackheath boys pull off a rousing victory over arch-rivals South London Harriers in the 37th contest for the Nicholls Cup.

Although SLH grabbed the first five places, 13 of the next 14 home were visitors. The final score was tallied on the first 76 men home from each team, and Blackheath's strength-in-depth won the day. The turnout of 107 represented a club record for an away fixture and Sydney finished sixth in 46:41. As the field trudged past Cane Hill asylum, an enormous Victorian-era hilltop institution, he was in cruise control and kept things steady for five miles in all, before taking off and hammering the final two-and-a-half miles at top speed. These had been the instructions of coach Hill, who was watching carefully from a vantage point halfway between the Farthing Downs and the main road to Brighton, near Hooley Farm. Sydney responded to Hill's shouts and his final mile was estimated at a remarkable 4:30. During the friendly banter afterwards SLH's winning runner Laurie Weatherill expressed his dislike of cross-country running when compared to track, while Sydney politely gave exactly the opposite opinion.

* * *

Meanwhile, Sydney's new status as a world record-holder inevitably brought with it an increase in requests to appear at schools, dinners and functions. He had no inclination or need to raise his public profile, but his sense of duty – and a desire not to disappoint people – meant he accepted most of them.

A typical example would be the annual dinner of London AC at the Restaurant Frascati in central London in early December 1937. This sumptuous and elegant venue was a real sight for sore eyes in Oxford Street: The façade comprised a handsome gold portico with gold metal work involving thousands of sheets of gold leaf framing the huge windows. A yellow and gold revolving door ushered privileged guests into a spacious lounge area with thick red pile carpets, vivid brocade settees and curtains and huge gilt chandeliers above. Functions such as this gala dinner would be staged inside the Louis XIV salon. A week or two later, Sydney would find himself returning here, a special guest at the South London Harriers annual dinner. He was becoming familiar with the Frascati high life at this point, but within a few years this magnificent venue would be no more, destroyed by wartime bombs.

Although there were toasts, speeches and a formal side to these functions, being in the company of other runners meant there was the opportunity to relax and enjoy a convivial atmosphere – particularly when the likes of magician Norman Major stepped forward and sparked great hilarity by relieving prominent guests of everything from their braces to their cloakroom tickets.

As ever, Sydney was more than happy to be a good team man and support his club at low-key cross-country events. On the last Saturday before Christmas 1937, any thoughts of seasonal shopping were banished in favour of rounding off his sporting year at the annual 7.5-mile match with Ranelagh Harriers. It was on home soil at Hayes and Sydney won so easily it was almost laughable – finishing in 45:31, he was more than a minute clear of all opposition. With 17 of his colleagues in the next 19 finishers behind him, it proved a comprehensive win for Blackheath – their 13th in succession in this contest for the Pelling-Ratcliff Cup. The victory earned Sydney the Davis Challenge Cup, which carried with it the title of Blackheath cross-country champion for 12 months.

On a grey and misty Boxing Day, the club staged a festive paper-chase in which a group of 'hares' set off in advance to lay a six-mile trail. Sydney set off alone five minutes later and came within a mere 15 yards of catching them as he arrived at the finish. All then repaired to the clubhouse in

Bourne Way for hot baths, followed by Christmas drinks accompanied by wives and girlfriends.

Although he'd competed in fewer than 20 events during the course of 1937, it had been a memorable year for Sydney, one that saw him bounce back from injury to cement a place in the record and history books alongside the world's elite. No matter that somebody would one day beat his world record, for now he was the fastest miler on the planet. And, at only 23, there was surely much more to come?

18

Winning Friends and Influencing People

BY now, every time Sydney Wooderson set foot on a running track it was big news… particularly when the venue was White City and the opposition from foreign shores. The way Britain's bespectacled little hero overcame his perceived physical inferiorities to take on and beat Johnny Foreigner had caught the public imagination unlike anything before in athletics. His fearless bulldog spirit, camouflaged by a shy, unassuming exterior, was a lethal combination.

Aspiring athletes latched on to him as a role model. If pale, puny Sydney, wearing those famous thick specs, could be a winner, surely everyone had a chance?

From his very earliest years on Blackheath's books, Sydney had been praised for attending even the 'bread and butter' fixtures on the club calendar. He never did this to simply garner popularity, but it certainly endeared him to clubmates.

Blackheath historians Dennis Saunders and Tony Weeks-Pearson, who both knew him well, would endeavour to explain his appeal when they joined forces in 1971 to publish a comprehensive and definitive club history, which was updated in 1989. Saunders had joined the club a decade before Sydney and was a colleague for decades, while Weeks-Pearson came along in 1949 and benefitted from personal coaching by Sydney. Within the 300 pages of their club history they did a fine job of analysing the unique Wooderson phenomenon. Their breathless and heartfelt tribute gathered speed like Sydney on the last lap of a mile race, with barely a comma or full-stop to slow it down:

> "That he should, for his generation, belong to the realm of legend, rather than that of celebrity, suggests something more than mere speed of movement. Sydney struck a spark in the ordinary Englishman who otherwise had no interest in athletics, perhaps by a combination of supreme competitive running ability with everyday normality and sanity which often maddened journalists avid for copy and which – though this demeanour contributed towards a delay in his recognition by the cognoscenti outside Blackheath – was nonetheless a potent link with a public who saw in these qualities an image of the reticence the English seem to prize above rubies, and a projection of their own romantic ambitions of excellence. The spectacles, with their suggestion of mortal weakness were significant in forming this image; not less so was the idea of the office worker with such accompaniments as the umbrella and the anonymous suit, the reluctance to stir to sensational utterance – thus characterising the rigidity of that famous portion of British anatomy, the upper lip, and altogether a bewilderingly conformist background of English commuting and suburban life that confounded the sensation-seeking, but reassured the public as a whole."

In the early days, when Sydney discarded all this camouflage at the start-line of a race, his diminutive stature – added to his solemn black racing kit – prolonged the obscurity even after the race had started. It was only when he unleashed his hidden power and speed in the closing stages that people sat up and took notice. By 1938, of course, this had all changed and he was recognised everywhere he went, but people nevertheless continued to marvel at how such a small, introverted character could explode past bigger, more powerful looking athletes and beat them with ease. However predictable it became, little Sydney going full pelt to victory down the home straight with his disproportionately long stride was always a remarkable sight. No wonder certain newspapers were compelled to fill headlines with nicknames like 'The Mighty Atom' and 'Cyclone Syd'.

He didn't have the physique or the good looks of an Alf Tupper or a Desperate Dan, but he did become something akin to a comic-book hero to many a young boy in the 1930s and 1940s. A number of runners who later achieved international fame would name him as the biggest inspiration during their formative years. Bill Nankeville, for example, who went on to win four AAA mile titles between 1948 and 1952, hero-worshipped Sydney as a schoolboy in the late 1930s. Nankeville's next-door neighbour in Woking would take the lad to White City just to see Sydney in action. Nankeville reflected later:

> "It was only through the generosity of Mr Burgess next door that I saw the great Sydney Wooderson in action, and Wooderson soon became as big a hero to me as Ted Medhurst, the Chelsea goalkeeper, had been in the days when I was mad on football. Sydney may have been shy and modest but he was a fantastic athlete."

In the immediate aftermath of the war, something similar would occur with fellow teenagers Roger Bannister and Chris Brasher, who, thrilled by the sight of Sydney in action, were inspired to strive for great things themselves.

Sydney, this quiet champion, was inevitably a source of constant fascination to Fleet Street's esteemed sportswriters. Was he an enigma, a calculating man of mystery, or merely an ordinary fellow who hated publicity? He was certainly polite and courteous at all times, as far as we know, but rarely chose to speak at length to journalists, or provide the juicy sound-bites they craved. In his more talkative moments Sydney would chat about athletics in general – admitting that outside of work it ruled his life – but he appeared ill-at-ease talking directly about himself. Author and journalist W. Capel-Kirby concluded that this was mostly down to nothing more than basic shyness. He wrote:

> "Wooderson looks like a small-time clerk destined to work from early morning till late at night in a dingy, ill-ventilated office. He looks at you from behind horn-rimmed spectacles with eyes which suggest a heart laden with sorrow. In fact, Wooderson's general appearance gives one the impression that he'd be ill for the rest of the day if he so much as broke into a trot to catch his train. Sydney Wooderson is the last person you would associate with running, let alone world record breaking.
>
> "We have journeyed many thousands of miles in the same company, in various part of Europe, yet [have remained] more or less casual

acquaintances. Snobbishness? No! Shyness? Most definitely! Beyond the customary polite everyday salutations, the longest remark Wooderson ever addressed to me was one of six words – 'I was beaten on my merits.' This was a more than generous tribute to rivals to whom, under normal circumstances, he would show a clean pair of heels. Never shall I forget that occasion in the packed Berlin Olympic Stadium. Wooderson was due to face the start in his heat of the 1500 metres Olympic event. Hitler and Goering just below me in the tribune of honour, sat up and took notice. Everybody strained to see the much publicised British miler. They expected a record shattering performance. I alone knew Wooderson was being sacrificed for the good name of British sportsmanship.

"He was a lame man. In my opinion he should never have stripped. The world could have thought what it liked. And yet, tragic though it was, I shall always regard the little fellow's plucky run that afternoon as the most outstanding of his many triumphs. What he did on one leg many could not have done on three. Despite a chipped ankle bone, Wooderson was up there with the leaders 50 yards from the finish. I almost wept as first one, then another, and another streaked past our champion – second-raters judged by Wooderson standards. 'I was beaten on my merits.' How it must have hurt him to speak those few words. And how those American critics squawked, jibed and wisecracked at the expense of the big-hearted Blackheath runner. Wooderson thrives on hard running of a nature which would spell *finis* to the career of more robust athletes. It is argued by experts that an athlete touches peak only once a season. Here again our little wonder scores: He is always at peak."

Jack Oaten of the *Evening News*, one of Fleet Street's most accomplished athletics correspondents, was a shrewd judge of an athlete. Oaten remembered his first sight of Sydney in action as a 17-year-old:

"I recall him then as a frail-looking boy, thin and apparently undeveloped, with a style as far removed from the classic as Salvador Dali from Rembrandt… It was hard to convince oneself that any runner with such an unlikely-looking physique and so uneconomical a style would do anything out of the ordinary in senior running. If only at the time we had known the courage and the fierce ecstasy of the fighter which lived within that frail frame, we might have been better prepared for what was to come... Evelyn Montague, coined, in the pages of the Manchester Guardian, the most expressive sentence about Sydney Wooderson I have ever read: 'He looks as vulnerable, and is as dangerous as, Jimmy Wilde.'

"The thing to remember about Sydney Wooderson is that he was never, even at the height of his career, anything other than just an ordinary chap. Champions, according to the great American coach Dean Cromwell, are never quite normal. This goes too, for most of the champions I have met, but Dean Cromwell could never have known Wooderson. He fitted to a 'T' those well-known words of W. S. Gilbert – 'an everyday young man'. Those of us privileged to have known Sydney believe that was part, and a big part too, of his greatness. Meek is perhaps the word that best described the effect he had on those meeting him for the first time. He rarely spoke first. In conversation he had little small talk, and in a journalistic sense he never ranked high as an interviewee. He answered the questions that were put to him but he rarely volunteered anything – in marked contrast to most of the athletes who have reached equal eminence. In all the years I have known him, I have never seen Sydney Wooderson seriously annoyed nor heard him raise his voice in anger. So far as I am aware, he made no enemies in the sport, but many, many friends. That meek exterior concealed an unassailable spirit. Behind the meek Jekyll was a Hyde imbued with unbounded confidence, resolution of purpose and immense courage. He was steadfast and exceedingly painstaking in everything he did, and he had a fanatic's belief in the superiority over all other forms of sport of the amateur athletics which he loved."

Being a proud amateur, and loyal to all that amateurism stood for in the 1930s, meant Sydney had no qualms about dropping training and competition down his priority list in the first half of 1938. He did squeeze a couple of cross-country events into his early-January schedule, but then embarked on a prolonged period of 'cramming' in advance of Law Society

Image of Sydney on a cigarette card for collectors, issued by R. and J. Hill of London

final exams due in June. By the start of 1938 the ship carrying his British international teammates to the Empire Games in Australia had already left on its long journey south, but there was never any question of Sydney being able to join them, for even without his exam preparations, a period of four months off work was never a feasible prospect.

Naturally he wasn't the only athlete to miss the trip for work reasons, meaning England took a much-depleted team to New South Wales for the February 5–12 competition. They would prove to be moderately successful in medal terms, however, and Sydney will have noted how Welshman Jim Alford won the Empire mile in a modest 4:11.6, a time well within his own capability. Alford had only been free to travel to Australia because he had time on his hands before starting at Loughborough College. Sydney, of course, will have noted that the AAA had increased the amount of international competition being staged in the summer of 1938, meaning he had plenty to look forward to once his dreaded exams were done.

As a serious young man with professional pretensions, and with a father who expected good things from him, there was little chance of Sydney taking shortcuts or treating his exams with disdain. An accomplished international runner of a later era who knows exactly how Sydney will have suffered is Tim Johnston, who qualified as a solicitor at a time when his appearance at the 1968 Mexico Olympics was looming. Tim told me the period before Sydney's Law Society exams would have been intense and pressurised. It is almost certain he would have spent many long hours at the premises of the 'crammers', the private law tuition company Gibson and Weldon, prior to the exams themselves. Over a period of nearly 100 years this London firm prepared hundreds of thousands of future solicitors and barristers in England and Wales for their exams, including famous names like Robin Day and Quintin Hogg.

It was a crucial time in Sydney's career development, as Tim Johnston explained:

> "Sydney is unlikely to have earned much during his time as an articled clerk at his London office, as those positions normally tended to be subsidised by the young man's father, and were not like the position of a Managing Clerk – nowadays called Legal Executive – who would have been at a similar level of seniority but paid a small salary. In Sydney's case everything would have been geared to him getting

qualified and it would have hung like a cloud over him for ages. He would have to learn about all facets of law in a family solicitors' business, doing years of prep before the big exams. There would be loads to remember, hence the all-important crammers."

Most articled clerks of Sydney's era will have started straight from school and signed up for articles for five years as he did, but subsequent years saw an increasing number of aspiring solicitors go to university before starting articles. The last hurdle for all of them were these final examinations, facing Sydney in June 1938, taken at the end of articles, and obligatory for all. His 1936 exam had been the traditional 'irritation' of a separate test in 'Trust Accounts and Bookkeeping', which most young men found irrelevant and eccentric, but which Sydney had taken and passed just a few months before the Berlin Olympics.

The Law Society of the day apparently had little interest in how articled clerks spent their time. That was a matter for the boss at their place of work. Sydney will have learned his trade by observing seniors at work – the 'sitting by Nelly' theory of education as practised in British industry from time immemorial. His final exams in June were basically to test knowledge of those rules and principles which the new solicitor would need to apply in his daily work. It consisted of a series of papers with a list of questions which candidates were expected to answer in essay form over three hours. The emphasis was on facts rather than theoretical analysis. There was huge pressure on the examinee during Sydney's era, for a failing in any one of the seven different papers meant you had to retake the whole lot again.

Solicitors' offices often provided no training or preparation for the final exam, hence the need for long stints at the 'crammers', most commonly the private company Gibson & Weldon in Guildford or Lancaster Gate. Its critics believed cramming led to a system resembling the breeding of battery hens, some believing it was merely a way to guarantee the least talented students would get through with a minimum of effort. The notes dictated by an instructor were the key – if the student memorised these successfully they would pass. Afternoons were often free to memorise the work of the morning and at the end of each week they would be tested. It would be a grim four months for outdoor types like Sydney, but once done and dusted the relief would be enormous and a large chunk of summer would still remain to be enjoyed.

Sydney's abandonment of running for this period of study was in stark contrast to Tim Johnston, who chose to blow away his exam blues with daily hell-for-leather runs in Central London. Tim recalls:

> "With the Mexico Olympics looming, I was determined to pass the whole lot in one go. I sat the exams in the second half of 1967 and passed all seven papers. Shortly afterwards I was on the plane to Mexico for acclimatisation tests and training. I've never worked so hard before or since. I kept fit with daily flat-out 4.5-mile runs round Hyde Park and Kensington Gardens, using Queensway Baths as changing rooms. The result of all that was a PB of eight minutes dead for 3,000 metres at White City."

19

Escaping into the Garden of England

BEING cheered to the rafters by 50,000 at White City, or being barely acknowledged by one man and his dog in the fields of Kent – both scenarios had become part of Sydney Wooderson's world. If truth be told, he generally preferred the latter. For him, satisfaction and pleasure from running was not contingent upon praise and glory. It was therefore no surprise – three months after his thrilling world record at Motspur Park – to find our hero tackling the very different challenges posed by mud, ditches and hedgerows.

Personal glory was taking a back seat to teamwork when 23-year-old Sydney, at the start of 1938, agreed to pull on the black singlet of Blackheath for the first time in a major cross-country contest for senior runners. The occasion was January's annual Kent County Championships, this year staged in the 1,000-acre medieval deer park surrounding Knole House in Sevenoaks. Sydney had won the Kent junior title at Dartford six years earlier, but this was his very first crack at a senior county championship.

His admirers often said Sydney ran the last lap of a mile race "like a startled deer", so this former royal hunting ground naturally meant he looked perfectly at home! My modern-day tour of his racing venues took me into Knole Park on a mild and dry Boxing Day morning, one of at least a dozen runners roaming the paths and grasslands to shake off seasonal excesses. To run in the footsteps of 'The Mighty Atom', my first task was to find a landmark known locally as 'The Hole in the Wall', which marked the point where Sydney and the cream of Kentish runners gathered on Saturday 8 January 1938 for the start of their two-lap battle. First home after seven seriously undulating miles would be county champion for a year, but the collective focus was on team placings, with Blackheath desperate to lift the club crown, and hugely boosted by the presence of Sydney.

I found 'The Hole in the Wall' after directions from a local runner, but it seems my predecessors from Blackheath Harriers 77 years earlier had a tougher job locating it… drenched by rain, they missed the start of the junior race altogether as a consequence, and one official was still in a grumpy mood about race arrangements when he put pen to paper some days later.

Sydney's capabilities in two-and four-lap track events was beyond doubt, but a race like this would pose all sorts of difficult and intriguing questions of his capabilities. He'd won two out of three club cross-countries earlier in the season, but this county race looked a tougher nut to crack – a difficult hilly course, unpleasant weather, and the tricky tactical decisions over if and when to help teammates during the race.

I struggled to work up much speed when I ran through the wide downhill valley where they started their first lap back in 1938. Reports suggest Sydney had no such trouble, and he was well to the fore early on as the field shot off at 3pm in the rain. From there they slowed considerably as they went uphill, through the woods to Keeper's Cottage, past a farm and to the top of Godden Green footpath and back towards the start across the golf course. Spectators offering encouragement were at a premium as the rain clattered down, and to make matters worse, there was chaos at halfway when problems with the course markers saw everybody follow the wrong route, a deviation that shortened the race by at least 400 yards. Worse, in the eyes of Blackheath officials, was the general course layout near this spot, which was designed so that the leaders would hurtle down a steep 1-in-3 gradient, then be expected to negotiate a sharp right turn just yards from the finish-line.

Blackheath's experienced trail-layers attending Knole Park that day were agreed about the dangers of this: "They could not have picked a worse course had they tried… the genius [who designed this] should have been made to run up and down it for an hour or so!" was their unanimous verdict. They felt the hill and turn would be dangerous so close to the finish as runners would be hurtling along without caution at this stage. No accidents were reported, however, and perhaps Sydney's light and nimble frame gave him an advantage in such surroundings.

At around halfway Blackheath were clearly packing well and looking to have an advantage over rivals Aylesford Paper Mills. Sydney looked to be coping well and was at, or near, the front throughout, and into the second-half of the race found himself locked in battle with just one serious challenger, J. Hodges of Gravesend. As the rain continued to pelt down, this pair arrived at the so-called 'death trap' at the top of the golf course and flew steeply downhill at breakneck speed. They swept round the sharp bend and Sydney won a terrific battle for the tape by a mere two seconds to take his first major title over the country. There was no crowd to roar them in, but it was a thrilling climax nevertheless. With the first six from each club scoring, Blackheath's heroic half-dozen were all in the first 17 home, ensuring a substantial margin of victory over Aylesford and Cambridge Harriers. Stanley Wooderson came home 12th and among those braving the weather to see the family success was mum Nettie and elder brother Alfred and his wife.

It was a highly satisfying afternoon's work for both Blackheath and for Sydney. And if they needed bringing down to earth, the job would be done as the weary but jubilant finishers were told they must find shelter by trudging out of the park to nearby Sevenoaks swimming baths, where their allocated changing area was the cold, tiled floor of an empty pool!

Just because you are newly-crowned county champion, it doesn't mean you get an easy ride in subsequent races of course. In the mob match between Blackheath and Orion Harriers a week later, Sydney suffered the embarrassment of losing a shoe in the early stages and was overtaken by almost the entire field of 120. However – as many experienced runners will verify – incidents like this can get the adrenalin pumping even faster than normal, leading to near-miraculous recoveries.

So it was with Sydney, who located his recalcitrant shoe, jammed it back on and raced back into the fray knowing he now had a lot of overtaking to do. The trouble had occurred in a secluded area of bushes on the Hayes course, and there was little room to manoeuvre as he set off with about 300 yards to make up to regain a position with the lead group. At various points in the first two miles, the watching Blackheath supporters were surprised and concerned to see no sign of Sydney, but by the time the leaders hit the Blackness Farm area – about one-third of the 7.5 miles completed – he had clawed his way back into fourth place. It was a remarkable display and by halfway he'd improved to third, and was giving long-time leader, clubmate George Wilkinson, something to worry about.

'Wilkie' was a club enigma, a naturally gifted runner who did virtually no training at all, famously preferring the clubhouse where he would enjoy his pipe and tankard of ale instead of exerting himself out of doors! Today was a rare opportunity for him to beat the celebrated Sydney, however, and Wilkinson looked up for the challenge. As they hit the top of Fox Hill on the homeward journey, Wilkinson was still leading but Sydney had, ominously, closed the gap behind him. It was hard work in a relentless strong wind and some of those further down the field struggled to keep their balance in the exposed areas. By the time the two leaders reached Hayes Common they were side by side and they cantered to the finish apparently perfectly happy to share first place. They'd covered the tough 7.5 mile route in 47:21, a healthy 16 seconds clear of the next man. Sydney's brother Stanley continued his recent good form – he was one of eight Heathens in the top ten – and when all the calculations were done Blackheath were emphatic winners.

The visitors from Essex brushed off their big defeat by performing some entertaining 'turns' at the uproarious smoking concert and dinner that followed the race. Two particular items on the programme went down a storm and would, according to one Blackheath official, either make their performers a fortune or have them locked up. One of these opened with the lines:

"Dey almost got me Boss,
It's dem guys from Hayes.
They put a bullet through me pants,
An' took the ribbon off me stays!"

Blackheath president Rex Cross praised the unique enthusiasm and sporting outlook of the Orion club, who didn't run for medals, trophies or prizes and consequently had turned down the idea of a cup being competed for at this mob match. A toast was then drunk on behalf of Blackheath club captain Ronald Philo who was socialising for the last time with his running pals before setting sail for military duties in Iran.

Sydney allowed himself one more excursion across the Kent countryside before putting the spikes away for the year in order to concentrate on his law studies. This was on a sunny and relatively mild Saturday afternoon in February over a four-mile course near Maidstone, where he helped Blackheath trounce his *alma mater* Sutton Valence by 41 points to 97. Teammates Rex Cross and Sydney cruised home together to a mutually agreed tie for first place in 25:42, comfortably clear of the rest.

There was good news later that month when it was confirmed an IAAF meeting in Paris had ratified Sydney's Motspur Park run of 4:06.04 in 1937 as a world record. It must have been a proud moment to be made officially the king of the mile at the age of 23, and before long Sydney was tempted to mention publicly that he had his eye on being the first man to crack four minutes. In his book *3:59.4 – The Quest to Break the Four-Minute Mile*, John Bryant records:

> "In May of 1938, while the clouds of war were gathering over Europe, this shy solicitor's clerk stepped out into the sunshine of the White City track to begin his summer training and announced to the world that he was hoping to run the four-minute mile. 'It is the ambition of my life to be the first to do it,' he said. He indicated that if everything went well his first attempt at the barrier would probably be as soon as the August of 1938."

As well as letting slip his four-minute ambition, Sydney also admitted to a reporter that he considered American Glenn Cunningham as his greatest rival at the mile. Although the IAAF didn't recognise indoor times, Cunningham had in March 1938 clocked a sensational 4:04.4 indoors on a wooden track with no wind resistance. This track, in Hanover, New Hampshire, was known to be fast, being larger than most indoor venues, with only six-and-two-thirds laps to a mile and bends that weren't as tight as smaller tracks. The achievement was splashed across the front of the *New York Times* but never ratified for the record books. It did, however, convince many a sceptic that perhaps the 'impossible' feat of a four-minute mile was, after all, not very far away. "Given ideal conditions, I do not see why Cunningham's time should not be beaten outdoors," was Sydney's considered verdict.

The *Daily Mail* doubted that human pacemakers could be relied upon to take Sydney around a track at 60 seconds per lap and suggested mechanical

Midweek evening training at White City.

means – a 'mock athlete' circling the track in the same way as the artificial hare at greyhound races. This technology was already in place at White City, the paper pointed out. Sydney wasn't convinced, indicating he would rather tackle an all-star meeting on the August Bank Holiday at White City involving real-life runners such as Cunningham and San Romani: "That's the way most track records are recorded," he said.

20

The Thew and Thought Theory

AS in previous years, Sydney approached the summer of 1938 with the broad intention of peaking at mile and 1500 metres events in August and September. The difference this time was his intention to give extra attention to half-miling, a distance until now just a means of sharpening leg speed. Of course, his immediate priority was preparation for his final law exams which meant 'serious' track training would have to start later than usual.

Despite these amendments to programme, there seemed little reason to fear his performances would be adversely affected. His running during June confirmed that in addition to his widely accepted supremacy at the mile, he was clearly one of the fastest half-milers too. He appeared to have a great chance of the UK record at this distance, to add to the three-quarter mile, 1500 metres and mile records already captured.

Sydney was disciplined and organised enough – with the help of coach Hill – to temporarily put aside running issues in order to deal with the two days in June which involved the small matter of those exams in London. His career as a solicitor would last long beyond his days as an active athlete, and he knew where his priorities must lie. Blackheath officials publicly expressed approval that Sydney had put his work before his sport, while still thriving in both areas:

> "In former days it was no uncommon thing for an athlete to be adversely criticised for allowing his sport to interfere with his work, while the assertion that athleticism and brains never went

> together was frequently heard... [but it has] been emphatically demonstrated the development of the muscular powers never practically interferes with the development of the brain."

When it was subsequently confirmed Sydney had passed his finals, the club described Sydney as the perfect example of how the "thew and thought theory" had been vindicated to the full. The good news was made public through the columns of *The Times* during July, the paper naming 363 successful candidates, including Sydney, out of the 515 who had sat the exams.

As far as running went, Sydney kicked off his campaign at Blackheath's early-season evening meet on Thursday 8 June, where he successfully defended his club half-mile title and the Barclay-Essen Trophy. This first run-out for six months attracted much interest at Catford Bridge on a mild, humid evening, and his winning time of 1:58.4 was warmly applauded – John Furniss and Len King filling the places. It was a good start although the next outing a fortnight later, also a half-mile, would prove much tougher as the Southern championship title was at stake. This was at the United Services Sports Ground, a track situated in either Gillingham or Chatham, depending where you believed the boundary line to be.

Here the 880 yards required three heats to decide the finalists, Sydney, wearing No.9, cruising through his qualifier in second place behind Essex Beagles' Eddie Sears. For the final later that afternoon, conditions were unfavourable with a gusty wind and rough track to contend with. Sydney also found to his dismay that it wasn't just the track that was rough – the early pace was red hot and on the first bend he was seen to receive hefty jolts from runners either side of him, presumably accidental, which convinced him to slow down, get out of trouble, and cruise near the rear for a spell.

Title- and record-holder Arthur Collyer (Watford) and London AC's Brian McCabe were left to make the pace although Sears suddenly shot past them just before the bell sounded in 56.5. Sydney briefly looked boxed in at this point, but extricated himself without panic and moved up to the leaders. Sears had shot his bolt by now, and about 180 yards from home Sydney was able to effortlessly surge away from Collyer and McCabe. The pair, clad in all-white, responded gamely but when the man in black calmly kicked for a second time they had no answer and Sydney took the southern title by an eight-yard margin in 1:56.4. It was a highly impressive display of controlled and astute tactical running, particularly the unflappability after those early shenanigans. The time was superb in the circumstances and among the crowd, wearing a proud smile, was mum Nettie. Sydney quietly indicated he was confident of securing the British half-mile record and, judging by this performance, it was only a matter of when.

With exams done and dusted, Sydney was now more footloose than usual and accepted the opportunity to test himself in an invitation mile handicap at the Derby and County AC Sports at the end of June. It proved a relatively easy win in 4:23.7 and he took home an impressive Crown Derby bowl as his prize. More than 50 years later, interviewed for *Athletics Weekly*, Sydney would name this as the most extravagant prize he ever won during his strictly amateur career ("We still have it! I bet that's worth something now..."). There was an impressive turnout of athletes at this showpiece gathering, including Olympian Godfrey Brown and international cross-country champion Jack Emery.

At the beginning of July 1938, an interesting debate was sparked when columnist 'Ubiquitous' of the *Sporting Chronicle* appealed to the AAA to alter their entry policy for the forthcoming national championships. He wanted an end to the way some lesser athletes ("who have not the remotest chance of making a show and have no intention of competing") would obtain a competitor's entry ticket simply to mix with the stars and gain privileged vantage points. Ubiquitous also called for the AAA to start seeding entries to prevent race 'walkovers' which did the sport and its public appeal no good at all. He said the public of 1938 were nowadays only satisfied by high-class athletics and had no time for 'passengers' on the track. It was a well-made point.

The perfect warm-up for the season's first international match – Norway were bound for White City on the weekend of July 8 and 9 – presented itself in the shape of the 'Victory' 4 x 1 mile relay at Lee Green. Here heavy showers greeted the popular Ravensbourne Sports and its usual eclectic mix of lawn tennis, a donkey derby and flower show, to mention just three.

Sydney took the relay anchor leg with John Poole off first followed by Stanley Wooderson and Derek Reynolds. By the time the baton was thrust into Sydney's outstretched hand, Blackheath were a good 100 yards or more behind the leaders. The star of the show put in a sterling effort and closed the gap considerably as he recorded a swift 4:11 but it wasn't quite enough to overhaul Southend-on Sea's fourth runner, who himself was 25 yards or so behind the winning Polytechnic man. The winners were given a time of 17:33 for their four miles. Despite Blackheath only managing third, Sydney was by far fastest of the day and his 4:11 represented one of his best-ever miles, although of course came from a moving start. It underlined his fine form ahead of three big races at White City during the following fortnight.

Sydney hadn't taken part in Britain's 1937 defeat by Norway in Oslo, but toed the line in the White City return match a year later and showed the Scandinavians just what they'd missed. Two men from each team contested the 1500 metres, the press suggesting beforehand it would be a miracle if Sydney didn't add to his growing list of victories. And so it proved. This two-day match was closer than anticipated, the lead swapping hands throughout, until Britain pulled clear in the final couple of events to win by a mere five points, Sydney playing a key role. His 1500 compatriot, Midlands champion Jack Emery (Achilles), a much taller man who also ran in glasses, led the way for the opening two laps, then Sydney took over in business-like fashion and nobody posed a real threat from then as he sped home in 3:58.6. Emery rallied brilliantly near the end to pip Hans Lehne, meaning GB had the first two places (gaining 8pts to 3) at a crucial point in the contest when the team scores had been dead level. Lehne had fought hard but had no answer to the Brits' finishing power; he presented a more muscular athletic frame than Sydney, wore shorts that didn't flap around and modern light-coloured lightweight shoes. He made Sydney look dated in comparison, but, as one correspondent noted, the Englishman was this summer showing more vigour and confidence than ever before.

Some of the Norwegians stayed in town for the AAA championships the following weekend, and were joined by an array of talent from France, Belgium, Iceland, Germany and, unusually, Italy. Nearly 500 entries were received for the prestigious event and Sydney was going for his fourth successive mile title, knowing he might need to get close to his own championship record to hold off Italy's former Olympic champion Luigi Beccali. It rained heavily on the evening of Friday 15 July but Sydney qualified for the next day's final with ease, coming home just behind Southend's Bernie Wright, who had led the whole way. Veteran Beccali duly won his heat and a crowd of around 25,000 made its way into the

Shepherd's Bush area the next day to see if Sydney could give the famous Italian a beating in the nine-man final scheduled for 4.40pm.

Wright took them through the first quarter in 60.8 seconds and the halfway point in 2:08. Beccali found himself well down the field and Denis Pell looked the biggest threat to new leader Sydney, wearing No.15, as the bell sounded on 3:12.2. Empire Games champion Jim Alford made a bid for glory on the final lap, but Sydney held him off and surged himself, hitting the line in 4:13.4 a stride or two ahead of Pell and Alford but always in control. Beccali was a disappointing fourth, suffering defeat in England for a third time.

Away from the hurly burly of international competition, Sydney put his name down just four days later for a crack at the 440 yards in Blackheath's second evening meeting of the summer at Catford Bridge. It was a delightful evening, the Private Banks Ground bathed in sunshine, but Sydney's opting for the quarter-mile frightened off several colleagues who would normally have attempted to win the Reay Challenge Cup. On the horseshoe-shaped track, Sydney sped to a predictable victory, his time of 49.3 seconds amazing onlookers with the way it seemed so effortless.

21

Half-Mile Glory at White City

DURING Sydney Wooderson's era as Britain's favourite runner, and for many years either side of it, there were two major sporting venues within 400 yards of each other in the same district of Birmingham. On investigation, I found the one that hosted Sydney's well-publicised visit in summer 1938 continues to thrive 80 years later, but its neighbour was wiped off the face of the earth a while ago to make way for a shopping centre.

Sydney and his clubmates travelled to England's second city on a quest to lift the Waddilove Trophy, a popular annual contest that pulled in spectators by the thousand. It was staged at Perry Barr Stadium the same day the Law Society made their exam results public via the columns of *The Times*, meaning Sydney would potentially have double cause for celebration. He was down to run the half-mile and a medley mile relay and to be here had turned down an invitation to represent the AAA in Dublin on the same day.

Today's track was first created on the site of a rubbish tip in 1929, mainly to provide a home for crack local club Birchfield Harriers. In the decades since it has hosted cycle racing, dirt-track and speedway, equestrian events such as show-jumping, and more recently greyhound racing. In between the ground would be requisitioned by the War Office for use by the Home Guard and also accommodation for Italian prisoners of war.

In athletics terms, one of its proudest claims involves the installation of floodlighting, which allowed it to stage the first floodlit athletics meeting ever held in the UK in September 1948. The crowd that evening gasped in wonder when the lights came on for the first time towards the end of a meeting which had overrun into dusk.

Ten years before the lights were switched on, Sydney made his usual quiet and dignified way on to the track, but most of the excitable 7,000 crowd only had eyes for him – and there was no hiding place. He was becoming accustomed to such attention by now, and only too well aware of pressure to pull off a spectacular performance every time he stepped on a track. The odds were against any records on this July afternoon at the Alexander grounds, for the cinder track had only recently been re-laid and had not settled down as well as expected. It was lumpy and not likely to encourage fast times.

There were six events scheduled in all, with Sydney's half-mile the big feature. It would be all about the race today, and not a run against the clock, especially after Sydney found himself boxed in for much of the opening lap. When the bell sounded at the start of the second, he forced himself clear of danger and treated the crowd to one of his electric finishes. He flew across the line in 2:00.6, less than a second clear of plucky chasers John Powell (London AC) and A. A. Bird (Belgrave Harriers). The winning margin was only three yards, but Sydney didn't look seriously troubled. It was a fine run on a poor track and as such won him the Alexander Memorial Cup for best performance of the day.

Later that afternoon the crowd was delighted to see the great man in action again when he took the opening leg for Blackheath in a four-man medley mile relay, staged this time on the adjacent grass track. It had not been properly measured, so no times were taken. Sydney passed the baton on after forging a good lead, and teammates Wiard, Ransome and Chappell maintained this till the end, holding off Belgrave. After the points were added up, Belgrave lifted the Waddilove Trophy, narrowly pipping Blackheath.

A week or so after Birmingham, Sydney's fourth train ride in 23 days across the capital to race at the White City stadium would herald one of the highlights of summer 1938, both for participants and spectators alike. Groundstaff had worked furiously over three days to have the track re-laid for the Bank Holiday Monday showpiece on August 1 – at which 18 nations would be represented. *The Times* called it "the strongest foreign challenge ever encountered at White City" and estimated at least a third of the finest athletes in the world were here in London.

Winning relay team: Wiard, Chappell, Wooderson and Ransome.

In glorious uninterrupted sunshine, it was a repeat of last year's inaugural International Athletic Meeting, only this time bigger and better, and organised for the British Amateur Athletic Board largely by the energetic new AAA Honorary Secretary E. J. 'Billy' Holt. He had secured a mouth-watering entry list from the USA and all across Europe and all the trouble and expense was seen as fully justified, not just for the entertainment value, but for the high standard of competition it provided Britain's developing talent.

As temperatures soared, the dozen events listed in the sixpenny programme were preceded by a parade of athletes before an excited, bumper crowd. Sydney, to some surprise, decided to tackle his first major half-mile on this day, having earlier weighed up the pros and cons of running a mile in which there was a shortage of really testing opposition. He'd recently expressed his desire to attempt a British half-mile record and this seemed as good an opportunity as any. Despite not having faced many top-class men at 880 yards, he was thought well capable of improving his relatively modest PB of 1:54, given the right opposition and conditions. The British record was 1:51.6 at this point and the world's best 1:49.6, both possibly within reach. In today's heatwave he would be up against Italy's Olympic silver medallist Mario Lanzi, AAA title-holder Arthur Collyer and Dutch champion Sjabbe Bouman.

Wearing No.6 on his all-white GB kit, Sydney and the others had to suffer an annoying delay to the scheduled 3pm start after it emerged the USA's Chuck Fenske had made a very late decision to withdraw to concentrate solely on the mile, causing officials to fuss around amending arrangements on the start-line. Fenske, known back home in Wisconsin as 'Monarch of the Mile', will have heard about Sydney's recent outing of 49.3 seconds for 440 yards, and evidently decided to steer clear of him. Soldier Alf Baldwin of the East Lancs Regiment was called in at short notice to complete the line-up of six men. It was a frustrating and distracting episode for Sydney in particular, who might well have preferred to do the mile himself had he known Fenske was to run it, thus giving him the serious challenge he needed over four laps. Nevertheless, he wasn't the type to make rash or hurried decisions at this late stage and stayed put in the half-mile.

When everybody was finally ready, Lanzi shot away in trademark fashion, young Frenchman Jacques Leveque hot on his heels. The pair quickly spread-eagled the field and built a big lead and there was a period of worry for Sydney's fans when he appeared to take a hefty thump in the ribs as the chasers jostled for position. He allowed himself to drop back a little, presumably for reasons of personal safety. He was briefly boxed in as Lanzi completed the first furlong in 25 seconds. Sydney rectified matters with sudden acceleration and by the time Lanzi had passed halfway in 53.2 seconds – which seemed highly impetuous – Sydney was settled and back in touch. Like a small but cunning bird of prey, Sydney picked his moment and swooped with devastating effect halfway round the second lap. Victory looked inevitable as he picked off Bouman and Leveque and then, after the final bend, exploded past Lanzi with almost arrogant ease and strode home smoothly in 1:50.9, looking for all the world as if he could have gone faster had there been the need. Lanzi came in a shocked five yards adrift with Bouman third and Collyer grabbing fourth. It was the fastest half-mile ever run on British soil, beating Otto Pelzer's 1:51.6 at Stamford Bridge 12 years earlier, and obliterated the English native record (1:52.9) by Fred Handley of Salford at this venue a year earlier. Elroy Robinson's 12-month-old world record of 1:49.6 in New York would surely be Sydney's property shortly too. The *Daily Herald* commented:

> "Thus does our little Mister Wooderson continue to confound the experts and keep everybody guessing as to the real extent of his capabilities. He got his nose in front and running like a thoroughbred, he gradually increased his lead to the tape, even having time to look round before the worsted wrapped itself round his chest. You couldn't call a win like this effortless – all the same, Wooderson had something left."

It was a display that left nobody in any doubt, the *Sporting Chronicle* proclaiming: "Thus Wooderson proved himself the greatest middle distance runner Great Britain ever produced." Sydney and Godfrey Brown in the 440 yards were Britain's only winners from 14 events on this scorching hot day. Much later in the afternoon the mile race went ahead without Sydney and there were mocking jeers from the big crowd when Chuck Fenske's relatively slow 4:19.4 winning time was announced.

Record Wrecker

WOODERSON finishing his record half-mile yesterday.

WOODERSON, A WONDER RUNNER

New Figures For Half-mile

Sydney sat on the infield grass to cool off after his race, leaning back and placing a tracksuit top over his head to keep the burning sun at bay. He looked shattered in the photos of this little scene, but his stern expression was probably more a reaction to being crowded by cameramen.

There was no time to rest on his laurels, and Sydney had no intention of doing so during this rich vein of form. A well-publicised attempt on the 1500 metres world record had been lined up for him just five days later, 400 miles north at the annual Rangers Sports at Ibrox Park, Glasgow. On the morning of this meeting, Saturday 6 August, Harold Abrahams wrote at length about athletics' golden boy in his weekly newspaper column:

> "If someone were to point S. C. Wooderson out to you on the running track and tell you that he was the athlete who had run a mile more quickly than any other human being, you just wouldn't believe it. If you were to see that tiny 5ft 6in figure running with a dozen others, buffeted hither and thither, and almost apologising for occupying any space at all, he would be the last person you would pick out as a king among milers. That is until he released that incredible burst of stored-up energy. Then, and not till then, he looks for what for the past two years he has proved to be – unbeatable."

Abrahams admitted he'd initially thought Sydney to be a flash in the pan, but was by now completely won over, and likened him to a "small-bodied light car with an extremely high-powered engine."

A record-breaking Ibrox meeting, attended by around 50,000, saw Sydney narrowly miss the 1500 world record, set by Lovelock in Berlin, although his valiant effort was the fastest ever run in the UK, or by any Briton, at 3:49.0. However, as the authorities didn't recognise 1500 metres as an official distance in the UK it couldn't be called a British record in their eyes, meaning this performance was barely acknowledged at the time, the reports concentrating solely on his failure to beat the world record.

Sydney had travelled north by train for this event, a specially-framed handicap designed solely to assist his quest. Cheered on by his enthusiastic Scottish audience, he made an almighty effort to catch the man up ahead, Denis Pell (given a 30-yard start), but ended up 12 yards or so adrift and missed Lovelock's record by 1.2 seconds. It was an overcast humid day, although there was no wind or burning sun, and although the track was a little loose underfoot, surely the main reason for the 'failure' was Pell's start being a tad too generous. Had it been 20, not 30 yards, it might have had the desired effect. Sydney ran a cracking first lap but hadn't clawed any of the 30 yards back by 400 metres. Into the third lap he was still chasing Laidlaw, Griffiths and Pell, and with less than 400 to go momentarily seemed to waver, although quickly got back into his normal stride. The closing stages saw a terrific attempt to get on terms and his every stride was roared on from the packed terraces. Onlookers detected a very slight slowing in his final few yards, indicative of the fact that Pell was already home by then and the all-important 'chase' was over.

In some ways it was a glorious failure, for in only his third serious attempt at a 1500 metres his 3:49.0 was the fastest ever on British soil and had rarely been bettered across the world. His splits were 57.7 seconds for 400 metres, 2:04.4 at 800 and 3:04.1 at 1200. He may have missed his target today, but the signs were highly encouraging for the European Championships 1500 in Paris now just a month away.

Moments after flopping down on the Ibrox grass to take a post-race breather, Sydney was surrounded by other athletes, officials and footballers, all desperate to get his autograph. One photographer captured the moment well, showing around 15 bodies clustered around him, pressing forward as he dutifully signed their programmes and assorted pieces of paper.

22

Six Records in Six Weeks

THE simple beauty of the mile – the distance Sydney had conquered and upon which his fame was built – continued to be sidelined as this hectic summer progressed. On returning home to London, Sydney's thoughts turned from 1500 metres to 880 yards; his next record attempt would be at the half-mile, on 'home' turf at Motspur Park on August 20. But, before then, another massive audience would await him at White City for the fierce annual battle between Britain and France.

He'd been selected to run the mile against the French, but told the powers-that-be he preferred the half-mile on this occasion. His wish was granted, it seems, with a minimum of fuss. Other, lesser runners were shuffled around to accommodate the changes and it was announced Sydney would team up for GB with Arthur Collyer at 880 yards and Denis Pell and Jim Alford would fly the flag in the mile. With September fully committed to action across Europe, and hence non-Imperial measurements, it was now clear Sydney had run his last mile for nine months or more.

On a humid afternoon at White City the crowd cheered a fairly convincing home win, Britain doing enough by dominating the nine track events even though a rather feeble return from the field events didn't bode at all well for the upcoming Euros. Sydney won the half-mile convincingly by six yards, albeit in a rather modest 1:55.8.

The Times had recently introduced large news and sport pictures in its Monday morning editions, and there on the back page was a prominent action shot of Sydney, coming home ahead of 20-year-old Jacques Leveque, with Arthur Collyer well back in third. Although heavily bumped near the end, he was not overly exerted in advance of the planned record attempt a week later. Young Leveque, the pride of France, gave a fine account of himself, not at all overawed by Sydney as he seized the lead on the first bend. Sydney was content to remain last for a while before drawing level at halfway, the clock showing 57.9. On the second lap the two raced together up the back straight with Sydney slightly ahead and Leveque desperately trying to regain the lead. He managed this at the end of the back straight and then immediately cut in, long before he had attained the theoretical two-yard lead – the result being that Sydney was very nearly bowled over and for a second or two completely lost his stride. He somehow stayed composed and after checking and regaining full balance he immediately went for his man again, catching and passing him within 50 yards to win emphatically.

There was little time to bask in the glory of victory over the French, for Sydney had to get straight back to racing the clock and a return to his beloved cinder path of Motspur Park for his half-mile and 800 metres world record attempt a week later on Saturday 20 August. This was another specially-framed handicap and prior to the start the track looked in tip-top condition and the wind helpfully dropped after being blustery earlier on. Everything looked set for a very special afternoon. The BBC would be broadcasting "a description" of the world record attempt on its National Home Service channel.

Nothing was being left to chance, Sydney starting ten inches behind the line in case the track was found to be a little short. Blackheath's treasurer Ted Lymbery had initially been due to fire the starting pistol, but decided he'd be better placed on the gate taking the entrance money, although even he deserted his post so that he could share the excitement of the half-mile.

Everything went off like clockwork: The six runners lined up ahead of Sydney with starts of varying distances did a perfect job and made his task simple. Sydney blasted out a new world record for the half-mile of 1:49.2 which, remarkably, would stand unbroken for 17 years. His brother Stanley had the longest start under the handicapping and it was he who crossed the finish-line first, Sydney chasing furiously and achieving a world record 'double' by passing the 800-metre mark in 1:48.4. This was technically not a 'British record' as metric distances were not formally recognised then. Stanley, with his 85-yard start, was chuffed to have achieved the unusual feat of finishing ahead of a man setting two world records. Frank Whittingham (70 yards start) crossed the line third.

Elroy Robinson (USA) had broken the 800 world record in 1937 with a surprise performance – but today there was almost a sense of inevitability about Sydney's eclipsing it. He had been quietly confident himself and coach Hill always knew it was well within reach. The 3.15pm race had been timed for early in the programme and the crowd saw Sydney set off at a staggering pace, going through 220 yards in 25.7 seconds, having caught the first of the handicap men after just 30 yards.

The halfway point was reached in 52.5, meaning he was well inside schedule. He seemed to bide his time a little in the third furlong – some onlookers wondering if he was tiring having overcooked the first lap – but then surged to close the big gap to his brother and Whittingham, passing the latter and finishing only 1.2 behind Stanley at the end. The furlong splits were 25.7, 26.9, 27.8 and 28.8, and he was able to run the whole thing in the inside lane, always with someone to chase to keep him at full stretch. The other pacemakers were John Furniss (Blackheath) eight yards ahead, Jack Emery (Achilles) 40 yards, A. D. G.White (Thames Valley) 45 yards and Ron Henderson (Polytechnic) 65 yards. There were six timekeepers, three timing Sydney at 800 metres and three at 880 yards.

The packed crowd of approaching 5,000 made a huge din throughout and Sydney hadn't let them down. There were 3,049 paying customers, plus a stand full of competitors, officials and pressmen, plus all those congregated on the infield. Among the VIPs present were Guy Butler and Jack Lovelock. An enthusiastic Harold Abrahams did his radio commentary with a fine view of the track from the top of the stand, and Sydney would briefly join him up there to speak to the nation.

In the aftermath, after Sydney had changed his shoes and pulled on a tracksuit, he was hoisted high by fellow runners and assorted others nearby. Sydney had never bettered 1:54 prior to this summer, so it was a remarkable feat although not a real surprise given his good form. Looking back it was clearly not a genuine race, with the arranged handicapping all geared to Sydney's goal – but of course these were the days before governing bodies frowned upon and indeed banned record attempts that were paced. Sydney's achievement meant 50 years after Frank Cross clocked 1:54.4 at Oxford, a Briton was at last back in possession of the 880 yards world record. As things would turn out, this would be Sydney's last world class performance at the half-mile and he could now return to miling again with mission accomplished.

Another, less celebrated success that day was credited to a Blackheath member called Spray, who had predicted – exactly – the correct time of Sydney's mile world record a year earlier, and amazed everyone by doing the same thing this time! When the dust settled, many of the key figures at Motspur Park, including all three Wooderson brothers, repaired to Gourmets Restaurant for an informal celebration dinner. A total of nearly 60 diners included 12 from the visiting French party of athletes and officials. A sign of the times was the newsworthiness of the number of female diners present, the club *Gazette* pointing out: "It is not often that our austerity allows ladies to partake in our conviviality, but this was an occasion in history, and they deserve their names to be placed on record." Things got fairly raucous during the evening and when the traditional 'club cry' rang out, it was performed in perfect unison at enormous volume.

Horse and Hound magazine expressed astonishment at the record, their correspondent admitting a few years earlier he would have 'staked his oath' that the absolute limit had been achieved when American James Meredith ran the half-mile in 1:52.2 in 1916. He added:

> "A remark passed by a friend of mine who saw Wooderson break the record was rather illuminating. 'He doesn't look like an athlete,' he observed. Today many of our athletes do not conform to the 'Greek God' conception. Rather they are ordinary men and women, perhaps not gifted by any special physique, who, by sheer application and concentration upon certain principles have succeeded in disciplining their bodies to attain these amazing speeds. This is all to the good for it may encourage the young people of this country to do likewise. At the present time we have a lamentable shortage of running clubs and other sporting organisations."

A world record by a popular British athlete was, of course, guaranteed to reach the parts other sporting news items couldn't reach... and sure enough Sydney found himself featuring on the pages of the famous weekly satire magazine *Punch* before the month was out. Many politicians and social climbers of the day would have given their right arm to be the subject of a full page *Punch* cartoon – and in the August 31 edition this accolade was afforded to Sydney, the most unassuming, non-seeker of publicity anywhere in politics, entertainment or sport!

The caption to Sydney's cartoon stated: "A curious feature of Mr Sydney Wooderson's record-breaking half-mile run was that, unlike Mr Corrigan and the Queen Mary, he meant to do it." The references were to Douglas Corrigan, the well-known transatlantic pilot, and the RMS Queen Mary, the Cunard-White Star ocean liner that had recently made the fastest transatlantic crossings.

★★★

In the 1930s the European Athletics Championships were a new addition to the sporting landscape, steadily growing in stature but certainly not at this point a 'be-all and end-all' to anybody's season. Indeed some wondered whether there was room for another 'major' when there was already the Olympics, Empire Games and AAA championships. Nevertheless there was prestige at stake and the chance to become a European champion was not to be scoffed at.

Britain had not fielded a team at the inaugural Europeans in Turin in 1934 but did name a squad of 23 for the second staging in Paris in early September 1938. Controversially, the selectors chose not to field anybody in events in which Britain was not especially strong. This included the 10,000 metres and steeplechase. This attitude struck some newspaper correspondents as short-sighted, as it meant young and upcoming talent would miss the chance of gaining valuable experience on a major stage. As I write this, nearly 80 years later, the very same issue was being debated after Britain decided not to send any senior men to the IAAF World Cross-country Champs in Kampala. *Plus ca change*!

The three-day competition at the Stade Olympique de Colombes in Paris opened on Saturday 3 September 1938 for male athletes from 26 different nations, with the women's inaugural championships taking place around 750 miles away in Vienna a fortnight later. The British party in Paris included medical officer Sir Adolphe Abrahams, Harold's elder brother, an experienced former athlete and a man soon to be knighted and acclaimed as founder of modern sports science. His expertise was supplemented by that of masseur Mick Mays.

In perfect weather on the opening day, Sydney, wearing No.114, lined up for heats of the 1500 metres. Among the VIPs looking on was France's elderly President Albert Leburn. Sydney was aware the attention he normally got at home would be replicated here in Paris as his was one of the feature races. He was under pressure to complete a magnificent hat-trick of world records – within little over a year – by adding the 1500 mark to his mile and half-mile marks. With the Americans not involved he was hot favourite to take gold, so it was not really a matter of if he would win, but by how much, and how gloriously.

In recent years he'd rarely, if ever, looked the sort to buckle under pressure, but there was consternation during his heat on the Saturday when he continually encountered trouble and for a while looked ruffled. The first five finishers would qualify for the final, but Sydney did things the hard way, failing to steer clear of buffeting and boxing. He had to travel the long way around opponents so often that there was great relief when he finally settled down and came home in third place. He clocked 3:58.1, behind Belgium's Joseph Mostert and Finland's Toivo Sarkama. *The Times* scolded him for "Running deliberately into all the trouble there was going – and there was plenty of it."

The 1500 final was staged two days later on the Monday, with a field of ten doing battle in windy conditions. After the rough and tumble of the heats, there was concern in the GB camp over what Sydney would come up against. Had he been unlucky on the Saturday, or was it possible that opponents, particularly foreigners, were deliberately ganging up on him? The inscrutable Sydney certainly wasn't complaining – in public at least – and it was hoped his skill and judgement would steer him clear of further trouble.

As far as the public was concerned, records were what they wanted to see, a desire stoked up by the press. But given the ragged nature of Sydney's heat, plus the unfavourable weather, the chances of a world best in the final looked minimal. Sydney would confirm later:

> "Directly I started I knew it was hopeless to try for a world record on account of the wind. Furthermore I had no means of finding out my lap times. The track was very good, perhaps slightly on the loose side, but otherwise all right."

Sydney banished the concerns by doing his country proud, running the final his own way, choosing his pace and almost contemptuously indifferent to repeated crowding and changes of position. Beccali chose to set the early pace and Jan Staniszewski of Poland pressurised him. Sydney mostly ran at their heels with Mostert of Belgium and Niilo Hartikka of Finland occasionally in the mix. Jim Alford, GB's second runner, was never really in the picture. Sydney took the lead just before the bell and a pack led by Beccali pursued him purposefully, although the Italian stumbled badly at one point and Staniszewski faded. They battled the stiff wind in the back straight and Mostert made the best effort to push Sydney, straining every sinew but failing to get past. Sydney crossed the line in 3:53.6, around five yards clear of the Belgian, who was just 0.9 of a second behind with Beccali third in 3:55.2. The times were well short of the record many had hoped to see, but the manner of the victory proved again that Sydney was tougher than he looked and knew how to win in potentially tricky circumstances.

"Sydney played with the opposition," purred a delighted Jack Crump. Lovelock's world record (3:47.8) and Miklos Szabo's European mark (3:48.6) were safe for the time being, although Sydney's effort was a championship best and improved Britain's gold medal haul to four.

Later there was speculation Sydney might step forward and save the day in the 4 x 400 metres relay when the British team were agonising over a replacement for absent star Bill Roberts. However, Sydney decided two big efforts in one day would be too much, and it was left to Jack Barnes, Alf Baldwin, Alan Pennington and Godfrey Brown to carry the baton. They were beaten into the silver medal position by the Germans by just 1.2 seconds. Germany topped the final medals table with 12 golds and 32 in total, ahead of Finland (five and 11) with Britain third (four and eight).

Directly after the final evening of proceedings, Sydney was part of a contingent moving on to compete in internationals in Milan and then Oslo, meaning he would jet from Paris to Milan via Turin, and not return home like some of the Blackheath Harriers party, most of which had been watching rather than competing. Sydney's urbane and rather glamorous travel schedule caused great glee among his less celebrated clubmates and the banter flew around: "Little Sydney is nothing if not up to date," said one of them.

With the athletics over, the other Blackheath boys were, unlike Sydney, now free to enjoy what the French capital had to offer. One of them headed south for a holiday, but several extended their hotel stays in Paris some pretending they had business to attend to, others admitting the city's after-dark entertainment scene was calling them. One group visited the Alcazar de Paris Music Hall where the naked female flesh was appreciated by all – except the elderly Blackheath man who, to his fury, had left his spectacles at his hotel!

Sydney, meanwhile, was en route to Milan with other members of the GB team for a three-day competition, thrilled by the view from the plane's windows when crossing the Alps. The track on Sunday 11 September for the 1500 metres proved tricky due to rain and Sydney found himself leading for the first lap-and-a-half, simply because everybody else refused to do so. Home favourite Luigi Beccali then moved to the front and stepped up the pace but at the bell Sydney regained first place and Beccali and Chuck Fenske challenged him hard in turn. Sydney kept the American at his shoulder round the last bend and then sprinted away to win by less than five yards in 3:58.4. It was a modest winning time for Sydney, but the finish provided a great spectacle for the crowd, his two challengers less than a second behind, both given 3:58.8.

Sydney's continental adventure continued without delay, flying direct from Italy to Norway for another three-day international. Oslo's Bislett Stadium had first staged international athletics 14 years earlier and a world record was set that day, kicking off an astonishing trend in this atmospheric little stadium, where more than 60 would be broken in susbsequent years. After the pedestrian pace of Milan, Sydney was keen to run close to record pace on this occasion and lined up with high hopes in the 1500 metres on the evening of Thursday 15 September.

The track was in excellent condition, although this was offset by bitterly cold winds. Although nowadays the marvellous atmosphere generated by floodlighting and noisy fans at Bislett is seen as a bonus for competitors, at least one reporter at Sydney's race reckoned that running here "under electric light at 8pm" was a distinct disadvantage. Sydney certainly wasn't complaining however, and once underway made the most of some excellent pacemaking. The enterprising Finn Kauko Pekuri, roared on by his home crowd, led for three laps (61, 61.5 and 63) setting Sydney up for a fast final 300 metres which gave him a phenomenal winning time of 3:48.7.

It was the fastest ever by a Briton and only missed Lovelock's world record by a mere 0.9 of a second. He came in three metres clear of Joseph Mostert of Belgium, with teammate Jack Emery third in 3:53.4. As he crossed the line both hands shot up in front of his face – not in celebration, but to protect himself from the finish-tape which had been fixed at eye level! Towards the end of this three-day festival, Sydney was feeling fresh again and happy to take part in the 4 x 400 metres relay, running his leg in 49.1 to help GB take third place behind the Netherlands and Norway.

★★★

After setting half-a-dozen records in less than seven weeks in summer 1938, it is unlikely Sydney had any lingering doubts about his place among the world's elite. But if he had, they would have been banished by the unlikely sight of a tablecloth being brandished in his direction!

This infamous white linen cloth belonged to a well-known character from Birmingham, Dorothy Neal, who regularly attended major athletics meetings around Europe – and always took the tablecloth with her. Her aim was to get only the very best track and field stars to autograph the cloth – and being asked to do so was regarded as confirmation that the athlete in question had indeed reached elite level!

Dorothy explained: "I'm quite ruthless in my selection. Only an outstanding few have a place on the cloth." She had begun collecting the signatures at the 1934 Empire Games and one of the first asked was Jack Lovelock as he sat on a bench beside the White City track. After signing, Lovelock asked her: "Do you want him too?" indicating Sydney, sitting quiet as a mouse nearby. But Dorothy responded loudly: "No not him."

Sydney evidently heard this put-down, but didn't react. Now, four years later, Dorothy was seeking out the same "quiet little chap" that she rejected in 1934 and she thrust the well-known tablecloth at him. Sydney is said to have grinned shyly and replied: "Ah, so I have now qualified then?"

Reaching 'tablecloth status' was just one small step during his highly eventful, rewarding and exhausting 1938 season, with unprecedented travel involved. He'd become a proven major talent at international level. As track competition had started and finished slightly later in the year than normal, he decided to withdraw from cross-country racing during the winter of 1938–9 in order to be fully fresh for the following summer.

He told clubmates at their annual dinner that he still firmly believed cross-country was hugely beneficial to all runners, but there were special circumstances behind his own decision to drop out for one winter. He was responding to a toast proposed by track captain Charles Woods, who had prompted hearty laughter when he thanked Sydney for running in Paris, as this had given club officials a perfect alibi to enjoy a weekend in the French capital.

Blackheath's redoubtable membership was evidently in jocular mood, but the bigger picture in Britain was not quite so cheerful. War clouds were gathering. In the autumn of 1938 it was confirmed the 1940 Olympics was to be switched from Tokyo to Helsinki, Japan having forfeited the Games because of the ongoing Sino-Japanese war. Britain's Olympic prospects looked strong for 1940, with the likes of Sydney and one or two others measuring up as genuine gold medal prospects. However, there was no avoiding the very sinister rumblings taking place outside the world of sport.

Some wondered if those Helsinki Olympics would actually take place at all. In Europe war was beginning to look inevitable following the manner in which Hitler reacted to all attempts by western democracies to appease him. Plans were even being drawn up to evacuate British children from town to country and air-raid shelters being built. But Prime Minister Neville Chamberlain insisted war could be averted and embarked on his famous 'shuttle-diplomacy' programme, meeting Hitler three times in September 1938.

For a spell, it seemed Chamberlain might be succeeding in his quest to preserve "peace for our time" and Blackheath Harriers' newly-elected President Arthur Thwaites even issued an autumn message to the membership expressing his delight:

> "We have no doubt that all members feel with us a sense of relief and thankfulness that we are to be spared the havoc and horror of another European or world war... we remember with pride and gratitude those older members who kept the club alive during the years 1914-18, but ask yourself whether such self-sacrificing achievements would be possible today? Another war would affect the club even more, and only a person of vivid imagination can picture what might have happened [here] in London and its environs had hostilities broken out."

The relief and optimism of Thwaites – who had been wounded in the 1914–18 War himself – would soon evaporate. Hitler reacted to the diplomacy by simply continuing to increase his demands. The infamous carve-up of Czechoslovakian territory in the Munich agreement of autumn 1938 was followed within weeks by a nationwide pogrom in Germany and the intensifying anti-semitic climate led to a stampede to get out of the country, producing a refugee crisis. Poor Chamberlain was left feebly calling for 'moderates' in Germany to restrain Hitler before it was too late. It looked a forlorn hope.

23

'The Yanks Are Out to Get You!'

PETER Wilson was a revered sports writer, known via his by-line 'The Man They Couldn't Gag.' Harrow-educated and larger than life, Wilson loved to be controversial and outspoken, but was also regarded as an astute and canny observer of British sport. When he issued a grim warning to Sydney Wooderson that he needed to watch out for his safety, it was a view that couldn't be ignored.

Wilson published the open message to Sydney at the beginning of 1939, warning in no uncertain terms that the top American runners were "out to get him" – and he must learn from lessons of the past as he planned his 1939 summer season. He warned Sydney not to accept an invitation to run in the so-called 'Mile of the Century' race in the USA in the summer if there was any chance of him not being at his absolute peak:

> "They'll be out to get you. Glenn Cunningham may have announced his retirement, but I have a hunch he'll come back if there's a chance of meeting you in his own home straight. You'll have to be as fit as a whole orchestra of fiddles because you can bet the spikes out of your shoes that the Americans will gang up on you – and you know better than I that as many international races are won with the elbows as with the legs."

Wilson was concerned Sydney's lack of muscularity, his sense of fair play and his gentlemanly attitude might hamper his chances in big international clashes away from home territory. He was also keen to emphasise admiration for what Sydney had recently achieved – however, at the end of his piece there was a sting in the tail. His message was clear – Sydney must only take on the Americans in their own back yard if fully fit and committed – to repeat his Berlin fiasco would be unthinkable:

> "I'm not only congratulating you on your record breaking in 1938 but also on what you have done to further the cause of 'Fitter Britain'. A lot of money has been spent in trying to boost this campaign but a little man in a black tracksuit has done more than all the advertising and all the committee have been able to achieve. And that little man is you. Most athletes look the part. They seem to have the kind of electrical energy which marks them off from the ordinary fellow who has to earn his living working in an office. I'm sure that you won't mind if I say that you look just like the 'man in the street' who only runs when he's late for the 8.30 in the morning. But by sending up more records in smoke than when a gramophone factory catches on fire, you've proved that one doesn't need special physique or special advantages to become a world beater. You do a proper job of work in a solicitor's office and at the same time you can take on the picked athletes of the world and beat them over any distance from 800m to the mile.
>
> "I've only got one thing against you. You let us down in the Berlin Olympiad of 1936. It wasn't your fault. Your ankle was in no condition for you to run but you allowed yourself to be persuaded into it. That fortnight was a pretty dreary time for GB. But the worst five minutes of the lot was when you failed to qualify in a heat which you could normally have won running on your hands."

The rumours and gossip surrounding whether or not Sydney would take on the Americans in New Jersey were clarified a few weeks into 1939 when he was formally granted permission by the AAA to participate in the Invitation Games on Saturday 17 June at Palmers Stadium, Princeton. Sydney was quietly determined to go up against Cunningham and prove he was the world's best miler, especially after having turned down the

Princeton organisers a year earlier due to work commitments. This time the 'Mile of the Century' was definitely on!

The prospect of little Sydney venturing into the lion's den to put the Yanks in their place was a thrilling prospect for British sports fans and press alike. And there was jubilation in the USA too, for this would be a huge money-spinner, with their top men under pressure to lower the colours of the world's fastest miler. This news meant plans for a July contest between GB and USA teams in New York had to be abandoned, its promoters deciding that Sydney making his much-heralded USA debut in Princeton would cause their event to suffer badly in terms of gate money.

* * *

There was plenty of snow and ice in southern England during the winter of 1938–9, particularly around Christmas, but it wasn't this that persuaded Sydney to avoid cross-country altogether this season. His six-month break was geared towards being fresh for the summer. Doing little or no cross-country had worked well in early 1938 – old-stager Walter George had recommended that – and judging by all the planning and gossip surrounding his 1939 summer calendar, this repeat hiatus was a good thing too. He was motivated and raring to go.

At this stage Sydney certainly couldn't be accused of hiding or steering clear of pressure situations. In addition to the big American date, there was also talk of travelling to race in Australia in the near future. In fact this would never materialise, nor would a trip to Helsinki which had been a strong possibility for June. Closer to home, he entered talks with Fred Williams, secretary of Manchester AC, about attempting a world record on their Fallowfield track. Once those details were thrashed out it was made known that Sydney would go for a record in the rarely-run distance of three-quarters of a mile (1,320 yards/1206 metres) at Fallowfield on the gala evening of Tuesday 6 June. It created a rather hectic schedule for him and raised a few eyebrows: this record attempt would be just eight days after the British Games, and 11 days before the Princeton mile.

Sydney and Albert Hill designed his 1939 programme with the aim of peaking at Princeton. The first fortnight of February was taken up with easy off-road runs of four or five miles at weekends, this giving way to steady evening runs on the roads when the weather improved, three or four times weekly. By April he was travelling regularly to White City to begin trackwork in earnest under Hill's watchful eye.

His typical working day in much of 1939 involved a session of deep breathing exercises and a brisk walk early in the morning, before his commute to start an eight-hour day in his city office at 10 am. The evening track sessions would typically last between 60 and 90 minutes on Mondays, Wednesdays and Thursdays, plus another most Saturdays. They began with three slow warm-up laps before Hill put him through his paces, rehearsing starts, and tackling various types of run. They varied between 60-yard sprints to medium paced five-lappers. Invariably brother Stanley would be there to help pace him. Stanley would also provide company two evenings a week for a brisk five-mile walk somewhere in South London, and again on Sundays for the long-standing countryside hikes they loved so much. Often the latter stretched to 20 miles or more.

Of course, Sydney's plans to conquer foreign fields unfortunately coincided with an increasing likelihood that war was coming. Before long it looked a matter of 'when' rather than 'if'. By April, the Government had delivered enough Anderson air-raid shelters to protect 1.5 million citizens. Sydney was still a relatively young 24, but must have seen the way the wind was blowing and considered the possibility that time was running out if he wanted to add more records and major victories to his tally. His was not a 'reserved' occupation, meaning he'd be among several million young men eligible to be called up to fight if he passed the medical.

Studying his morning paper at breakfast and on the train into town each day, he will have read about Hitler's plans to hugely expand German naval power. This was followed by headlines about the creation of the pro-German Slovak Republic, provoking dissolution of Czechoslovakia. Germany had violated the Munich Agreement and established the Protectorate of Bohemia and Moravia. Shortly after UK and France offered a guarantee of Polish independence, the Soviet Union proposed a tripartite alliance with the UK and France which was rejected. Yet another step on the road to war saw Hitler publicly renounce the Anglo-German Naval Agreement and German-Polish Non-Aggression Pact. Then followed the 'Pact of Steel' between Germany and Italy. Less than

21 years after the end of the Great War, Britain was teetering on the edge of conflict again.

Despite all the grim news bulletins, daily life in Britain had to continue. The 'Keep Calm and Carry On' mentality meant sport and special events went on regardless... Sydney was one of several VIP guests at a London Press Club dinner in the February, and a few weeks later agreed to run an exhibition mile, paced by five well-spoken young gentlemen from Alleyn's School in Dulwich. The track was an unfamiliar five laps to the mile and Sydney knocked out a modest 4:37, giving the relay runners a day to remember as they did their 352 yards each alongside the great man.

More of Sydney's legion of schoolboy fans got to meet him when he returned to his old stamping ground, Sutton Valence School, for a tree-planting ceremony conducted in front of the school's chapel. The idea was to commemorate his two world records in the past two years. After shovelling in enough earth to keep the sapling upright, Sydney took a look around his old school and signed autographs for a huge queue of boys. Having visited the spot nearly 80 years later, I can confirm the tree in question is a silver birch (*betula pendula*), which remains in good health and has reached a splendid height of around 40 feet.

With all the talk of war, perhaps it was appropriate Sydney's first competitive appearance on British soil for more than eight months should finally come at the Royal Military College, Sandhurst on Saturday 29 April. Attractively positioned on the Berkshire/Surrey border, the college track played host to a remarkable victory by Sydney, who was certainly not overawed by his surroundings, where men of the calibre of Churchill, Montgomery and the Duke of Gloucester had done their cadet officer training. Blackheath pipped the young officer material by just two points, 60-58, after 12 events. In the showpiece mile, the Heathens' John Furniss grabbed the lead early in proceedings, but the pace wasn't too hot and Sydney needed to make his own running. He took over relatively early on and eased away at the halfway point to record an emphatic solo victory in 4:14.8. He came in a massive 160 yards clear of his nearest challenger and his splits were 61, 68, 65 and 60.8.

The Sandhurst opposition was only of modest calibre, but nevertheless this was a startlingly comfortable victory that left the well-heeled audience gasping. The omens were good for Sydney's 1939 season. The *Sunday*

Planting a silver birch at his alma mater.

Mirror certainly thought so: Their scribe reckoned the only people with any chance of overtaking Sydney these days would be "those roller-skating blondes from Harringay Arena!"

By the time May arrived, Sydney and his coach would set aside time, usually on a Thursday, to discuss tactics in forthcoming races. Often they would agree target times for each lap, with little regard for who the opposition might be. Their attitude seemed to be that if he kept to his planned schedule the opposition wouldn't cope anyway, whoever they were. Sydney would memorise the schedules but would usually have Hill at trackside in races to call out his times as he passed.

Things had started in highly promising fashion at Sandhurst, but before Sydney faced any of his biggest challengers there was club business to deal with – a couple of Blackheath evening meets in May. The first saw him go off scratch in a mile handicap in Charlton Park, Greenwich, in which he improved marginally on his Sandhurst time with 4:14.6. The handicapping left him crossing the line in third place, but he will have been pleased with the even-paced splits of 64, 64, 65 and 61.6. Clubmate Haslehurst was first home but had the considerable advantage of a 195-yard start, with Parrott second off 190 yards. Sydney couldn't quite overhaul that pair, but did pass the man given a 260-yard start. He confirmed to reporters afterwards he was now in strict training for the Princeton race in June. A week later there was a chance for further sharpening in a half-mile victory over club colleagues in 2:01 at the Catford Bridge track.

24

Making History Over Three Laps

THERE wasn't just the sweet smell of chocolate in the air when Sydney pitched up at Bournville Village on the overcast afternoon of Saturday 20 May 1939. There was excitement and tension too, a bumper crowd of over 12,000 turning out for the best athletics meeting staged in the Birmingham region for many a year. Many of them were workers and families attached to the nearby Cadbury chocolate factory, whose huge Rowheath sports ground was hosting the big day.

It was a joint promotion by Midland Cycling & Athletic Club and Bournville AC, in the form of a 'Coming of Age' jubilee carnival meeting and involved a bumper four-hour programme of no fewer than 106 track and field events. Sydney was star attraction of the day and given a marvellous reception as he trotted on to the impressive sportsground next door to the famous chocolate factory. By then the big crowd had begun to tire of all the heats and lacklustre races, but were livened up by their first tasty morsel of action at 4pm – the AAA 4 x 440 relay championship, surprisingly won by South London Harriers. Then followed the big one – the mile invitation race in which Sydney was hot favourite to win the huge Coronation Bourneville Bowl.

Ignoring the pull of the chocolate tour and gift shop, I visited the area in 2016 and found the Rowheath venue still looking impressive and the area largely unspoilt. The facilities were opened in the early 1900s for the large Cadbury workforce, most of whom lived locally at the specially-created 75-acre Bournville Village. There were 14 pitches for football, 13 for cricket, four for hockey, two for rugby, 31 tennis courts, two croquet lawns, a green for clock golf, a boating and fishing lake and, of course, the athletics track. The stylish-looking pavilion served as a clubhouse and often held elaborate balls and dinners too. All in all, a remarkable set of facilities for the time. Eventually the pavilion would fall into disrepair, but was reborn in more recent times as the HQ of a church organisation.

The site of the old Rowheath running track – according to the evidence of my research – was now somewhat overgrown, but had not been built on and was easy to find. A pathway has been trodden along its original oval-shaped route and although no runners were around during my visit, there was one big lad determinedly following in Sydney's footsteps at walking pace. He was the only sign of life in the entire vicinity and his continual lapping suggested some sort of weight-loss programme. Seventy-seven years earlier he wouldn't have had such a tranquil and undisturbed setting for his solo exercising. The enormous crowd that gathered here in May 1939 had been buzzing in anticipation, waiting to be entertained.

There was an enormous howl of anguish when it was announced Olympic gold medallist Godfrey Brown was withdrawing from the quarter-mile, which meant even more pressure on Sydney to give them value for money when the milers gathered on the start-line. His brother Stanley – who from a distance of 50 yards was a dead ringer for Sydney – set off like a rocket, making the pace until halfway, clocking contrasting laps of 58 and 68 seconds. Many in the crowd cheered him on, thinking it was Sydney. Stanley then retired, leaving Sydney to lead. He passed the bell on 3:11.8 and threw in a final lap of 60.2 to win easily in 4:12.0, ten seconds clear of Surrey AC's Frank Close. It was well short of his very best, but a good workout nevertheless and announced as the fastest mile ever seen in the Midlands.

* * *

As the big showdown in Princeton grew ever closer, Sydney prepared himself for the important British Games Bank Holiday event at White City by agreeing to run in a club relay the preceding Thursday. It proved a perfect warm-up, Sydney taking the anchor leg in a 3 x 880 yards contest as part of the Herne Hill Harriers 50th Jubilee meeting. Opening up for Blackheath, John Poole recorded 2:02 and John Furniss took over with 2:00. Sydney set off with the baton marginally ahead as Denis Pell took over for the hosts. Sydney maintained his lead all the way, recording 1:57 to bring the Heathens home first. They were jubilant at beating their South London rivals on their own track, particularly as internationals Pell and Aubrey Reeve had been involved.

Sydney went into the big Whit Monday Bank Holiday fixture at White City in confident mood, even promising he would beat his recent Birmingham time of 4:12 by more than two seconds. He and Hill had worked out a schedule designed to get him a 4:09 (laps of 61, 63, 64, 61) provided conditions were reasonable. They were pleased when Monday 29 May dawned fine and sunny for the British Games, organised by the *News of the World* and incorporating the Inter-Counties championships. It promised a great holiday gala for Londoners, in perfect conditions.

The attractions of the day included demonstrations on the in-field by various emergency services, with the intention of reassuring the public of the nation's readiness for war. The Auxiliary Fire Service – who would later feature prominently in the Sydney Wooderson story – showed off their portable water tank, designed for when fires occurred at places with no water supply, but unfortunately it burst and flooded the track. The huge programme of events was already running late and this new delay lasted nearly five minutes as the fire engines and ambulances made their way out of the arena and groundstaff rushed around feverishly. Fortunately the dampened cinders on the track didn't seem to hamper Sydney too much, nor did the fact his race began with smoke still pouring from wreckage of a dummy plane involved in the demonstration.

Athletes in Surrey colours had a good day, retaining their Inter-counties crown, but highlight of the event was undoubtedly the stunning mile victory by Sydney, one of the best performances of his career. *The Bystander* magazine reckoned he almost broke his own mile record that day "by accident" – while other papers acclaimed a "sensational start to Sydney's season proper", and "a solo run of power and electric magic".

Wearing a huge No.13, rather awkwardly pinned on top of the large 'K' for Kent on his singlet, he clocked a brilliant 4:07.4. It was a time he'd only ever bettered once, at the carefully-manufactured record attempt at Motspur Park. It left his nearest rival Jim Alford trailing around 80 yards behind at the finish. Plenty had been going on in the stadium that day, but this eclipsed anything else on show even though Sydney had set his own pace and there were no late dramas near the finish-line.

En route to a brilliant Inter-Counties victory.

With 27 county teams involved, the field events had kicked the day off in mid-morning, followed by a parade of the athletes at 1.30, with the band of the Scots Guards adding to the lively atmosphere. In the afternoon, a huge gang of starters, 30 in all, lined up for the mile. Sydney's desire to chalk up a good time rather than get involved in a 'race' was crystal clear as he uncharacteristically took the lead from the start. He went smoothly away with a first lap at 61.2, was 20 yards clear by halfway in 2:05, and accelerated slightly on the all-important third circuit. A lonely final quarter of 59.4 gave him an inter-counties record of 4:07.4 and left Welshman Alford a massive 12 seconds adrift, closely pursued by Frank Close. *The Times* congratulated itself for predicting he would go under 4:10, and called him a "bespectacled phenomenon" who had performed like a track version of the pugnacious little American boxer Henry Armstrong.

The emphatic nature of the victory sent a clear message that Sydney was in great shape, full of confidence, and more records could soon be on the way. Word will also have reached the USA that Cunningham and his countrymen would need to be at their very best on June 17 when Britain's 'Mighty Atom' swept into Princeton.

On the eve of Sydney's scheduled departure for the States – literally the night before – he would be attempting to create a new world best for three-quarters-of-a-mile up in Manchester. Getting back down south in time to catch his ship for New York would entail flying between London and Manchester immediately before and after the race. It was all made possible thanks to Associated Newspapers who paid for the air travel. Part of the pay-off for the sponsors would be exclusive access to Sydney for their *Daily Dispatch* staff for interviews and pictures. Sydney and coach Albert Hill would fly from Heston Aerodrome in West London to Manchester's Ringway Airport on the afternoon of Tuesday 6 June, attempt the world record in the evening and then hurtle straight home again. They would be spending less than four hours in Manchester.

It wasn't the type of adventure Sydney, or anyone else for that matter, attempted very often in the 1930s and the sportswriters made much of what they called Sydney's "hustling". Running flat out at Fallowfield and then suffering the stresses of long-distance travel and a lack of proper acclimatisation in the USA all sounded rather unsuitable preparation for Princeton, and several newspapers weren't slow in pointing this out. They seemed to have a point, but coach Hill didn't agree and seemed mildly insulted by all the criticism. He scoffed at the doubters: "[Sydney and I] have worked together successfully for so long – so how, and why, should anybody else know what is best?"

Sydney may have received free plane tickets for his Manchester trip, but no such luxuries came my way when resuming my tour of his old race venues: I ventured into the city knowing Fallowfield Stadium had been a site steeped in sporting history, but was sadly demolished 40 years before I got there. It was a case of slipping back into 'psychogeography' mode and drifting around southern Manchester for a couple of hours to look for clues. Perhaps the best known present-day psychogeographer is author Will Self, whose explorations on the Thames foreshore and beyond lauded the practice of walking and wandering through remnants of the past. My wanderings in Sydney Wooderson's footsteps could be likened in some ways to Self's journeys, but probably differ significantly from the original brand of psychogeography introduced by Guy Debord, enigmatic Frenchman of the 1950s beat generation. Its central activity in Debord's eyes was to carry out the *derive* (the drift), the conceptual reimagining of a place, by soaking up its essence, and wandering around without a plan or purpose. In my case, there was a specific purpose – garnering material for my blog and for this book!

Whatever the name for my behaviour, it took a lot of 'drifting' before I could pinpoint the actual spot where for many years Fallowfield staged top-class athletics, cycling and even the 1893 FA Cup final. It was a site standing on what is now University of Manchester property, the running track on land now occupied by a huge hall of residence called Owens Tower and the rather more attractive Firs Pavilion. Vast sportsfields and facilities are still in evidence nearby, however, and in modern times this site welcomed top athletes when it housed visiting teams for the 2002 Commonwealth Games.

Appropriately I was here on a sweltering day, just like 75 years earlier when Sydney tackled his special invitation three-quarter-miler on a track sparkling in pristine condition. A stadium record crowd for athletics turned out that hot June evening in 1939, underlining how Manchester had looked forward to this event for months. It was even broadcast live on the BBC's Northern Home Service radio, coming directly after 30 minutes of melodies from 'The Little Orchestra' fronted by soprano Dorothy Pearce. The ground had been recently improved with the installation of a judges' stand and a pressbox. Manchester AC had instructed its members not to use the inside lane for training at any time to ensure it would be in tip-top condition for Sydney. The track looked good, the air was still, the scene was set for a world record.

The 'race' involved Sydney starting from the scratch mark, with four men given starts of various length up ahead for him to chase. At the 8pm start time it was still very warm, a thermometer showing 76 degrees F. The four pacemakers shot off at lightning pace, Sydney looking to shelter behind them in pre-arranged fashion. Half-miler Austin Littler (Pilkington Recs) led the way early on and Sydney closed to within eight yards of him, completing 440 yards in a swift 57.9 seconds. On the middle lap he moved confidently into second place, passing the half-mile point in two minutes exactly. The record was most definitely on. The pacemakers had done a sterling job and halfway through the third and final circuit Sydney lengthened his stride to surge past leader Kierans of Salford, the crowd roaring him home over a sensational final 200 yards.

Across the nation people crouched close to their Bakelite radio sets to hear BBC commentator Richard North getting highly animated as he described the scene:

> "A little figure in black surrounded by a sea of white… perfect little steam engine… lengthens his stride, head up, arms going like pistons, putting on the steam… left right, left right, oh marvellous! A marvellous long stride like a racehorse… sprinting for all he's worth… left right, left right, left right. A perfect exhibition of the human body in motion!"

Sydney hit the finish-line with a 15-yard lead and, more importantly, beat his own world best by 1.34 seconds. The crowd went wild. He'd run 2:59.5 to become the first man in the world to run three laps of a standard running track in less than three minutes. According to the *Daily Telegraph*:

> "It was one of the greatest efforts Wooderson has made in his career, and no man could have put more into his final running than he did after coming into the last bend."

Sydney's laps of 57.9, 62.1 and 59.5 brought him home well clear of the rest, the crowd paying scant attention to moustachioed Arthur Collyer, reigning AAA half-mile champion, Jim Alford, Kierans or Littler by this point. Onlookers were visibly amazed as Sydney appeared barely out of breath when a microphone was pushed into his face and his calm voice was heard through the loudspeakers. He spoke of the track being in excellent shape and said had the weather not been so hot he would have taken a bigger chunk off Blaine Rideout's previous world best of 3:00.4.

It had emerged by now the three-quarter mile was a distance that would no longer be recognised by the IAAF for records purposes. But this didn't take the gloss off things for Sydney's run had still created history as far as the Fallowfield crowd was concerned. He'd already been widely touted as a strong contender for 1500 metres gold at the proposed 1940 Olympics in Helsinki, and tonight had only underlined that fact. He was besieged by people wanting to shake his hand, slap him on the back and wish him well for his forthcoming American adventure. It had been a great night and, in his quiet way, Sydney enjoyed proceedings immensely. He would ultimately return to Manchester to run on a further six occasions, and his friendship with the people at Manchester AC would later see him become an honorary member of that club.

There was widespread interest in the fact that directly after the race Sydney was flying south, grabbing a few hours' sleep and then stepping aboard the *SS Normandie*, bound for America. One reporter noted that he had legged it around the track at 15 mph and would then jump on a plane to fly home at 130 mph, and also pointed out:

> "This will not conclude his hustling! It will continue with training spins round the promenade deck and odd moments spent in the ship's gymnasium. Then only a few days after arrival in the States he meets a bunch of the world's best middle distance runners in the famous Princeton Mile of the Century contest."

Another revealing article sprang from the pen of W. Capel-Kirby, who put together a substantial piece after gaining exclusive access to Sydney and coach Hill as they sat 4,000 feet in the sky on the London-Manchester-London flights. As WCK probed Hill for technical information about Sydney's remarkable turn of speed, the man himself sat a couple of feet away, his face pressed to the window enjoying the fascinating sight of towns and countryside beneath them. Hill explained that Sydney had

"Insignificant but extremely powerful thigh muscles to propel his spindly legs and provide the terrific driving force to so slight a frame."

The real secret of his success, proposed Capel-Kirby, was that Sydney acquired perfect style by virtue of his very lack of robustness. He had a high sprinting action compared to the long loping stride of rivals and that is where 'The Mighty Atom' got his pace. He possessed the ideal balance of ingredients for a sprint action and long-distance stamina.

Comparing running to bike gearing, Capel-Kirby said the average miler ran in middle gear, conserving energy to assist stamina by using a lower leg action than that of the sprinter. Sydney, however, was an exception: His lack of inches prevented him relying on length of stride, but his big heart and spacious lungs enabled him to carry out long distance sprints. It was comparable to a bicycle being able to climb a stiff gradient while in high gear.

Medical scientists had found nothing abnormal about Sydney, according to Capel-Kirby, apart from remarkable staying power concealed in a body so sparse as to weigh only 8st 12lbs when stripped. Although he could sprint for long stretches, Sydney's style never suffered until the final dash for the tape when his head often fell back and he rolled a little – otherwise his poise was perfect. He had performed so well in the oppressive heat of the Manchester race because the human machine functioned more smoothly and with better rhythm when well warmed up, cold muscle equalling poor lubrication. Capel-Kirby added that Sydney also took in 'central heating' provided by sugar, hence his pre-race meal of a sweet omelette eaten three hours before he broke the record.

The following morning, as Sydney paid a quick visit to his chiropodist before packing his bag for the train to Southampton docks, the *Daily Herald*'s A. B. Austin swooped on him and walked alongside, quizzing him about his chances in the USA. Austin was told the sea trip would take around five days and the only training Sydney would manage on board ship would be gentle jogging on rubber matting on the promenade deck. Austin was fascinated by his interviewee and described Sydney as having "a shy, schoolboyish voice" and whenever he agreed about something he always commented "Rather!" with only slightly more emphasis in his voice than usual. Austin continued:

> "It was clear he hates talking about himself and it is not an assumed modesty but his defence against the acute discomfort of having to answer personal questions. But on this occasion he was a little annoyed and in his diffident, jerky, low-voiced way said: 'I wish [the papers] would get things right!' when referring to press reports that he would have run better if it hadn't been so hot: 'Actually the hotter it is the easier it is to run. Warmth makes breathing easier. You are breathing warm air into your lungs instead of cold, your breathing is better regulated. Of course you feel the efforts of the heat after the race. But while you are running it is a help.' When he arrives in New York he will go straight to Princeton with Hill and continue quietly with training – using his unvarying pre-race routine: 'After a normal breakfast I sit and read the papers for a bit. Then I go for a two-mile walk. I come back to a light lunch – fish or omelette – read quietly for a little afterwards and then settle down to try to sleep for an hour-and-a-half. I usually manage to sleep for half an hour anyway. Finally I go to the track and have a warm up before the race. By warm up I mean a trot round.'"

Before disappearing into his Calais Street home, Sydney gave some detail about his normal day-to-day routines, pointing out that hobbies and relaxations, apart from reading and some swimming in winter, did not exist for him as his office work kept him busy until six every evening and he trained up to four nights a week. He was not engaged to be married or likely to be soon, he said, as running was currently his life. The pair shook hands and Austin wished him luck at Princeton, Sydney replying "Rather!"

Although Sydney was well used to press attention, the spotlight this week had intensified to new sky-high levels. The sports pages publicised his trip to the USA with remarkable fervour and jingoism. He must have felt like a lone soldier heading to unfamiliar foreign fields. On the surface his usual cool and calmness was evident, but underneath it all he will have been feeling well outside his normal comfort zones. This was a man who hated letting down a handful of ordinary clubmates, let alone an entire nation whipped up by pre-race excitement in the papers. His ability to triumph at Princeton was not in question, but could he maintain a coping mechanism to ensure pressure and tension didn't hamper his chances?

The trip across the Atlantic was a real eye-opener for 24-year-old Sydney, who had never left European soil before. The *SS Normandie* was a huge French liner of 83,000 tons, travelling direct from Southampton for New York on Wednesday 7 June. Sydney and Albert Hill's tickets had been obtained from the CGT offices in Cockspur Street in central London, and the company promised them "private cabins, wonderful food, deck sports, a perfect dance-floor, an atmosphere of French gaiety and sea sickness abolished". Among the cabaret acts on board to keep passengers amused was 'Deveen the Deceiver and His New York Blondes'. Also making the journey west was a party of 21 magicians heading for a Magicians' Congress at Battle Creek, Michigan.

The *Normandie*, just like Sydney, was a record breaker. Two years earlier it had crossed the ocean in a new east-to-west record of 3 days, 23 hours and two minutes, and a west-to-east record of 3 days, 22 hours and 7 minutes. On its arrival in Southampton on this occasion the vessel brought in sacks of mail from long departed exiles and loved ones in the USA, as well as a handful of celebrities including actress Mary Pickford and her husband Buddy Rogers who were besieged by fans as they disembarked. The ship had had an eventful trip, answering an SOS call en route from the Greek vessel *Kalliopi*. A steward needed emergency assistance following an incident involving a gun. The *Normandie*'s medical man was lowered down in the nick of time and saved the man's life.

Sydney left by train from Waterloo to meet the ship at Southampton, accompanied by brother Stanley and Albert Hill. The trip would take the best part of five days and he would train during that time with some gentle running on strips of rubber matting laid for him on the main deck. Hill publicly predicted his man would win the Princeton race in a new world record of 4:03 – a statement which had the Americans in a lather of excitement, although Sydney himself hinted that to simply win was more important than setting records.

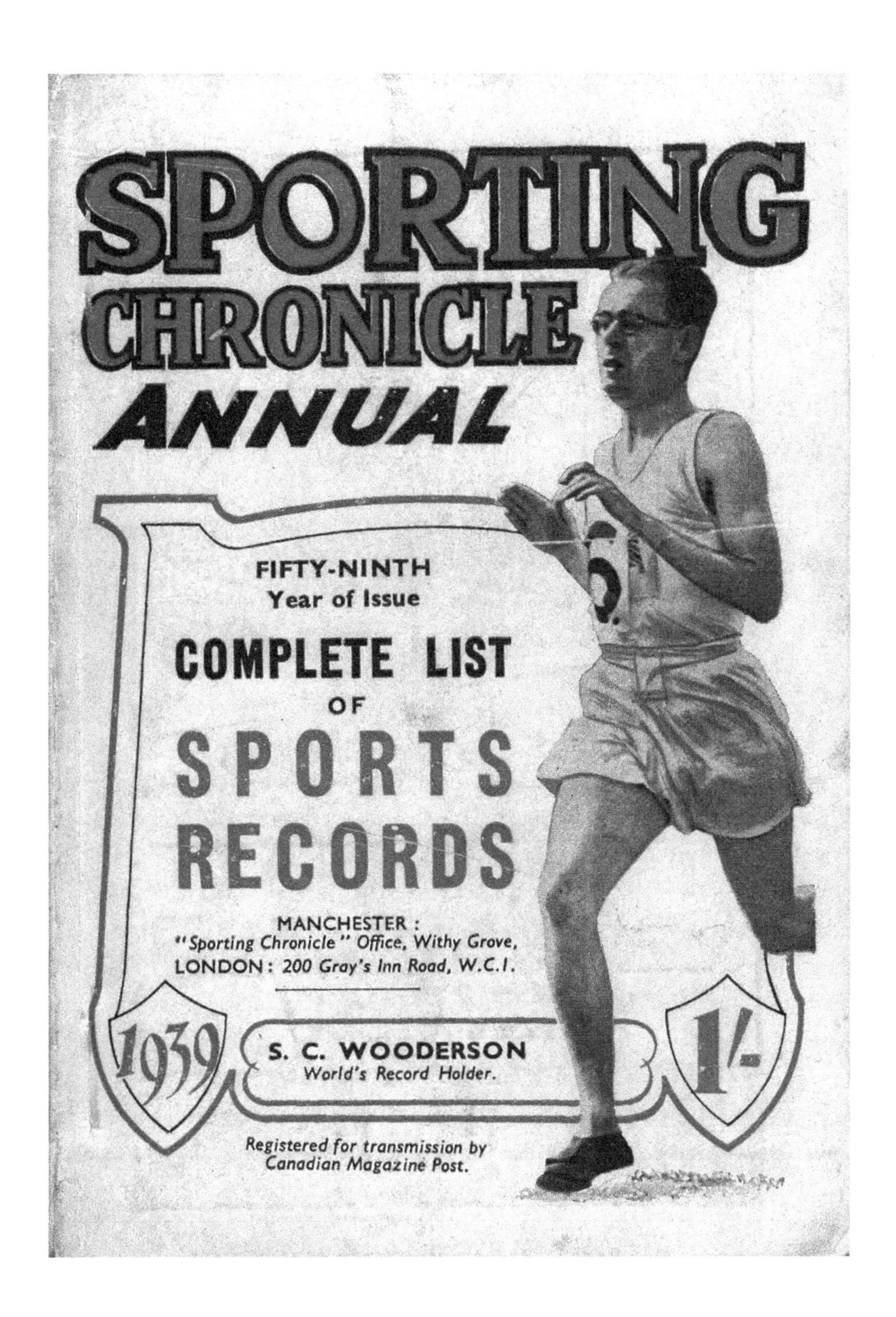
SPORTING
CHRONICLE
ANNUAL
FIFTY-NINTH
Year of Issue
COMPLETE LIST
OF
SPORTS
RECORDS
MANCHESTER :
"Sporting Chronicle" Office, Withy Grove,
LONDON : 200 Gray's Inn Road, W.C.1.
1939
S. C. WOODERSON
World's Record Holder.
1/-
Registered for transmission by
Canadian Magazine Post.

25

Mayhem at the Mile of the Century

MAKING Princeton's annual mile his first appearance in America meant world record holder Sydney was emulating Jack Lovelock, whose debut there had been the equivalent race at the Palmer Stadium in July 1933, billed 'The Mile of all Time'.

The following year it was renamed 'Mile of the Century' – a title it retained throughout the 1930s. Main organiser of this series was Asa Smith Bushnell III, a full-time athletics administrator whose approach attracted criticism from the old guard in the UK. They poured scorn on what they called 'stunt-making' by Bushnell and his colleagues. But the 39-year-old was showing that miling was no longer the prerogative of the English/Oxbridge set, despite their historical ownership of the event. These Princeton events changed the face of world miling and kick-started the debate about the prospect of a four-minute mile, which before long would escalate into a global sporting obsession.

Although hyperbole and pizzazz were certainly not Sydney's style, he was happy to take on US darling Glenn Cunningham on home ground now that the timing of the challenge suited him. He left the sound-bites and predictions to Hill, and stoically resigned himself to more rounds of press interrogation. On arrival in New York he faced a barrage of cameramen and reporters unlike anything he'd experienced before. Uncomfortably, many of them probed for personal information, rather than the race itself. Sydney politely tried to cooperate but found it all rather difficult. A typical reaction in the following day's papers was: "He's a slight, anaemic-looking chap who does not look capable of running round a corner without swooning!"

Setting off for the USA with reporter Joe Binks (left), brother Stanley and coach Albert Hill (right).

Back home a nation awaited. Blackheath club colleagues and the boys of Sutton Valence School were among thousands making plans to tune into the race via their Bakelite radio sets. The BBC's National Service network announced it was planning an 11.15pm broadcast from the USA on their regional wavelength, which would incorporate a description of the June 17 race. Live sports commentary was not commonplace at the time, especially at such a late hour, with only Test cricket in Australia normally persuading people to stay up beyond bedtime.

The esteemed *Time* magazine hit the newsstands and joined in the hullaballoo:

> "For two years US sport fans have been reading about Sydney Wooderson, a bespectacled little London solicitor. Within 22 months the 125-pound Briton smashed the world's records for the mile, the three-quarters, the half-mile and 800 metres… at Princeton's Palmer Stadium, 28,000 US foot-racing enthusiasts get a first squint at England's beloved 'Leather Legs'. After two refusals-with-regrets, he has accepted Princeton's invitation to run on its super-fast track against US miler Glenn Cunningham in its famed Invitation Track Meet."

Cunningham had long been the man Sydney was desperate to beat. Not since the days of Lovelock had it been so important to him to vanquish one particular rival. Although the 29-year-old from Kansas had an inferior outdoor mile time, he had chalked up a sensational 4:04.4 indoors in March 1938. On paper it was the quickest mile of all time, but was rejected as a record by the IAAF due to his being paced by four different quarter-milers. The record books showed Sydney was still top dog, but to erase any lingering doubts he really needed to beat Cunningham in this first confrontation on a track.

Although the race was viewed as a head-to-head between the two fastest men in history, the other three participants were certainly no slouches – Cunningham's countrymen Chuck Fenske, Blaine Rideout and Archie San Romani. Sydney's world record stood at 4:06.4 and only Rideout of today's line-up had not been within two seconds of that time. It was a sparkling array of talent to be gathered on a single start-line. Sydney would need to be at his very sharpest to avoid being bullied by the four bigger

Americans around him. Many of his fastest runs thus far had been achieved with the carefully planned help of other runners, but today he would have no friends. The 28,000 crowd was furiously partisan, and if ever there was a day when Sydney had cause to feel lonely and intimidated on a track, this was it.

On race day some ominous black storm clouds passed over the Palmer Stadium but the threat of rain looked to be gone as the clock ticked towards the 6.20pm start time. The evening remained hot and humid. Row upon row of terracing climbed skywards beside the track and space was at a premium, both in the stands, on the bleachers, and at track level. The atmosphere was both claustrophobic and electric. The sense of anticipation was palpable, noise levels and tension slowly building as the lesser events came and went. Shortly before his scheduled start time, Sydney could be found outside the stadium, jogging along gently in an attempt to warm his muscles and clear his head without thousands of eyes upon him. He slipped back inside and finally it was time for the big one: the so-called Mile of the Century.

In his black club kit and size four shoes, Sydney presented a rather unprepossessing sight on the start-line, which must have surprised the orange-clad college alumni looking on. Was this small, undemonstrative figure really the fastest miler in the world? As he wandered around quietly, eyes cast downwards, Sydney had "the guileless look of a schoolboy" according to sports historian John A. Lucas. Finally the five runners were called to attention and sent on their way, 28,000 pairs of eyes eagerly examining every change of position, every jostling elbow, every little move that might be significant.

Sydney, positioned centrally with a pair of Americans either side, jumped ahead in the opening yards and then… nothing. If the crowd had expected the unexpected, they certainly got it: over the next three laps or so nothing happened! Sydney stayed ahead without extending himself, the others content to sit behind in a bunch. What nobody had anticipated in the noisy build-up was three almost completely incident-free laps. It was tactical deadlock. For more than three minutes none of the five men was brave (or foolish) enough to commit to a surge of any kind.

Nobody wanted to take the initiative and put their neck on the line. They ambled along completing the first two laps in 64 seconds each. The chance of a 4:03 world record, as predicted by Albert Hill, had vanished into the sticky evening air long before halfway. Fenske moved to Sydney's shoulder but showed no interest in passing. Cunningham and Rideout ran side by side and San Romani brought up the rear. Remarkably, the third lap was even slower (66 secs, 3:14) and still little was happening. Surely Sydney would kick at any second and give us his familiar long sprint for home?

With barely 300 yards left it was becoming worryingly clear that the pace was nowhere near fast enough to suit Sydney against such a formidable field. Positioned as they were, it was clear – either by accident or pre-planning – the four Americans were ganging up on their diminutive visitor. Why hadn't Sydney accelerated free of them before now?

At the penultimate turn, with just 220 yards left, the pace of all five men visibly quickened and the real race for home was finally on. Sydney had left his famed sprint very late indeed, but managed to get narrowly ahead. Then came the final bend and the drama the crowd was craving, and with it the moment of the race that changed everything – 'a bump heard around the world' – as one writer would put it.

As they hit the final bend, Rideout, wearing No.22 on his all-white outfit, the least fancied of the five, spurted to get past Sydney and in doing so cleared a path for his closely packed compatriots. But in his eagerness to grab the lead Rideout appeared to cut in and brush Sydney's upper right arm. Startled, Sydney wobbled, regained some balance but found himself badly hemmed in and his left foot stuck the kerb. Simultaneously he flung his right arm out. For a split second this gesture looked merely a means of keeping upright, but on repeated playbacks of old British Pathe film footage it looks very much like Sydney tried to shove Rideout away in retaliation. Uncharacteristically petulant maybe, but surely understandable?

The crowd rose in amazement as Rideout ploughed clear of the tottering Englishman and into the lead. Fenske found the room to surge past them both just as Sydney began to regain his stride, and at last hit top speed. Sydney was then able to re-pass Rideout, and move into second place, but Fenske was away and out of reach. Sydney visibly faltered as he realised the race was lost, Cunningham flew past him and the game was well and truly up for the Englishman. San Romani and Rideout also passed him in the agonising final few yards. If it had been an American plot to unseat Sydney it had worked perfectly; they'd gone in for the kill just as Rideout boxed him in, and he'd had insufficient time and opportunity to recover properly.

Sydney had wriggled out of similar melees and trouble spots many times before, but this time the damage was done too close to the line by fast-finishing opponents. All four Americans had beaten the fastest miler in the world: after three-and-a-half laps of nothing happening, the frenzied fans couldn't believe their eyes at this incredible climax.

Fenske, whose last lap was timed at 56.8, had won in 4:11, the game Cunningham just six-tenths behind, San Romani third in 4:11.8, then came Rideout in 4:12.8 and Sydney fifth and last in 4:13. The place was in uproar. Thousands of miles away BBC listeners slumped beside their radios in disbelief that Sydney had come in last. Martin Carter, speaking in 2007, was a pupil at Sydney's old school Sutton Valence in 1939 and remembered the moment clearly:

> "We all stayed up late to listen to the commentary. We were intensely disappointed when he failed to win and we suspected foul play."

The initial feeling, among Brits at the Stadium at least, was that Sydney had been seriously impeded, although he was possibly guilty of tempting fate by running a poorly-judged race and not imposing himself at an earlier stage. He shouldn't have been bumped, but perhaps he could have prevented the circumstances that allowed it to happen? In the immediate aftermath, referee Asa Bushnell ruled that no foul had taken place and the result would stand.

But if the Americans thought the controversy would quickly disappear once the dust had settled, they were very wrong. The episode would be analysed endlessly over coming weeks and months and one correspondent suggested this race had become the single most-discussed in athletics history. Joe Binks of the *News of the World* filed a report that concluded:

> "Rideout cut too sharply across... it seemed to me as if Rideout came across too soon in making his desperate effort to catch Wooderson, for their shoulders touched and the lighter Wooderson stumbled and his left foot hit the boards on the inside of the track... The scenes at the end were astonishing. Some of the crowd applauded the American winner – but only half-heartedly – while the remainder maintained a deathly silence. Wooderson was approached afterwards by Rideout who first of all apologised, but later in the dressing room said Sydney had rather contributed to the

> mishap by running on too straight at the end. While I must extend my own sympathy to Wooderson for being baulked in such a way, I also feel he should have sprinted earlier and so prevented any such occurrence."

Although grim-faced Sydney was seen to disappear very quickly into the changing rooms, Binks somehow obtained a quote from him:

> "I was fouled by Rideout and could not do it, though I know I would have won had the race been run properly. I was just preparing to make my dash home when Rideout pounded into me. It can't be helped I suppose and Blaine has apologised, but I feel I have not done myself justice and let my country down."

Coach Albert Hill called it "disgusting" and said they had not expected the others would gang up on Sydney as they did. He hinted it was unlikely after today's scenes that Sydney would take up invitations to run in New York and Buffalo before returning home. Sydney's brother Stanley joined in, saying Fenske had admitted to him that Sydney would have won had he not been impeded. Ibrox Park supremo Bill Struth was looking on too, part of a touring Scottish party, and he was emphatic in his view that Sydney had been badly fouled.

The accused Rideout, however, told reporters he believed Sydney was at fault: "Sydney hit me as we were rounding the curve. He kept straight ahead instead of turning with the bend. His right arm struck me under the arm. The collision may have thrown him off his stride somewhat but I am sure that it was not my fault." Matty Geiss, a Princeton-based coach who had been instrumental in signing Sydney up for the race, thought there had been a foul but it was entirely unintentional.

The debate raged on, many who had not even seen the race concluding Sydney had been ganged up on, and accusing the American of tactics that were unsporting and unfair. On the other hand, a number of experts gave credence to the view that, whatever the rights and wrongs of the melee, Sydney possessed the best leg-speed and shouldn't have allowed it to become a slow race, but, if so, should have been more prepared for what occurred late on. The wire-services crackled for weeks over the incident. Newspapers and magazines printed a series of blurry stills of the film footage. Nobody can say what was in Rideout's mind in the crucial key moments, but all the pictorial evidence pointed to him being at fault. The Princeton meeting, already famous, gained a new dimension of international notoriety.

Whether or not Rideout cut in deliberately, or even cut in at all, remained a split verdict despite the evidence of the newsreel film. AAA official George W. Smith, in his 1955 book *All Out for the Mile*, an experienced miler who had raced against Sydney in the past himself, was not entirely convinced that Sydney had been unlucky or badly treated. He concluded: "No miler who has been subjected to rough treatment, as alleged against the Americans, could have covered the last quarter of a mile in 59 seconds [as Sydney had]." He pointed out that throughout the history of modern athletics people had often been eager to disparage American sportsmanship.

Smith, bearing in mind his major role in athletics officialdom, was perhaps being diplomatic in his book. On the other hand, the now-retired Jack Lovelock, had made it clear in his journals that the Americans carried a reputation throughout the 1930s for deliberately intimidating visiting star runners.

There was huge British disappointment at the outcome, several sources chiding Sydney for inadequate acclimatisation in the USA after his busy racing programme and hurried travel arrangements. The New Zealand writer A. F. Ingram reckoned that, despite his speed, Sydney was clearly flawed as an out-and-out racer:

> "It seems strange to state that an athlete holding three world records, and credited with being the first runner to break three minutes for three-quarters of a mile, should have doubts cast on his ability as a racer, but that is the position. Wooderson's best efforts have been made in races in which he has received the benefit of pacing from competitors on marks scheduled to pull Wooderson out and assist him to run his laps in preconceived times. In actual competition, against classy milers, Wooderson has yet to prove himself, although he has many fine times to his credit."

For a day or two there was fevered talk of a re-run of the Mile of the Century just seven days later on Randall's Island, New York, if Sydney would agree to stay on. It could raise funds to be shared between the under-privileged children of New York and London, suggested local promoters desperately. *The New York Journal* called for Sydney to agree, saying by this one little gesture he could make himself the most popular Briton across the entire USA: "Wooderson, from a personal standpoint, will gain nothing by posing as a martyr, or by refusing to run in this country again," they said. But, as Hill had hinted, Sydney was not in the mood to remain in the States to run more invitation races, and they cabled London to confirm he would be back in time to defend his AAA mile title at White City on July 7 and 8.

Other gossip suggested Fenske and Cunningham had been urged by Albert Hill to race Sydney again in the August Bank Holiday event in London. Fenske was interested, but the idea lost traction when Cunningham refused to commit either way.

The controversy was still bubbling by the time Sydney disembarked the *Normandie* at Plymouth on Monday 3 July along with 500 other passengers. He came down the steps wearing a light raincoat, a wry smile on his face, to be met by another round of flashbulbs and questions. He told them he'd never considered lodging a formal protest and praised the hospitality he'd received and the warm reaction of American fans after the race. He felt very fit for the AAAs big event in four days' time and said the whole Princeton thing was now best forgotten. But he added that he hoped Fenske and the other Americans would come to England soon to race... "And then we can see who is the best!"

With the benefit of hindsight it could be argued Sydney's programme of training specifically aimed at Princeton – covering the months of April and May – was simply timed wrongly. Perhaps he peaked too soon? He'd pulled off two magnificent performances at White City and Fallowfield in the nine days before flying out to the USA, but then lacked sparkle on the big stage. This had now happened twice – at Berlin and Princeton – although there were mitigating circumstances in both cases. Was there a possibility that stage fright had been a factor? Or was it merely random problems cruelly coinciding on the occasion of a really big race? Sydney had certainly faced pressure situations before and not crumbled – but maybe everybody has a breaking point.

World Sports magazine would, eight years later, publish Sydney's recollections of Princeton, in which he again played down what happened – even suggesting no physical contact – and refused to apportion blame:

> "It was the luck of the game. We were bunched, which was natural enough, but Rideout did not touch me as he went by. [But] he was so close that in trying to avoid him I hit the rail and stumbled, and I ran into trouble and there's nothing more to it than that."

That may have been his view years later, but there is no doubt in the immediate aftermath he was a bitterly disappointed man, harbouring a sense of injustice, not least for having let so many people down. On top of this, Cunningham was by now only months away from retirement and Sydney had lost his only chance of beating the great American.

26

Five in a Row

ALTHOUGH he'd only been back in England four days, the Friday evening qualifying heats for the AAA mile final came more than two weeks after the Princeton fiasco, so Sydney was physically well rested and eager to race again.

He cruised in second in the third heat in a trouble-free 4:20.6, beaten by Frank Close of Surrey AC by four-tenths of a second, and a second or so ahead of Birchfield's Ernie Lansdale. He had made the pace during the middle two laps and looked fresh as a daisy at the finish. The wild and wet weather of earlier in the day had dissipated into a pleasant sunny evening just in time. Denis Pell would be his big rival in the final, and the Herne Hill man had an easy ride in qualifying.

Gusty winds and intermittent heavy showers threatened to spoil things on the Saturday afternoon, but with an excited 30,000 people inside White City, the weather was soon forgotten as Sydney and Pell produced a truly magnificent contest in the mile. That morning's papers feared for Sydney in his attempt to lift the AAA crown for a fifth successive year: *The Times* called Pell a very serious threat, especially if Sydney was stale and without the zest to set a killing pace, which had looked the case in Princeton. Their correspondent also accused Sydney of becoming an 'anarchist' by experimenting with different distances instead of concentrating solely on what he did best – the mile.

The opening lap of the final saw Birchfield's Ernie Lansdale lead the way in 61.8 with Sydney back in seventh in the following pack. Lansdale maintained his position beyond halfway (2:09.4) but by now the crowd was roaring delightedly at the sight of Sydney surging through to second place in the blink of an eye. There were gasps as he stumbled when moving off the inside to avoid being boxed – but it was only a momentary problem and he grabbed the lead halfway through the third lap, followed closely by Pell and Frits de Ruyter of the Netherlands. On the back straight of the final lap, Pell unexpectedly battled past Sydney in dramatic fashion, but Sydney refused to let him open a gap and came again on the home straight, winning a real thriller by less than two yards in 4:11.8. Pell was given 4:12, Arthur Collyer of Watford next in 4:15. Twenty-nine-year-old Collyer had a good run but was disappointed not to get closer to Sydney, having switched to the mile instead of his usual 880 yards convinced he could pull off a shock at these championships.

Sydney had needed all his strength and speed to withstand the intense pressure from Pell and win in a championship best time. Unlike some of his victories, this time he'd left absolutely no margin for error – and had never looked in real trouble, even when conceding the lead on the last lap. He crossed the line, having parted company with his number, a look of fierce determination on his face. It was hugely satisfying to have produced a brilliant final lap that blew away the bad memories and self-doubts evident in the USA. Nobody else, before or since, had won the British mile title five years in a row. Apart from one occasion Sydney had achieved this feat by getting progressively faster at each successive championship: 1935 – 4:17.2, 1936 – 4:15.0, 1937 – 4:12.2 (event record), 1938 – 4:13.4, 1939 – 4:11.8 (event record).

His was one of 12 titles claimed by home nation runners from the 23 up for grabs. He attended the traditional post-championship dinner in Central London along with relay clubmates Cotton and Ransom. There was a celebratory atmosphere, with many in the room fearing it could be the last such dinner for a while with war on the horizon.

The following weekend looked set to be another hectic 48 hours after Sydney confirmed he'd run in Worthing on the south coast on the Saturday and then appear in a GB shirt in Belgium barely 24 hours later. To ensure he would be at his sharpest for the latter, he asked organisers of the Inter-Counties event at Worthing's Homefield Park if he could withdraw from their mile and run an 'exhibition' 880 yards instead. Under sunny skies he duly completed this in a modest 2:07, with the exercise nearly backfiring when he managed to spike himself – his right shoe somehow inflicting a cut on his left ankle. It needed attention from St John Ambulance, but he was declared fit for the Brussels fixture the following day.

Sydney and the British team flew out from Croydon at 9.45 on the morning of Sunday 16 July for the afternoon's meeting – an international gathering to mark the 50th anniversary of formation of La Ligue Royale Belge d'Atletisme. In front of 4,000 at the nine-year-old Jubilee Stadium (later renamed Heysel), Britain – with guest of honour Lord Burghley proudly looking on – won the Challenge Cup by a clear nine points from France.

Sydney went into his 1500 metres race as hot favourite, having just heard the news that his world 800 metres record had been eclipsed the previous day by two seconds, by Rudolf Harbig in a match between Germany and Italy (1:46.6). With local favourite Josef Mostert his main danger, Sydney got himself in a poor position early on, surrounded on the inside lane, but was able to drop back to avoid being impeded and had no trouble subsequently returning to the thick of things when he was ready. It was vintage Wooderson, as he moved up for the kill, surging with 200 yards left to destroy the field. As they motored up the finish straight Sydney even had time to look over his shoulder and check on Mostert's progress. The Belgian pressed hard and the crowd roared him on, but Sydney's 3:54.8 was good enough to win by two-tenths of a second.

One of Sydney's Blackheath clubmates was delighted to hear news of this victory on a crackly radio many miles away in a Calcutta hospital… D. Burton-Jackson, serving with the Gurkha Rifles, had been suffering badly from dysentery and was confined in the Carmichael Hospital, Calcutta, for nearly four weeks. Some of his misery was lifted when the report of the Brussels race came through on his bedside radio at 4.40 in the morning local time.

After flying back from Brussels on the Sunday evening, Sydney clocked up a good few more miles the following day, having accepted an invitation to attend the start of Leamington Fitness Week in Warwickshire. Wearing the white GB tracksuit he used at the weekend, he spoke to a gathering in the spa town's Victoria Park at the launch of the event. He gave a demonstration run of half-a-mile along the perimeter path that had been made exactly 880 yards for local runners when this riverside park was created 40 years earlier. Accompanied by Tommy Green, race-walking gold medallist at the 1932 Olympics, Sydney then gave coaching advice to youngsters and presented trophies after a series of races. The organising committee's assistant secretary Laurence Wyles beckoned Sydney to the microphone and invited the watching youngsters to shout out questions – but such was their enthusiasm they instantly swarmed forward and surrounded Sydney, firing their questions at him from close range. Said Wyles:

> "It was a grand sight to see Sydney giving tips to these kids and answering questions by the dozen – including some about America which would have made excellent newspaper copy!"

A *Coventry Evening Telegraph* reporter grabbed Sydney for a chat, and ruefully reflected on what many sports journalists had already pointed out – Sydney was devoted to athletics and happy to talk about all aspects of the sport apart from himself! Asked about his 800 metres record being smashed by Harbig 48 hours earlier, Sydney said he wasn't despondent and admitted the German had chalked up a time that he [Sydney] would probably never emulate.

Two days later he was back on home turf, running on the Wednesday evening at the Blackheath club championships at Catford Bridge – and surprising a few by putting his name down for the 440 yards. He sped round in 52 seconds, but it wasn't quite enough to unseat Chappell, a specialist quarter-miler. If nothing else, it was a good sharpener three days ahead of the popular Kodak Sports, where he would be running a special 1,000 yards race in front of a big crowd.

War seemed to be looming ever closer, the July weather was a big disappointment, and Sydney Wooderson was suffering with a head cold as he lined up to run on a notoriously difficult track. Not a happy weekend for our hero as he made his competitive debut in the Harrow and Wealdstone district on Saturday 22 July 1939.

The annual Kodak Sports were staged on the photographic company's sportsfields, adjacent to their factory dominating the NW London skyline just down the road from Harrow and Wealdstone station. I visited the site on my tour of Sydney's race venues and was confronted by an industrial wasteland. Kodak had been slowly downsizing in recent times and the

Meeting fans in the Midlands.

massive site was being redeveloped. The factory and its recreational area flourished for much of the 20th century but in the new digital world Kodak is apparently no longer the big player it once was in these parts. The sportsfields and old clubhouses were disappearing bit by bit as workmen got busy in 2016.

Sydney came here with a host of other top London runners to contest a 1,000 yards invitation handicap. The gossip suggested he would attempt a new British record at this distance. The weather was dull for the time of year, windy, overcast with precious little sunshine. Sydney set off from the scratch mark at precisely 2.30pm, his nine opponents all given starts of up to 50 yards. The handicapper's adjustments looked like they might conjure up a close finish to please the crowd, but would they help engineer a record? A bumper turnout estimated at 10,000 packed the ground and Sydney was, as usual, centre of attention before, during and after the race. But the chances of a world record looked distinctly unlikely in Sydney's eyes once he'd become aware the long back straight of the track was actually uphill – its top bend some six feet higher than the lower bend! Although this 'hazard' posed the same problem for all the runners, it wouldn't be much help in a battle with the clock.

The pace was fast in the opening quarter-mile and just before two circuits were done, Sydney was close to overhauling local favourite Arthur Collyer (Watford Harriers) who had started 10 yards ahead of him. However, Collyer responded well and held him off. By this time Eddie Sears of Essex Beagles (25-yard start) had a good lead and any chance of catching him disappeared when it became clear on the final lap that Sydney was either unable, or unwilling, to throw in his customary late sprint.

Sears clocked a finish of 2:11.1, Collyer 2:13.9 and Sydney – having run the full 1,000 yards – was fourth to cross the line in a slightly disappointing 2:14.5. He'd fallen well short of the GB record of 2:11.2 set by Cyril Ellis (Birchfield Harriers) at Stamford Bridge ten years earlier. He was warmly applauded but a sense of disappointment hung in the air. As if to placate record-hungry athletics fans, the very next day saw an announcement that Sydney would attack the 13-year-old world best time for 600 yards in August. The best time of 1:10.8 for this rarely-run distance was currently the property of D. G. Lowe, and Sydney would attempt to better it in Priory Park, Chichester.

Invitations to run were flooding in this summer and Sydney's merry-go-round continued just four days after the Kodak Sports with a trip to Northumberland. Elswick Harriers was hosting a special evening of sports to mark its golden jubilee year and wanted Sydney to star in an invitation mile handicap. Once he'd accepted, tickets began selling well and the organisers made hasty arrangements for special buses and free car parking at their homely little stadium in Cowgate, Newcastle. With a 6pm start, the crowd would have to wait two hours before Sydney's appearance in what was cheekily-billed 'North of England's Mile of the Century.' In all, the day featured 500 entries from runners and cyclists, including many schoolboys, and there was also cycle polo and netball.

Sydney's long trek north for this specially-framed handicap pitched him against the pick of the locals. Nearly 40 years before the likes of Foster, Cram, Spedding and Sharpe caught the imagination of Geordie fans, the arrival of this bespectacled London solicitor persuaded a ground record of 7,000 to squeeze into the Co-op Welfare Ground. The place had never seen anything like it. His brother Stanley accompanied Sydney and ran an early-evening, less-heralded two-mile race, which he won. His close resemblance to his brother and identical black running kit meant many in the crowd thought they were watching Sydney – and it took an announcement over the public address system to clarify matters.

In the mile, Sydney ran from the scratch mark and conceded generous starts to Potts and Wylie of Darlington and Burns of Elswick, in a field of 12 runners. It looked a tough task with his nearest opponent starting 65 yards up ahead. During the first three laps Sydney ran smoothly and was content to bide his time, but on his final circuit accelerated sharply and delighted the crowd by moving clean through the field like a knife through butter. He won by a good ten yards in 4:15.2 which was immediately announced as the fastest mile ever seen in northern England. It was around six seconds' improvement on the previous best – 4:21 by Fred Bacon in 1895 at Berwick. The *Newcastle Evening Chronicle* called Sydney's display "Truly a lesson in grace of style as well as judgment in timing."

When Sydney received his prize from the Lord Mayor of Newcastle, Alderman Wallace, it became clear he was limping heavily. This would later be identified as a calf strain that had occurred mid-race, but which hadn't hampered him until after the finish. Sydney played down the problem, but it would prove serious enough to signal the end of his season. What he wouldn't have known, of course, is that the impending outbreak of war would mean he not only missed the rest of the 1939 summer, he wouldn't participate in serious competition again for another six years.

The immediate implications were that he was out of the big White City international on the August bank holiday which had created the prospect of a re-match with Blaine Rideout of the USA. Subsequent medical advice from a Harley Street specialist confirmed he should also withdraw from the Chichester race, and, more importantly, Britain's match with Germany in Cologne on August 20, a fixture which in the current political climate was attracting much controversy. Directly after the Elswick race Sydney was due to appear at the New St James Hall in Newcastle to be introduced to the ringside crowd before a major bout between boxers Ginger Sadd and Jim Berry. Limping heavily and keen to protect his injury, it appears Sydney quietly made his way directly to the railway station instead.

The expert advice was to stop running indefinitely and not risk permanent damage to his right calf and achilles area. It was a blow, but at least meant Sydney and his coach could start planning earlier than expected for the Helsinki Olympics due the following summer.

During the enforced lay-off, the Wooderson flag was flown by Sydney's two brothers, notably at the 37th annual Fire Brigade Sports at White City. They ran in the London Auxiliary Fire Service Mile Relay, Alfred and Stanley both representing the 'E' district. Stanley opened on the 880-yards leg and Alfred went third at 220 yards and they helped their team to an emphatic victory. *The Times* reflected on the fact that Stanley physically resembled his famous brother, while eldest sibling Alfred looked more like a sturdy little footballer than an athlete.

In Sydney's absence, Denis Pell, the man he thrillingly beat at the AAAs, stepped up and gained some sort of revenge for what happened to Sydney in Princeton by beating Blaine Rideout at White City. The British track and field team's appearance in Cologne went ahead despite the political tensions, and the visitors were warmly welcomed by a 45,000 German crowd. Pell again rose to the occasion, running a lifetime best of 3:50.2 in the 1500m. It was remarkable the match took place at all; obtaining flights proved tricky and the atmosphere in Cologne felt 'unreal' according to team manager Jack Crump. The sense of drama was heightened when a violent thunderstorm broke over the ground soon after the start. Britain fielded a somewhat understrength team and failed to win a single event, apart from a dead heat in the 110m hurdles, and were hammered by 93.5 to 42.5 points. In his autobiography Crump recalled his impression of things happening around the German team:

> "[Everything was] all very serious and highly planned, and to my mind the antitheses of amateur sport… I did have serious feelings that some form of stimulant might have assisted the German athletes."

By the time the Brits had arrived home at Croydon airfield, via Belgian airline Sabena, tensions had increased further. After what he'd seen and heard in Cologne, Crump was convinced war in Europe was probably just days away. That horrendous prospect took a huge step towards reality just three days later on Wednesday 23 August when the Soviet Union and Germany signed a non-aggression pact. This led to an Emergency Powers Act being passed the next day in Britain. Poland was thought to be under immediate threat and a mutual defence treaty with them was formally signed.

On Thursday 31 August the British fleet was mobilised and civilian evacuations began from London. Early the following day German troops crossed into Poland and less than two hours later German planes bombed Warsaw. At 9am on Sunday 3 September, a British ultimatum was delivered to Berlin but expired two hours later. Britain, France, Australia and New Zealand promptly declared war on Germany.

27

Serving on the Home Front

THE very able-bodied Sydney Wooderson, by now 25, was among those available for active military service, but at his medical was declared unfit due to his poor eyesight. Within a few days, a role in the immediate war effort was found for him on the home front – he would join the Auxiliary Fire Service and be conveniently based close to home.

By the end of September 1939 he had moved out of the family home in Camberwell to live three miles away in West Norwood in an orphanage that had been requisitioned for the London Fire Service as a training centre.

At this point the Government undertook the massive task of listing the details and address of every civilian in Britain and Northern Ireland, in order to properly coordinate the war effort at home. It became known as 'The 1939 Register'. This massive document showed that Sydney was sharing accommodation with four other men, including head of household 28-year-old produce broker Fred Mason. Also on the premises was Sydney's brother Stanley, described as a fruit salesman, barrister's senior clerk Arthur Bayliss, 28, and counting house clerk Alf Taylor, 29. Sydney and Stanley's three housemates were all married men, but clearly unable to live with their wives while stationed at West Norwood.

The accommodation was known as the 'Gabriel and Jane Arnold Home' in Wolfington Road, built in 1911 to house 50 children as part of a complex known locally as 'The Jewish Orphanage'. It was an imposing three-storey edifice, with the appearance of a Jacobean palace. The children of the orphanage had recently been evacuated to private homes, mostly in the Worthing area, and orphanage staff had departed to enlist or help elsewhere in the war effort. The vacant orphanage buildings were quickly reorganised to become a regional hub for the training of fire service personnel.

The three Wooderson siblings would all sign up with the Auxiliary Fire Service and looked smart and fit in their distinctive uniforms, which included a peaked cap. The thick spectacles they wore gave away the reason they were here and not away with the military services. As AFS men they were part of the Civil Defence Service, and will have been among the fittest on the books, as the AFS largely consisted of men and women too old or too young to go to war.

The AFS and 1,600 local authority brigades would soon be merged to become the National Fire Service. Firefighting in wartime would, of course, become a hugely important job, particularly during 'the Blitz' which would begin exactly a year further on. By that time Prime Minister Winston Churchill was lauding fire service personnel as "Heroes with grimy faces" – but in the early days Sydney and his colleagues had to suffer unwarranted and inappropriate jibes from certain quarters that they were merely 'army dodgers' and not heroes at all.

Being classed as a civilian meant Sydney was one of 41 million Britons issued with an identity card after they had provided Government enumerators with their details for the 1939 Register. The legal requirement to carry these ID cards remained until 1952. The Government needed to know who and where everyone was in wartime, as well as keeping track of births and deaths. The 1939 Register would emerge as a key document of 20th century Britain, helping not only the war effort, but formation of the National Health Service, and replaced the censuses of 1931 (destroyed in an air raid) and 1941 (never taken).

Even though the early months of the conflict would be a relatively quiet 'phoney war', day-to-day life was disrupted for everybody, and of course the runners of Blackheath Harriers were no exception. A hefty chunk of the membership was called up to serve the nation, but it was hoped enough members would still be around to keep the club alive during the first autumn of wartime. Sadly the advertised opening day of the new cross-country season came and went with no club run taking place, and for a long spell there was no word from the club regarding future plans. The committee found itself in limbo because it was feared the club's HQ

A fireman in wartime.

would be appropriated by the Civil Defence authorities. The AGM was pushed back several months, but eventually an all-clear came after several idle weeks to reopen the premises and club life resumed with an average weekly attendance of about 30 runners.

It would be a mix of old and young faces with many of the 'middle range' age group away on military duty. Sometimes morale on club nights would be boosted when members serving in the Forces turned up unexpectedly for a run while on leave. On the other hand, occasionally the atmosphere would be deflated by news that a colleague or acquaintance had been lost in action.

Many who did attend regularly began to lose enthusiasm for aimless training runs when they knew there were no races to prepare for – but this all changed in December 1939 when it was announced there would be a five-mile handicap race before Christmas and more fixtures in January and February of 1940. The AAA showed similar bulldog spirit at a meeting in Birmingham, announcing they intended to carry on normal activities throughout wartime as far as they possibly could. It would need more than Adolf Hitler and his expansionism to close down British athletics!

★★★

Blackheath's clubhouse was alive with good cheer on Boxing Day 1939 as a group went out for a training run and an even bigger group stayed in the warm to toast an early end to the war and happier times ahead. A few days later, around 30 members, including Sydney and brother Stanley, turned up again for a road run, and were not put off when it was found a damaged boiler and the freezing weather had combined to render some of the facilities useless. As if the general privations of wartime weren't enough, the runners now had to forego their usual post-run bath and wash with water heated in kettles.

Sydney was keen to run some cross-country to maintain a modicum of fitness during these uncertain times. January 1940 and subsequent weeks saw some of the worst weather in living memory but Blackheath officials stayed true to their word and helped lay on a number of races, including what ended up being an 8.5-mile handicap road race on Saturday 20 January in freezing conditions.

Although he didn't normally do vast amounts of road work, Sydney was put on scratch along with clubmate Len King. The big freeze had ensured the clubhouse water supply was still out of action, so they set off knowing there'd be no warm bath on their return. Undaunted, they headed off and were well strung out by the time they reached Addington Church. The leaders pulled away on the snow-covered roads and with Sydney exercising caution in the dangerous conditions, first over the line on this bitterly cold day would be another Heathen, Laurie Hamill, in 49:42 (from a 45 seconds start) with King second and Sydney, in his first race for six months, cruising home third in 51:41. Despite the weather, a good number turned out to watch the action, including Sydney's mum.

A week later at Petersham it was back to traditional cross-country for the first time in just over two years for Sydney. Although the course was mostly heavy and in a state of semi-thaw, he will have felt good to be running the paths around the edge of Richmond Park and beside the Thames that chilly and misty morning, even though much of the famous park was out of bounds due to wartime restrictions. Another bonus for the runners was the camaraderie and hospitality in the old pavilion behind the cosy Dysart Arms, home of hosts for the day, Ranelagh Harriers. The size of the turnout had allowed a mob match of 7.5 miles to be set up, in which Blackheath would take on the combined might of Ranelagh, Orion and South London Harriers. Initially some Heathens expressed dismay at this, but settled to their task and subsequently put on a great show to win by a big margin. Sydney was full of beans and drew away from the pack with a mile to go and won in 46:54, holding off a spirited challenge from Arthur Stansbury of Ranelagh. Sydney's fine showing prompted press chatter over whether he might take up cross-country seriously from now and gradually relinquish track. One correspondent pointed out Sydney and his brother looked to be carrying a little extra weight having not raced properly for so long – they were "positively burly" he wrote.

Encouraged by these races, the South of Thames CCA adapted their usual annual championship into a five-mile contest on Wimbledon Common a fortnight later on Saturday 10 February. Some 16 clubs sent in the names of 130 runners, a healthy number with so many men away on military service, and a field of 99 subsequently toed the start-line near Belgrave Harriers' HQ.

It was a demanding five-mile route from Belgrave Harriers' HQ and 13 men never made it to the finish. Frank Close (Surrey AC) took the title in

29:50, cruising home comfortably after pulling away from Sydney and the rest in the first mile on the Common, before leading the excursion to more open country. Belgrave's Hewitt and Thames Hare & Hounds' Coggins filled the other places. Sydney was not at his sharpest and happy to just enjoy the trip, coming in 16th, some 90 seconds behind the winner. Asked about his unaccustomed position well down the field, Sydney brushed this off saying he hadn't taken things too seriously and treated it as "just a training spin."

Northern Europe was still in the grip of intensely cold weather but this, and the complications of life during wartime, didn't prevent plenty of sport taking place that weekend in the London area. In addition to the cross-country there was football between teams representing The Army and The Empire, a number of rugby fixtures, boxing, rowing, and greyhound racing.

After his low-key performance on Wimbledon Common, Sydney went down with flu and his doctor advised him to take things easy for a spell. He rejoined his AFS unit in the first week of March 1940, with the plan in mind to begin serious track training in April. Around now the idea of formally requesting extra time off to train was forming in his mind.

In the mean time, the occasional public appearance to meet his fans and support local causes were deemed necessary, and he made himself available as guest of honour at the annual supper of the 88th London Company of the Boys' Brigade, of which one of his cousins was captain. In responding to their welcome, Sydney stood up and said:

> "I fully realise the good work which is being done here in this company and in other companies throughout the Boys' Brigade. Self-discipline and physical training do help in your life, especially in these difficult times."

After his bout of flu and his private concerns about needing time off work to train, the last thing Sydney needed was an injury, but a foot problem occurred in mid-March and he was forced to take the best part of a month off to recover. Around this time he will have noted that in the USA John Woodruff ran the fastest half-mile in history (1:47.7), but as it was indoors in Hanover, New Hampshire, it wouldn't displace Sydney's place on the world record list. Another of Sydney's best times – his three-quarter mile record at Fallowfield – was beaten in April when Paul Moore of Stanford University clocked 2:58.7 in Paolo Alto, California. This rarely-run three-lapper was no longer an IAAF official distance any more, meaning it gained relatively little publicity.

* * *

With war having been underway for some six months – albeit still a 'phoney war' so far – it was becoming clear there was still a need for organised running events in the capital for the spring and summer of 1940. The annual peace time events had been put on hold, but there were still enough keen men around on any given weekend to support and enjoy races. An additional benefit would be cheap entertainment and a morale boost for the wider public.

Thus athletics began playing its part in keeping the nation's pecker up, just like football was already doing. To start with, sport had to stop because the fear of air attack had meant the Government closed most sports grounds, along with cinemas, theatres and other entertainment venues.

Matthew Taylor, professor of history at De Montfort University, says Home Office files of the time demonstrate that while few ministers or senior civil servants had much time for sport themselves, the Government of the day recognised its positive effect on public well-being. This was particularly true in relation to vital groups such as servicemen and workers engaged in war production. During this early part of the war, social research organisation 'Mass-Observation' told the Government a programme of football, for example, was far more useful in raising morale than expensive propaganda campaigns urging the public to 'stay cheerful'.

Restrictions on crowd sizes and the preponderance of 'guest' players meant wartime football often lacked the excitement and competitive aspect of peacetime, but many of the athletics events that went ahead would prove hugely popular. With Sydney Wooderson the main flag-bearer, these rarely lacked a competitive edge.

Athletics stood up to be counted in early 1940 and played its part in the London area with the formation of a special regional squad of runners known as 'The Combined Clubs' (TCC). Ferdie Gilson, historian of South London Harriers, says that in April 1940 H. C. Lomax, secretary of London Athletic Club, wrote to the SLH and Blackheath clubs, suggesting that they, along with LAC, should join together to form The Combined Clubs – a team of athletes to be active "during hostilities only". A meeting was called at The Devereux Hotel in central London (a regular Blackheath committee venue, which would soon fall victim to German bombers) where it was decided to go ahead with this idea. TCC was launched under the Presidency of Jack Densham, a former sprinter and one-time President of both SLH and LAC, and a committee comprising two members from each of the three clubs. C. E. Jones, the new Hon. Secretary, quickly secured the use of the City of London School's cinder track in Marvel's Lane, Grove Park, Lewisham.

The formation of TCC stimulated similar projects elsewhere, and helped enormously to keep athletics alive during wartime. Amalgamations in the London area in 1940 would include 'The North Middlesex Harriers' (Highgate, Shaftesbury and Southgate), 'The Watford Combination' (Watford, St Albans and Vale of Aylesbury) and 'The West Middlesex Triangle' (Finchley, Southall AC and Thames Valley).

Sydney would subsequently appear in TCC events on around a dozen occasions over that first summer of the war, and would be responsible for many of the best individual performances, with his fame ensuring large enthusiastic crowds. Of course, once the war continued beyond 1940, the number of athletes available for TCC and other matches would inevitably start to dwindle due to the armed forces' need for more recruits.

Ferdie Gilson and Brian Boulton, two pillars of the SE London running fraternity over the years, shared their personal memories with me about the days when TCC began using Grove Park as its home base. Boulton, a former Kent mile champion and President of Kent AAA, used to live and run in the district and he recalls:

> "Much of that City of London School sportsground is now owned by Eltham College. For more than 20 years I lived nearby with my parents in a house backing on to those CLS grounds. For many years I used to train by exiting our back gate to gain access to the College playing fields. I was athletics captain at the College in the late 1950s and later trained there with Glynis Goodburn, whom I coached before she married fellow long-distance star Keith Penny. The track I recall was not a standard shape, but pear-shaped."

Gilson, a budding young runner who would blossom after the war, has colourful memories of that time:

> "In those days, the space between Ridgeway Drive and Grove Park Railway Station was a huge allotment, where people enthusiastically grew vegetables. Like most others with a garden, we raised chickens for eggs, as each person's ration was only one fresh egg per week – if available – but often only one per fortnight. Alternatively you could have one packet of dried egg powder to make 12 eggs every four weeks. However, vegetarians were allowed two fresh eggs a week, if available. Children and some invalids were allowed three per week and expectant mothers two!"

Just as the TCC idea was being launched in early May 1940, and home-based runners such as Sydney sought to step up their training, the so-called 'phoney war' came to an end as Germany invaded France and the Low Countries. This was a grim reminder that any pretence at 'normal' athletics taking place would have to stop and the AAA reprised its actions of the 1914–18 war by setting up an emergency committee to run things. For several years hence there would only be meetings involving the *ad hoc* groups such as TCC or the military services, and for these the pre-war stars who were available – notably Sydney and sprinter Cyril Holmes (an Army PT instructor at Sandhurst) – would be urged to appear wherever they could.

Sydney went along with all this, pleased he could head off and run somewhere and break the often dull routines of his new life with the fire service and, later, the Army. Sometimes he needed to ask for time off, but mostly arranged his normal leave allowances to coincide with events. Jack Crump of the AAAs would later pay tribute to the way Sydney and Holmes regularly turned out, fully fit or not, particularly at the events raising cash towards the war effort. By merely participating Sydney added many hundreds to the crowd numbers and also helped lift the general morale of the watching public and the other participants. Crump said:

> "I believe that in those anxious times [Sydney Wooderson and Cyril Holmes] both did a service to British athletics of a value far in excess of anything they have themselves realised."

The summer 1940 track meetings would be limited, but on a wider scale than in the first world war. The usual inter-services matches went ahead, as did a series between the AAA and combined Oxford and Cambridge teams, the University of London and the services. The three main services approved of these arrangements as they recognised the importance of athletics as a recreation and fitness-producing medium.

28

A Difference of Opinion

WHETHER you knew Sydney Wooderson well, or merely admired him from afar, the man had one characteristic that was crystal clear: Away from the running track he was mild-mannered and not in the least bit confrontational.

Therefore it was something of a shock when news emerged in 1940 that Sydney had challenged his bosses at the Auxiliary Fire Service, and then – unhappy with their response – had resigned on the spot.

The conflict blew up in the spring, roughly six months after war had been declared. By now Sydney had been able to complete several cross-country races and had received several invitations to races fixed for the summer of 1940. War or no war, he knew that to fulfil these fixtures without letting people down he would need to step up his training and at least get somewhere near normal race fitness if he could.

But when it came to allowing time off for training and showing flexibility regarding leave, the AFS management were nowhere near as cooperative as Sydney's employers had been in 'Civvy Street'. Their uncompromising attitude annoyed Sydney, who felt there was room for manoeuvre, and during May he took action to try and get things sorted out.

Instead of speaking further with his immediate managers at the AFS, Sydney felt it more appropriate to write to the secretary of the Fire Brigade Amateur Athletic Association to seek advice. In his letter he asked about obtaining authorisation for a little extra leave over coming weeks to allow time for twice-a-week training, and about getting permission to split his 12 days' leave period to allow him to take part in races that summer. A week later his superintendent at West Norwood called Sydney into his office and accused him of "going over my head". Sydney defended himself, saying he felt he had done things by the book and felt the superintendent's complaint was unjustified.

Sydney was now ordered to appear before a divisional AFS officer – a meeting at which he was again reprimanded for his actions. He was in no mood to back down on this matter, and continued to insist that he failed to see how he'd been in the wrong by writing to the sports secretary to ensure correct procedures were followed. The divisional officer was reportedly not impressed with Sydney's position and told him to go away for 24 hours and think things over. Sydney said this wouldn't be necessary and resigned from the AFS on the spot. His younger brother Stanley backed him up by quitting too.

The story was leaked to the press and received widespread coverage. Sydney explained that although he badly wanted to continue training and racing, he would obviously now seek to honour his responsibilities and serve his country at this time of war by finding a new role. He revealed that he had now registered for the services and hoped to be called up to join the RAF. Given the choice, many men of the era preferred the 'collar and tie' option the RAF could provide, along with its more glamorous appeal above the other services. But the RAF wasn't in the business of accepting people for superficial reasons, and demanded people of some standing, high skill levels and excellent health. Sydney may have been an intelligent, super-fit young specimen, but he will have surely suspected his poor eyesight would again stand in his way?

While waiting to hear where he would be sent, Sydney found himself with the time to channel plenty of energy into running. He would manage to cram in a remarkable 15 races between 18 May and 23 July 1940 (just 66 days), which would turn out to be the most prolific period of racing in his entire career.

One of the race invitations that had contributed to his conflict with the AFS bosses was to a Public Schools meeting in Manchester on Saturday 18 May. Once he'd walked out on the AFS, Sydney was free to head north for this event at his leisure – and duly ran an exhibition mile at the Fallowfield stadium in 4:20.6, having been paced for the best part of three laps by Blackheath clubmate Flight Lieutenant W. Becker. During his business in Manchester talks about a return visit took place, leading to an announcement that Sydney would come back for a special 1,000 yards invitation race organised by Manchester AC on Saturday 22 June, which would be a specially-framed handicap to help him attack the world record.

Less than 48 hours later, he was back down south on familiar territory, winning a half-mile at an evening gathering in New Beckenham, on the Midland Bank sportsground. He clocked 2:01 to hold off clubmate Len King (2:02.4), while brother Stanley romped to an emphatic win in the two miles.

Sydney's biggest race since the outbreak of war took place the following Saturday when a crowd of around 5,000 turned out for the Midland Cycling and Athletic Club Sports, in aid of the Lord Mayor of Birmingham's War Relief Fund. It was held at the Bournville track in Birmingham and robustly advertised beforehand with posters proclaiming: "The greatest sports meeting of the year on the most beautiful sports ground in the UK!" The host club was donated £160 to cover the cost of trophies, thus allowing them to donate all gate monies to the War Relief fund. Punters paid a florin or a shilling to get in, according to which part of the ground they chose, and events got underway at 2.30. They had been warned beforehand the appearance of Sydney and others was only "Subject to services duties allowing" and were promised "Ample air raid shelters area available at the ground, and within minutes of the ground".

In windy conditions, Sydney won the mile in dramatic style in 4:20.4, narrowly pipping Welsh champion Jim Alford by less than half-a-second with Frank Close a very close third. Sydney had been trailing this pair into the final straight and needed an almighty effort to pass and stay there to win by just four yards at full speed. The local *Sports Argus* called it Birmingham's best ever meeting with the mile the feature and talking point of a great day. It was a nice escape from the misery of war for the excited spectators.

And so June 1940 dawned with the new Prime Minister Winston Churchill having taken office, and the dramatic and historic evacuation on the beaches of Dunkirk. But on home soil Sydney's immediate priorities lie with a 1,000 yards record bid scheduled for Manchester three weeks hence. His build-up to this would involve a busy programme of five appearances in just 20 days for The Combined Clubs.

First up, on Saturday 1 June, was a match between TCC and Belgrave at Grove Park in which Sydney won the 880 yards comfortably in a speedy 1:56.7 by a 20-yard margin from teammate John Furniss (2.00.7). Around

48 hours later at the Lloyds sportsground in New Beckenham, TCC took on Woodford Green and Ilford: In the 440 yards Sydney got himself boxed in early on and also seemed to have problems with the wind. Nevertheless he ran a highly respectable 52.7 but was pipped on the line by a mere two-tenths of a second by Thompson of Woodford Green. In a medley relay that evening (440, 220, 220, 440) Sydney was anchor leg for the winning team, running his 440 yards in 52.4. This time he held off Thompson, to ensure victory for TCC.

The following Saturday saw TCC hosting again at Grove Park, with Jack Crump's AAA team the visiting opposition. Sydney said he was aiming for a half-mile of 1:54, and set off smartly, brushing off some rather ugly jostling early on, to give himself a good test over two laps. He roared home 20 yards clear of Teddy Mead of Herne Hill Harriers in 1:53.9, his best time since the Motspur Park world record of nearly two years earlier. It wouldn't be the only time Sydney was able to predict his finish time correctly to within a tenth-of-a-second or two.

The TCC meetings were proving popular and another decent crowd gathered at Grove Park on the afternoon of Saturday 15 June as TCC entertained Herne Hill and Mitcham. Sydney couldn't repeat his previous week's impressive effort, but beat Mead again without really extending himself in 1:55.4. Columnist 'Insight' of the *Daily Mirror* turned up at Grove Park and was impressed by Sydney's demeanour, and defended him from any suggestions that lately he'd been allowing his athletics to interfere with wartime public service duties. Some unscheduled 'entertainment' for the crowd at this event was provided by activity overhead involving fighter planes. Elsewhere that afternoon, more than 60 long-distance men also defied the fear and restrictions of the war by heading into Windsor Great Park for the first wartime Polytechnic Marathon. They tackled three laps within the park, Les Griffiths of Herne Hill winning in 2 hrs.53 mins.

Sydney's final preparations for his record attempt three days later in Manchester saw him win a 440 yards contest in 52.5 seconds at Hackney, running for TCC against Victoria Park: "I am quite satisfied with my display and, given fair weather conditions, I am confident of creating a new record [in Manchester]," he said.

Manchester AC were staging a War Fund Sports at Fallowfield, on Saturday 22 June and Sydney's appearance in the invitation 1,000 yards received widespread publicity, described as an attack on the unofficial world record. His time to beat was Elroy Robinson of the USA's 2:09.37 set in 1937, with the British best held by Cyril Ellis (2:11.2) since 1929. Officials and local fans were delighted to see Sydney back on their patch and 5,000 assembled for the 2.30pm start, despite inclement weather, many donating generously to the local War Fund. One local paper praised Sydney for single-handedly boosting athletics in Manchester by creating all this interest.

Sydney's 4pm race was "described" live on Home Service radio by Richard North of the BBC. With one or two entrants unable to get there, just four men toed the line, Sydney taking the inside. Alongside was another bespectacled runner, the RAF man Austin Littler, plus late inclusion Eric Holderness wearing a white T-shirt, and on the outside B. Fishwick. The quartet shot off and Sydney found himself in last place after 440 yards, despite a time of 56.5. At this point local pacemakers Holderness and then Littler (both Salford AC) began to slow and dropped out, meaning Sydney had the lead with 500 yards left, but nobody to chase. His second lap of exactly 60 seconds left him far too much to do, and even an impressive final 220 yards of 17.6 wasn't enough to seriously threaten the old records. He crossed the line in 2:14.6 amid anti-climactic groans. Holderness and Littler had done a good pacemaking job for the first lap, but the absence of experienced runners Frank Close and Eddie Sears, who had cried off, meant Sydney had no help when it mattered. This was the major factor behind his failure, and there was no attempt to blame the rain-lashed track.

Eric Holderness' son Robert told me his father was called up for this race at a very late stage and was asked to pace Sydney over the first 440 yards, something he managed exactly to schedule:

> "Just before war broke out my father Eric had been selected as the fourth member of the 4 x 400 relay team for the [postponed] 1940 Olympics. He was only 20-years-old at the Manchester record attempt and soon after was posted to Burma to serve until 1945 in the intelligence corps, reaching the rank of Sergeant Major. On his return he just failed to make the 1948 Olympic team but in 1949 ran a PB of 48-something. For me the significance of the Manchester record attempt by Wooderson will always be that life went on regardless – for it took place shortly after the evacuation of troops from Dunkirk and shortly before the start of the Battle of Britain."

The Manchester 1,000 yards record attempt gets underway.

Manchester would be the first of two big disappointments within 48 hours for Sydney. On the following Monday he received the perhaps unsurprising news that his poor eyesight had meant another medical had been failed – this one with the RAF. Having burned his boats with the Fire Service, he would have to wait a little longer to find out where he would end up serving his country. On the bright side, this rejection at least meant he was still available for the foreseeable future for TCC fixtures that were coming thick and fast this summer.

29

Hitler Defied by Ponders End Charlie

BY the beginning of July 1940 the first German bombs had begun falling on Britain. However, on Saturday 6 July even the threat of Adolf Hitler and the Luftwaffe couldn't stop the Ponders End annual Fete and Gala taking place in a leafy corner of NE London. And that was very good news for runners and sports fans.

Amid the coconut shies and home-baked cake stalls, the highlight of the day would be the programme of races put on by the local athletics club. Since the 1920s Ponders End AC had used a cinder track in Durant's Park in Hertford Road, Enfield, for training and racing and whenever the park's annual fete and gala came along, the club would give the big crowds some races to watch. Many of Southern England's best runners would grab a slice of the action.

This year's date for the 25th meeting fell at a time when the war had been underway for almost a year, but the fete organisers saw no reason to cancel and there was general approval when the go-ahead was announced. The first Nazi daylight raids on Britain had occurred within the past week or so, a prelude to what became known as 'The Blitz' later on. By the end of that summer more than 1,000 British civilians had been killed by bombings, sparking Churchill's War Cabinet to give Bomber Command the order to attack Berlin. While all this was brewing, Fete and Gala chairman Charlie Baker – a colourful character who once worked in a circus himself – stuck two metaphorical fingers up to Hitler, saying the silver jubilee show must go on, and assembled a massive programme of track and field athletics.

As start-time approached on July 6, however, the rain bucketed down to such an extent the whole thing was put in jeopardy. Luckily the weather improved just in time and athletes and public headed for Durant's Park in big numbers. Sydney was the top attraction and on a busy afternoon, twice wore the colours of Kent against opposition from Essex and Middlesex and then changed into Blackheath kit for his third race. His two inter-county contests were a half-mile comfortably won in 1:56.4, and the mile where he was first in an untroubled 4:30, with Essex Beagle Eddie Sears runner-up in both. In an open mile relay Sydney contributed a fast-looking 220 yards (time unknown) to help Blackheath take second spot.

My own visit to Durant's Park in more recent times meant another venue ticked off on my tour of Sydney's race venues. The site of the now-defunct Ponders End AC's cinder track was easy to find, even though it's been disused for years. It is covered in rough grass now, although I stumbled across a small hole where evidence of the old cinders could be seen. I did my customary run in Sydney's footsteps, coming down the former six-lane home straight somewhat slower than he would have done!

Just two days later Midland Bank officials welcomed TCC to their New Beckenham sportsground once again, this time for an evening meet in which Sydney took a roasting from the handicapper. A handicap mile was set up which involved 14 starters, with unknown youngster Cornford given a massive 190-yard start; Sydney had given this lad coaching sessions recently and probably knew he would struggle to catch him in these circumstances. Cornford came home first and Sydney – off the scratch mark as usual – had to be satisfied with fifth place despite running 4:22.5, easily the fastest time of the night and producing a last lap described as "electrifying." The handicapper had the good grace to admit he'd got this one wrong, as everybody watched four runners with starts of over 100 yards all beat Sydney to the line. It had been an impossible task for the champion, but nobody was too upset on this otherwise perfect English summer evening in a lovely setting.

A mere 48 hours later came the start of what would be widely known as 'The Battle of Britain', a phrase coined by Churchill in the House of Commons. The primary objective of the Nazis was apparently to compel Britain to agree a negotiated peace settlement and an air and sea blockade began, with the Luftwaffe initially targeting coastal-shipping convoys, ports and shipping centres. Bombs landed on Plymouth, Cardiff,

Southampton and Portsmouth. And it was in mid-July – as the bombing slowly began to intensify – that Sydney heard the armed forces had finally found him a role.

His call-up papers instructed him to report for duty on Thursday 25 July with the Army's Pioneer Corps, whose work was generally light engineering tasks of various sorts. Brother Stanley had been in a similar limbo and was told he was required by the Royal Army Pay Corps, who took care of military financial matters in Surrey not far from the family home. Although their lives were continuing to take very similar paths, this was the first time the two brothers had been split up.

★★★

Shortly before these developments, a Thursday evening contest at Southall saw TCC take on the host club, plus Thames Valley Harriers and Polytechnic Harriers. Sydney won the half-mile in 2:00.5, two seconds clear of teammate Len King. This proved a handy warm-up for a bigger gathering two days later at Portsmouth. Sydney and his mum were part of a cheerful party of 40-plus representing TCC who headed for the busy naval base where a good crowd of around 2,000 assembled beside the Pitt Street track. The Royal Navy/Royal Marines athletes joined forces to take on TCC, with entry costing sixpence, or a shilling for a place in the stands. The crowd was the second largest the ground had ever held, and most were here to see Sydney tackle the half-mile and the first leg of the relay. In the former, the Navy runners were given 40 yards start but Sydney chased them down in determined fashion and had caught most by halfway. He took the lead with almost a lap left and came in relatively comfortably in 1:56.4, a time considerably better than the Navy record, although never challenging his own best of 1:49.2.

In the final event of the afternoon programme, Sydney went up against talented Sub-Lieutenant John Loaring of the Royal Canadian Navy, an Olympic half-miler, on the opening 440-yard leg of the relay – and they enjoyed a thrilling tussle. Sydney, clutching his baton, prepared himself to start adopting an upright posture, but just as the starting pistol sounded found himself bumped heavily by the neighbouring runner and almost fell. The starter didn't recall them, however, and this helped Loaring get off to a dubious flying start.

Sydney eventually closed the gap and halfway round attempted to pass only for the Canadian to respond well and hold him off. It was neck and neck for the remainder with Sydney inches down at the handover. Things got worse at this point for his handover to teammate Whittingham was little short of dreadful. The remaining legs involved the hectic format of 12 runners from each team doing 110 yards each. A great battle ended with a narrow win for TCC despite some very rough handovers which exposed their lack of relay experience. It had been a comedy of errors really, but brilliant entertainment for the crowd to round the day off. The Navy won only five of the 13 events, but still triumphed overall by a handful of points.

Sydney won't have been happy at the bumping, but was impressed by the speed of Loaring, a relative unknown in Britain but a big star in his native Canada where he was revered as a track runner and swimmer. Loaring was in Portsmouth as a temporary Navy radar officer, and had recently lived up to his hero status in Canada by saving the lives of civilian survivors on a torpedoed ship: After being assigned five tiny lifeless bodies, three were revived under Loaring's direction, leading to official commendations being awarded later on.

* * *

With barely a fortnight left on Civvy Street, Sydney managed to squeeze in a further four meetings representing TCC. First up was a contest at the impressive Surrey home of the Met Police athletes, Imber Court in Thames Ditton, on Saturday 13 July. Sydney and teammates were impressed to find the police had asked qualified AAA personnel to run the event, which suggested they were taking the day's races more seriously than expected. Sydney was able to win the mile in a new ground record of 4:17.0, a huge 18 seconds (about 80 yards) clear of teammate Moynihan.

News of Sydney's Army call-up made the newspapers and sparked debate over whether this would rule him out of his well-publicised record attempt at Ibrox Park, Glasgow, due for August 3. But any doubts were erased when Rangers' manager Bill Struth told a reporter he had made discreet enquiries and understood that Sydney's first posting for basic training would actually be in the Glasgow area, meaning he would be very handily located to take part at Ibrox.

With his immediate future sorted out, Sydney headed over to Tooting on Saturday 20 July for an AAA open meeting and conjured up the fastest mile run in Britain that summer. He was second to cross the line in 4:13.4, the man ahead, Doug Wilson (Polytechnic Harriers) having been given a generous 75 yard start in this handicap event. Sydney looked in good shape and clocked 2:07 at the halfway point when he began to accelerate past opponents who had all started ahead of him. At the three-quarter mark he was still lying 10th, some 80 yards behind the leader and despite a 60-second final lap he couldn't quite get his man, but finished more than happy with his time. Reporter W. Capel-Kirby called it "a grand performance" on a track that was a long way short of first-class standard and pointed out that 4:13.4 would have been equal to 4:10 at places like Ibrox, Fallowfield or White City. Capel-Kirby went further and said he was sure one day Sydney would stagger the athletics world with a record-breaking three-mile run, if and when he chose to move up from miling. He added the sad but salient point that were it not for the behaviour of Mr Hitler, Sydney would not have been running at places like Tooting this week, he would have been winning 1500 metres gold in the Helsinki Olympics.

Sydney's last athletics engagement before reporting for Army duty came three days later, just 48 hours before he would begin basic training in Glasgow. The event saw TCC visit Kent House in Penge, the well-appointed ground used by Beckenham County School, on the evening of Tuesday 23 July. It was a big night for the school, who had never hosted first-class opposition before and it provided fine entertainment with most events arranged on a handicap basis. Blackheath supplied an experienced race starter but all other personnel were provided by the eager school and a crowd of over 1,000 looked on. Sydney won the mile in 4:22.5 off the scratch mark, overhauling all opposition about 300 yards from home, winning by 50 yards in what he considered a good time given the rather uneven grass track. Teammate Len King, who started 60 yards ahead, was beaten into second place by nine seconds. If Army duties were about to curtail his running, which must have seemed a real possibility, then this wasn't a bad way to sign off.

30

A Soldier's Tale

SO it came to pass that on Thursday 25 July 1940 – a day German bombers launched fierce attacks on shipping in the English Channel – that Sydney Charles Wooderson began life as a soldier; service number 13058865, reporting for basic training with '2 Centre Pioneer Corps' – a unit that had very recently moved from Caister in Norfolk to Glasgow. He was pictured in one morning paper disembarking his train, still dressed in his smartest civvies and looking a tad pale and nervous.

Earlier that week he had spoken of looking forward to Army life as he was convinced the field training would improve his running. However, that first day must have been nerve-wracking for someone who'd never lived far from home before. Many times he'd shown steel and confidence to perform well in front of big athletics crowds, but this was something well outside his comfort zone.

Many athletics fans will have been heartened to read in their newspaper about Sydney joining the Army, as here was a sporting legend doing his bit for the nation alongside the ordinary men and women. Some will have recognised he was joining one of the least glamorous regiments, an outfit with, arguably, an unfair image foisted upon it in recent months.

The Pioneer Corps was often portrayed as a motley collection of men dragged into the Army by the war's insatiable hunger for bodies, any bodies – clerks, light labourers, intellectuals and incapables, unfit to fight, but fit to prepare the way for, or clean up after, the 'proper' soldiers. The job of the Pioneers was seen by many as merely tidying up the war, according to writer Padraig Colman, whose own father served in the regiment. But Colman challenges the view that the Pioneer Corps was merely a dumping ground for the untalented or rejected. He points out that many highly celebrated people served with them: artist Sir Eduardo Paolozzi, dramatist Christopher Fry, writer Alfred Perles, Professor Jack Cowan, founder of the Architectural Review, Hans Coper, the sculptor and potter, and of course, athlete Sydney Wooderson.

The 'music hall' image was surely rather harsh, for the Pioneers did essential work that often went unseen and unappreciated; they handled all types of stores and ammunition, built camps, airfields and fortifications, cleared rubble and demolished road blocks, built roads, railways and bridges, loaded and unloaded ships, trains and planes, constructed aircraft pens against enemy bombing and a host of other jobs.

Unglamorous work or not, Sydney was nevertheless in the British Army, and as such would effectively come under Lieut. General Harold Alexander, commander in chief of Southern Command. Satirical magazine *Punch* pointed this out in one of their issues, without realising the two men had another common link – Alexander was a former member of Blackheath Harriers!

In one way, at least, Sydney's start to Army life was made easier when he was granted time off in his very first week to compete at nearby Ibrox Park on Saturday 3 August. Rangers manager Bill Struth is thought to have used his friends in high places to help secure Sydney's availability. A telegram to Struth from Sydney confirmed he was clear to take part, and Struth quickly passed this news to local pressmen so they could make it public. An equally important factor in getting the sports on came when the cival authorities who had requisitioned Ibrox announced they were moving out.

Prior to the big meeting, Sydney was pictured in the pages of the *Daily Record* sitting in the changing rooms at Ibrox in full Army gear, chatting with British youth sprint champion Allan Watt of Shettleston Harriers, prior to going for a training run. As there had been no major London meetings that summer, interest across the UK in this 54th annual Ibrox Sports was sky high. Sydney was said to be aiming at a new Scottish allcomers mile record, which would mean consigning to history the five-year-old mark of 4:12 held by Maryhill's Bobby Graham.

Seventeen men signed up for the mile handicap, including record-holder Graham, who was given a 50-yard start. Sydney would naturally be on scratch, with the slowest-ranked man up ahead on 145 yards. Wearing No.1 on his all-black kit, Sydney was the centre of attention and received a huge welcome in the famous stadium, which was populated by anything between 25,000 and 60,000 according to which report is to be believed.

Struth was praised for getting the meeting on in a time of war and although the overall line-up was clearly not the strongest seen at this venue, the afternoon would prove highly entertaining. Proceedings started around 2.45 with the mile due at 4pm. Meanwhile, the local press issued reassurance:

> "Ibrox has excellent air raid shelters – and if it should happen that Mr Goering is in a nasty mood, stewards will see that everyone in the ground is shown in orderly fashion to a place of safety. Manager Struth has made all arrangements to meet this contingency."

Eight lined up for the mile and over the opening two laps Sydney was able to chase four top men – Frank Cross (Surrey), Bobby Graham, Morris Carstairs (Edinburgh University) and Maurice Bingham (Finchley) – to get off to a strong start. At 440 yards he was timed at exactly 60 seconds, and by halfway the clock showed 2:05.5 as Graham dropped out. By now Sydney was comfortably placed with only Andy Coogan (Maryhill) and Ian Stokoe (Edinburgh University) still up ahead after their 80 yards and 115 yard starts, respectively. Covering three-quarters of a mile in 3:10 left him needing a final lap of under 62 seconds to beat the Scottish record; it would be tough but definitely within his capability. He never faltered and by the time he entered the home straight he had all the field beaten. Despite their local favourites being trounced, the home crowd was in tremendous voice. Sydney passed Stokoe and then homed in on young local lad Coogan, drawing level and passing him with less than 20 yards to go. He steamed across the line to a huge ovation, beating the record by one second. Bobby Graham was among the first to shake his hand. Sydney said afterwards:

> "I was pleased with my run, but was hoping for a faster time. Considering I have been sleeping in a tent [lately] the time was

> quite satisfactory. It was a very good day, but quite a strong wind. Close, Bingham and Graham helped me considerably for three laps and then two long markers pulled me out till 100 yards from home. Quite a nice fast last lap. I was able to train during the week on the Ibrox track and hope to keep in fairly good trim [in the Army] by training about twice a week – just to keep fit and for something to do."

Twenty-three-year-old Coogan was so proud to have met and run alongside the champion that he would clip a picture of the race from a local paper and carry it in his wallet for the rest of his long life (he died less than a fortnight short of his 100th birthday in 2017). Unfortunately his commanding officer in the Lanarkshire Yeomanry saw the same picture in the local paper and Coogan was court-martialled for sneaking out of barracks to run at Ibrox. Much worse was to follow: Coogan would later be captured in Singapore by the Japanese, and during a horrific period as a Prisoner of War would twice suffer the ordeal of being ordered to dig his own grave as well as enduring a mock execution by a Samurai sword-wielding officer who threatened to behead him.

Coogan's miserable ordeal would be lessened one day when a Japanese guard noticed the newspaper cutting Coogan carried around. The guard was also a runner and recognised Sydney Wooderson in the photograph. It allowed the young Scot to form a rare bond with one of his captors; thanks to having run with Sydney, Coogan's three-and-a-half years of hell suddenly became slightly more tolerable. He survived the ordeal and would live to the age of 99, by then an uncle to cycling legend Sir Chris Hoy. The tale of Coogan's connection to Sydney Wooderson would appear in his remarkable memoir *Tomorrow You Die*.

Coogan fondly recalled leading the way during their Ibrox race:

> "The atmosphere in the stadium was amazing. I wasn't sure where Wooderson was, but I knew he was coming up by the way the crowd were roaring. I wasn't racing, using the head, I was just desperate to get to the finish. With about ten yards to go, Wooderson came level, then passed me. I was happy to be in second place and, to tell the truth, just happy to be in the race, as it was a great honour to run against Wooderson. Afterwards, he was very encouraging. He

told me I had a good future in athletics and gave me his pins and his number as souvenirs. He was a proper gentleman and he put me at ease as I chatted with him. It was the biggest crowd I had ever seen, and when I came out of the tunnel everybody started clapping. They thought I was Wooderson – I was very like him and we both wore specs!"

Incidentally, another of the many British soldiers captured as Japanese Prisoners of War was Fergus Anckorn, a Blackheath clubmate of Sydney's who ran with and against him often. Anckorn is said to have survived his ordeal as a PoW largely by virtue of his skills as a magician. Due to celebrate his 99th birthday in December 2017, Anckorn had the distinction of being both the youngest and oldest member of the Magic Circle during his lifetime.

Ibrox had been a first-class outing for Sydney and an event that helped thousands briefly put aside nagging worries about the war. Things had by now reached a critical point with the Luftwaffe working to achieve air superiority over the RAF. A few days after Ibrox, it shifted its attacks to RAF airfields and infrastructure and as the battle progressed, also targeted factories involved in aircraft production and strategic infrastructure. Before long it would be employing terror bombing in the UK on areas of political significance and on civilians.

An invitation to run at another famous football ground came Sydney's way as arrangements were made to stage the Everton FC Sports at Goodison Park on Saturday 10 August. Once again Sydney was able to arrange Army duties to allow him to take part. The meeting would be in aid of the Lord Mayor of Liverpool's War Fund and organised by councillor McLachlan, a long-time supporter of athletics. Attractions included foot and cycle races, boxing and music by the Liverpool Passenger Transport Band, with Sydney very much top of the bill. It was announced racing would begin at 3pm with Sydney on track an hour later. Tickets went on sale at five shillings and half-a-crown for seats and a shilling for the terraces – half price for men and women wearing services uniform.

Unlike the well-filled Ibrox a week earlier, a disappointing crowd of less than 3,000 was inside Goodison when the action got underway. A special invitation mile was on the programme for Sydney's so-called record attempt but when only one of the appointed pacemakers turned up this was cancelled and Sydney switched to the mile handicap. Here he was up against men of considerably lower pedigree, but several were given starts of well over 100 yards.

Of more concern to Sydney than the 13 men up ahead was the nature of the track made available for the contest – which was basically the space around the four sides of the football pitch, meaning they all had to run five laps and negotiate four corners of 90 degrees each circuit. All this tricky cornering, added to the strong gusty wind, would surely rule out a good time, let alone any records. To his credit, Sydney simply got on with the job and made light work of the unusual conditions.

He set off from scratch and flew around each 320-yard lap, steadily passing opponents as he went. Slowing down was inevitable at each corner but he still came home in 4:22, lauded as a remarkable feat in the circumstances. It won him kudos and superlatives in the next day's papers; his attitude and application had gone beyond the call of duty for an elite athlete and made it all the more disappointing that such a small crowd attended. Coach Albert Hill addressed the ground via the loud speaker system and expressed disappointment the sporting people of Merseyside had not come along in greater numbers. It seems the reason was at least partly a clash of dates with a services athletics meeting less than five miles away in Allerton.

For his part Sydney was pleased with his performance, believing it was the equivalent of 4:12 on a more conventional track. He added that he'd enjoyed enormously the TCC events of the summer, confirming that now his season was over. He wouldn't seek further Army leave in order to race, but did intend to keep fit throughout the coming winter and hoped to occasionally get down to Hayes to run with clubmates.

Less than a week later the nature of the war changed significantly for people in SE England, particularly in Sydney's native South London: the first Luftwaffe bombs to be dropped on the capital exploded with great loss of life close to where Sydney had until recently been based with the Auxiliary Fire Service. On the afternoon of Thursday 15 August they hit Croydon Airport and surrounding factories – a handful of airmen and more than 60 civilians lost their lives.

A number of sources reported that Sydney had been invited to run on Saturday 31 August at Imber Court in Thames Ditton to raise funds for the London bomb victims but the mounting tension over incoming air raids appears to have forced a cancellation. Around this time Sydney did squeeze another appearance into his season, representing an AAA team against London Colleges & Medical Schools and winning the half-mile in 1:59.8.

31

The Blitz: London Runners Can Take It!

THE novelty of having a sporting superstar soldiering in their midst no doubt soon faded for Sydney's colleagues in the Pioneer Corps. Particularly as he rarely talked about his achievements unless seriously pressed.

Occasionally, however, there would come a reminder of his celebrity status. One example during his Glasgow Pioneer Corps days would be a guest appearance he made in a boxing ring, introduced to the audience at a charity event for employees of a local munitions factory. This gala night featured old-time champions donning the gloves again – Larry Gains, Jim Higgins and Johnny McMillan among them. Sydney only agreed to appear because the event raised much-needed funds for the Central War Relief Fund.

Just as the eventful summer of 1940 began to fade, Hitler's bombers initiated what would soon become known as 'The Blitz' – a deadly aerial bombardment of London that started on September 7 and went on for eight dreadful months until mid-May 1941. At one point the Nazis dropped their fiery payloads on 57 consecutive nights, incinerating vast areas of the capital. These raids were part of the Battle of Britain, Hitler's plan to destroy the RAF in advance of an amphibious invasion. The RAF prevailed, of course, and German ground forces would never get beyond the lightly protected islands in the English Channel.

With the start of the Blitz inevitably came episodes to adversely affect club life at Blackheath. Enemy action took tiles off the roof of the Hayes HQ, bringing down part of the ceiling of the adjacent cottage and incendiaries hit the car park. The bombing was far heavier elsewhere in London and one notable victim was the Devereux hotel, used for many a committee meeting in pre-war days. The act of wasting paper was by now a major wartime sin, so paper trail-laying for cross-country jaunts was stopped and in some cases powdered lime used instead. This meant some of the trails laid were faint and difficult to follow – but it was wartime after all, and few complained.

Athletics and other sports in the capital were naturally wound down during the Blitz, but Sydney's club issued a newsletter in late 1940 in which interesting points were made about the resilience and spirit of Londoners in general – and Blackheath Harriers in particular – during the crisis:

> "Whatever the future history of this club, the first year of this war will rank always as one of its greatest years of achievement, for despite the absence of many of our best men in the services, curtailed and erratic travel facilities, blackouts, rationing and blitzkriegs, both the summer and the previous winter season were carried through to a successful conclusion."

"London can take it!" as the Government's 1940 propaganda film reminded everybody. The bulldog spirit was certainly evident at Blackheath, with officials and members heeding the distant call of their captain from his army outpost. He sent a simple rallying call to the club: "Carry on!"

Sydney, for his part, ran more than 20 races during 1940, underlining how he'd "done his bit" as Jack Crump and the AAA would appreciate, for this figure even exceeded his tally for most seasons in peacetime. And it wasn't just racing either, for he dutifully made public appearances to conduct coaching demonstrations and meet fans. A typical example would be a Games Week staged by the Kent National Fitness Committee at Orpington at which Sydney was chief guest, spending time showing youngsters how to improve at all aspects of athletics.

During the autumn Lance Corporal Sydney Wooderson was posted south to Bicester in Oxfordshire and shortly after that to Wiltshire, meaning he was now based much nearer home following the Glasgow stint. After his unit (2 Centre Pioneer Corps) was disbanded in October, he was sent to join 205 Coy Pioneer Corps based at Bicester. After a stint working at Swindon, a few weeks later Sydney and 205 Coy moved south to Wilton, near Salisbury, where the stately home Wilton House had been requisitioned as the new HQ of the British Army's Southern Command.

Vital early work for Sydney and his colleagues at this time involved laying 750 miles of telephone cable in and around Wilton House, linking the centre of operations with all units in the area. The Pioneer Corps were nothing if not versatile. Nissen huts were set up in the grounds for use as extra offices and accommodation for the humbler lower ranks such as Sydney. Nearby, the Pembroke Arms Hotel became an Officers' Mess and the Estate Office was converted for the soldiers to use as a canteen, which was run by the stout-hearted Lady Beatrice, Countess of Pembroke, and her helpers. Much of the planning for D-Day would be done here at Wilton House.

The ongoing Blitz meant Sydney was unable to get back to Hayes to run with his clubmates as often as he would have liked over the final few months of 1940, and he wasn't around when the club's cross-country season opened in rather tentative and low-key fashion in the November.

With typical understatement, a club official recorded that the winter cross-country campaign "Opened in circumstances that which could be considered inauspicious." London was being subjected to heavy bombing raids every night, the air-raid sirens starting to wail just after dusk night after night. Some Blackheath runners turned out regularly in defiance of all this in a desperate bid to sample "the old winter enjoyment" of pre-war days.

Travelling around was difficult and prevented many members getting to Hayes, but the club soldiered on and by Christmas a number of races for the new year were optimistically arranged. These were difficult days, but whatever Hitler threw at London, Sydney and his clubmates could always browse their fixture lists and find something to look forward to.

★★★

Before long it had become obvious to family, to fellow runners, and to the Press: Little Sydney Wooderson, racing snake, was putting on weight! The deprivations of war, instead of leaving him looking gaunt, pale and undernourished, seemed to be having the reverse effect. One newspaper even ventured the suggestion that he was nowadays looking "chubby."

By the start of 1941, the fastest miler in the world hadn't raced for five months and his normal training regime had gone into dysfunctional mode. It wasn't a lack of motivation or desire, it was simply that Britain was being blitzkrieged and more important issues were at stake.

Army life was active enough, indeed far less sedentary than his previous office-bound occupation, but it seems his new daily grind – and swapping mum's cooking for Army food – had seen him pile on the pounds.

His first serious test in running kit since the previous summer came on Saturday 11 January 1941 when a five-mile cross-country match was arranged from Belgrave Hall, Wimbledon, between hosts Belgrave Harriers and Blackheath. Nine Heathens faced 13 Belgravians with the first eight home from each side to score. Cross-country is typically a sport that attracts precious few spectators, but following publicity about Sydney's comeback and people's need for entertainment to take their minds off the war, a good-sized crowd came along.

Several newspapers previewed the race in that morning's editions, some printing pictures, presumably deliberately posed, of Sydney running along a road dressed in full Army uniform… one of the captions suggested this was Sydney running after a bus ("The poor bus didn't have a chance!"). Sydney's mum Nettie was among the spectators on chilly Wimbledon Common that day, as were a number of reporters and photographers, who gleefully noted the fact Sydney, famous for being puny and pale, appeared to be carrying more bulk than usual.

Surrey's reigning six-mile champion, the in-form Tom Carter, led after the first lap of around a mile, with Blackheath's gutsy Harold Thompson hanging on like a limpet. Soon Thompson slipped back and ran alongside Sydney but they were unable to close the gap. Carter was seeking a seventh win in the same number of weeks, and looked untouchable. Sydney ran smoothly but was clearly not race-sharp and eventually came fifth, more than a minute down, but not unhappy in view of his long lay-off. Blackheath got four men in the leading half-dozen but the home side still won the day by a 30-point margin.

A fortnight later Sydney featured more prominently when Blackheath joined forces with Ranelagh for a mob match against Orion and South London Harriers. It proved a tough 7.5-mile ordeal in torrential rain, run from the Royal Forest Hotel, positioned above Chingford Plain on the edge of Epping Forest. The dreadful weather was relentless and only 25 runners mustered at the start. It was not a day for spectators but among the brave few was Frank Rye, former Loughborough MP and Mayor of Westminster, the son of Walter Rye, the founding father of modern cross-country running. Also clambering enthusiastically across ditches and pathways to get the best vantage points was Sydney's formidable mum.

Jack Stubbs (SLH) forged an early lead but was soon hauled in by Sydney and clubmate Thompson, who worked together to build a good advantage for the rest of the contest. Many found the course difficult to follow and some back markers went completely awry. Sydney and Thompson cruised in side-by-side, recorded joint-first in a time of 49:00. This would be one of four appearances at this fine Essex venue, not a happy hunting ground for Sydney, the only time he was not beaten.

Getting back to barracks, and to the serious business of helping defend the country, Sydney's unit in the Pioneer Corps began supplying guards at the Army's Southern Command HQ at Wilton House, and at Government House and Radnor House, both in Salisbury, while others were deployed on fire-watch duty. There was a lighter side to Sydney's personal duties at this time, for he agreed to write a regular article on athletics for the *Pioneers Calling* in-house magazine.

He penned a column called 'Searchlight on Sport' for the St. Valentine's day issue in February 1941. The magazine carried an interesting mix of reading matter, including a series of humorous asides (example: "There is no truth in the suggestion that certain Italian generals have issued a challenge to Sydney Wooderson…"). The publishers were confident it would appeal to more than just the internal Pioneers audience and advertised it for public sale at 6d a copy. Indeed, the editorial quality prompted one newspaper to marvel at how the Pioneers must have remarkable talent among their ranks, and were clearly "not just pick and shovel men".

Meanwhile, the makeshift cross-country season featured a couple more outings for Sydney, the first a 7.5-mile Blackheath handicap event staged from the Hayes clubhouse. Sydney pipped in-form Harold Thompson by a few feet to win in 46:26. A few weeks later Sydney was unable to get time off and missed a cross-country match at his old school Sutton Valence. He might have been glad about missing out after hearing of the wartime transport problems they faced: First headache saw the group forced to board their train at Victoria without his brother Stanley, who was left on the platform embroiled in problems concerning army passes and booking clerks. Then, when the group finally reached Maidstone, a policeman stopped them walking into town for security reasons; it would take considerable persuasion to convince him they were visiting runners and had no evil intent.

These problems no doubt sparked banter at the clubhouse afterwards, but there was grim news to absorb too when it was discovered 19-year-old clubmate Gregory Lygo, an RAF sergeant, had been killed in an accident on home soil that same weekend. A few years earlier Lygo had been personally recruited for Blackheath by Sydney, who had spotted his talent in schoolboy races.

Later in March Sydney obtained leave and headed back to race at Chingford for the second time this winter. The nation woke up that chilly morning to dreadful news from Plymouth, where many civilians had been killed during a night of German air raids, an estimated 20,000 incendiaries and hundreds of high explosives raining down on residential and commercial areas of the city. But life went on elsewhere, and on the edge of Epping Forest, 95 men, representing 12 different clubs, lined up for a Southern Counties Inter-team competition. Orion Harriers officials had designed a brand new route that was supposed to cover 7.5 miles, but sadly things failed to go to plan and the race ended in farcical circumstances.

It was unclear whether runners took wrong turns or whether the route was simply badly mis-measured, but, led by Reg Gosney (Eastleigh), the runners began crossing the finish-line in little over 30 minutes, meaning they'd barely covered five miles or so. There were confused and angry faces, many of the leading men having based their tactics on a run lasting at least 45 minutes. This was possibly the reason Sydney, so well-known for his fast finishes, only managed fifth. Any ill feeling over the fiasco probably dissipated quickly, as most of them would have been grateful to simply get out at all for recreation and exercise in these dark days.

For Sydney it was a strange and disjoined winter season to say the least, but the runs he did complete would have helped his fitness for the summer ahead. A year earlier he'd spoken openly and optimistically that in 1941 he hoped to have the required fitness to run fast miles again, and there was even talk of chasing another record or two. What he had perhaps not anticipated was the amount of weight he put on over the first 18 months of wartime, and the frequent problems incurred in planning and obtaining leave to get to races. He confirmed to friends that he'd put on 19 pounds since war began, a dramatic increase for a man of such small, sinewy build.

Sydney's first public appearance on a track in 1941 caused great surprise and delight as the hosts – University of London Tyrian Club – plus some of his TCC colleagues, had not expected to see him at all at Tooting on May 10. He was granted leave at the last minute and dashed to the ground eager for action. He ran the 440 yards and will have been reasonably pleased with 53.8 seconds, which saw him take third spot, behind winner Palmer of Tyrian (52.7). The home side won nine of the 12 events to beat TCC comfortably. Sydney, later that afternoon, ran the opening leg of 880 yards in the mile medley relay, recording 2:07.5 as TCC (3:56 in total) were beaten by just three seconds. The *Gazette* noted that he looked in rude health ("positively chubby"), confirming the remarkable statistic that he had put on one-and-a-half stones in 18 months.

There would be time to shed the additional ballast, for Sydney's next public race was ten weeks away in mid-July, by which time the Blitz had finally ceased and his Army duties had changed. The Pioneer Corps' guard duties at Southern Command HQ were handed over in July, after seven months, to the 70th Battalion, Royal Warwickshires, and the following day Sydney's 205 Coy moved on to Wotton Underwood, near Bicester, from where they began working on a railway line near the villages of Ambrosden and Arncott. Other important projects included building a Prisoner of War camp in the hamlet of Sedrup. Before the move, Sydney was the inevitable winner of the 440 yards and mile races at his inter-company sports, and also tried his luck at 220 yards in a relay. Asked how he'd got on, Sydney modestly told the *Gazette*: "I think I had a good day."

Being based in the Bicester area made life a little easier when it came to attending race venues in the London area, and on Saturday 19 July Sydney made it to Epsom when the Armed Forces took on Civil Defence Services, organised by AAA man Jack Crump. A good gathering of top athletes saw £150 taken at the gate and, added to programme sales, raised a healthy sum for war charities. Sydney appeared for the mile, both ankles heavily strapped. He took the opening laps gingerly by all accounts, getting the measure of this five-laps-to-the-mile grass surface. In a blanket finish just 1.4 seconds separated the first four, Austin Littler (RAF) winning in 4:23.4 and Sydney fourth in 4:24.8. It emerged afterwards he'd been a doubtful starter due to ankle trouble sparked by a pulled muscle. He explained that wearing heavy army boots most of the time was the root of the trouble, and admitted he'd defied doctor's advice to turn out at Epsom.

It was crystal clear he was not moving as freely as usual and after finishing was seen to be hobbling. As well as the boots, he said training on hard tracks hadn't helped. The discomfort troubled him for several weeks and contributed to changes of plan here and there – including crying off a meeting in Palmer Park, Reading, in aid of the Red Cross and a revival of the old annual Nottingham Forest FC Sports.

The *Sunday Mirror* said Sydney had nursed an ambition to be the first man to run a mile in four minutes and had earmarked 1941 as the year he might go for it. They speculated that the twilight of his career might be coming and that if he also missed the Bank Holiday Rangers Sports at Ibrox through injury he would be missing what might have been the greatest day of his life.

The ankle damage slowly improved, however, and Sydney didn't rule Ibrox out. His plans were hit, however, when an Army order was issued restricting military leave and travel over the Bank Holiday weekend. Nobody outside his inner circle knew what was happening and just before Ibrox *The Daily Record* reported that his coach Albert Hill had arrived in Glasgow expecting to meet his man, but Sydney was nowhere to be seen. Three AAA athletes did arrive on time, others were said to be coming on a night train, but Sydney's movements remained a mystery. Communications were not easy at this time, and the Glasgow public held its breath.

On race day there was a huge collective groan among a bumper 45,000 crowd when it was announced Sydney wouldn't be running. However, a lively meeting wasn't entirely spoiled and the Scottish fans enjoyed the performances of charismatic John Addison, currently stationed in Scotland with the 7th Canadian Forestry Corps, a lumberjack and former speed cop, who won the 880 and 220 yards finals in fine style.

Glasgow's loss turned out to be Watford's gain, for Sydney was able to overcome the travel restrictions and get into Hertfordshire for some Bank Holiday action. The crowd at Watford were delighted when he appeared unannounced, ready to take part in the mile medley relay for TCC against Watford Harriers, St Albans, Vale of Aylesbury, Shaftesbury Harriers and Finchley Harriers. Clearly not fully fit, Sydney looked far from his best and was unable to hit the front before handing over the baton, outpaced on his opening leg by an inexperienced 20-year-old.

This summer was not going according to plan and there was an unwanted four-week hiatus before Sydney's next track action. This came at Maidstone on Saturday 30 August when, representing an Army and RAF team, he pulled out of the mile and restricted himself to another crack at 880 yards in a mile medley relay against the home team, Police and Medical Services. On the grass track that is nowadays used by Kent's county police HQ, Sydney looked in better shape than of late. He handed over in the lead to teammate Harold Wickerson, and the team went on to win by 20 yards. The afternoon's activities raised funds for the RAF benevolent fund.

Sydney's most disjointed and least satisfying track season since leaving school drew to a close with a rather pedestrian victory in West London on Saturday 6 September. The Royal Army Pay Corps Detachment's sports and gala, which featured Sydney and a Pioneer Corps team, was staged at the Liverpool Victoria Sports Ground in Acton. It was a successful afternoon, but Sydney only needed a modest 5:01 to win the mile, in which brother Stanley was runner-up, representing the hosts.

By now carrying the rank of Corporal, Sydney and his unit were on the move again in early September, transferring the short distance to an HQ in Bicester, but still involved in Prisoner of War camp construction and railway line work for the time being. During this period good news came through from the IAAF in Sweden that they had formally ratified his world records of two years earlier – 1:48.4 for 800 metres (875 yards) and 1:49.2 for the half-mile, both at Motspur Park in August 1938.

With Sydney unable to get to Hayes very often to train and race with clubmates, he was glad to accept an offer from friends in Manchester to become an honorary member of Manchester AC in the latter half of 1941 – a status that would give him the occasional opportunity to run outside of the Army environment. He took part in a road race, finishing third, and was runner-up in a six-mile cross-country while wearing Manchester colours.

To ensure some action early in the winter of 1941–42, Sydney and Stanley were able to exert some influence and engineer a repeat of the Pioneer Corps–versus–Pay Corps fixture at Acton, but this time in a cross-country setting over a four-mile course on Saturday 22 November. The result of Sydney first and Stanley second was repeated. Stanley was probably not too upset at being beaten for the umpteenth time by his brother, for this month he was celebrating getting engaged to his 29-year-old wartime sweetheart Miss Jessie Anne Round.

The brothers were in opposition again the following Saturday when a five-mile cross-country was fixed up at Hayes, involving Blackheath, the Met Police, London Fire Service and the Royal Army Pay Corps. Blackheath were effectively fielding a 'B' team as they had also sent a strong team to tackle Oxford University at the Shotover Hill course the same day. More than 50 starters assembled at Hayes, many lacking cross-country experience, but a good race ensued. Sydney grabbed the lead after a mile, only to be collared by Police runner Saunders on a hilly road section. Sydney looked a little fitter than of late but was unable to hold Saunders, who opened up a gap on Fox Hill. He finished second, 80 yards down on Saunders who recorded 28:27 and led the Police to the team prize. It would prove Sydney's last race for six months.

He was one of 200-plus Blackheath men enrolled in the armed forces at this point in the war. Many would pop up unexpectedly at the clubhouse while on leave, but others would sadly never be seen again. Some would be mentioned in connection with remarkable adventures on foreign soil. One member brought with him some lemons collected in Tunis and these were raffled to raise clubs funds. Another three were incarcerated in Oflag VI-B, a prisoner-of-war camp for officers in north-western Germany: the trio of Lee, Lymbery and Sewell were held alongside Wing Commander Douglas Bader of the RAF, the legendary legless air ace. On hearing the news of their capture, Blackheath sent them 'tobacco parcels' and a few months later received word these had got through. The camp was the setting for a remarkable escape in December 1941 when 12 PoWs disguised themselves as Germans, complete with dummy rifles and most managed a successful getaway.

December proved pivotal in the progress of the war, Britain and the USA declaring war on Japan after the attack on Pearl Harbour, Hawaii. This was followed within days by Germany and Italy declaring war on the USA, meaning the European and South-east Asian conflicts had become a global war and Japan, Germany and Italy were now united against Britain, USA, France and their allies.

32

Long and Awkward Journeys

THERE it was, as clear as day. Discoloured grass forming the elliptical shape of a running track abandoned many years ago. Not quite another Sutton Hoo, but it felt like an important discovery all the same!

The path of the faded lanes could be followed across what are now football pitches on a nondescript recreation ground just up the road from Tottenham Hale railway station in North London.

Avoiding the occasional scampering dog and stray football, I kneeled down to examine the grass and the cinder beneath, and felt sure this was the site of another of Sydney Wooderson's wartime races. Another venue ticked off my list, I jogged a few laps of Down Lane Recreation Ground and tried to imagine the scene on this very spot around 75 years earlier.

It was overcast and relatively quiet during my visit, but for Sydney on Saturday 22 August 1942, this field was alive with a noise and colour all too rare among war-weary residents of North London. The occasion was the Prince of Wales Hospital Sports and Sydney was by far and away the most famous face in attendance.

Funds were being raised, and people being entertained, and Sydney was only too pleased to get the Army leave necessary to come and play his part. He was supporting a hospital that opened its doors to the sick and injured for around 120 years in total. As hospitals go, it was an interesting sort of place – apparently at one time a donkey called Nellie was a popular member of staff, for example. And in its later years, it was the setting for Dennis Potter's landmark TV drama *'The Singing Detective'*. The grounds extended to four acres, but my research indicated the sports day of 1942 took place nearby on the cinder running track on Down Lane. Created in the 19th century, this track would remain in use until the 1970s, and its footprint can still be made out today via satellite imagery.

Back in summer 1942 the mile handicap race here saw Sydney and leading Welsh runner Philip Dee pitted together, both placed on the scratch mark. Sydney beat the Newport Harrier by around eight yards in 4:21.6, but wasn't quite able to catch Kingsley of Hoffman AC, who'd been given a generous 165-yard start by the handicapper. It was a good workout and the crowd appreciated his efforts, cheering him along every step of the way.

The event brightened up this corner of North London for an afternoon at least. Elsewhere the news was not good. Just a day or two earlier more than 3,000 men had died in the failed Allied invasion of Dieppe. The raiding force was trapped on the beach by obstacles and German fire and within hours all Allied troops had been killed, evacuated, or left behind to be captured. The bloody fiasco suggested France couldn't be successfully invaded for a long time.

* * *

Attending or participating in a Blackheath/TCC athletics fixture during 1942 meant you always stood a fair chance of glimpsing something rather unusual: A world champion turning up on his pushbike!

Due to the wartime travel restrictions, putting on cycle-clips and pedalling from his barracks would often be Sydney Wooderson's best bet if he wanted to reach a Saturday afternoon athletics fixture. Even the world's fastest miler couldn't afford to put on airs and graces in these troubled times.

Pedalling furiously for miles along undulating roads probably didn't do much for his track performance, but Sydney's attitude pleased his club no end. To show their appreciation of Sydney's commitment to the cause, they 'went public' by publishing a statement:

> "It is a source of great gratification to the club that Sydney Wooderson, world's record holder for the 880 yards and the mile, should go to the trouble and inconvenience that he does in making

> long and awkward journeys in order to support TCC meetings. The opposition that he meets in these matches is seldom such as to fully extend him, but despite this he does turn out to run whatever race is required for the benefit of the club and the others associated. All honour to him who could so easily find much more attractive afternoon's racing. It is an example we commend to all our members, for our champion shows no signs of being temperamental – which is more than could be said for some champions who have in the past shown signs of almost as much temperament as ability."

Early in April 1942, after more than four months without competitive running, Sydney had been transferred by the Army from 205 Coy Pioneer Corps to the Royal Army Ordnance Corps (RAOC). It was a move that brought him a little nearer home and while based in barracks at Aldershot he would find that a good number of races were within cycling distance.

The RAOC was basically a supply and repair corps with responsibility for weapons, armoured vehicles and other military equipment, ammunition and clothing and certain minor functions such as laundry, mobile baths and photography. Their important repair work functions were absorbed in 1942 by the Royal Electrical and Mechanical Engineers (REME) and a huge array of temporary depots built to meet the rapidly changing pace of war. Much of Sydney's work would soon involve repairing radio equipment.

By now the first American forces had arrived in Britain and it was an ever-changing picture. The sporting press regularly suggested Sydney might be appearing here or there at various track events, but many would never take place. A programme of sport stumbled on throughout the hostilities, but nothing could ever be guaranteed.

Sydney's first taste of competition in 1942 didn't materialise until Saturday 16 May when TCC took on the Met Police and Tyrian AC at Thames Ditton – but his appearance was a close-run thing. He had planned to run the mile, but arrived at the track several minutes too late for this. After discussions with officials he was able to switch to a two-miler, which he duly won in a time of 10:03.0, by the comfortable margin of 150 yards.

A fortnight later, on the same weekend the RAF launched massive bombing raids on Cologne, Sydney put on the racing shoes again. At Tooting Bec, he was part of a strong AAA team that beat London University on the council track. *The Times* called it "a very interesting contest" as 22-year-old

Doug Wilson (Polytechnic) took the mile race by the scruff of the neck and opened a substantial gap on the chasing Sydney. The latter's fast finish gave the spectators a thrill but wasn't quite enough to reel Wilson in. The Londoner won in 4:20 by less than a second. During the war Wilson would emerge as a major talent, a highly promising miler who had also been coached by Albert Hill for a spell.

Three events were cobbled together during the month of June, the first thanks to Jack Crump who recruited an AAA team to tackle the Metropolitan Police at Thames Ditton in midweek. Sydney arrived direct from his depot in the nick of time to win the mile in 4:28.4. Three days later, on Saturday 13 June, the TCC tackled the RAF at Halton Camp in Buckinghamshire, Sydney getting a relatively easy ride to win the mile in 4:24.2. A fortnight further on, Crump's team took on the Officer Cadet Training Unit at Sandhurst and won 11 of the 13 events that afternoon. Sydney triumphed in the half-mile in 1:58.9, beating Kierans of Gravesend by three seconds.

Meanwhile, as British athletics continued in understandably haphazard fashion, over in neutral Sweden major drama was occurring. Runners Gunder Hagg, 23, and Arne Andersson, 24, set about Sydney's world records with gusto. Suffering far less war privation and inconvenience because of their homeland's neutrality, the pair would race each other 23 times at distances ranging from three-quarters of a mile to 5,000 metres over the period, setting an astonishing 20 world bests. They ultimately took five seconds off Sydney's mile record of 4:06.4 in six separate steps. The first came in the Slottsskogsvallen stadium in Gothenburg on the evening of Wednesday 1 July 1942 when Hagg, in his first race of the season, clocked 4:06.2. Andersson came second, equalling Sydney's record. Then, just nine days later, Andersson would equal Hagg's new record in Stockholm.

After three years and 10 months as the world's fastest miler, Sydney Wooderson had been knocked off his perch. When he raced at Sandhurst on June 27 Sydney had been announced as the world record holder – but by the time of his next outing three weeks later, he was only No.3 on the world list. This would be a low-key affair in London, a half-mile on the Parliament Hill track on the edge of Hampstead Heath, where he ran 2:01.8. It was quickly followed by the biggest athletic event of the summer in the London area, a meeting to raise funds for the Duke of Gloucester's

Red Cross Appeal, on the grass track at Epsom. The sun blazed brightly on the afternoon of Saturday 25 July and a big crowd attended.

Sydney was by now showing better form and delighted the crowd by clocking his fastest mile for two years, coping superbly with the slightly bumpy grass track and the need to run five laps to complete the 1,760-yard journey. Facing opposition from the Navy, RAF and Civil Defence, Sydney led for most of the race, resisting a determined late challenge from Jim Alford (Roath Harriers) to win in 4:16.4. It was a long way short of what the new Swedish stars were doing, but a fine effort in the circumstances nevertheless.

Officials of TCC were struggling by now to arrange fixtures, hampered by the fact more and more men were being conscripted into the armed forces. The TCC idea had worked magnificently in the early days of the war, but with the war intensifying, the only event of note in the second half of 1942 came on Saturday 15 August in West London when the Army's Pay Corps provided the opposition. On the Boddington Gardens track in Acton – just off what is nowadays known as the North Circular Road – Sydney won a half-mile in 2:05.2, eight seconds clear of all opposition. In a mile medley relay later that afternoon he anchored TCC to victory by running the final two laps and beating his brother in the process.

Before the summer disappeared, Sydney grabbed opportunities to test himself twice more over his favourite distance – on very different types of track at Dorking and Portsmouth. On Saturday 12 September at the Pixham Lane sports ground the people of Dorking welcomed him to their five-laps-to-the-mile grass running path – and he rewarded them with a ground record and comfortable victory in 4:22.8, running that day for an Army team and helping raise funds for the Duke of Gloucester's Red Cross fund.

A week later he was leading light in an AAA team visiting the Pitt Street ground in Portsmouth to face a combined Hampshire, Sussex, Royal Navy and Marines team, in another fund-raiser. Also lining up for the mile was Doug Wilson, meaning Sydney had the chance to avenge his defeat in May at Tooting. A good crowd cheered him first over the line in 4:18.4, a decent time in the circumstances, although Sydney confessed he'd hoped to go a bit quicker.

And so the fourth long winter of war loomed, bringing runners the prospect of another seven or eight months with precious few competitive or social gatherings to look forward to. Sydney will have welcomed the fact that a rare pre-Christmas cross-country race was arranged at Charterhouse School, just six miles or so from his barracks in Aldershot. He cycled over to meet ten of his Blackheath brethren for the five-mile contest against a rather makeshift School team. Sydney and brother Stanley shared the honours, crossing the line side-by-side in 31:00 with the School's Patrick Trollope some 20 seconds down, their nearest challenger.

The School had been hit by illness and could only put up seven lads for the race, which led to Blackheath loaning them two of their younger runners for the day. Trollope, a future President of Oxford University Athletics Club, had been allowed to lead for about two miles before the Woodersons decided enough was enough and cruised past. There was a lively atmosphere as everyone enjoyed the tea and hot baths laid on for all. The majority of the Heathens team then strolled down to Godalming station to make their way home, no doubt chuckling at the sight of Sydney clambering on his trusty bicycle for some more exercise!

33

Lifting Spirits and Raising Funds

GETTING settled in barracks not far from home, finding he was able to do some serious training, and benefitting from an improvement in diet all led to better wartime running during 1943 for Sydney Wooderson. Even so, the twin enemies of illness and injury would never be far away this year.

After a few relatively idle weeks, leaving him a long way short of pre-war fitness levels, Sydney made a quiet comeback to competitive action at Hayes on Saturday 16 January. A closely fought and well enjoyed 7.5-mile cross-country contest was staged between Blackheath, the London Fire Service and Tyrian AC. Sydney treated it as a training spin, being piloted around the course by his brother. They finished in joint-seventh in 48:04 and it was clear that if he wanted to knock off some decent mile times in the summer this was only the start of a long road back to full sharpness.

A week later the brothers linked up again with clubmates for a long and steady sociable training run from Hayes. Participants on these runs always made the most of the occasion, for wartime duties meant many could only join in occasionally, and of course nobody knew what the future held. The average age of the pack had obviously crept up as most of the younger men were away fighting. Those on foreign shores missed these runs with a passion. The club historians noted:

> "The appetite for a run at Hayes again of many away from home was whetted by the rare appearance of a photo in the *Gazette* of a

leafy lane towards the common in a full blown English summer – a nostalgic sight which gave rise to correspondence from overseas betraying surges of homesickness."

The club was able to put on another 7.5-mile handicap over the country before the season, such as it was, came to a close. Sydney and Stanley ran gently together again, having recently both suffered a bout of flu and in no condition to race hard. The outing seemed to be doing Sydney good until the point where he suddenly twisted his ankle rather badly and had to limp back to base. It would need several weeks to heal.

These bleak days must have felt a million miles from the glorious record-breaking runs in front of big, adoring crowds in the late 1930s. But a reminder of those heady times came along when *The Times* announced in February that the AAA had pledged that once the war ended it would purchase three special commemorative plaques from the IAAF to present to Britain's three world-record breakers, Sydney Wooderson and long-distance walkers Harold Whitlock and Fred Redman.

Spring training generally went well, mostly done in Sydney's own time, and the extra pounds were shed. The rewards would be evident as Sydney went on to perform at a consistently high level in no fewer than 11 races between May and August of 1943. This period would also see, at long last, the emergence of a young pretender who looked capable of seriously challenging Sydney's 10-year supremacy as Britain's top miler – the 23-year-old office worker Doug Wilson from North London.

On the same May weekend that 617 Squadron's Lancaster bombers performed their dramatic 'Dambusters' attack on the Mohne and Eder dams in Germany, Sydney turned out for an Army team to do battle at the Pixham Lane sportsground in Dorking in aid of the RAF Benevolent Fund. The opposition came from the RAF, Met Police and Civil Defence. Headed by the band of the Queen's Royal Regiment, a parade of athletes carried the flags of the allied nations prior to the action on the track. Sydney was a popular winner, taking the mile in 4:25 with little difficulty, and was presented with his prize by Mrs Ruby Touche, wife of the Reigate MP.

Sydney followed this up on Saturday 22 May by looking very sharp in a half-mile victory (1:57.4) on the Iffley Road track in Oxford. His efforts helped a strong AAA team beat a combined Oxford and Cambridge university team by a huge margin, although the home team were down to the bare bones after at least five of its top young men cried off due to illness. The nearest challenger to Sydney was his AAA teammate Pettit, the Police mile champion, from whom Sydney accelerated away to win by 35 yards.

The summer raised spirits among what was left of the home-based athletics community. Normal annual niceties such as Easter eggs, holidays by the sea and Guy Fawkes' night may have temporarily disappeared for now, but 1943 did see a number of good quality sporting events able to go ahead – including the British Games at White City. War be damned – this Shepherd's Bush show must go on!

Although the attendance was lower than pre-war, and the strength of competition a little watered down, hard work behind the scenes saw the event go ahead on the Whit Monday Holiday, June 14. The stout efforts of officials and volunteers were rewarded when nearly 20,000 came through the White City gates and Sydney, for one, certainly didn't let the war-weary public down with his performance on the track.

He won his mile in spectacular style in what was widely trumpeted as his best track performance since peace time. The condition of the track did the milers no favours but Sydney was in good shape and shot into the lead with Doug Wilson snapping at his heels and this pair spread-eagled the field. The first 440 yards were done in 61.2 and they still led at halfway in 2.07. At the bell Wilson made a plucky challenge and they entered the home straight neck and neck with the crowd roaring them on. Sydney was able to gradually ease ahead and the younger man couldn't find an effective response, Sydney taking the prize by a single yard in 4:12.8. Apart from his 4.11 at Ibrox Park in 1940, it was his fastest mile in more than four years.

The same weekend – by a strange and sad quirk of fate – saw the death of Denis Pell of Herne Hill Harriers, who had been the last young Englishman to give Sydney a good race in the mile before Wilson came along. Pell was killed in a flying accident while training as a pilot at RAF Cranwell in Lincolnshire. This 26-year-old sergeant had represented GB on 12 occasions before war broke out, and his best performance had been finishing two-tenths-of-a-second behind Sydney in the brilliant 1939 AAA mile. Sydney would later reflect that Pell had possessed the natural ability to be better than him, but lacked the vital single-minded determination that Sydney possessed. Pell had always shown a refreshing attitude to his sport, putting enjoyment ahead of achievement, the thrill of racing more important to him than clockings. He was buried with full military honours at Margate on Friday 18 June.

After White City Sydney had 11 days to prepare for another big test on a major stage: Saturday 26 June would be his fourth visit to the Fallowfield ground in Manchester, this time for an event that would prove so popular it would morph into the annual 'Manchester Mile'. The adverts proclaimed: "Come and see a repeat of the Great Race at White City between Wooderson and Wilson," and gave details of extra entertainment from the likes of the CWS Band and a special schedule of trams from Piccadilly Station to the ground. Hopes were high the event would raise a four-figure sum for Mrs Clementine Churchill's 'Aid to Russia' project. Sydney had been signed up to star in the handicap mile, which headed a programme of 24 races. It caught the public imagination and a substantial entry list was assembled.

The Prime Minister's wife had launched her Russian aid campaign a few months earlier to help provide medical aid and clothing to alleviate the horrific suffering of civilians after Germany went to war with Russia in the summer of 1941. Her commitment was endorsed by the British public, and such was the enthusiasm that by the end of hostilities it was estimated the Empire had donated more than £7 million to the cause.

Somebody had the bright idea of calling the Fallowfield feature race 'The Stalin Mile' and a silver rose-bowl worth 130 guineas was put up for the winner. Presented by city councillor Harry Sharp, it was decided the race would be repeated every summer and the first man to win it three times could keep the huge rose-bowl for good. Before the races began the Soviet flag was unfurled in the centre of the packed ground by locally-based Sam Wild, well-known commander of a British unit that fought the fascist army in the recent Spanish Civil War.

Sydney lined up for the handicap mile wearing No.1 but in an unfamiliar pale-coloured kit. He rose to the occasion and won from scratch in a superb 4:11.5, beating a field of 14 lined up at various points ahead of him. Doug Wilson had to be satisfied with third this time, having been given a five-yard start. What was unexpected was the quality of Sydney's time, as he had not appeared to extend himself unduly or be 'towed' to the line, cruising home around 50 yards clear. It was a classy display and hailed the fastest mile ever seen in Northern England, comfortably out-ranking Sydney's own performance in Newcastle in 1939.

It had been achieved on the back of some good recent training and an improvement in Sydney's diet this year. Reporters gleaned the dietary information after one of them chatted to Sydney's brother Stanley as he crouched trackside shouting lap times to Sydney. Stanley revealed that his famous brother had drastically cut down the bread and potatoes in his stodgy Army diet and his weight had returned to normal. He also pointed out that Sydney received few privileges, having done all his recent training in his own time and this trip to Manchester was part of normal weekend leave. Stanley's revelations confirmed what everyone had suspected – that prior to this summer Sydney had piled on the pounds after being forced to swap mum's cooking for the efforts of Army kitchens.

Although Sydney would only return here once more in his career, the Manchester Mile would go from strength to strength – stopping in 1952, not because of lack of interest, but because Frank Evans won the rose-bowl for a third time meaning it was his for keeps. In 1949 it was won by local newspaper reporter David Coleman (Stockport Harriers) the only non-international to do so. Coleman, of course, went on to become a renowned BBC sports broadcaster – but would often refer back to this victory as one of the greatest thrills of his life as he'd emulated his boyhood hero Sydney Wooderson. The story of the Manchester Mile didn't end in 1952, however, for after Frank Evans' death in 2013 his family returned the rose-bowl to Manchester AC and it was decided to relaunch the Mile as an annual summer event open to all. Naturally this writer couldn't resist and I took part in 2016, taking the opportunity of a close look at the rose-bowl Sydney won in the inaugural year.

★★★

On July 1 Arne Andersson ran a world record mile of 4:02.6 in Gothenburg, beating Gunder Hagg's best of 4:04.6. It brought the four-minute mile closer and quietened cynics who had scoffed, calling it physically impossible. One man who believed it could be achieved with Sydney's involvement was 'Lilywhite', a sport and stage columnist at the *West London Observer*, who wrote:

> "I do not think four minutes will ever be done for the mile until Hagg and the present world champion Andersson of Sweden can

> meet Wooderson… with a meeting of these three fastest runners in the world, it would be possible. I can visualise big meetings after the war and promoters will fall over each other for the honour of staging a match between these champions."

After the excitement of his return visits to White City and Manchester in June 1943, the next few weeks would be immensely busy, but a case of 'after the Lord Mayor's show' for Sydney. He chalked up half-a-dozen races during July, although venues like Banstead, Harrow, Tooting Bec and Camberley couldn't provide huge crowds or elite-level opposition. Nevertheless, he welcomed the regular competition which got him back in the groove in terms of consistency, although predictably short of personal bests and records. Had his motivation suffered, the big meets scheduled for White City and Glasgow later that summer would have stirred the blood again.

He may have been the country's top miler, but Sydney continued to get the occasional tough ride from the handicappers. At the Harrow Civil Defence Sports on Saturday 3 July, for example, he faced a field of 12 given good starts, and could only manage fifth, Main of Belgrave taking advantage of his 110-yard advantage to finish first. A week later, the playing field was a little more level when Sydney lined up for an AAA Select to challenge the Royal Military Academy at Sandhurst. He won the half-mile in a highly respectable 1:56, and looked on from the sidelines as teammate Doug Wilson took the mile in 4:17.

A very special challenge then presented itself when, for the first time, Sydney performed at two separate meetings in one day. First up on Saturday 17 July was the mile race at an Air Training Corps meet at White City, which he won in 4:17.4. With the clock ticking towards 4 pm, Sydney then dashed off for Banstead in Surrey, around 15 miles away, using train and car to reach the local Hospital Sports, which was raising funds for Royal and Merchant Navy charities. Here he fulfilled a promise to run a three-quarter-mile 'exhibition' and clocked 3:12.2 helped by four pacemakers. It was a strong performance and just three seconds short of his own British record. As well as Sydney, the Banstead crowd enjoyed the appearance of 'Hitler' in a comic ceremony in which the Führer was shaved and bathed in a huge tank of water. Earlier, the meeting had been addressed in more serious fashion by local MP, Commander Sir Archibald Southby, who reminded spectators of the importance of both the Royal and Merchant Navy, saying that not only did the outcome of the war depend on them, but so did British people's very existence.

Having raised £400 for charities at Banstead, the public also got behind an event barely a mile away the following Saturday too. Billed as a wartime alternative to the annual AAA championships, much hard work was needed to put on this inter-services charity match at Epsom. A strong line-up entertained the big crowd as teams from the Army, RAF, combined Navy/Marines/Allied Forces were beaten by a Civil Defence squad. Doug Wilson tried to dominate matters in the mile, making the running early on, but Sydney sat back in third place before moving up and easing clear to win in 4:13.8. Wilson held on for second ahead of Jim Alford. Looking on was Prince Olav of Norway, who thoroughly enjoyed the sight of fellow countryman Sakarias Johnsen winning a discus and javelin double. The Prince was by now exiled in England following his heroic resistance in 1940, holed up for two months in the forest after his homeland's German invasion.

Buoyed by his Epsom performance, Sydney was confident of getting close to 4:10 in August, and decided to sharpen his speed with an outing at 880 yards when TCC took on the Royal Navy/Marines and Tyrian AC at the Tooting Bec on Saturday 31 July. On a less-than-perfect track, he won in 2:03.9 in front of a good crowd, holding off a strong challenge by Watts of the Navy to win by five yards. He hadn't gone flat out as a big meeting at the White City beckoned just 48 hours later.

Sports fans were delighted to see the traditional August Bank Holiday athletics back at White City, this time an Allied Forces meeting with a very strong line-up, including many foreign internationals. Starting at 2.30 there were 15 events and profits went to British Red Cross and services charities. Around 25,000 went through the gates, the Duke of Gloucester was guest of honour and the band of the Royal Scots Guards provided a stirring musical backdrop. It was just like pre-war days. Norway, Poland and Czechoslovakia were well represented and a number also wore the colours of the Netherlands, New Zealand and South Africa.

In the mile, Sydney, wearing No.47, was in no mood to mess about and shot ahead from the gun. The crowd was entranced as he gave an almost perfect exhibition of style, grace and speed, winning by the huge margin of more than 70 yards from Jim Alford in a fast 4:11.8 while still apparently having plenty in reserve at the end. It was his fastest mile on English soil for more than four years. The Duke presented the prizes and when Sydney stepped forward, there was a huge cheer to confirm his ongoing popularity. The subsequent edition of upmarket magazine *The Tatler* featured a fine picture of Sydney bowing humbly as he received his reward.

Sydney's good form won him plenty of headlines in the wartime press and whetted the appetite of his fans in Scotland ahead of his appearance at the Rangers Sports at Ibrox on Saturday 7 August. After the difficult matter of obtaining Army leave was sorted out, Sydney promised his best time of the season if conditions allowed: "I am in form and the Ibrox track suits me as well as any I have ever run on."

The 57th annual staging of this event featured the usual five-a-side football tournament involving Scotland's top clubs, plus athletics involving two teams representing the AAA, and clubs such as Bellahouston, Maryhill, Victoria Park, Shettlestone and Garscube. Around 35,000 were inside the ground to witness Rangers beat Clyde in extra-time in the fives final – but the high point of the day would be the fascinating mile handicap that one expert called "One of the greatest miles ever run."

The handicapper did his sums and decided Sydney should concede starts of up to 145 yards. It looked a tall order, but this was one of Sydney's favourite tracks and if he timed things correctly that man with the huge advantage might be a 'hare' to help him clock a fast one. The only worry as start-time loomed was the weather. It was truly atrocious – rain and fierce swirling winds. *Dreich* didn't begin to describe it.

The crowd played their part, roaring Sydney on as he closed in on the men ahead. He'd caught most, including Doug Wilson, by the end of the third lap, but at this point it was clear those who'd gone off with 90 yards' start or more could not be overhauled in this wind. Sydney's final furlong was a tremendous effort but he just failed to reach the leading trio and crossed the line in 4:15.2. On the printed page it looks a relatively ordinary time, and combined with his finishing fourth, is often overlooked by athletics historians. However, the bare facts don't tell the full story and the horrendous conditions meant this was a far better run than was realised – even by many who witnessed it.

The *Daily Record* of two days later appreciated how well Sydney had run and disregarded the wartime ban on reporting the weather by mentioning how bad conditions were: It was the worst day for track times this annual event had ever seen, they said, and highlighted the views of correspondent Joe

Binks who was convinced he'd seen the best mile ever run in Britain because of the circumstances. Sydney had actually slowed a little in the home straight on realising he couldn't catch the last three opponents, making his time all the more remarkable. Perhaps his only mistake had been to speed around the first lap in just 60 seconds in such conditions? When that time had been called by the announcer, the crowd had roared enthusiastically, believing some sort of record was on the cards, which of course was never likely.

Binks, who identified Sydney as "Sixty-six inches of athletic dynamite", acknowledged that the bare facts of the run didn't make stunning reading, but was at pains to point out the remarkable adverse circumstances in which Sydney achieved his 4:15. Because the ban on reporting weather conditions lasted ten days in case it was useful to the Germans, it wasn't until a fortnight later that Binks explained why he regarded Sydney's run as so magnificent: "I can assure you the weather at the Rangers' meeting was atrocious," he wrote.

For the record, Gordon Monshall (RAF) actually came in first off his 90-yard start, Cameron (Army), off 105 yards, was next, followed by James Fleming (Motherwell YMCA) off 125 yards. Sydney had actually drawn alongside Fleming with 75 yards to go, but the Scotsman leapt forward in shock at seeing him, and put in a burst that a tiring Sydney couldn't match. Sydney's splits were given as: 60, 66, 65 and 64.2.

AAA team manager Jack Crump was among those stunned by Sydney's wind-battered performance. He said the story of his mere participation at Glasgow exemplified the man's "modesty, exceptional ability and quiet willingness to help a good cause." Crump said Sydney was in great demand everywhere during these times and had proved the biggest single attraction in athletics over the whole period of the war. It was clear if you could get Sydney to run, a big crowd was guaranteed. Rangers' request to have Sydney participate had initially been rejected, he revealed, as his allocated Army leave for athletics had been used up, and the commanding officer felt he couldn't provide yet another pass, in fairness to Sydney's less famous colleagues. But when this bad news was passed on, the Lord Provost of Glasgow had intervened and pulled a few strings – with the result that Sydney was given leave from 6pm on the Friday night to first parade on the Sunday morning.

The main body of the AAA squad headed north during Friday daytime but Sydney was travelling alone later on and Crump worked hard to secure a sleeping berth on the night train for him. Nothing was available and on a crowded train Sydney had to spend the entire journey in the corridor. To make matters worse the train reached Glasgow several hours late and a tired and hungry Sydney reported to the hotel in the middle of Saturday morning, only three hours before his race. Crump managed to organise a meal for him, for he'd had no breakfast, and found him a quiet room in which to attempt a couple of hours' sleep. Crump confessed later that if weary Sydney had asked to miss the race he would have happily agreed. He wrote:

> "It was a terrible afternoon, very wet and windy and from the scratch mark he was conceding big, in fact unreasonably large, starts to all opponents. Against the very strong wind he ran magnificently. [Afterwards] the party managed to get sleepers back to London that night but they were late arriving at Euston on Sunday morning and a dash across London by taxi to Waterloo was necessary for Sydney to catch his train to the barracks."

Sydney was given a letter for his commanding officer which explained his lateness for morning parade. Crump was immensely grateful Sydney had gone to so much trouble to run, and reminded him he hadn't asked for reimbursement of his travel expenses between his barracks and London. Sydney said that he wouldn't bother Crump over this, because the Glasgow meeting was on behalf of war charities. Crump was stunned:

> "To have gone to all the trouble and discomfort involved, to run a tremendous race without any reward, and then to give up claim to entirely justified expenses was typical – his popularity was founded upon the best of all grounds – complete integrity in every way."

In addition to donating his expenses to charity, Sydney was of course mindful that he didn't jeopardise his amateur status and spoil his record of never taking a penny from athletics. He had always been very strict about never accepting anything that could be construed as 'payment'. High-profile athletes of the past had landed in trouble over such matters and Sydney was not a man to take risks.

Sydney's brilliant run would prove to be a fitting farewell to Ibrox, for he would not run at this great stadium again. He'd appeared there five times in all, each a memorable occasion for both athlete and fans. Running in this arena in front of the raucous Glaswegians was a unique experience, and I was given a flavour of what it was like by Scotsman Hugh Barrow (Victoria AC) who recalls taking part in a mile race on the Ibrox track a few years after Sydney:

> "On the day in question you were told to report to the primary school on Edmiston Drive, where you changed. Then the athletes warmed up on the training area under the Ibrox main stand, sharing that arena with the City of Glasgow Mounted Division, so you had to be careful. The half-time whistle would blow out on the pitch and this was the signal for the athletes to head through the tunnel towards the pitch with the players coming off in the opposite direction. When you took to the track surrounding the pitch, what an atmosphere! Not even an Olympic champion would experience this.
>
> "You had been cautioned from wearing either blue or green vests [Rangers and Celtic colours] – and that was a pity as my club normally wore blue and white hoops. Time was at a premium so you were on your marks immediately – the gun went, although you could hardly hear it, and you were off heading round the Copland Road bend. Then came the first surprise, the track was lined with police, sometimes actually on the track, so it could become an obstacle race. Suddenly, halfway up the back straight, a police snatch squad rushed out in front of us across the track, heading for the crowd. On the next lap, the snatch squad were on their way back across the track with a culprit, so you had to swerve to avoid them for a second time. It wasn't exactly made for fast times, however on this occasion I managed to win over my old rival Ian McCafferty, who went on to greater things, including the 1972 Olympic 5,000 metres final in Munich. For my endeavours I was presented with a transistor radio by [Rangers manager] Scot Symon and a cold wash back at the Primary School!"

* * *

Assessing Sydney's wartime efforts on the track, Jack Crump's admiration knew no bounds. He pointed out:

> "Both Sydney and Cyril Holmes ran well during the war time period but their service duties hardly allowed them the full measure of training needed and the type of competition available was not of the standard which world class athletes need. But how greatly they helped British athletics during this time… it would be difficult to compute how much money these two raised for war charities by their appearance in meetings but it would certainly aggregate many thousands of pounds."

Buried in the avalanche of praise coming Sydney's way during this period was a cautionary note about the manner in which he usually achieved his best times on a track. It was not the first time it had been suggested that Sydney only achieved 'world-class' times when being paced and helped by others, and he wasn't quite so quick in straight championship races. These views emerged from the rather unlikely sources of services papers '*Eighth Army News*' and '*The Crusader*'. It was a view rejected yet again by his club's *Gazette* who countered by quoting several performances from the past when Sydney ran sub-4:10 for the mile in difficult conditions and against tough international fields, and underlined the indisputable fact that as a miler he'd been in a class of his own in Britain for years.

The remainder of the disjointed 1943 summer season would be played out in the south of England for Sydney, and he must have been relieved to resume in West London in far better conditions than he faced at Glasgow a week earlier. At the Liverpool Victoria sportsground's immaculate grass track in Acton he responded with a ground record. In a mile relay contest, he covered five laps (reportedly amounting to 1 mile and 23 yards) in 4:36.1, beating brother Stanley by a good 25 yards. Groundsman Nobby Clark had promised the track would be in tip-top condition for the champion's return here, but wisely warned the public not to expect records.

Another ground record was smashed a week later on Saturday 21 August when Sydney returned to Imber Court in Thames Ditton, winning the mile for an AAA team against the RAF and a Police/Civil Defence team. Sydney signalled his intentions from the gun, forging a lead he never relinquished. Doug Wilson was several yards behind throughout and never seriously threatened. Sydney's 4:14.8 beat Wilson's seven-day-old ground record by almost two seconds and Wilson was also able to squeeze inside his previous time.

By the beginning of September 1943 Sydney had been moved again within the Army. He remained a corporal, but now found himself helping maintain and repair radio equipment at the Royal Electrical and Mechanical Engineers workshops in Crookham, near Aldershot. Word of his transfer to the REME soon reached Fleet Street and the *Sunday Post* sent a photographer along to take pictures of him hard at work with radio sets. REME had been formed less than a year earlier to tackle various technical and engineering tasks and Sydney was among many home-based soldiers to be transferred into the new environment.

Although he was running well during this period, Sydney was of course not in the best possible shape due to the stresses, strains and privations of life during wartime. Problems associated with rheumatism dogged him on and off and he needed hospital treatment and the occasional break from training to deal with this. It meant there was never really any chance of him racing the great Gunder Hagg, who stopped off in Scotland in September, en route home to Sweden from the USA, and made it known he would love the challenge of a race against Sydney. Even the excitable sections of the sporting press could see this was highly unlikely during a time of war; they rued the fact that "the race of the year" would not be possible for the foreseeable future.

Despite all this, Sydney was able to fit in three more competitive afternoons before 1943's makeshift season came to a halt. At Stanmore on Saturday 4 September he won a half-mile comfortably in 2:05 from a field of seven on a grass track. A fortnight later he made a late decision to compete at the Pitt Street track in Portsmouth for the AAA Select against the Navy and a Hants/Sussex team and won the mile in 4:19.6. Finally, on Saturday 25 September at Reading he ran from scratch for Blackheath in a mile handicap, but was well short of catching Ruddock of Surrey-based club Airscrews AC, who benefitted from his generous 153-yard start to get home in 4:15.4, 14 seconds ahead of Sydney.

Meanwhile, across Britain around now, widespread hopes that the war would be over by Christmas 1943 were proving mere wishful thinking. Intense and heavy RAF bombing of Berlin, the invasion of Italy and the German surrender at Stalingrad had all given cause for optimism, but as another winter closed in there looked to be some way to go yet before peace returned.

CHURCHMAN'S CIGARETTES
S. C. WOODERSON

34

A Year Like No Other

THE year of 1944 would be like no other for Sydney Wooderson. There would come pivotal moments in the progress of the war, mixed with episodes of personal bereavement and serious illness. On the running front he would only manage a meagre seven races over a year that included his landmark 30th birthday. Then, as 1944 began drawing to a close, he found his very future as an athlete was hanging by a thread.

The year had started well enough: On Saturday 22 January at Roehampton he returned to action after a four-month break from racing and his first proper run of any sort for ten weeks. The University of London at Roehampton hosted a 4.5-mile cross-country involving their own Tyrian AC, Blackheath, Thames Valley Harriers, and London Fire Service. Sydney and a good collection of clubmates were able to obtain leave and head over to the chilly start-line on Wimbledon Common.

The wind felt bitingly cold on the Common as the start was delayed by a handful of late arrivals. Harold Thompson of Blackheath got off to a fast start and led for the best part of a mile at which point he was caught by a pack. Les Phipps (TVH) seized the lead and maintained his position for some distance, but undid all his good work by taking a wrong turn. Sydney, looking in good shape, took advantage and increased his lead across Putney Heath to win impressively in 26:30, 17 seconds ahead of the rest. Having done so little since the previous summer Sydney was delighted with the outcome. The fast course had suited him well, although TVH managed to take the team prize. Hosts Tyrian entertained their visitors afterwards at a nearby café.

Three weeks later the Blackheath clubhouse was alive with noise and banter for a mob match of 7.5 miles for which the visitors were Orion and South London Harriers. With the normal trail-layer unable to attend, the route was 'limed' by Baggy Hargreaves. The Wooderson brothers helped the home team win this annual affair for the first time since 1940, having mustered 25 runners, far more than expected. The Heathens' man Enfield emerged from an unholy scramble at the start to be early leader but by the time they reached Layham's Farm, Sydney had taken command. To the delight of most of the healthy crowd of spectators – which included the mothers of both Sydney and future star Gordon Pirie – he came home to win in exactly 46 minutes. Enfield stuck with it to finish a good second only 11 seconds adrift.

The good attendance, and fact that a fair number were able to stay afterwards for a convivial supper, made this a rewarding day reminiscent of those good old pre-war days. Runners were able to relax and go through the many messages received from exiled members and other absent friends who were clearly badly missing club life. One example was a missive from Clay Thomas, who told them he was currently looking after dozens of cadets and trying to turn them into runners. He said even at the ripe age of 61 he still looked forward to returning to the clubhouse for another of those "Runs with the old man's pack, then bath, tea, grub, chat, leg-pulls and a sing-song!" Another long-distance greeting had found its way home from member Harold Rainbird, who'd seen action in Salerno and Naples, suffered a dose of malaria, and was badly missing the camaraderie of the English running scene. Rainbird was currently enjoying leave in Egypt, the highlight of which had been finding a copy of the *Egyptian Mail* carrying a photo of Sydney Wooderson on its sports pages.

Blackheath came up trumps again three weeks later, agreeing to stage a Southern Counties team race at Hayes over 7.5 miles. It attracted 70 starters who were sent on a lap of Hayes Common before proceeding along the usual club route. Reg Gosney of Eastleigh led from early on with Sydney in relaxed mode, running easily much further back and subsequently cruising home in eighth, more than two minutes behind Gosney's 45:11. Blackheath's Will Vercoe made a surprise appearance, following his recent adventures in El Alamein and Italy, using it as a training run.

Blackheath's annual general meeting on April 1 was attended by just 26 of its 823 membership, who held a few moments' silence as a mark of respect to members recently killed in action. Defiantly, the club announced there would be no further cutting of the fixture list, as they felt a strong responsibility to carry on regardless of the war. Tributes were paid to all who had worked to keep the club alive during the conflict and to Sydney and others in the services who made the effort to run whenever they could.

Sydney was able to launch his 1944 summer season on Saturday 20 May at Cambridge, winning a mile in AAA colours against the Combined Universities in a time of 4:28.8. It wasn't lightning quick but emphatic: he was never seriously pressed and left Oxford's Gray trailing around 100 yards in his wake in second place.

★★★

BEATEN by an art college student who was sporting a beard! That was Sydney Wooderson's rather unlikely fate on his first visit to the bomb-scarred city of Coventry.

There were mitigating circumstances of course. The race in question was a half-mile handicap in which the hirsute victor had been given a 15-yard start. Not only that, the track was in very poor condition, and – perhaps most significant of all – the champion was a few weeks away from succumbing to an illness that would lay him low for nearly four months.

Sydney's appearance pulled in a big crowd at the Coventry Godiva Sports at the Coundon Road stadium on the afternoon of Saturday 27 May 1944. It was his first run in this part of the country and one that helped boost morale of local people after nearly five years of war and the various restrictions that went with it. Coventry had taken a real battering from the Luftwaffe (1,236 locals killed in bombing raids over a two-year period) and days like this were to be enjoyed.

Accordingly Sydney received a big ovation and his trademark fast finish made it a dramatic two-lap race, even though he couldn't quite catch two of the opponents given starts. Some reports made much of the fact that, unusually for a track runner of the era, winner Harold Fox (Leicester College of Art & Technology) was sporting a beard! Fox had stormed off from his mark 15 yards ahead of Sydney, with other, lower-ranked runners even further ahead. The local paper called Fox one of the most stylish local half-milers seen in the Midlands for years.

It proved a great race on an uneven, hard-baked track, with Sydney putting in a brilliant late burst 300 yards from home, surging just as Fox appeared to falter. Frank Froggatt (Small Heath), who'd started 38 yards ahead of Sydney, momentarily looked set to grab the lead, but Fox revived and kicked again. All the time Sydney was closing dramatically – getting ahead of Willetts (Godiva) in the process – but ultimately ran out of track. The first four crossed the line in a blur, just two seconds covering them all, Sydney third in 1:58.4.

I wanted to include Coventry on my tour of Sydney's venues, but as this 1944 track had long since disappeared, I needed help from another star athlete to pinpoint its location. Colin Kirkham, locally-based 1972 Munich Olympian, came to the rescue, explaining Coventry's complex sports venue history: In Sydney's day Coventry Godiva AC was based at Rover Sports Ground at The Butts (they used a 360-yard grass track squeezed inside a cycle track), but during the war this was taken over by civil defence authorities. It meant Godiva had to look elsewhere, hence the May 1944 meeting being held at Coundon Road, long-time home of Coventry Rugby Club. Coundon Road's versatile facilities would eventually be demolished in 2004, and when I ran down to the site on a rainy afternoon I found it covered by new housing. But at least the sporting connection remains visible, as apartment blocks and streets are named after the former rugby stars who once played there.

★★★

The war took a significant turn at the beginning of June 1944 when Operation Overlord was launched, 5,000 tons of bombs dropped on German gun batteries on the Normandy coast. D-Day (June 6) saw many thousands of Allied troops land on French beaches ready to push inland as part of the largest amphibious military operation in history.

As positive and heartening news of what was happening across the Channel continued to flow in, Sydney headed north to Lancashire from his barracks to take part in the Preston Allied and Combined Services sports meeting, schedule for 2pm on the Saturday after D-Day. It was to raise money for Prisoner of War and Red Cross funds and would take place on the famous Preston North End football ground at Deepdale, the programme including added extras such as sack and obstacle racing. Running on grass held no fears for Sydney and he tackled the mile handicap with gusto from the scratch mark, motoring along nicely and hitting the front in the third lap. The big crowd rose to cheer him home as he won by a healthy margin of 50 yards in 4:24.1 with Goodbury (Surrey ASC) runner-up off a 60-yard start. The *Liverpool Echo* remarked that Sydney looked in the sort of form that a few years ago had people finally believing a four-minute mile was possible.

Barely 48 hours after Sydney had returned to the London area, the capital came under attack from a new and frightening source – V-1 flying bombs, or 'doodlebugs' as they became known. It was Hitler's response to the D-Day landings and marked the start of a terror campaign that continued through June. They were launched from along the French and Dutch coasts, peaking at more than 100 per day over SE England, and amounting to 10,000 in total. Everyone in London was affected by the doodlebugs and the Wooderson family were of course no exception. Simon Amos, grandson of Sydney's half-sister Rhoda, recalls being told about events in the Wooderson household from this period. He told me:

> "I was told about a family visit to Calais Street, Camberwell, in summer 1944. Doodlebugs were dropping and Stanley was using his stopwatch, which he normally used for running, to measure the time it took between the flying bomb's engine stopping and the explosion on impact. While everyone sheltered in the cellar, [Sydney's father] George stayed upstairs until Rhoda went up to ask him to join them. Apparently George was very touched about his daughter's concern for his safety. Early the next morning my uncle Ted went out to buy fish for [Sydney's mother] Nettie, which would normally have been in short supply. But due to the doodlebugs the streets were deserted and the fishmonger was not sold out. My uncle remembers trams being pulled from Camberwell depot with shattered windows around that time. Railway goods wagons were derailed at a bridge there, and women were loading their prams with the spilled coal."

The continuing assault by the doodlebugs badly affected all aspects of life in the London area and the track season was seriously disrupted with many cancellations, including Blackheath's evening meetings. Some club members began steering themselves out of built-up areas towards the countryside for training runs whenever possible… the Blackheath archives reveal that "Pastures new were delighted in" over this period, allowing members to forget the war occasionally:

> "There were some quiet, idyllic nights, while there is description of one occasion when the President was observed having a quiet afternoon browsing among the Club archives and so peaceful was the club room that the war seemed far away."

American army uniforms were observed at Blackheath's clubhouse for the first time in mid-1944: "You fellows sure enjoy taking your punishment," joked the GIs – possibly referring to London's continual bombing, or maybe the long distance running, or maybe both! Although it was by now widely believed the war was nearly over, the national joy at Allied advances in France had the shine taken off it by the dreaded doodlebugs in London. However, Blackheath runners could find solace down at the club, where it was becoming evident that more and more familiar faces were by now re-appearing after long absences earlier in the war. This was hugely encouraging for those who had feared for the very future of the club during the darker days.

Sydney prepared well, training hard in his spare time, for the biggest date of his summer, the so-called Stalin Mile in Manchester. A big crowd and serious competition was guaranteed at the Fallowfield ground on Saturday 24 June, with Britain's top milers Sydney and Doug Wilson the main attractions as more funds were raised for Mrs Churchill's Aid to Russia project. Lining up in the invitation handicap mile he had the rare experience of being joined on the scratch mark by Wilson, with the others at various points up ahead. It created a new dimension to Sydney's usual task of simply having to catch inferior runners.

Sydney looked strong throughout and Wilson couldn't get within five yards of him by the end. Sydney wasn't quite able to overhaul Clifford Bunton, who had the run of his life in 4:10.8, albeit from an 80-yard start. Bunton, a Derbyshire-born assistant lecturer at the University of London, was 20 yards clear by the end. Known as 'Bunny', he would go on to make his name as an academic, moving to California at the height of the British 'brain drain'. Sydney was second in an excellent 4:12.8, the fastest time of the year in Britain, and one that would have won most AAA championships in peacetime.

It was a pleasing performance, but the enjoyment quickly wore off when Sydney noticed afterwards that his legs were becoming painful and swollen. It wasn't clear exactly what the trouble was and he is said to have visited more than one specialist to find out, eventually being told the most likely cause was a form of rheumatic fever. Within days he had to be admitted to the Army hospital in Aldershot as the problem intensified, and the tentative initial diagnosis was confirmed. It was far worse than his previous experience of rheumatism, and he would end up spending the best part of four months in hospital.

At one point doctors warned him he may never run again, and with his 30th birthday looming in August, Sydney had to cope with the very real prospect his sporting career was over. The news only became public after he wrote a letter from his hospital bed to the secretary of 'Bristol's Own Fund', apologising that he would not be available for their sports meeting in late July. Initially he stated "I may be in hospital another week or so," but time passed and the problem persisted. There was to be no quick cure.

Before long the Fleet Street sportswriters were hinting darkly that Wooderson was finished – Peter Wilson of the *Daily Mirror* particularly outspoken on the subject. Sydney kept his counsel but confirmed later he had read the stories. The problem particularly affected his back and legs and, apart from the physical discomfort, he had to cope with a demoralising lack of activity like no other he had ever experienced. His hopes of making a full recovery and returning to running must have fluctuated, but on the more optimistic days will surely have convinced himself the looming end of the war would be a huge step forward as he could then leave the Army, get back to a normal healthy diet and work towards re-establishing old routines.

Keeping up with news from the outside world from his hospital bed, he would have heard all about Doug Wilson winning the annual Ibrox Park mile in 4:13 and Arne Andersson bringing the four-minute mile a step closer by clocking 4:01.6 at Malmo.

In August Sydney underwent surgery and was obliged to write to Billy Hughes at Worthing Harriers declaring himself unavailable for a sports meeting scheduled in the seaside town for September. He'd always hated letting people down like this, but must have hated even more the wretched incarceration indoors which meant he missed simple pleasures such as his regular walks in the countryside.

Victory in the war looked imminent throughout the summer

– key events included the liberation of Paris – but the end remained tantalisingly out of reach. September came and went with Sydney still confined to bed and his misery would deepen further when his father George died at home at the age of 79 in early October, shortly after suffering a bad fall.

Writer Norman Harris records that Sydney's response to warnings his career may be over was non-committal, and under his inscrutable exterior he always refused to believe the experts. He would simply be patient and wait and see how things went. He'd now passed 30 and his chances of being the world's first four-minute miler had been dealt a savage blow – but Harris believes a notion had been strengthening in his mind that, providing the war soon ended, he could make a comeback and maybe try longer distances. He was still unmarried and running meant everything to him outside of his work. He felt he could still be a top performer after all this was over and felt he had ability within him that had not been fully realised. By this he meant moving up to distances of around three miles (5,000 metres), and possibly having a serious crack at winning top-level cross-country events. Despite ten years of brilliance over half-miles and the mile, there was some truth in the suggestion he'd never actually won a truly great, major race. He had unfinished business to attend to if he could shake off the wretched rheumatic problems.

As Harris would point out, in his favour over these miserable months, Sydney was able to call upon a wealth of experience, self-reliance and patience. He was a well organised and sensible athlete; if anyone could plot their way out of this horrendous scenario and make a good comeback, then Sydney Wooderson was surely that man.

Years later it would be suggested Sydney had been annoyed by a piece in the *Daily Mirror* by Peter Wilson – known for his no-holds-barred journalism – in which he predicted Sydney was finished. This may have motivated him all the more to prove people wrong and get back to his best.

Meanwhile the press announced that Sydney's father had left £8,112 in his will, with the family fruit and veg business based at Covent Garden left to his three sons. With Sydney not wishing to abandon his legal career, the business would end up jointly in the hands of his two brothers. This would subsequently lead to problems, as Sydney's son Philip explained to me in 2017:

> "Stanley and Alfred were made partners, but before long the two of them fell out. Stanley was no businessman, his heart was always in repertory theatre and light opera, and when his side of the business failed Sydney had to give him much of his own inheritance to bail him out. Alfred made a success of his half, but there was a rift between them that only Sydney could bridge."

Stanley's daughter Jill Gunn, meanwhile, told me her recollection of what happened:

> "My brother Richard and I certainly think Stanley's heart was in the business, but his and Alfred's approach to running it differed greatly, which we think was the cause of the rift. Sydney certainly kept a good relationship with both his brothers although he was much closer to Stanley. If Stanley had not inherited the business I think he might have gone to university and then become an Anglican Vicar or possibly a school teacher."

Jill said Stanley had been a shy man like Sydney, but not so retiring, whereas eldest brother Alfred was none of these things:

> "Stanley and his wife Jessie would become good amateur performers, he a leading actor in straight plays, she a soprano singer playing leading roles in musical comedy, later joined by Stanley."

Sydney, of course, would never have contemplated performing on stage – even speaking at running events filled him with dread – but in addition to their running and walking, he and Stanley shared a common love of reading and crossword puzzles.

By the end of October 1944 there was light at the end of the tunnel for Sydney. He was finally allowed home from hospital and it was reported he would be returning to his army unit during early- to mid-November. He was still suffering to some extent from the rheumatic trouble in his legs, but was on a slow road to recovery after being told to steer clear of all athletic exercise for a further three months.

35

A Most Honourable Defeat

AFTER seven miserable months of illness and slow rehab, Sydney Wooderson must have struggled to feel cheerful as the new year of 1945 got underway. The war was still not over, and nor was his absence from the sport he loved.

His patience would finally be rewarded in February when a doctor gave the all-clear to resume light training. The swelling on his legs had gone and he felt ready to run again. From gentle beginnings things progressed well and within a couple of weeks he could circle his training track at 4:25-per-mile pace. This was, he declared with typical understatement, "All rather encouraging." The comeback was on.

All he needed now was for this wretched war to conclude, a quick demob from the Army and maybe a summer just like the old days could be around the corner? It was wishful thinking, but the indications were promising: From his bunker, Hitler's new year message was poorly received by his own people, some suggesting it had been pre-recorded or even faked. Berlin suffered more devastating bomb attacks and it looked as if the game was nearly up.

While Sydney slowly and quietly regained fitness, one of the main protagonists in miling's new world order – 26-year-old Gunder Hagg from Sweden's northern forests – stopped off in London en route to an eight-week tour to compete in the USA indoor season. Hagg did some training in Hyde Park, and told reporters he was certain the four-minute mile barrier would be beaten in the very near future, modestly hinting his friend and compatriot Arne Andersson might be the man to do it. There was no mention of poor Sydney.

Early in April Sydney felt ready to emerge from his personal wilderness and make a public return to competitive running. He chose an event organised largely by Joe Binks of the *News of the World*, a 12-mile relay at Mitcham in SE London. Ten months had passed since his last race, by far his longest period away from the sport since boyhood. Representing the REME he tackled a stage of around three miles and passed the baton on after a very pleasing time of 14:11. His brother Stanley's RAOC team won the event, but for Sydney the day had been a huge personal success. Suitably encouraged, a week later on Saturday 14 April, he ran another road relay leg – this one 2.5 miles of a 12.5-mile event staged by Worthing and District Harriers from Sompting, on the edge of the seaside town. Sydney recorded 13:45, which was 16 seconds quicker than any other runner on the day. REME were beaten by Eastleigh, but Sydney was called forward to receive a medal for fastest clocking. George Hogsflesh, who'd been working as an AAA caretaker-manager through the war years, then invited him to present the remaining prizes.

Unable to get to club nights due to Army duties in Hampshire, Sydney wrote to Blackheath Harriers during April to update them on his good progress. He reported being fit again and finding he could now do plenty of training without adverse effects – adding the news that brother Stanley, also a Heathen of course, had received a commission and was now serving in the Far East.

April was a pivotal month in many respects, for events in Europe now signalled the war really was ending. Hundreds of thousands of German prisoners were taken on the Western Front, Mussolini was executed, German forces surrendered in Italy, and the month ended with Hitler reportedly committing suicide in Berlin. A week or so later followed the inevitable formal and unconditional surrender of all German forces. Victory Europe (VE) Day was marked by mass celebrations throughout the western world on Monday 8 May.

There was, of course, no prospect of Sydney being able to leave the Army immediately and years of general austerity would continue in Britain well beyond the end of the war. However, the sporting world could begin to get back on its feet and athletics administrators were already making efforts to reinstate championship and international fixtures for later that summer.

As far as Sydney was concerned the next red letter day would be Saturday 23 June when an AAA regional challenge match between Midlands and South would take place at Rugby – his chance to return to track racing and test himself again over a mile.

Excellent weather greeted the big day, which incorporated a Hospital Sports event on the impressive sportsfields owned by engineering company British Thomson-Houston (later GEC) on Hillmorton Road on the eastern edge of Rugby. Sydney's presence helped swell the crowd to a bumper 5,500. There must have been pre-race nerves after so long away, but Sydney looked unruffled as he led the mile from the start. He was only seriously challenged once, when Sgt. L. G. Brown (Midlands) got close at the beginning of the third lap. This had the crowd roaring, but the famous corporal ran away from the lesser-known sergeant to win by at least 20 yards in a highly satisfactory 4:20.8. Midlands won the team prize by a narrow margin after nine events.

A short walk away from the BTH sportsground was Rugby School, and it is said Sydney's race was watched by teenage pupil Christopher Brasher, who was so captivated by what he saw that his life was never quite the same again. According to Brasher's biographer John Bryant, the sporty young men of Rugby were visited by luminaries from many different walks of life, but the only one to make a real impression on Brasher was Sydney Wooderson. Bryant describes how Brasher was fascinated by how Sydney looked more like a man who had been mugged for his ration book than an elite runner:

> "Brasher took one look at the puny figure, his hair Brylcreemed back, his short-sighted eyes peering through thick horn-rimmed wire glasses, and declared: 'If he can be a champion, so can I.'"

Brasher would never look back, going on to win Olympic gold, and becoming a high achiever in sports journalism and business, and founding father of the London Marathon.

A further four weeks of good training for Sydney culminated with an appearance at the Army athletics championships at Aldershot on Saturday 21 July, before which he confidently predicted he was ready to run 4:15. He then proceeded to smash the old Army mile record by almost ten seconds, clocking 4:14.8. It was achieved despite a stiff wind blowing across the Queen's Road stadium, and having to run virtually solo most of the race, all 15 opponents trailing way back from the end of lap one. His nearest challenger was Jimmy Fleming, second by a massive 16-second margin. Speculation that Sydney would soon be ready to confront the flying schoolmaster from Stockholm, Arne Andersson, was confirmed this weekend: the two would meet at White City on August Bank Holiday in 16 days' time. A duel between these recent world record holders was a mouth-watering prospect.

Before then Sydney had adequate time to tackle two more tests over a mile, the first on Saturday 28 July at the Bristol's Own Fund Sports on the Aero Engines Ground in Kingswood. In an invitation scratch contest for the Bristol Mile Trophy he romped to an easy win in 4:19.6, never seriously threatened and leading for almost the entire race. It resembled a time-trial. Afterwards Sydney said he felt extremely fit but hadn't enjoyed the track, which was six-laps-to-the-mile:

> "I am behind on my training as I didn't really start racing until June but I think I shall improve. I aimed today at 4.18 to 4.20 and think I could have done better."

The following Wednesday Sydney made it three out of three, winning the mile at the 2nd Group Anti-Aircraft Command athletics meeting at Southampton. In stormy, humid weather on a grass track, he cruised home comfortably in 4:24.0, a good 70 yards clear of runner-up Jimmy Fleming. He decided that was enough racing prior to White City and wrote to Bill Struth in Glasgow explaining that because he needed to be in best possible shape to face Arne Andersson he would miss the Rangers' Sports at Ibrox scheduled for 48 hours earlier. This meant the hot Bank Holiday weekend of August 4–6 was clear for him to prepare quietly for the race on the Monday afternoon.

And what a holiday weekend it turned out to be.

As historian David Kynaston points out, the pleasures of peacetime returned to Britain with a vengeance that weekend: There were record numbers of sun-seekers on trains to Blackpool, BBC's new 'Light' service took over from wartime programming, and people swarmed to sports grounds and other entertainments in tens of thousands. On the Monday 30,000-plus descended on London Zoo and a short walk away 10,000 were turned back from a sold-out Lord's cricket ground before the fourth Victory Test against Australia. Even these scenes were superseded at the White City where 52,000 managed to squeeze in to see Sydney versus Arne (thanks in part to a gate collapsing), with an estimated 20,000-plus being turned away. The Stadium had hosted some big occasions before the war, but had never witnessed mayhem and excitement on this scale. Many who failed to get inside would have to dash home and make do with the BBC radio commentary of Harold Abrahams.

Arne Andersson and Gunder Hagg had arrived earlier by plane at Croydon – the latter rather disappointingly opting to avoid Sydney by entering the two-mile race. His first words at the airport: "Too hot. I shall do nothing but rest till [my] race on Monday." Andersson was also reticent: "All I want [now] is a quiet stroll in the country." The papers were full of talk of records and even the possibility of a four-minute mile. Asked about the chances of a super-fast time in his duel with Sydney, Andersson said everything depended on the condition of the track. Bill Oakley, senior groundsman at White City, reckoned it was in fine order and there was no faster track in England, but he sagely played down talk of a four-minute mile.

This was the biggest athletics occasion in Britain for six years and work had been underway on the track for three weeks, involving much rolling and repairing, but the groundstaff were unable to get hold of some of the materials needed to make it near-perfect, owing to the war shortages. Wise old heads like Joe Binks and Harold Abrahams agreed records were unlikely on this surface, the latter predicting a 4:05 winning time. Andersson and Hagg grabbed the opportunity to inspect the track and declared it was "A little too hard in some places, and a little too loose in others."

People started queuing outside the Stadium at breakfast time. Interest in Sydney's duel was unprecedented, and even *The Times* was prompted to investigate the reasons for the 'magic' surrounding this and other big mile races:

> "Of all races [the mile] seems to us to have the most essentially classic quality. Before every great battle on the track there comes a breathless hush of waiting – ominous, delicious, insupportable; but at the shorter distances once the pistol has cracked, everything is soon over and the onlooker has barely time to savour the joyous anguish

> he is suffering. The four laps of a mile give him space to breathe, to alternate between hope and despair, to luxuriate consciously in his own feelings. The first two laps are by comparison a thrilling 'mark time' with the third the cumulative excitement rises almost to fever heat, and the last is one long misery until, if he be lucky he can murmur 'he's got him' and sink back in huddled relief."

As journalist and author David Thurlow points out, on paper Sydney-versus-Arne seemed an ill-made match, with Sydney's PB set eight years before and some five seconds slower than the Swede had recently run. Andersson was a picture of health and physical fitness after six years of good living in his neutral homeland and hard racing against compatriot Hagg. The pair between them had been able to bring the world mile record tumbling down by five seconds. Andersson had recently underlined his form by clocking 2:22.7 for 1,000 metres. Sydney on the other hand looked exactly what he was: a 30-year-old soldier who'd survived on sub-standard food for six years and was not long out of his sick bed. It really was David and Goliath stuff.

The day's programme featured battles between men representing the AAA, Army, RAF and US Forces, but most of the huge crowd only had eyes for Sydney and Arne in the mile at 3.20pm. When it arrived the air was thick with tension.

Nine men were spread across the start-line. Sydney and the Swede stood in the centre side by side, Andersson the tallest and most athletic-looking of the entire field. He was literally head and shoulders above the little figure of Sydney, whose slight frame was exaggerated by the baggy shorts and dark shoes that looked from a bygone era compared to the slick white footwear of his opponent. Sydney had swapped his black club kit for the all-white of the Army, but the crowd had no problem picking him out.

Starter Fred Hulford's pistol sent them on their way. The usual jostling took place before they settled and after half-a-lap Andersson's big powerful stride took him to the front. Sydney was dwarfed as he trailed behind the Swede, who completed the first circuit in 60.8. Positions remained unchanged and they went through halfway in 1:03.1 having opened a substantial gap on the other seven men. The pace was strong but both men looked to have something left, which was great news for those who'd worried about Sydney's readiness for this day. The third lap was a little slower (65) and the tension mounted as the two contrasting figures remained close together but clearly gathering themselves for the climax. Photos in the next day's press would show Sydney clinging on fiercely as they rounded a bend together, looking half the size of his opponent, whose long powerful legs seemed to start at Sydney's armpit level.

Around 50 yards before the bell the little man sensationally surged ahead and started the final lap three yards to the good, the clock showing 3:08. It was a courageous and surprising move, but had he made it too soon? Not for the first time, this type of sudden spurt would have the sportswriters questioning the wisdom of his tactics. It was probably the sight of Andersson looking over his shoulder and slightly losing rhythm that prompted Sydney to react as he did. The 52,000 crowd loved it, however, and were in absolute uproar.

If Andersson had under-estimated Sydney's capabilities this would have been his wake-up call. On they went, positions unchanged as they hit the home straight. But Andersson was not panicking and he dug in when it became clear Sydney didn't possess another kick, looking to be at maximum effort and tiring. The Swede duly strode by to win by just a couple of strides in 4:08.8. It was a defeat, but Sydney went down with honours. His time of 4:09.2 was his fastest since the Inter-Counties race of 1939 when he'd been at his peak, and it was an astonishing performance given the intervening circumstances. On a track that was loose in places and not fast, plus a troublesome wind, it had been the second-fastest mile ever run in Britain, only beaten by Sydney's carefully-paced world record at Motspur Park eight years earlier. The RAF's Jim Alford worked hard to come in third, but finished a distant 4:19.2.

Bevil Rudd, an expert 'insider' writing for the *Daily Telegraph* marvelled at the scenes:

> "It was the most honourable of the few defeats our champion has suffered... He matched Andersson all the way with terrier tenacity and sublime courage and confidence but he had not quite the youth and physique to cover the Swede's ferocious burst over that last 100 yards."

Although the overwhelming verdict was that Sydney had run a marvellous and courageous race, Joe Binks would put forward the theory Sydney may have spoiled his chance of actually winning by "delivering his challenge too soon". In the *News of the World*, Binks argued:

> "Before the event our great little champion had agreed with my suggestion that he should trail the giant Swede until 300 yards from home and then turn on his finishing burst which had always proved successful and which he could sustain to the tape without falter. But things didn't turn out that way… About 50 yards before the end of the third lap Wooderson caused the great crowd to yell frantically when he sprinted past the Swede. It was a big shock to me. Our champion, however, bowled along in his usual devastating style on the back stretch and for a time I noticed Andersson swaying a little. Yes, the Swede was being pushed to his utmost to hold his little opponent… then, as I feared, strength began to tell, the long-striding burly Swede grinding his teeth and shaking his blond mane, literally forced himself to the front by sheer power."

Binks said most of the 'old-timers' agreed that Sydney made his final burst too soon. He could never have outstayed such a formidable opponent by hitting top gear 500 yards from the post:

> "Sydney explained to me after the race that he felt well and decided to take the lead when he did in an effort to slacken Andersson off. He believed that if he had waited any longer Andersson would beat him more easily."

Hagg, meanwhile, lowered the GB allcomers two-mile record by finishing alone in 9:06 and the day ended in a very narrow win for the USA Forces, just a point ahead of the Army.

Athletics icon Sir Roger Bannister would later reflect on Sydney's performance in this race as the moment he was inspired to become a miler. Bannister was a 15-year-old schoolboy watching wide-eyed up in the stands alongside his father and the sight of little Sydney bravely going for victory left an indelible impression. He recalled how he'd earlier emerged from White City underground station into a huge milling crowd and suffered the crushing disappointment of being told to turn back because the stadium was full. Suddenly a barrier collapsed, along with a police cordon, and people – Bannister and his father included – flooded into the packed stadium. Sir Roger would confess:

> "I wouldn't say I broke down the gates personally, but I gave a shove behind the people who were breaking the fence and we just managed to get in and found a little corner at the back of the Stadium. When Sydney hit the front on lap three the stadium was filled with a roar such as I had never heard before. The drama of this confrontation crystallised my sporting ambitions. I resolved then to become a miler. As boys we all have our sports heroes, and Wooderson from that day became mine."

In subsequent years others would echo Bannister's sentiments and name this as the race that inspired a lifetime's devotion to athletics – accomplished authors and historians Peter Lovesey and David Thurlow among them.

As if all this wasn't enough drama for one day for the people of Britain, news bulletins suddenly began issuing startling announcements that evening indicating an atomic bomb had been produced by Allied scientists and one had already been dropped "On a Japanese army base" which subsequently turned out to be the city of Hiroshima.

★ ★ ★

Eight days after Sydney's White City heroics, events in Japan culminated in VJ Day, the point at which the war was widely seen as officially over – even though Japan's formal surrender would come three weeks later.

Among the frenzy of celebration and chatter of that day it was reported that the 'Desert Rats' of the Seventh British Armoured Division were planning to stage a 'mini Olympics' at the Olympic stadium in Berlin later in the month – and they wanted Sydney Wooderson and Arne Andersson to race each other as the big feature of the event. The huge *Olympiastadion* had suffered little serious damage in the bitter fighting for the Reich capital and the authorities were urged to formally invite Sydney and Arne to take part in this 'Victory Sports'. Asked about this, Sydney told a reporter:

> "All I know is what I read in the papers. Yes, I want to go all right. What would you do? [gestures in frustration at his Army uniform]. I

ran the mile on the Berlin track before the war. It's a lovely stadium, built up around the arena so that no wind reaches the track at all."

He added that he would be likely to get time off for such a venture, but would have to continue training in his spare time, as his Army regime involved only PTI and precious little running. Speaking uncharacteristically candidly, he went on to reveal how a reliable source had told him he could be out of the Army by the end of September, although this wasn't yet official. As it would turn out, the plans for a Berlin mini-Olympics died a death, and Sydney's September demob also proved a non-starter.

However, there was plenty more athletics action for him to look forward to in 1945, and August featured an untroubled 4:26 victory in the mile at the midweek Anti-Aircraft Command Championships at Sudbury Hill in Middlesex. This was little more than a stretching of the legs just three days after the White City race, and two half-mile races later in the month would provide a more serious test.

On Saturday 18 August an invitation half-mile at Worthing football ground in Woodside Road was attended by more than 5,000 – and Sydney delighted promoter Billy Hughes by winning in 1:58.4, quicker than he'd expected on grass. A week later on a better track he improved to 1:56.2 when representing the AAA against the RAF at Somerset Police's sportsground in Taunton. Another 5,000 crowd turned out, with sprinter Macdonald Bailey an added attraction. After a first lap of 55.2 seconds Sydney shook off all opposition and won with ease. Funds were raised for the RAF Benevolent Fund and prizes were handed over by local MP Victor Collins. The *Taunton Courier* marvelled at the power of attraction Sydney could command, referring to the fact a meeting planned for Manchester that day was cancelled purely because Sydney had already agreed to run in Somerset.

The end of hostilities in Europe prompted enthusiastic overtures by liberated France to resume the athletics challenge matches with Britain that had been so popular before the war. The British were only too happy to oblige. Team manager Jack Crump recalled that the AAA had been pressed by Government sources to lose no time in fixing such a match. However, getting a team to the Colombes Stadium in Paris for Sunday 2 September proved somewhat tricky. Bridges were down, communications difficult and air travel not possible. Wrote Crump:

"Nor could we secure railway accommodation for the whole team to travel together. We took some rations with us – eggs, tinned milk, tea and biscuits – for food was still a great difficulty in France at that time. We were given a tremendous welcome by the French public and a terrific hiding by their team. We had similar difficulties getting back to London and it was certainly the most unforgettable and most fatiguing international match journey any British team had ever experienced."

Sydney and about half the team arrived in Paris at five in the morning on the Saturday, following exhausting journeys by boat and train. They immediately went to bed and later did some gentle loosening up exercises before being guests of Racing Club de Paris in the evening. The transport difficulties meant Doug Wilson and the rest of the party arrived on the Sunday morning.

That same day Imperial Japan signed formal documents of surrender to make this the 'official' end of World War II – and how nicely this welcome milestone in history was marked by Corporal Wooderson of the REME: He romped to a stunning 1500 metres victory in 3:48.9, a French allcomers record and Britain's solitary success in the day's 12 events.

It was the 15th international between the two nations, the first since 1939, but if ever a result did not matter, this was the occasion. Sydney's personal triumph came despite fairly heavy traffic and a stiff wind, beating Jules Ladoumegue's 15-year-old French record by just three-tenths of a second. Andre Wartelle had made the early pace, followed by France's new wonder boy Marcel Hansenne, but Sydney took the lead on the third lap, and had a tough time fighting off Hansenne to win by two yards.

Paris would prove to be Sydney's very last mile or 1500 race in ten GB international matches of this sort spanning the ten years since 1935, and he'd achieved victory in the lot – a perfect ten out of ten. He was now 31, didn't have too much time left at top level, and it seemed to make sense to now confirm his earlier hints that he would move up to longer track distances in his final two or three seasons in the sport. With that decision taken, and his running now firmly back in the groove, all he craved now was a quick exit from the Army and a full return to normal life.

But, to his dismay, hints about a September release proved to be false and the prospect loomed of more weeks, perhaps months, in uniform.

Britain did not completely demobilise in 1945, and release class was generally determined by length of service and age. Releases had begun in June 1945, and the last of the wartime conscripts wouldn't exit until 1949. Urgently-needed men – particularly those in the building trades – were able to return to Civvy Street quite promptly, but the likes of Sydney would have to bide their time.

In the meanwhile, he had to focus his mind on a re-match with Andersson in Gothenburg, which was hastily fixed up for Saturday 9 September, just a week after Paris. In return for Sweden having sent their stars to White City in August, the AAA agreed that Sydney and sprinter Cyril Holmes could appear in Gothenburg at short notice. Sydney had a chat with Jack Crump and assured him that after recent events he believed he had an outside chance of upsetting Andersson and Hagg. There was precious little time to prepare, but Sydney was unfazed and welcomed the challenge. Andersson and his Swedish stablemates welcomed it too, and the public certainly did. It promised to be a cracking spectacle.

36

Cheered Through Swedish Streets

AFTER the debacle of the tortuous journey to Paris, the small AAA party travelling to Gothenburg a week later were pleased to be able to secure a handful of seats on a military plane. But there was mild panic ahead of departure when it emerged their Swedish hosts were expecting Sydney to race over 1,000 metres, and not at his favoured mile distance.

Sydney quickly put his foot down and a message was relayed insisting that if his race wasn't over four laps as he'd anticipated, then he wouldn't be coming. The matter was quickly sorted, the Swedes explaining it was all a misunderstanding and their 1,000 metres invitation had been intended for Frenchman Michel Hansenne and not Sydney.

For all his heroics and records of the past, Sydney was very much the underdog as he flew in from London on the day before the race. He was greeted on arrival with the news that Gunder Hagg wouldn't be running the mile, but the showdown with Arne Andersson was still on. Sydney would be attacking the giant in his own lair.

After their four-hour flight, the small visiting party took a stroll around Gothenburg and were wide-eyed at the shop windows filled with the sort of fruit and confectionery not seen back home for years due to rationing. It was like another world, recalled Jack Crump. A senior army officer commandeered a Mercedes Benz to take the Brits to the Slottsskogsvallen stadium and with the vehicle being open-topped, Sydney was recognised and given a great welcome as they drove through city streets. The forthcoming race had created enormous interest and was being billed as an attempt on the world record. There was even a special technical team at the ground to broadcast live radio commentary to British troops stationed across Scandinavia.

Crump, who reckoned he was the only man alive to have seen all of Sydney's major mile races, said the track was in superb condition compared to those in Britain, even though Sweden had suffered wet weather during recent weeks. During the final few hours before the race, Sydney confided in Crump he would aim for 59 seconds on lap one and 60 for the second. When Crump let out a surprised whistle and frowned, Sydney's response was simple: "I'll need to do that to win." Asked about his intentions on the third lap he quietly said he would have to see how it went!

Sydney received a huge ovation from the 12,000 crowd as he stepped on the track wearing No.1 on his white GB vest with the traditional two hoops of blue and red, and once again looked positively frail in his flapping white shorts alongside the tall Andersson in his modern kit. All Sydney's opponents were Swedish, the others Rune Persson, Rune Gustafsson and pacemaker John Ilberg. It meant three of the world's four fastest milers during wartime were up against him – only Hagg was missing.

There was a terrific rush from the gun and Sydney, as often happened, took a buffeting in the inside lane and found himself in fourth place once things settled down. He made early efforts to improve on this and avoid getting boxed in, and visibly winced when taking a spike to the right leg. Sheer determination got him into third place by the end of the first lap, but the pace was hot. Ilberg clocked 58.4 seconds at 440 yards, Andersson on his shoulder and Sydney next in 59 dead. Crump admitted later to continuing astonishment at how Sydney could hit his pre-race predictions so accurately, time after time. There was no visible slowing on lap two and they reached halfway in the same order: Ilberg leading in 1:59.6, his pacemaking job now done, Andersson on 2:00.1 and Sydney 2:00.5. Crump clearly recalled thinking at that moment that the four-minute mile could be about to happen.

Ilberg dropped out and the two main protagonists hit the front to an almighty din from the crowd. They continued on at four-minute-mile pace, faster than Sydney had ever experienced at this stage of a race. But he was right behind Andersson and seemingly quite unperturbed. He was still there at the bell which Andersson hit at 3:02.8 just two-tenths of a second ahead. It was so absorbing nobody dared blink let alone look back at the rest of the field. Sydney would not be shaken off and stuck doggedly to the big man as they swept round the penultimate bend. Then, with just 200 yards left, suddenly and sensationally, Sydney found an extra gear from somewhere and went past his man.

Officials had erected equipment at the 1500 metres mark in addition to the mile finish-line, and as Sydney flew past them and broke the first of the two finish tapes, he was recorded at 3:48.4, the fastest-ever 1500 by a Briton. With only the home straight left, there was still little to separate them and Andersson seemed to be summoning up all reserves of strength and youth to hang on. With 50 yards left Sydney was still ahead but the extra kick he now needed simply wasn't there. Andersson, looking desperate, hauled himself level and they were neck and neck for some yards, the Swede's flailing left elbow suddenly appearing to strike Sydney. The crowd gasped as the smaller man checked slightly but recovered, and remained in the race for the line. Andersson, looking anything but a picture of grace and power, clattered over the line. Sheer strength had won the day after one hell of a battle. His time was given as 4:03.4 and Sydney finished less than a second behind, no more than three yards, in 4:04.2.

Sydney's last lap of 61.2 seconds had not been quite enough for victory but gave him a personal best and the fourth fastest mile of all time. He'd come so close to victory against all odds, and if ever there was a 'heroic failure' this was it. The other times were academic, but for the record Gustafsson took third in 4:05.8 and Persson 4:10.0.

The bumping near the end never became a major talking point as it had looked accidental and Sydney was not too badly hampered. But, just like at Princeton, for a split second it had appeared serious and there was again the sight of Sydney's arm seemingly flying up in retaliation, or maybe for protection. Inevitably he was asked about it and Reuters reported his diplomatic answer: "Andersson left me plenty of room as he passed me. I only threw out my arm to warn him to be careful."

Crump was not so dismissive however. He would say later that Andersson's desperate effort to pass had seen his left arm catch Sydney and it "Flung him half round and almost stopped him in his tracks." He agreed it was accidental but firmly believed it cost Sydney any chance of victory. He pointed out that the capacity crowd sympathised with the visitor, some of them booing their own man Andersson, who seemed quite upset about the incident.

Sydney's performance exhausted watching colleague Holmes so much the sprinter said he had no energy left for his own 100 metres final later on. And Crump had been so excited he hadn't stopped his watch properly and was "left trembling for the next half-an-hour." He had never witnessed a pluckier race or a more glorious failure, he said.

Sydney knew this was likely to be the final serious mile race of his career, the distance at which he'd once ruled the world. But he seemed to quickly and happily accept that the disappointment of ending on a losing note was more than compensated for by having run a brave and stunning lifetime best. He would never forget the stunning level of support from this knowledgeable and committed home crowd, the best he'd experienced outside his homeland.

A special consolation prize was arranged for him, a sailing ship made of glass with his name engraved upon it. Returning to his hotel in the open-topped Mercedes, he was cheered through the streets like a hero on a victory parade. There would be another ecstatic reception the following evening, at a meeting in the town of Uddevella, 40 miles to the north, where he ran a gentle exhibition lap to protect sore heels, shyly acknowledging the cheers as he went.

Gothenburg had, arguably, been his greatest performance on a track and represented a marvellous way to end his years as a miler. He could look back over a career during which he'd run the elite time of sub-4.15 at least 24 times – a far superior tally to any contemporary and which underlined how the war had surely deprived him of the Olympic title he deserved. His 4:04.2 took him to the top of the all-time GB mile rankings where he would stay for nearly eight years, until deposed by Roger Bannister's 4:03.6 at Oxford. It would keep him in the all-time British top ten for 13 years.

Around two years later, Sydney would reflect on Gothenburg in an interview with the journalist and author A. V. Selwood:

> "Gothenburg was my greatest ever race – the mile I will never forget. It proved to me that the Army, illness and rationed food hadn't crippled me as a runner. Andersson tempted me to have a go before I should, and then, in a wonderful sprint left me two-and-a-half yards behind him at the finish. I'd looked forward to Gothenburg tremendously. It would be my return match. It would help resolve the doubt that persisted at the back of my

mind – are you finished with first-class running? A suddenly-understanding Army had given me a week's leave in order to get tuned up. Gothenburg's track is better than anything we have in Britain – it is smooth and fast, set in beautiful surroundings. As I sat down to an early supper – an austerity one, for I was afraid a sudden invasion of Swedish food would have a bad effect on my stomach – I considered my plan of campaign.

"From my previous experience I knew that Andersson was a strong runner and thought the best way to rob him of his deadly last-minute sprint was to start fast and keep fast... [as] we came into the final straight the crowd were cheering, giving us an amazing ovation. I kept on – then from the corner of my eye I saw the arms and shoulders of the Swede pull level, working furiously to get more speed, moving like pistons as he struggled for a last sprint. I remember thinking: Will I do it? And abstractly pondering on the huge size and amazing strength of Andersson. We were side by side. The tape stretched just ahead, then those arms and shoulders surged just a little more forward. We crashed through the tape – Andersson was ahead of me, he had beaten me again this time by two-fifths of a second [sic]. But as we shook hands and as the spectators crowded round I realised that despite my disappointment at not winning, my doubts were resolved. I had made the mile in 4:04.2 against the time when I won the world record with 4:06.4 at Motspur Park."

There was plenty of post-race soreness around his 31-year-old body after Gothenburg and he would steer clear of any more serious competition for the rest of 1945. Scheduled races at Epsom and Liverpool continued to be publicised in the press, but Sydney cried off both due to a nagging achilles strain, although did make a 'meet and greet' appearance at the former, not wanting to let them down entirely.

★ ★ ★

The autumn of 1945 saw Blackheath Harriers stage their first annual meeting since the end of the war. Sydney was elected vice-president and the club put on record its admiration of his efforts against Andersson, stating they were proud to have in their midst a champion who transcended mere athletics and had become a much-loved figure beyond the realms of sport. Sydney's place in the *zeitgeist* around now would be endorsed by author Richard Holt in his definitive social history *Sport and the British*, when he wrote: "The small, thin, dowdy, bespectacled man in Blackheath's all-black strip represented the courage and endurance that had defeated Hitler's armies." The general affection for Sydney had never been more prevalent – and his image as a brave and tenacious little underdog was even acknowledged within Royal circles, as we shall see later.

Shortly before Christmas 1945, Sydney was informed he would be released from the Army a few weeks into the new year. It meant he could look forward to resuming the more predictable weekly routine of his legal career in the city, and plan properly his training for longer distances such as three miles and five kilometres. Although they still kept in touch, he and coach Albert Hill nowadays saw less of each other than in pre-War days and Sydney would embark on this new phase of his career as a largely self-coached athlete. The intervention of war had seen Hill lose regular involvement with various aspects of London athletics, and once hostilities ended there was little sign of this being reversed. The man who Sydney called "a guide, philosopher and friend" would soon emigrate to Canada to join family members running a market gardening business.

The sporting press was fascinated by Sydney's decision to push on with his career and tackle longer distances. With his famous fast finishing ability, his patience, and his success at strength-sapping cross-country, many reckoned he would take to three-mile track running like a duck to water. One of his many admirers in the Fourth Estate was an entrepreneurial 36-year-old called Jimmy Green who, operating from a bungalow in Kent, took the bold step in 1945 of launching a monthly athletics magazine. Called simply *Athletics*, it proved highly popular and within a few years was re-branded as *Athletics Weekly*, and is still thriving more than 70 years later. An early edition gave a good basic description of Sydney's unusual running style:

> "Running very upright with a high arm action, proves great feats of speed and endurance are possible with a slight frame and stature. He's no stylist but his style suits his physique. Tremendous leg

> drive. A retiring disposition, could be described as the elusive scarlet pimpernel of the track!"

As Britain slowly and painfully recovered in the immediate post-war months, Sydney likewise adopted a circumspect attitude, making a quiet comeback to racing in a low-key cross-country in mid-December 1945. This five-miler from Hayes saw Blackheath take on Herne Hill Harriers and the Met Police. The latter arrived with only four men so combined forces with HHH. Equal first in 29:16 were Tommy Rowe, the Canadian George Norman, and guest runner Lawson, all wearing HHH colours. Sydney finished 37 seconds later in equal sixth alongside clubmate George Wilkinson, content to take things easy on this sociable occasion.

Sydney and club colleagues were keen to enjoy the special atmosphere surrounding this first post-war Christmas. They responded in good numbers to the club's invitation to a Christmas party which urged them:

> "Bring your wife or your girlfriend (both if you like)… there will be dancing to Don Reedo's Dizzy Fingers and other frivolous entertainments and a bar to lean on."

It was a big success, the clubhouse vibrating for hours with post-war shenanigans. Six years of war was over, and although a significant number of pals had been lost in action and Britain was still in the iron grip of austerity, Blackheath Harriers demonstrated that their club was alive and kicking.

37

A Roar Heard Across London

IN COMMON with thousands of other British servicemen, Sydney Wooderson wasn't able to return to civilian life until long after the war ended. His demob took place in mid-February 1946, some nine months after hostilities in Europe had ceased.

As a 31-year-old bachelor, he emerged from the Army to return to home life with mum Nettie, by now aged 71 and a widow for the best part of 18 months. Sydney found himself attempting a return to normality in a world where post-war austerity was hitting harder than expected. There was even a housewives' revolt when the Government announced cuts in bacon, poultry and egg rations. Things failed to improve during early 1946 and rationing of bread soon followed.

Day-to-day existence was tough, and many people looked to sport to bring some colour to their lives. League football would be welcomed back in 1946 by huge attendances, but before that was a summer of athletics and cricket to look forward to. The new magazine *Athletics* ran an editorial in which it relished the prospect of "Record-breaking performances by Sydney Wooderson at longer distances."

Meanwhile, an article by Jack Crump in *Look and Learn,* a newspaper for children, confirmed that Sydney was treating summer 1946 as his final track season, partly because of age, injury and illness, but also because he needed to concentrate on his career and not have the constant problem of needing time off for training and racing. Sydney was nothing if not sensible and pragmatic. Crump's article called him the finest runner Britain had ever produced – truly a Blackheath Harrier "with a frail body and the heart of a lion."

Sydney knew that before embarking on serious three-milers on the track he must boost his stamina levels and that meant some cross-country and road-work in the opening months of 1946. A mob match between Blackheath and South London Harriers in January saw him finish a solid eighth, covering the gruelling 7.5 miles in 50:40, the race won impressively by teammate Humphrey Nunns. Then came his final race as a serving soldier, in which he unsurprisingly won the midweek AA Command cross-country championships on the edge of Epping Forest at Chingford. The cross-country season would culminate later on with an enjoyable club run, Sydney was one of 24 Heathens tackling a 12-mile route over West Wickham territory untrod by most of them since the start of the war. It was followed by supper, music and billiards in the clubhouse.

The club was by now back to pre-war normality with a busy calendar of training, racing and social events. It was in good shape and membership at a healthy level, soon to exceed 800, a figure which included life members. To underline their pride in the exploits of their most famous member, and mark the occasion of his fastest mile the previous year, they presented Sydney with a testimonial in the form of an illuminated address in scroll form. A large gathering marvelled at this beautifully executed item on vellum, which incorporated the club badge and motto and Sydney's initials in a border of oak leaves and acorns. The message referred not only to his mile at Gothenburg, but his conscientious training and personal character as well as service to the club since 1931. Soon after this was handed over, Sydney attended his first Bohemian Concert put on by the club, along with more than 200 colleagues at the Bridge Hotel at London Bridge. The night featured many happy reunions following the war, but there was a poignant moment when the widow of one gallant member arrived alone.

Sydney enjoyed a rare slice of competitive action on the roads in mid-April when he took on a leg of the inaugural Cambridge Harriers 20-mile invitation road relay. Nine teams tackled six legs of around 3.3 miles each, the event based at Bexley Cricket Club with the start and changeover in nearby Glenhurst Avenue. Finchley Harriers won in 1:45.30 and Blackheath were second in 1:47.17. Derek Reynolds brought in the baton on the fourth leg, handing over to Sydney who covered the circuit in 17:53, looking relaxed until sprinting the last quarter-mile in view of an enthusiastic crowd.

He lunged forward to hand over to teammate Dick Choat who shot off and maintained second place to the end. All six Blackheath men clocked between 17:37 and 18:29.

As the new track season got underway in late spring, the chatter in the sporting press turned towards the 1948 Olympic Games to be staged in London two years hence, and Sydney was talked about as the nation's big hope in the 5,000 metres. His main British rival would likely be stylist Peter Ward who was back in athletics after being inactive since 1939. All this was pure conjecture, because by now it seems Sydney had privately decided he would hang up his track shoes long before the Olympics.

To kick off his 1946 season he made the short journey on Monday evening, May 13, from home to the Roan School in Lee where Blackheath were taking on the school team. A good crowd braved surprisingly cold and windy conditions, most supporting the school. There was great delight that Sydney had agreed to come, and a huge queue of autograph hunters built up outside the changing rooms. Due to the age gap between the teams, generous starts were conceded to the schoolboys in most races and for the mile it was decided Sydney would run but not score. He took things steady and was fastest in 4:49. Afterwards everyone retired to the warmth of the pavilion for a dance organised by the school's entertainments secretary.

Things got a little more serious three days later when Blackheath's club championships at Catford Bridge saw Sydney win the two miles in 9:47.2 to lift the Morgan Cup. It was again noticeably cold for May, but a bumper crowd attended to see Sydney launch his campaign at distances over one mile. He moved up to three miles on Monday 22 May, winning in 15:33.4 as Blackheath took on Cambridge Harriers at the Charlton Park track. His final appearance of the month involved a long trek north which yielded victory in 4:28.2 in an invitation mile on Teesside at the inaugural Billingham Synthonia open meeting on Saturday 25 May.

For Sydney this summer was all about building slowly towards a handful of big races in a six-week spell at the back end of the season. These included the AAAs, a match with France at White City and the European championships in Oslo. He was also considering the idea of rounding things off for good with a 'final hurrah' at Motspur Park at the end of August. It meant working hard now to achieve optimum sharpness and fitness later – and to this end he raced no fewer than eight times during the month of June.

On the first day of the month the Kent three-mile title was duly added to his personal honours list at the Police sportsground in Maidstone despite a deluge of rain that left the track sodden and unsuited to fast times. Nevertheless Sydney's 14:59.2 was just 1.2 seconds outside the championship best and represented his first county title for nine years. On Thursday 6 June, Blackheath pulled in another big and noisy crowd when visiting Beckenham County School on a warm evening, Sydney winning a handicap mile in 4:35 narrowly from teammate Dick Choat.

On the same weekend that TV broadcasting by the BBC resumed after its wartime suspension, and a victory parade was staged in London, Sydney took part in an open two-mile team race at the Dartford Hospital Sports. Proving his running was bang on target in this important year, he came home two-fifths of a second inside his pre-race prediction of 9:35. This was followed by Friday night action on June 14, representing the AAA against a Combined Services outfit on a heavy Catford Bridge track. Sydney was quickest miler in 4:19.2. More speedwork followed the next day, Sydney clocking a sprightly 1:57.6 for 880 yards in the Kent mile medley relay for the Camden Cup. Conditions at the Charlton Park track didn't favour speed but Sydney worked hard on the opening leg to give the Blackheath quartet what would prove a winning lead (team time 3:46.3) at the Siemens sportsground.

Sydney was by now mixing up his distances and the days of running four-lap races week in and week out were long gone. On Wednesday 19 June Blackheath took on a combined South London Harriers and Met Police side at New Beckenham and in the mile Sydney won in a modest 4:38.2. Three days later he headed north for the second time this summer, accepting an invitation to run a three-mile handicap in the Rotherham Hospital Sports. He triumphed in a superb 14:32.2 from scratch, pipping Sheffield United Harriers' Wilson who had a 155-yard start and Ellis of Hallamshire Harriers who'd been given 130. Speaking afterwards, Sydney revealed he'd run to a specific schedule and had hit his target perfectly in 14:32. It was highly encouraging considering his relative lack of experience at the distance, for he'd come close to Peter Ward's British record. Among the people who sat up and took notice was the Essex Beagle Jim Peters, who realised he'd have no chance against Sydney at the AAA championships and quickly switched his plans to the six-mile race. With hindsight, that move by Peters would prove a vital stepping stone en route to his becoming the world's fastest marathon runner over the next few years.

Back in SE London, on the evening of Thursday 27 June Sydney tried his luck again at two miles, winning for Blackheath against Southgate Harriers in 9:38.0 by a huge 80-yard margin on the Catford track from visitor Edward Nankivell. There would be no let-up in his racing schedule and 48 hours later he enjoyed another easy victory in the mile, in a special AAA fixture involving members of the Services, past and present. He came home in an impressive 4:19.2 on a less-than-perfect Sudbury Hill track, nearly 100 yards clear of nearest rival Clifford Bunton of London University. He was clearly in good shape following the ups and downs of the past few years and his performances, on paper at least, appeared to be steadily improving as the weeks went by. The business of peaking around the end of July looked well on course. His careful planning included opting out of big fixtures such as the British Games, the Kinnaird Trophy meet and the Southerns, but he kept the AAA champs and Waddilove Trophy firmly in his sights.

Ten days before the AAAs at White City he set off to Ireland for the first time, part of an AAA representative side invited to Dublin for the Clonliffe Harriers Diamond Jubilee meeting. On the Trinity College grass track at College Park, Sydney captured an Irish allcomers record with a superb display, clocking 9:05 for two miles. He beat the old record by J.J. O'Connor of 11 years earlier by a huge 13.6 seconds, and it was suggested he'd also achieved a world best time for two miles on grass. His nearest challenge came from Steve McCooke in the distinctive hooped colours of East Antrim Harriers who crossed the line 14 seconds down. His 440-yard splits were reported as: 66, 72, 71, 66, 70, 67, 68 and 65.

Sydney's final run-out over three miles before the year's important races saw a 'Kent Clubs' combo take on their opposite numbers from London at Gillingham's United Services Ground. On a soft and slow track he won in a relaxed 15:01, beating Charlie Smart of Belgrave comfortably. He'd taken the lead after a mile and was never in trouble despite the relatively slow time. Apart from training spins this signalled an end to his main preparations.

It was time to focus his thoughts on White City a week hence and the exciting prospect of a first major three-mile outing. Wim Slijkhuis, a talented Dutchman, had accepted an invitation to run the race and a mouth-watering duel with Sydney was in prospect. Sydney spent the last few days beforehand quietly, venturing out to the Tooting Bec track to support his clubmates from the sidelines at a match with Herne Hill and the Met Police.

★★★

The first AAA championships since the war, after a break of seven years, generated enormous interest and the weather was warm but overcast for most of the two-day event. Sydney was again top of the bill, the supporting cast featuring stylish West Indians Emmanuel McDonald Bailey and Arthur Wint, and Nigeria-born Prince Adedayin. The centrepiece of day two, Saturday 20 July, was Sydney's bid to establish himself as a world class three-miler: he wouldn't be troubled by the ace Swedes Hagg or Andersson – recently banned for contravening the amateur code – but 23-year-old Slijkhuis was sure to be a tough nut to crack. The Dutch champion was the new name on many people's lips, even though few knew how to pronounce it.

The championships were again spiced up by plenty of foreign entrants among the 400-plus participants. There would be a new mile champion for the first time since 1934 – Sydney had taken that title on five successive occasions before the war. Now he had a brand new challenge, the British authorities making sure he had a fast race by inviting Slijkhuis, a tall, dark, bony-faced sports outfitter from Amsterdam. A time of close to 14 minutes, or maybe under it, would be needed to win – and Sydney knew his relaxed 15:01 of the previous Saturday wouldn't be anywhere near good enough. Today was the real deal and what a thriller it would prove to be.

It was a race that lit up an otherwise shambolic day at the White City; even the AAA annual report would admit afterwards the overall organisation had been "rusty" following the long break. The infield was constantly cluttered by people, the announcing was disjointed and the scheduling went badly wrong, notably when the marathon leaders entered the stadium while the steeplechase was still in progress. To cap it all, at the end of Sydney's race, the steward responsible for the finish-tape was apparently caught unprepared (a photo of the moment shows him frantically holding it up 'manually', a yard or two from where it should have been tied!). Fortunately all this chaos was overshadowed by the sheer excitement generated by the race.

Sydney, in his black kit, wore number 17, with Slijkhuis wearing 15. Sydney was drawn on the outside with the 14 other starters inside him. As they milled around waiting to be called to order, clutching little cards detailing their starting positions, Slijkhuis showed Sydney his card apparently unclear where he should stand. Sydney helpfully pointed him towards the inside of the track. They shot away fast from the gun but after half-a-mile of cat-and-mouse Slijkhuis jumped boldly into the lead and opened up a gap. Then he seemed to deliberately slow and Sydney, working to his own schedule rather than reacting to the Dutchman's antics, went smoothly past and led after four laps in 4:40.6.

Now the pace quickened, and the noise from 25,000-plus crowd increased accordingly. Sydney, with Slijkhuis working watchfully behind, passed the 1.5-mile mark in 7:00.6, then two miles in 9:23.4 and 2.5 in 10.45.4. The rest of the field were by now out of serious contention. Sydney still led as the bell sounded (mile splits: 4:40.6, 4:42.8, 4:29.8.), but Slijkhuis at last made his move on the bend with 300 yards to go and gradually began to open a gap. The crowd screamed at Sydney to respond.

Slijkhuis looked the smoother and more composed of the two, but Sydney got back to his heels. Slijkhuis looked anxiously over his shoulder hoping he'd broken the little Englishman, but was out of luck. On the final bend, timing his effort perfectly, Sydney passed as they entered the home straight, his arms pumping and his opponent had no response. The winning margin was six yards, exactly one second, and his final lap of under 60 seconds gave Sydney a wonderful British record of 13:53.3, beating the allcomers' mark by more than six seconds and the English native best by around 15 seconds. The noise from a delighted crowd in those final yards must have been heard all across West London and beyond. One Sunday paper correspondent called it the loudest he'd ever experienced at any athletics event.

Some who witnessed events during that heart-stopping last lap pondered why Sydney hadn't adopted similarly patient tactics in Gothenburg in 1945, which would surely have seen him beat the great Andersson. Such thoughts possibly passed through Sydney's mind too. The best three-mile run on British soil by Taisto Maki of Finland (13:59.4) had been blasted out of the water, and Jack Emery's English native record (14:08) completely

'Sydney went smoothly past'.

annihilated. Sydney's lap times were 69.8, 72.2, 68.4, 70.2, 69.6, 70.4, 71.0, 71.8, 70.0, 72.0, 68.6 and 59.2. The degree of control he exerted over proceedings made it one of the very best races of his career and it would win him the AAA's coveted Harvey Memorial Gold Cup as best champion of the year, and also the C N Jackson Memorial Cup, for best display at the championships. *The Times*, not normally given to hyperbole, reported: "No finer race, or at any rate duel, over the distance has ever been seen in this or perhaps any country."

Just like a year earlier, when Sydney's performance at this stadium inspired a young Roger Bannister to take athletics seriously, so today's race had a huge and lasting impact on a 15-year-old spectator called Gordon Pirie. This impressionable young man lived not far from Sydney and would later break five world records and run at three Olympic Games. Pirie's biographer Dick Booth records that during 1946 Pirie would attend the 75th anniversary dinner of South London Harriers where he would listen awe-struck to Sydney, "the best-loved runner in Britain."

Sydney's victory, followed by Doug Wilson's in the mile and Squire Yarrow's marathon triumph, came in quick succession during the afternoon, and provided perhaps the most thrilling sequence of top-class athletics ever witnessed by British fans. Yarrow strode into the stadium for the last 540 yards of his 26 miles and 385 yards matching McNab Robertson stride for stride and in a thrilling finish breasted the tape just two-tenths of a second ahead of the Scotsman.

Wilson, suffering from the after-effects of an abscess on his jaw, had looked decidedly unwell beforehand. He won a real thriller against Dutch wine merchant Frits de Ruijter, both given the same time of 4:17.4. Wilson thus became the first man, apart from Sydney, to take the AAA mile title in 12 years. Wilson would later acknowledge Sydney as undisputed king of the mile through this era, admitting he never realised his own full potential because of a tendency to over-train, which was in sharp contrast to well-organised Sydney:

> "We [sometimes] trained together and got on very well. Sydney was a very nice chap, very quiet, but very determined and I was never in his class."

Two days later the British team was announced for the forthcoming

Sydney comes in ahead of both Slijkhuis and the finish-line official!

European championships in Oslo and Sydney was named for the 5,000 metres as expected. It would be his very last track championship race and he was desperate to do well but a shade nervous too. On the rare occasion that things went wrong for Sydney it usually occurred in big races abroad. If only this was in London where his normal routines wouldn't be upset!

But before Oslo there was the small matter of the traditional annual battle with the French – this year a revenge mission following the trouncing they gave GB in 1945. It would be on the early August Bank Holiday Monday and White City would be packed for this sporting summer highlight. Sydney had two relatively low-key mile races and a two-miler on his schedule prior to White City: First up was victory at Catford Bridge on Thursday 25 July, his mile of 4:23.5 enough to win Blackheath Pash Cup, his presence swelling the crowd considerably. A lively evening concluded with a Ladies' Egg and Spoon race.

It was a good warm-up ahead of the Waddilove Trophy at Perry Barr in Birmingham less than 48 hours later. Delays on the trains meant a late arrival and a hurried journey between station and the Birchfield stadium. Sydney wasn't unduly stressed however, and won the two-miles at a canter by 100 yards in 9:35.6. The large crowd on this sunny afternoon enjoyed seeing the champion but realised it was little more than a training spin as Sydney toyed with nearest rivals Stan Cox and Bobby Reid. The hurried start was matched by a hectic climax when proceedings ended late, creating an undignified dash to catch the train home, meaning some of the team didn't have time to enjoy the fine tea laid on by the home club.

In the days that followed, Sydney tried to divorce himself from the hullabaloo surrounding the forthcoming Bank Holiday showdown with the French, and quietly toned up with a mile victory in 4:36.8 on the Thursday evening of August 1 at Catford Bridge. Meanwhile, the visitors from France were holed up in a hotel on the Surrey/London border and all was not well within their ranks. It would emerge in the French press that some of them were distinctly unhappy over their hotel and "a surprising lack of hospitality from the AAA" during this trip. Their party of 35 (including a 400 metres runner named Robert Chef d'Hotel) was apparently required to sleep in dormitory fashion in a basement that had been converted from an air-raid shelter. Their spokesman felt this accommodation did not compare well with what was provided for the British a year earlier in Paris, although he did admit the food in London hadn't been as bad as expected. The hotel manager reportedly hit back, claiming the furnishings were luxurious and the only evidence of austerity was the whitewashed walls.

Despite their unhappiness, the French reportedly "enjoyed a long lie-in" on the morning of Monday August 5, in sharp contrast to the public who wanted access to White City that day. Thousands made an early start and arrived hours before the scheduled start. Nearly 50,000 were said to have made it inside. The British weather rose to the occasion, helping to make it a day to remember in London for this first international match on British soil since the war.

The very tiny number of British homes who by now contained a TV set (less than 0.3 per cent) could watch grainy BBC footage of a number of events during the afternoon. Team manager Crump confessed the squad representing GB was rather "experimental" and one morning paper pointed out the real 'spice' surrounding this long-awaited meeting was the fact not a single event contained a certain winner – not even Sydney's race for once.

Once the pre-event parade got underway in the sunshine there was surprise and dismay that the hosts were not wearing matching tracksuits or uniforms. *Athletics* magazine criticised the AAA for this, saying it should have at least been possible to borrow a set from the Army even in these austere times. Although the British athletes were not exactly scruffy, it did seem inappropriate they were not better dressed for the occasion. Once the formalities were done and the clock ticked towards the three-mile start of 3.30pm, Sydney appeared in his all-white racing kit to big cheers, a bold No.1 pinned to the front. The opponent most likely to upset his charge for victory was seen as Raphael Puzajon, a man described by one paper as "this brown-skinned son of France", who had won the international cross-country title easily at Ayr earlier in the year and was reigning 5,000 metres champion of France.

The starter Edward Vowles, a leading Surrey official, fired his pistol and after the usual early jostling the three-mile contest was underway. Apart from quick opening and closing laps, the 12 circuits of the track would be tackled in even-paced style by a confident looking Sydney. He spent much of the race in front, with Puzajon sitting menacingly on his shoulder. They looked impregnable and Sydney's teammate Steve McCooke (East Antrim Harriers) and France's Rene Breistoffer were never really in with a shout.

Puzajon's impudence in grabbing an early lead lasted for less than three laps, Sydney taking over with minimal fuss and going through the mile in 4:39.6 and two miles in 9:23.6. With 220 yards left he kicked on and Puzajon had nothing to offer and the victory margin was a good 35 yards. Sydney recorded 13:57 and Puzajon was 5.8 seconds adrift, Breistoffer a further 28 seconds down. Sydney's lap times were reported as: 65.4, 72.6, 72.0, 69.6, 70.2, 70.6, 71.6, 71.6, 70.0, 71.0, 71.4 and 61.0.

It hadn't been quite the thriller everyone hoped for, but was heartily cheered anyway. McCooke came in a despondent last of the quartet, having endured a nightmare race due to a stitch; he'd actually quit and left the track at one point but was pushed back on by team captain Dave Grigg! Britain gained revenge for the previous year, winning by 72 points to 57, helped by Trinidad-born McDonald Bailey equalling the 23-year-old GB record of 9.7 set by Eric Liddell in the 100 yards.

By now Sydney's plans to close his track career at the end of this summer in a blaze of glory had been firmed up and made public: After bidding for the 5,000 crown at the Euros on August 23, a week later he would bow out with a world record attempt over two miles at Motspur Park. Oslo was an elite championship while Motspur Park was a mere club event, but in some ways the latter seemed more important to Sydney. Signing off by completing a hat-trick of world records at events staged by his own club had very special appeal for him, even though Oslo would involve a bigger audience and wider interest. Typically, Sydney wanted to deflect some of his personal glory to the benefit of his club.

Prior to Oslo, he agreed to run the mile when Met Police hosted a match at Imber Court against Polytechnic Harriers and Blackheath. It was a dull, cool afternoon with a fierce wind crossing the grass track, but Sydney and Doug Wilson both saw it as a nice leg-stretcher before the Europeans and chatted amiably beforehand, Sydney agreeing he'd help Wilson by dragging him to something like 4:16. They set off briskly and went through 440 yards in exactly 60 seconds, Wilson leading for a spell before Sydney passed at halfway in 2:07. Nothing changed after a 68-second third lap and after exchanging a few words and glances they agreed to finish side-by-side, clocking 4:22 in what looked like a dead heat. The officials disagreed and gave Wilson the verdict. Both runners seemed mildly annoyed at this and Sydney told reporters: "We wanted to dead-heat but apparently the judges thought otherwise." And so the result went into the record books as a rare defeat for Sydney, but perhaps it was really a case of the officials sending a message out to runners who blatantly manufactured results in this way?

It was of no real consequence as far as Sydney was concerned, for he now had far bigger fish to fry. A week later he'd be heading to Scandinavian soil for the final international appearance of a 15-year career. The IAAF's third European championships were over four days at Bislett Stadium, for the first time a combined event for both sexes. Nearly 400 athletes from 20 nations would be vying for the limelight, but all eyes – certainly all British eyes – would be on one small figure in the 5,000 metres.

38

Astonishing Scenes in Oslo

THE Great Britain track and field squad – with both Sydney Wooderson and team captain Bill Roberts making their final appearance – was given a cheery send-off by pressmen and other well-wishers at King's Cross station on the rain-lashed London morning of Saturday 17 August.

Their train to Newcastle was the first leg of a laborious journey to the IAAF European Championships in Oslo due to begin five days later. The party boarded their Norwegian Line steamer later that same day by which time the sea was smooth and weather excellent. Much of the 36 hours was spent sunbathing on deck, enjoying the type of food most had not seen in years due to rationing: "A very hearty dinner that evening was indulged in by at least one British official," Sydney would write later in his notes for Blackheath's *Gazette*, hinting at scenes of over-indulgence without actually saying so.

Just after dawn on the Monday morning the captivating scenery of Norwegian fjords could be seen up ahead. The party was joined in Oslo by press and AAA officials who had arrived earlier by plane, and then came a bus ride to rather spartan accommodation which would be home for the next week or so. It was a former German anti-aircraft station at Smestad, high in the hills outside Oslo, and Sydney described their quarters as a "three-roomed hut". It was rough, ready and not very roomy, but would prove conducive to team spirit and friendship. The athletes had to make do with uncomfortable bedding made of straw-filled pillows and straw palliasses. Poor Alan Paterson, a six-foot-plus Scottish high-jumper, complained he couldn't fit in his bunk and suffered further misery on finding no porridge was available either!

There was a large canteen on site, with separate tables for each team above which were displayed the national flags. Food was plentiful with lashings of butter and milk despite the fact Norway was struggling like Britain for fresh produce in the wake of the war. Each team was paying for its keep at the camp and the Danish were said to have paid their way by supplying eggs for everybody. Pictured soon after arrival, it was noticeable the GB team didn't have a proper uniform; although officials Jack Crump and H. S. Oliver were smart enough, the runners sported open-necked shirts and in Sydney's case a dark sleeveless sweater. After dropping off their bags the Brits headed to a nearby running track in the city's Jordal neighbourhood to loosen up, where they found other teams already doing light training.

Sydney cruised a very easy three miles that Monday afternoon and did the same the following day, deciding that was quite enough exertion prior to Friday's big race. He'd never been one to churn out pointless miles, and wasn't about to start now, however bracing the air, or interesting the surroundings. His caution was in marked contrast to half-miler Tom White who took advantage of the fast track and clocked the quickest 660 yards of his life (a few days later he would finish half-a-second short of taking gold in the 800 metres). Wednesday was treated by most Brits as a rest day and they went sight-seeing among pine-clad hills, visiting the well-known Holmenkollen ski-jump hill, and seeing some Viking ships at close quarters.

Back at the camp in the hills, an embarrassing diplomatic situation arose when a party of Russian athletes turned up unexpectedly, despite having been warned earlier they couldn't compete as they hadn't affiliated to the IAAF. Lord Burghley, leader of the IAAF, backed down and let them stay despite the rules. One sharp newspaperman pointed out: "Britannia not only rules the waves, they waive the rules!" The 23 Russians quietly settled into their part of the camp, their only special request being a sewing machine and a flat iron!

Obviously Germany was not taking part so soon after the war, but a small Italian team did attend. Norwegian organisers were said to be flabbergasted by this, and there were debates in the press over how a country that had lost the war was able to afford the luxury of air travel to sporting events, and why they'd been allowed to compete at all. There would be adverse public reaction at the opening day parade on Thursday 22 August with the Italians receiving an ice cold reception as they marched past King Haakon of Norway, the 30,000 crowd's cheers suddenly ceasing. In striking contrast was a great roar to greet the British, led out proudly by skipper Bill Roberts, the 34-year-old Salford quarter-miler. One of Sydney's clearest memories from the day was the playing of the Norwegian national anthem, which he described as "very lovely." But he wasn't so happy about the GB team's general appearance: "Ours was the only team which had not been provided with a proper outfit – even the Poles and Italians had magnificent training suits." The opening day's proceedings were witnessed by a capacity crowd with many locked out, those outside content to sit and listen to results relayed out to them on loudspeakers.

Team manager Crump admitted that Sydney's fate in the 5,000 metres was Britain's "major interest" in these games and he'd never known a team associate itself with one single athlete as intensely as this one had with Sydney. He wrote afterwards:

> "I am sure Wooderson never fully realised how much the whole team was anxious for his success, but when Heino [planning a 10,000/5,000 double] won the 10,000 quite easily the tension grew. Two days before the 5,000 Mick Mays came and reported to me that Wooderson was having trouble with an ankle and he was seriously concerned as to whether he could keep Sydney fit for the race. We agreed we would say nothing to anyone but I did speak to Sydney and asked him if he was in pain or greatly worried by his injury. To my surprise he told me he was not so much worried about the 5,000 metres for he felt he would be all right, but was worried about his [forthcoming] two-mile race at Motspur Park because it meant so much to his club."

Many people were nervous for Sydney and desperate for him to win this Oslo swansong. The source of some anxiety was the well-known cat-and-mouse tactics of the Scandinavians whereby they would gang up to make opponents run wide or at unfamiliar pace. "Wooderson's only hope of beating a possible team-up is to make the pace so hot from the pistol that his opponents will be too preoccupied to give thought to spoiling tactics," wrote W. Capel-Kirby.

The big day, Friday 23 August, dawned fine and bright and Sydney was up and about early. He recalled:

> "I had an early breakfast and short stroll into the country. Back to a light lunch and rest in the afternoon before leaving just before 5 o'clock for the stadium. I didn't feel particularly nervous, but of course rather 'strung up' [when we had to] wait on the starting line for Reiff of Belgium who arrived late."

Crump had arranged a special late meal of steamed fish on race day and sat with Sydney while he ate it – noticing for the first time since he'd known him that he was definitely nervous. He only ate half his meal, then had a short rest before being taken to the Bislett stadium. Crump was not allowed trackside to call lap times, but wrote down Sydney's planned schedule anyway and promised he would shout out times from the sidelines as best he could in the hope Sydney might hear. Their plan was based on a winning time of 14:10. Knowing Sydney's hatred of too much fuss, and his strong desire to be fit for Motspur Park eight days later, Crump and May discussed the possibility that the very pro-British Norwegians would probably grab Sydney at the end if he won, and toss him into the air in the same exuberant way they'd dealt with earlier winners. This could not be allowed to happen and they hatched a plan to get to the track to rescue him if necessary.

In the final couple of hours before the race Sydney went to considerable trouble to stay away from crowded and noisy areas, determined to stay calm and relaxed. A fascinating snapshot of these moments is captured by a translation into English of an account by Henry Eidmark, covering the event for Swedish magazine *All Sport*:

> "I left the press box and went round the small clubhouse to find a better viewpoint for the high jump which was taking place at the other end of the stadium… In the relative calm behind the great concrete stand, a solitary figure in a black track-suit lay stretched out on the grass with his hands behind his neck. A short, slightly-built gentleman in glasses, nothing spectacular about him, not

> unlike a grey mole waiting in front of his hole. I crept silently by in my rubber-soled American golf shoes, but in passing I had time to take a snapshot of the half-asleep sportsman. Because here was none other than Mr Sydney Wooderson! How could [local favourite Viljo] Heino be threatened by this weak-looking oldie? He did not sit on the sun-scorched grandstand waiting to start as the other competitors were doing, nor did he want to stay indoors in the stuffy, stale changing room, from whence the Finns Heino and Perala had just vanished. He lay there totally relaxed in the relatively refreshing shade, disturbed by no-one, collecting himself perfectly for the forthcoming battle of giants. At that moment I knew that Sydney Wooderson would be European Champion in the 5,000 metre race!"

Eidmark may have been convinced of the outcome, but Sydney himself was a bag of nerves. The field was strong, even without the banned Hagg and Andersson, for it included the likes of Slijkhuis, Reiff, Puzajon and Heino. Would they gang up on him and force a repeat of Princeton? He expected he would probably have to dictate the pace for long periods himself this time, and thought a fairly even-paced 14:10 would be good enough to win. That represented the equivalent of 13:42 for three miles, i.e. better than his own UK record earlier in the summer. It was an ambitious target but he was confident it could be achieved, particularly if Crump could help by shouting his lap times from trackside. Once he heard the level of the noise being generated by this raucous Bislett crowd, he suspected – correctly as it would turn out – that there would be little chance of hearing Crump. This was a setback rather than a disaster, and Sydney wasn't overly worried about having to trust his instincts and judgement rather than a clock.

The atmosphere was electric as they set off, Frenchman Puzajon leading after completion of the first stampede of a lap, then giving way to Heino who would remain at the front until the closing stages. Sydney kept well out of trouble early on and, as planned, appeared to be running to his own schedule and largely ignoring what was happening ahead of him. He was back in 8th place at 400 metres, improved to sixth after three and found himself fourth by halfway. By the two-mile point he was part of a four-strong leading pack detached from the rest, alongside Heino, Reiff and Slijkhuis. Heino, who went into the event under a cloud of controversy following suggestions he'd infringed the amateur code, now began to feel the effects of his 10,000 metres earlier, and Slijkhuis seized the lead. Sydney would confirm later that the crowd noise ("the most enthusiastic I've ever known") meant he heard nothing from Crump from start to finish. However, the sight of Sydney coolly and steadily working his way into a challenging position without undue chopping and changing delighted his supporters. His career might now be in its twilight days, but he'd never looked better on a major stage.

Slijkhuis continued to lead into the final lap as the bell prompted another rise in decibels from the frenzied sidelines. But Sydney had him in his sights and around 250 metres from the finish he pounced, finding another gear and passing the Dutchman in explosive fashion. He was on his way to a final lap of 59 seconds. Onlookers were stunned, including Henry Eidmark, the Swedish journalist, who wrote:

> "He shot forward suddenly in the easiest, most relaxed final rocket finish anybody could imagine. At that moment there was not a single spectator at Bislett remaining seated. Such cheering had never before been heard as the ovations that day for an athlete from abroad."

Sportswriter Norman Harris described the dramatic final stages:

> "He started sprinting into the last bend. He was running faster and faster. It was amazing after that tough pace. And faster still. Then, into the straight, he tore for the tape. His head was leaning back, his hands flashing up underneath his chin, he was rocketing. He did not spoil it by looking back or coasting. He burst through the tape."

It was a wonderful display. Sydney had annihilated a top-class field to become European champion and did it in a UK record of 14:08.6, the second-fastest of all time. Someone calculated it was equivalent to 13:42 for three miles, which, if correct, was better than his recent personal best at White City. Only Gunder Hagg had ever run faster and the Swede would be one of the first to send a congratulatory telegram. Sydney had run 14 seconds faster than the Olympic record for the distance and 23 seconds better than Peter Ward's previous GB record. Slijkhuis took the silver medal nearly six seconds behind in 14:14, and Evert Nyberg of Sweden passed the fading Heino to get bronze in 14:23.2. The Czech soldier Emil Zatopek, at this point an inexperienced 23-year-old, was fifth, 17.2 seconds adrift of Sydney.

As Sydney pulled up after bursting through the tape, Jack Crump was already pushing his way through to ensure his man had space to recover and wouldn't be mobbed. He immediately noticed from Sydney's ashen face that something was wrong: "Are you all right?" he cried out as Sydney appeared to shake his head. Crump and masseur Mick Mays leaped forward to grab him as he began to crumple to the ground. They were able to maintain some space around him, but this looked serious, for Sydney was never one for histrionics and always stayed on his feet as a rule. He lay motionless for a while on his back, concerned faces all around. Had he passed out, or merely stumbled over due to tiredness? Amid the hullaballoo it wasn't clear, but some reporters seized the moment and began filing stories suggesting the champion had run himself into oblivion and had blacked out. Before long he was back on his feet though, walking gingerly away.

Sydney would later put his own side of the story in Blackheath's *Gazette*:

> "There was lot of talk in the English papers about a black-out. I admit I was exhausted momentarily for it was the toughest race, both physically and mentally, in which I had [ever] competed, for throughout it was a battle of wits having to keep an eye on not only one but six opponents all of whom were capable of winning the race. But after a few minutes I was back to normal."

In the aftermath it was clear to Mays and Crump that Sydney had other worries: although his fragile ankle stood up brilliantly to the demands of a scorching 5,000 metres, it was stiffening and causing discomfort now the race was over. Sydney had felt it during the race, but ignored the soreness and had got away with it. But now, with thoughts turning to next week's Motspur Park finale, this fresh pain was taking a little of the gloss off today's triumph.

On radio Harold Abrahams had given the folks back home a remarkable, excited commentary and the race, it was universally agreed, had been a real classic. Sydney was widely praised for his brilliant judgement during those 14 minutes or so of action. W. Capel-Kirby called it one of the most thrilling races in the sport's history and added that near him a party of British women had slumped to their seats at the end through sheer exhaustion from cheering and screaming, tears pouring down their faces.

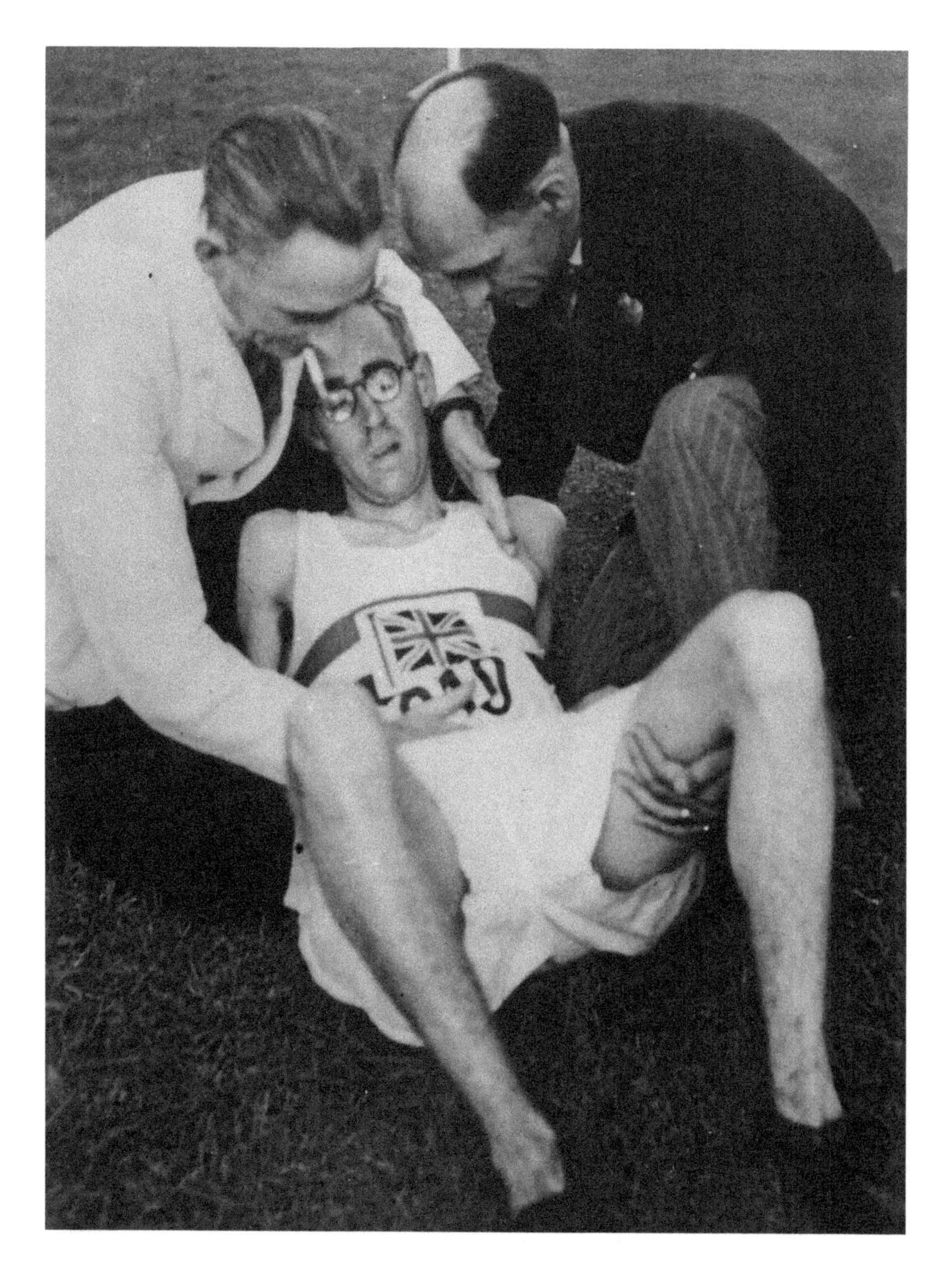

Mick Mays and Jack Crump rush to Sydney's aid.

Sydney explained how it had all been rather simple from his viewpoint:

> "If the race was slow from the start I [had] intended to get in front and make the pace. On the other hand, if it was fast I intended to keep my own pace and gradually work up to the front as the pace slowed down. This did in fact happen, which suited me. When Slijkhuis took the lead about three laps from the finish I went with him and then about 300 yards from the tape I must have felt him weakening for I decided to take the lead and go all out with a fast sustained burst. This of course worked very well, for as soon as I passed him he was beaten and all I had to do was to keep up the pace to the finish."

The race had been the debut at top level for the young Czech Emil Zatopek. He had captured various national records but had precious little experience outside his homeland at this point. Zatopek was stunned twice by Sydney that day – firstly by his general appearance on the start-line, and later by the nature of his victory. He thought Sydney looked more like "a near-sighted professor" than a runner, but he'd rocketed past him. According to author George Gretton, after the race a bewildered Zatopek described Sydney thus:

> "An elderly, serious gentleman who stepped out on to the starting line with shorts that reached nearly down to his knees, and a pair of glasses on his nose."

While Zatopek marvelled at Sydney's famously deceptive appearance, more experienced onlookers seemed to form a consensus that Sydney was only now, at the age of almost 32, beginning to appreciate and achieve good pace judgement, having moved up to longer distances. Most of his success at the half-mile or mile had been unevenly-paced efforts and owed much to explosive finishes. He was now in new territory but coping admirably. It was an immensely popular victory and his GB teammates were particularly delighted. Although not the most sociable of animals, Sydney was part of a squad that got on very well together on this trip – so well, in fact, they formed the exclusive 'Smestad Club' in order to socialise and reminisce in the years afterwards.

Some of the squad departed Oslo to compete in Bergen over the border in Sweden, but Sydney quickly headed back to London to get medical attention on his ankle and prepare for Motspur Park. He was photographed stepping off his plane at Northolt in Middlesex three days after his race, apparently having travelled alone. Despite his status as a new European champion, there was no-one to greet him bar a couple of journalists as he descended the steps clutching an armful of newspapers. It was hardly a returning hero's welcome. One writer observed:

> "Arriving home, he was a hatless, solitary figure in sports jacket and flannels; he walked across to the Customs House. Someone asked his name and made a tick on the arriving passengers list, someone else checked his luggage. He was back at his desk the next day in the office..."

Sydney confirmed his international track retirement to one of the reporters:

> "I would sooner retire while I am on the top note than after I have taken a beating. In winning at Oslo I was more exhausted than I have ever been in any race before. I shall keep on with club running but am definitely not going to tackle the [1948] Olympic Games."

Sydney's career was at a major crossroads, and there was also change in the air as far as athletics itself was concerned. Immediately after the championships in Oslo, the IAAF congress considered a proposal by the Scandinavian countries – supported by many – that compensation should in future be paid to athletes with families who had to take unpaid time off work to represent their countries at athletics meetings. Called 'the broken time controversy' it saw a strong argument put forward that current rules effectively prevented working-class men from representing their country.

British delegate Harold Abrahams was against major change, but did concede the sport's strict rules on amateurism perhaps needed modifying. Avery Brundage (USA) was much less flexible and said paying compensation was tantamount to encouraging professionalism. As around half the IAAF members were not present in Oslo, nothing could be decided. Frustratingly this important matter was shelved until the next congress, two whole years away.

39

Sad Farewell to Track

BACK in London after his tumultuous Norwegian adventure, Sydney found himself with just four full days to recover, get his injury treated and prepare for his Motspur Park 'farewell' the following Saturday, the day after his 32nd birthday.

The event involved a special meeting put on by Blackheath Harriers for more than 600 athletes, the centrepiece of which was Sydney's bid to run the fastest two miles the world had ever seen. The best on British soil to date had been 9:00.6 by Gunder Hagg at White City the previous summer, while the English native best was Jack Emery's pre-war 9:03.4 in Manchester.

Knowing it would be his very last serious track race, the club went to great lengths over the summer of 1946 to make sure the day was a success, and had even set up a special 'Prize and Expenses Fund' appeal. Saturday 31 August marked the end of an era, not just a summer season, and aroused enormous interest. Even the long-awaited resumption that day of League football, absent since 1939, failed to overshadow the occasion. One correspondent noted:

> "Motspur Park was like a garrison preparing for desperate defence – all the approaches and inner wards were manned by robust figures in uniform and there was an air of tension and expectancy."

There was only one grandstand and space was limited, but somehow the stewards squeezed in just under 7,000 people by 2pm on the big day.

Blackheath members had been able to apply earlier for seats in the covered stand at 5 shillings apiece and these were much coveted. There had been a big queue outside by lunchtime despite the ominous looking grey skies and the definite chill in the air. Things got underway at 2.30 with a 100 yards handicap race, by which time there was heavy rain and fierce winds from the south west. The people in the lower rows of the stand were soaked and the special press table awash. Conditions contributed to the man second on the bill – sprinter Emmanuel McDonald Bailey – withdrawing, although a muscle strain was officially blamed.

There were many anxious faces around, not least Sydney's, as this weather meant the track would clearly not be in great shape for Sydney's record attempt. However, none of this dampened the enthusiasm of the crowd who gave him a huge welcome when the moment arrived. As if on cue, the sun had just emerged, the winds had dropped and the puddles on the heavy track suddenly looked far less troublesome.

Sydney assured everyone he would give the existing records his best shot and brushed aside any mention of his ankle problem. He'd got through the Oslo ordeal without it breaking down and that had been a longer race. His target today would be to cover the eight laps in an average of 69 seconds each. Unless the injury resurfaced, that was surely not unreasonable. He lined up wearing No.21, with 19 others, five clubs each represented by a quartet of runners.

There was very little fuss or delay at the start, despite the significance of the occasion, probably because officials were anxious to get the race away while there was a window of favourable weather. The inevitable fierce dash for the first corner saw Sydney tucked on the inside and established in third by the bend. He then barrelled his way to the front in unusually robust fashion and by the time they'd entered the back straight had a lead he would never relinquish. The first lap was given as 61 seconds, the half-mile as 2:10, three-quarters in 3:19 and one mile in 4:26.6. At halfway he was bang on course. According to one observer, Sydney looked a little thinner than usual, but was showing no signs of fatigue after his recent Oslo heroics, in perfect rhythm as he increased his lead on the fifth circuit. If he could keep this up and finish with his usual surge surely victory and the records would be his.

All was looking well until suddenly there was an audible gasp from parts of the crowd – at the beginning of the sixth lap he could clearly be seen to be limping. He was still travelling at speed but all his usual finesse and rhythm was gone. The atmosphere was transformed and within a minute or two people were calling out urging him to quit, and this included officials. Nobody wanted to see the popular champion punish himself unnecessarily. If Sydney heard these shouts, and he surely must have, he was having none of it. He continued toiling away, his lead still significant, but occasional signs of pain and anguish flashed across his face. He was lame although not entirely crippled, and with just two laps left was not going to stop now – this was a team race after all and Blackheath's chances would be ruined if he jacked it in.

The crowd responded, but most of the applause was sympathy-based as he finally hobbled over the line some 110 yards clear of Belgrave's Len Herbert and was given a time of 9:12.8. It was a highly respectable clocking in the circumstances, but before the injury had looked set for something 15 to 20 seconds quicker. It was pointed out later that at almost the exact same spot Sydney had begun limping, the talented West Indian Arthur Wint had stumbled and injured himself in the 440 yards – this gave rise to unsubstantiated rumours that a hazardous section of track had been responsible for the two incidents.

Herbert (9:34.8) beat Finchley Harriers' Maurice Bingham by two seconds for the runners-up place, and there was some consolation for the limping Sydney to find that his efforts had ensured Blackheath won the team prize, by a single point. The pain had not been entirely in vain, but even so, he hadn't wanted his brilliant track career to end like this. The sight of 'The Mighty Atom' grimacing and hobbling had been a truly sad one. After the initial applause died away, a tremendous feeling of anti-climax descended on the ground leaving Sydney no doubt feeling he'd let people down. This was a long way from the truth of course, and many came forward to shake his hand and tell him so.

As a footnote to these events of August 31, a competitor named Alan Turing caused a surprise, winning the three-mile invitation race in 15:37. It was a great show by a 34-year-old running novice, unrecognised by most present, who was, of course, more famous for his wartime code-breaking work at Bletchley Park. *Athletics* magazine confirmed later this runner had been the same Doctor Turing "largely responsible for the so-called electronic brain machine."

Sydney's post-race plans now involved a couple of months' rest and rehab before giving full attention to cross-country competition. At 32 he still had a winter or two in his legs and wanted to make the most of that time – particularly while he was still a bachelor and had the luxury of weekends unhindered by family commitments. Summer 1946 ended with news that he'd been selected as winner of both Harvey and Jackson Memorial trophies for his performance in the AAA championships in July. The AAA ratified his 13:53.2 that day as an English native three-mile record, and the BAAB would follow suit for GB record purposes. During September he honoured a commitment in the West Midlands, attending an event at Tatchbrook Road sportsground in Leamington although not running himself due to his injury.

He may have quit top-level track racing, but his fame showed no sign of letting up: In just a matter of days in September he had the dubious honour of appearing in the satirical magazine *Punch*, and also as the subject of a clue in the *Times* crossword!

Punch columnist Charivaria commented on a recent press quote from Sydney which suggested that British athletes had suffered lately because their diets were affected by rationing. He thought if that was the case then Sydney had done very well to get himself "to the front of the queue" so often in races! Two days later, bowler-hatted city gents doing their *Times* crossword on the train (including possibly Sydney himself?) were confronted by the following clue for '15 across': "How Wooderson eventually sped to fame (2,3,4,3)." The answer was INTHELONGRUN.

With no serious running on the horizon until late November, Sydney could now make more time for other pursuits: a particular favourite were trips to see Shakespeare plays at the Old Vic Theatre accompanied by brother Stanley, who was especially keen on all aspects of the world of showbusiness. The brothers' favourite routine would be to assiduously read the play beforehand, then go and see it performed live by the likes of Peggy Ashcroft, Ralph Richardson, Laurence Olivier and John Gielgud.

40

Presidential Status

AFTER eight weeks or so out of the limelight, the final Saturday of October 1946 proved a significant one for Sydney Wooderson. During the day he set out on his first proper run since injury – a steady off-road five-miler with clubmates – and then spent the evening at Blackheath's annual general meeting, at which he proudly accepted an invitation to become Club President for the coming year.

He was a popular and unanimous choice. Accepting this honour in succession to George Mullins, there was great acclaim from the floor, and, as tradition dictated, a ceremonial chanting of the 'club cry.' Members were reminded how Sydney had given great support to club races over the 1946 summer season without being asked, despite his international and other commitments. Secretary Gordon McIvor marvelled at the way Sydney always ensured even the most humble club fixtures were noted in his diary in exactly the same meticulous manner as he carried out his training. He added:

> "And that training was carried out often at great personal inconvenience involving a combination of hard work, attention to detail and common sense, with no place for cranky notions. Sydney has held British prestige high in the whole world of sport. We are proud of him. We mourn the fact that his father, and that great Blackheath Harrier Sercombe didn't live to see his culminating triumphs. We are happy to hear the AAA have decided on an action

> unique in their history – namely, to honour our champion by a special presentation at a dinner to be given in his honour."

George W. Smith, in his book *All Out for the Mile*, says the high honour of the club presidency was recognition of Sydney's fame and his popularity, two things that did not always go together in a sportsman:

> "The secret of this double success is not difficult to penetrate. His fame was the outcome of a perennial eagerness to match himself against others; an utter lack of awe for athletic reputations, however great; the ferocity of a tiger in competition; and an insatiable appetite for hard-won records. His popularity derived from his attractive personality; his readiness to give his services to club, county or country; his impeccable conduct, on or off the track, and his constant fulfilment of the confidence placed in him. Throughout his versatile career he was champion of champions in his own right, yet his first thought was always for the well-being of the Blackheath Harriers, a club with a long history and splendid tradition. Never was a member so beloved by his club fellows and never did an athlete prove a better team man to his club."

True-to-form, Sydney's formal response after being elected President was not about himself or his achievements, but all about what he could do for them in his coming year of office:

> "The doubts I first felt at assuming such a high office in the club were soon dispelled when I found such loyal co-operation and willingness to help among officials, committee-men and all other members and I feel that herein lies the true strength of this club, and the reason for its continuing success. The year the emphasis is on the younger men taking their share of the responsibilities of office and this I am sure is a good thing now that our aim must be to build up our strength to even greater heights than before… we must be continually on the look-out for fresh talent and be ready to coach and encourage the many useful young runners we now have. I hope that any such members will come along to me with any training problems and with the experience I have gained over a

> long period I shall be only too willing to give guidance and advice at any time."

Prior to the 1946–7 cross-country season, Blackheath's captain George Wilkinson urged colleagues to improve on last season's fifth place in the English National, their best position since 1883. He urged better pack-running in races, and said he expected great things now more men were out of the Forces and available to run, plus both Wooderson brothers promising to be regularly available. Accordingly training facilities at Catford Bridge would open on Tuesday and Thursday evenings throughout winter with hot water and suppers available for afterwards.

The first significant date of Sydney's post-track career would be the traditional mob match for the Nicholls Cup on Saturday 16 November, when Blackheath took on South London Harriers on the windy downs at Coulsdon. This newly-revived battle over 7.5 miles was won emphatically by the gleeful Heathens who had 73 men among the 104 starters. Half-a-dozen Blackheath runners that day were even able to reminisce about taking part in the equivalent post-war race back in 1918. The 177 starters set off on Farthing Downs and tackled two long laps of farmland during which the field became very strung out. The going was generally good, if a little sticky, Sydney coming in a relatively modest eighth in 47:30, some way behind winner Humphrey Nunns (45:24). Gordon Pirie's mum supervised an excellent tea for all in the SLH clubhouse afterwards, where Sydney, as president, accepted the trophy from his opposite number.

A week later Blackheath fielded a 'B' team to take on Oxford University in a very muddy 7.5-mile contest at Hayes, won by visitor Peter Curry in 46:45, with Sydney third, exactly a minute down. This would ultimately prove the only occasion Sydney came up against Roger Bannister in a race. The 17-year-old student had taken off quickly at the start but as they reached Blackness Farm, Sydney and three others formed a lead pack just ahead of Bannister's group. At Layham's Farm Sydney and Gordon Monshall opened a big lead but failed to maintain it. Bannister eventually came home fifth, roughly 90 seconds behind his hero Sydney. Oxford packed well and won by single point.

Enjoying this regular Saturday competition over the country, Sydney put himself forward as a reserve runner for the Blackheath's trip to face

Cambridge University a week later, and during the week was asked to turn out. They gathered at Liverpool Street station just after midday, but due to hold-ups en route arrived late at Cambridge. In addition the start was at least a mile from the changing rooms, meaning things didn't get underway until almost 4pm and the run took place in semi-darkness. The 7.25-mile route was over heavy ground, one of the toughest Sydney had ever tackled. An innocent-looking ditch caught many out, causing unexpected mud-baths. Sydney ran a careful race and came in third, around a minute behind home winner Young.

On Saturday 7 December it was off to Charterhouse School for a 5.5-mile trek over Godalming's fields, Sydney enjoying himself in first place, beating Old Carthusian Coggins' course record of 30:11 by 37 seconds. The rest of the field were more than a minute behind, although Blackheath suffered defeat in the team contest. A fortnight later, the last Saturday before Christmas, saw 55 runners assemble at Petersham to tackle a range of hazards in snow-covered Richmond Park. Blackheath and home side Ranelagh contested the Pelling-Radcliff cup in their first mob match for eight years. The course was just under eight miles and hellishly difficult, much of it icy and uneven. Sydney came in equal-second, finishing alongside clubmates Dick Choat, Derek Reynolds and Keepex in 50:53. Another Heathen, John Poole, won by a 25-second margin, ensuring an emphatic away victory. It was almost dark before the last of the 55 men struggled across the line, and luckily the park-keeper had extended closing time to make this possible. It was an exhausting but exhilarating run in the snow and spirits remained high during a supper laid on in the nearby Dysart Arms afterwards.

It was a good way to end the year for Sydney, coming soon after he'd been guest of honour at South London Harriers' 75th anniversary dinner at the Bedford Hotel in Central London. Here he was lauded by fellow speakers, including Lord Burghley, President of the IAAF. The dinner was a highlight of what had otherwise been a relatively quiet few months for Sydney as he ensured his injury problems cleared up in good time for the serious cross-country races scheduled for early 1947. In the lead-up to Christmas it had become clear his fitness and motivation levels would be tested to the full by the severe winter that was setting in over Britain. The bitter cold would cause severe hardship generally, adding to the problems of rationing and austerity, and things would get even worse when a really severe freeze-up arrived during January 1947.

★ ★ ★

Runners of the modern era might find it a little hard to believe, but there was a time when cross-country races went ahead whatever the weather. In the Sydney Wooderson era, drifting snow and widespread ice were merely occupational hazards for organisers and competitors.

Consider the day of the 1947 English National championships: the nation was suffering the harshest winter in living memory but nobody fretted over health and safety protocol – they simply bunked off work and set off for the Hertfordshire venue a day early.

Britain may have been shivering under a blanket of snow that would last more than eight weeks, but the National was a big deal – this show must, and would, go on. Post-war austerity, rationing and fuel shortages had made matters even worse of course, but all this misery only fuelled the determination of runners to go ahead with their regular routines. The club mob matches, the regional champs, and definitely the National, would all go ahead whatever the weather.

Ten slippery miles of hills, snow, ice and slush awaited the 300 brave souls who beat snow drifts and treacherous roads to get to that 1947 National at Apsley, near Hemel Hempstead. It was the Diamond Jubilee staging of this famously tough race, but simply getting there would be the hardest aspect of all for many. An unprecedented 1,193 runners had signed up (49 teams plus 41 unattached men), but 17 entire teams failed to make it through the snow. Some – including the crack Tipton squad – did reach the venue intact but arrived just too late to take part.

A good number of the missing men were star runners of the era. This opened things up for unsung heroes to make a name for themselves. After all, the first ten finishers would automatically be selected to represent England in the international champs in Paris later on. It was suggested normal rules shouldn't apply because of all the absentees at Apsley, but the magazine *Athletics* dismissed this view, saying those who failed to arrive only had themselves to blame as there had been frequent warnings about roads being impassable.

European 5,000 metres champion and celebrated miler Sydney was one of those who did make it to Apsley. Rather unrealistically for his first crack at a National, the popular press named him favourite to win. Wearing No.41 and a long-sleeved top, his all-black outfit contrasted sharply with the sparkling snowy surroundings. Sydney was now 32, his glory days surely behind him, but he loved cross-country and relished the camaraderie of club events. This famous race – four laps of 2.5 miles each – would start and finish in Lower Shendish Park, close to Apsley Mills and the Grand Union Canal.

Despite the obvious hazards, some men opted not to wear spikes and tended to pay the price. The snow was very deep in places and a degree of awkward 'knee lifting' was needed to get through it. Reading AC's Bertie Robertson proved to be in a class of his own, forging a big lead on the first lap and eventually winning in 59:18, some 300 yards clear of Blaydon's Matt Smith. Sydney – his spectacles misted up and his black vest shimmering with frost – was seventh, impressive for a debutant, after moving steadily through the field as the race progressed. He coped well with the slippery conditions and his nimbleness meant he looked far more at home than many.

He was two minutes behind the winner, but it was a promising display from someone unused to ten-mile slogs in such conditions. Around 200 yards of plough on each of the four laps didn't help matters and it was perhaps surprising as many as 276 managed to finish. Each lap took them from the start area in the Lower Park near the railway line, around the grounds of Shendish House and the edge of Phasels Wood, and back to the Apsley Mills area, passing the vicarage. Just two places behind Sydney was clubmate Gordon Monshall, who was clearly benefitting from Sydney's help and attention in this and recent races. The pair ran together for much of this event.

The real stars of the day were the sleep-deprived Northern champions Sutton Harriers. They had set out the day before, driven through the night at a snail's pace, arriving with just enough time to grab a couple of hours' sleep in the Shendish Park changing rooms before the race's scheduled start. They sprang from their makeshift beds when called, and then roared to a highly commendable team victory. Blackheath were fourth.

Some 70 years later I jogged around the park in Sydney's footsteps and then relayed the tale of Apsley 1947 on social media. Plenty of 'old school' runners reacted robustly. One Hercules Wimbledon man suggested: "No

A ten-mile slog at Apsley.

way would it be allowed to take place these days. Imagine the horror if somebody fell over!" A Herne Hill Harrier added: "From a tough, hilly snow-covered course in 1947, we see the present day courses where at world level they run on almost bowling green conditions with fake hills and the occasional log to jump over, just to make it slightly harder. No wonder most present day athletes can't match or come close to what was done in the past!"

After the race Sydney told reporters he'd not felt happy throughout, despite his impressive display, and stated firmly he wouldn't be accepting an invitation to run for England in the international in Paris on March 30, despite qualifying for automatic selection. Some papers made a lot of these comments, but it seems they were not intended as a snub, merely Sydney sticking to his original plans for the coming months. The selectors named him anyway, but he declined and George Wicks of Bexhill was called up instead.

41

Severe Tests in the Big Freeze

THE dreadful weather across the UK in early 1947 seemed never-ending and runners began getting used to performing on snow and ice. The Southern Championships saw another freezing and hazardous ten-mile slog on exposed Ascot Heath where 275 starters made up 30 teams. They assembled, clapping gloved hands and breathing steam as they were called to the start area.

All the usual cheerful banter soon began to fade when it became clear they'd been summoned too early and would have to wait for junior runners to finish their race first. The huge field was kept standing around in the bitter cold for around 20 minutes and some made their feelings known. The start was delayed even further when a senior official was seen running around looking for Sydney, apparently so he could arrange a photograph to be taken with him.

Much of the snow around the Ascot course was compacted solid and very treacherous, the wind was bitter and more snow fell during the race. Across the Heath, scene of many a notable horse race meeting, regally patronised and otherwise, Sydney and teammate Monshall ran steadily together to maintain a place in the top 15 or so throughout. With less than a mile left, Sydney told his sidekick he thought he could make up a few places, and promptly accelerated away. He passed at least seven men with a wonderful turn of speed to thrill the frozen crowd at the finish-line. It was well worth the effort, for it pushed Blackheath into third place in a close team event.

Sydney was of course smaller and lighter than the majority and his nimble footwork suited the conditions. Aylesford Paper Mills took the team prize and Len Herbert of Belgrave triumphed in 54:04, just five seconds clear of Alec Olney (Thames Valley), with Sydney fifth in 55:11. Many finishers were disappointed to complete the ordeal only to find nobody had thought to lay on post-race hot drinks. Frozen and irritable, many departed for home quicker than usual, Blackheath among those rushing for the first train back into London.

Sydney's preparations for the championship races at Ascot Heath and Apsley had been blighted by a spell of flu and its after-effects, which kept him out of action for much of January 1947. That month had seen him tackle the Kent county championship at Aylesford over three laps of a very heavy course in constant drizzle and failing light. Until the final two miles Sydney was content to run in relaxed mode with clubmate Monshall, before pushing on in the latter stages to finish third behind Aylesford pair McCoy and Charlesworth. Monshall gamely stayed with him and they came in close together in the gathering gloom, barely visible in their black kit. A week later, Saturday 18 January, Kent won the inter-counties at Nottingham despite being without the flu-stricken Sydney. This event failed to run smoothly, starting late due to bad weather and other problems, and as a result the Sussex team missed a rail connection home and had to sleep the night on Victoria station platform.

What had already proved a cold and miserable winter got considerably worse on Thursday 23 January, when heavy snow began to fall on SE England, the start of Britain's most severe and protracted spell of bad weather in living memory. The big freeze soon assumed the aspect of an invading enemy, with soldiers turning out to fight it with flame throwers; Londoners' post-war blues deepened, for coal was already strictly rationed, gas supply reduced and electricity often cut off altogether. The adrenalin of fighting a war had gone, meaning this was relentless misery, blizzards day after day. The weather would be unrelentingly grim for the best part of seven weeks, a proper thaw not really taking effect until well into March.

It meant the ten-mile Blackheath Rowland Cup contest on the first day of February took place in thick snow, featuring a heroic little group of just 27 who made it to the clubhouse that grey day and bitterly cold day. They discovered the hill after about seven miles was severely treacherous, and struggled through snowdrifts more than a foot deep. Some runners went off course around halfway and arrived at the finish having avoided the hill altogether: whether deliberate or not, they were castigated by officials who promised the trail-laying had been of a high standard even in the awful conditions. Gordon Monshall won in 65:06 with Dick Choat second, more than five minutes behind. Sydney was back in eighth (73:25) taking things steady after his flu, and helping teammates. Remarkably there were no serious mishaps, although one runner risked frostbite by continuing after the sole of one shoe fell off.

Indoor pursuits were the order of the day for most of the country over this period and Sydney's diary featured several evening engagements where his famous face was required to put in an appearance. At London's Savoy Hotel in early February he stepped rather reluctantly into the spotlight when Minister of Health Nye Bevan announced he had been voted runner-up in the *Sporting Record* sportsman of the year competition. Mainly for the benefit of the photographers, one suspects, Sydney chatted with winner Bruce Woodcock, the British heavyweight boxing champion from Doncaster. Woodcock modestly told the smartly-dressed audience he felt Sydney should have won the award and not him.

Just over a month later, a couple of days after the National at Apsley, Harold Abrahams broadcast a tribute to Sydney's track career via a special 20-minute programme on the BBC Home Service, the show squeezed between music from Henry Hall and the BBC Northern Orchestra. Next day, Wednesday 12 March, the AAA prolonged the tribute by honouring Sydney with a dinner at the Holborn Restaurant. Life vice-president Arthur Turk told 150 guests that never before had the AAA honoured an athlete in this way in its 67-year history. Athletes and officials from all over Britain were in attendance to pay homage. Self-effacing Sydney will no doubt have found it quite an ordeal, steeling himself to listen and respond to the lengthy speech-making.

Several speakers beseeched him to come out of international retirement and go for the 1948 Olympics, one even suggesting he do this by moving up to 10,000 metres or even the marathon. Harold Abrahams handed over special plaques marking his world amateur records at 800 metres, 880 yards and mile, English native record for 3 miles and British amateur record mile. Sydney took to his feet and gave a characteristically simple speech, including an unexpectedly personal touch by thanking his mother for the care she had taken over his health and well-being during arduous periods of training. He said his ability would never have flourished if he'd not had a good home to return to afterwards. His Blackheath colleagues in the audience beamed when he emphasised his philosophy: "The team is more important than the individual, and the race more than the record". An unfortunate footnote to this gala evening was created when a car taking guests to the dinner was involved in a serious accident and never made it. Runner Peter Dainty had been in the car along with Kent officials, one of whom was seriously hurt.

During the dinner Sydney paid warm tribute to coach Albert Hill, to whom he was bidding farewell this year. Hill, now in his late fifties, had decided to emigrate to Canada to settle near daughter Alma, where he would work with her husband in market gardening. When the final parting came, there were sad farewells on the platform at Waterloo station, Sydney recalled later, and although the two men corresponded until Hill's death 22 years later, they would never meet again.

Unusually, Sydney had to wait for his fifth race of the 1947 calendar year before tasting victory for the first time. It came in the attractive and refined Berkshire surroundings of Wellington College on Saturday 15 March in a match against the student sons of Army officers. Blackheath's finest had gathered at Waterloo station bound for the Crowthorne venue, and found themselves squashed into a crowded train with rugby fans heading for Twickenham. Although a thaw had begun a few days earlier signalling the end of the big freeze, snow again began to fall during the race and runners found the 5.5-mile course rock hard and occasionally slippery, with a few short road sections thrown in. Once again Sydney and Gordon Monshall ran together and this time came in joint-first in 33:31 alongside teammate Wally Spencer. The college team put up a game display, but couldn't catch Sydney even though he ran cautiously and nowhere near flat-out pace.

Perhaps the visitors who enjoyed the occasion most of all were two Blackheath supporters who were given a ride around the course by the college's athletics master in his vintage Rolls Royce. At every stop the car picked up another of the college boys and by the end of its circuit of the route was packed, with bodies protruding from doors and windows. The visiting team enjoyed excellent bathing facilities and high tea afterwards, and were thanked profusely for coming, particularly Sydney, and the eager boys even accompanied them back to the station. It made a nice change from those problems encountered at the more austere Southern champs a few weeks earlier.

Sydney (left) on a goodwill visit to Dublin.

The harshest of winters had finally disappeared but the wind was fierce when the *News of the World* put on its first London-to-Brighton road relay event since before the war. On Saturday 19 April, 21 teams gathered beside Mitcham Common to tackle the 45.5-mile route to Brighton seafront, split into ten stages. The annual race had begun in 1924, championed by athletics correspondent Joe Binks, moving its starting point in 1936 from Westminster out to Mitcham due to traffic congestion problems. It grew in popularity and would become a national championship event during the 1950s.

As the 1947 race progressed southwards, Blackheath moved up from seventh to second thanks to some sterling efforts over the latter stages. Helped by the unfortunate roadside collapse of a Birchfield opponent, John Poole clawed his way into third position before passing the baton to Sydney, Blackheath's final runner. Sydney overtook Coventry Godiva's last man to occupy second, but although he gained two minutes on leader Lucas (Belgrave) it wasn't enough to close the gap entirely. Sydney flew along the seafront, and completed his journey from the Red Lion at Patcham in a stage record of 17:19. It meant Blackheath were runners-up in an aggregate time of 4:05.45, less than three minutes behind winners Belgrave.

The misery of the winter freeze-up would soon be forgotten as an uncommonly hot summer got underway. With his serious track running days over, Sydney's plan was to spend the summer merely keeping himself fit and helping his club. He would clock up just eight relatively minor races over the season, seven of them in May, and was subsequently forced out by injury anyway. He made it known he would be prepared to spare a couple of nights a week helping to coach some of Britain's hopefuls for the 1948 Olympics in London. The BAAB took up the offer and he and fellow 'veterans' Godfrey Brown and Sam Ferris were among those who helped out.

And so Sydney's deliberately low-key season – albeit one with a hectic start – opened on Monday 5 May with a 4:25.5 mile victory in good weather on a well-prepared grass track at the Roan School in SE London. It was quickly followed by a similarly comfortable win over two miles (10:00.7) against Cambridge Harriers in nearby Ladywell Park. Then, a few days later, a Blackheath evening meet saw another two-mile victory (9:50.5), a flawless run that won Sydney the club's Morgan Cup. His fourth outing in just 13 days saw him cruise to a 4:30 mile win as Blackheath took on Surrey AC and home side Gillingham & District. This was quickly followed by the annual Dartford Hospital Sports and another win at two miles, this in 9:36.4.

Sydney may have been out of the national spotlight, but he certainly wasn't idle. On the same day the British Games were thrilling thousands at sunny White City, Sydney could be found on this warm Whit Monday afternoon in an unlikely setting in South Wales. He'd accepted an invitation to the Pontypool Park meeting on May 26 which pulled in a reported 15,000, noisily enjoying the sight of Sydney winning a mile handicap off scratch in 4:28.8. He only had two opponents – Austin Littler of Pilkington, who was given 20 yards' start, and local favourite Harry Gallivan of Cwmbran Harriers, who had 70. Sydney caught and passed both before halfway to win by 12 yards. His seventh and final appearance in May 1947 was also many miles from home, at Billingham Synthonia's second annual meeting in fine weather in front of an enthusiastic 3,000 Teessiders. Having won the mile here a year earlier, Sydney kept a promise to return and duly won the two-mile team race in 9:25.2, a good 20 seconds clear of teammate Monshall.

Perhaps the frequency of his racing at this point was the reason it all went pear-shaped in early June when injury struck. Sydney's eighth track outing in a period of 33 days was at the Rotherham Hospital Sports in South Yorkshire where he set off from scratch but couldn't quite overhaul 18-year-old Doncaster runner Harold Palmer who'd been given a 90-yard start. Sydney worked hard in the closing stages and came agonisingly close to catching the tiring youngster. During the race he damaged his ankle but kept going, finding it very sore afterwards and a more serious problem than first thought. It put an end to his summer running, a disappointment for several clubs around the country who had him pencilled in to appear at their events.

Despite the injury, or perhaps partly because of it, the summer of 1947 turned into something of a pre-Olympics goodwill tour: Sydney visited various clubs and events as a guest and spectator, dispensing coaching advice, shaking hands and signing autographs rather than racing. Still a single man at the age of 32, he had the freedom to use his weekends to travel around in this way. A typical example was a visit to Northampton's County Ground in July when he took the salute at the march-past of competitors at the opening of the Northampton Y.O.C. Olympiad of Youth. He made a speech to the gathering and jogged a gentle exhibition lap of the cricket ground. Another occasion saw him lining up alongside HRH the Duke of Gloucester as a VIP guest at the opening of the newly-improved Ashton Playing Fields facilities, the HQ of East London club Woodford Green AC.

Sydney wrote to officials at both Torquay and Tamworth confirming his injury wouldn't allow him to race at their events as planned, but sportingly agreed to travel to both long-distance commitments anyway, to minimise any disappointment. This was also the case when he turned up at Dorchester for the Dorset Constabulary Sports; an appreciative crowd of 5,000 had assembled and gave him a warm ovation, with lengthy queues of fans seeking an autograph.

One Friday evening in July he went to Hastings to meet Anthony Pearson, the 15-year-old secretary of Hastings and St Leonards Cycling and Athletic Club, who took him to the Central Ground where he gave an hour's worth of coaching advice to the club's young runners. Pearson had been receiving coaching advice by letter from Sydney prior to this, but today was their first proper meeting. The pair would get on well and forge a lifelong friendship, Sydney becoming Pearson's regular coach. Pearson would sign up with Blackheath in 1949 and under Sydney's guidance became a top-class athlete, representing Britain in the International Student Games, setting a UK record at 3,000 metres indoors, running a 2:31 marathon and featuring prominently in cross-country.

Better known latterly as Tony Weeks-Pearson, he had a long career in teaching and would ultimately emulate his mentor by becoming Blackheath president in 1990. He remembered first writing to Sydney in 1946 for coaching advice and recalled the delight at receiving his first reply on Christmas Eve. Then when Sydney raced at Gillingham in May 1947, Weeks-Pearson and his mother bumped into Sydney's mum: "I remember meeting Sydney's mother before I met him or others of the family. 'He must go and introduce himself,' she told my mother in the stand at Gillingham… 'he's been writing hasn't he?'" From these shy, hesitant beginnings a strong relationship was formed. Before long Weeks-Pearson would come up to London for one-to-one coaching at the Ladywells Park track and stayed the night with the Woodersons, and the youngster recalled gazing in awe as his hero stood in the kitchen carving the joint of meat they were about to eat.

★★★

Just prior to the start of the 1947–48 cross-country season, Sydney scotched lingering suggestions he might be tempted back to the international stage at the 1948 Olympics in London. In an interview with journalist and author A. V. Selwood, Sydney said his working life must now be his top priority: "Thirty-three years old is a ripe old age for an international runner – but for a solicitor it's only the beginning!" Despite this, he was more than happy to continue serving his club, his year as President coming to an end in the autumn when he handed over the role to George Wilkinson.

Around now the club suffered internal scandal when cash was found to have been stolen from the clothes of members who were out training at the Private Banks track in Catford. Committee minute books reveal that subsequently a letter of apology was received by the secretary from a man admitting he took the cash while at the ground to play football. This confession didn't prevent runner Tony Poole resigning from Blackheath, however, dismayed at the loss of trust that the theft had created: "Everyone seems to have suspicions of others," wrote Poole. The Blackheath committee decided to drop their investigation, saying they didn't have enough evidence of guilt to prosecute. It had become a messy business, but was soon forgotten once the cross-country got underway.

With sporting matters now back to normality following the war, the last ten weeks of the calendar year featured a full fixture list of cross-country for Sydney and fellow mudlarks in the London area. Things kicked off at Hayes with a five-mile club match versus Surrey AC, in which Sydney finished a modest 11th in 28:11, taking care with his troublesome ankle. A fortnight later a sterner test came on Oxford's Shotover Hill where Blackheath's second string tackled the University runners, Sydney third in 40:24 behind home winner Peter Curry (38:26). Back at Hayes he was again third, over the 7.5-mile route in a mob match with South London Harriers, before returning to university territory on November 22 where he managed joint-first alongside teammates Gordon Monshall and Jack Braughton (all 42:19) in a seven-miler with Cambridge University. Finishing just six seconds behind them was future Olympic gold medallist Chris Brasher, an athlete who, as we have seen, considered Sydney his greatest inspiration in athletics. In the run-up to Christmas, Sydney and clubmate Nunns came in together to win a match at Godalming against Charterhouse School and then Blackheath's 'mass finish' trick was repeated with six of them (Sydney, Monshall, Choat, Reynolds, Spencer and Braughton) being given joint-first in an eight-mile mob match with Ranelagh at Hayes.

The club, and Sydney in particular, always received an enthusiastic welcome when they travelled to run against schools or college teams. A highlight of this period was their December 1947 visit to rural Essex for a five-mile match with the boys of Felsted School. The Blackheath team took a Great Eastern train and were met at the station by the captain of the home team who had organised taxis. They were ferried to Felsted Bury, a 16th century manor house used by the school as a centre of education for leisure and free time, and a building of great antiquarian interest.

The ground was soft but conditions good for racing: A fast start saw pupil Dodd steam into the lead, but after a mile Sydney passed and soon opened a big gap. Busby lost a shoe early on and manfully completed the race barefoot, coming in 16th and last as a result. The course record was broken by Sydney who finished to great cheers from the schoolboys in 31:10, around three minutes ahead of the battling Dodd. Boys stationed out on the course had provided a running commentary that was relayed over a loudspeaker system, providing great entertainment, particularly when one struggling back-marker was announced as a lad suffering from nicotine poisoning! A fine tea was laid on for the visitors afterwards and the school captain said a few words of appreciation to which Sydney responded.

One of the boys marshalling out on the course that day was John Moynihan, later to become a celebrated sportswriter and author, and for whom Sydney was a boyhood hero. Moynihan would recall this cold day clearly when writing for *The Oldie* magazine years later:

> "We frozen, bullied second formers at Felsted School had been detailed to act as markers… there was great excitement because Wooderson had agreed to take part. He may have looked like a spindly, bespectacled articled clerk, but once he donned the all-black running strip of his club there was no disputing who was going to win the race… Out in the murky countryside, I had taken up my place as a marker by a gnarled oak tree not far from

> the River Chelmer. It was difficult to see through an enveloping mist, but suddenly there was Syd, emerging like Omar Sharif in black, arms pumping, his legs pounding over the mud like steam pistons. For one magic moment he stopped, having hardly raised a sweat. 'I'm a bit lost,' he said, putting his hands on his hips. 'Where next?' 'Across the ploughed fields and you'll find another marker,' I replied, pointing vaguely in the right direction. 'Not far to go now sir.'"

Moynihan, like others, had begun his lifelong love affair with sport thanks to Sydney Wooderson's heroics two years earlier at the White City. Moynihan's parents had taken him as a treat to see the little man's duel with Arne Andersson. He recalled fondly:

> "The Yanks yelled for Sydney to beat the big Swedish bum as the pair veered away for the first lap [and] Wooderson suddenly acquired the stature of a Spitfire!"

42

A Serious Tilt at 'National' Glory

MILES from the nearest town, a remote windswept hilltop in North Kent provided a classic rural setting for many memorable cross-country battles either side of the Second World War. Yet the hundreds of runners who trod these punishing fields – famous names among them – rarely suffered any shortage of vocal support, for the venue was also the permanent home of scores of small boys rescued from broken and destitute homes.

The place in question was the Farningham Homes for Little Boys, a pioneering 19th century project comprising around 15 buildings which made up Britain's first 'cottage homes' establishment – seen then as a safer, healthier alternative to the old Victorian workhouses. This little hilltop complex, not far from the village of Horton Kirby, would survive until 1961, by which time attitudes to child welfare had changed. Some of the original buildings remain to this day, part of a private residential village called Southdowns. I visited the area in search of the place where Sydney triumphantly reclaimed his Kent cross-country title on the first Saturday of January 1948, ten years after last lifting the trophy.

I ran part of the course, under grey forbidding skies and relentless high winds, and found that traversing even the flatter of these fields overlooking the Darent Valley was tough going in such an open, exposed area. The important county and regional races staged here for many years were occasions that added colour and excitement to the lives of the boys from the Homes, and also gave a fascinating glimpse into another world for the visiting runners who came from more conventional domestic backgrounds.

More than a hundred senior athletes tackled a tough but popular course that day in 1948, one also used from 1926 to 1939 for the annual varsity contest between Oxford and Cambridge. Runners went through the goalposts on the sports field and out across the hedge-lined fields with the Horton Kirby millstream and River Darent prominent among the obstacles to be overcome.

Sydney caused a huge fuss on this, his only visit here. He was one of a big party of fellow Heathens, including club president George Wilkinson. The latter won admiration that afternoon for hiking more than a mile from the start so he could shout encouragement from a remote spot where he said he was "most needed and least expected!" The three-lap, seven-mile course featured many slopes and stretches of plough and tested 106 men to the full in the senior race. Sydney's main rival was an inspired Jack Charlesworth (Aylesford Paper Mills) who took an early lead. Sydney kept his tinder dry back in 11th place, looking for all the world like he would leave things late and make use of his famed explosive finish. But, unexpectedly, at the start of the second lap, he stepped things up and within the space of barely 200 yards had gone smoothly past nine men to the shoulder of leader Charlesworth.

This seemed to demoralise most contenders and before long the leading pair looked unassailable. Reigning county champion, Sgt. Tommy Macoy of the RAF, drifted outside the top ten, suffering from lumbago. A nice piece of downhill grass at the start of the third lap presented itself and Sydney shot away from the younger Charlesworth to cross the line at least 70 yards clear, winning by 16 seconds in 39:45. It was his fifth successive triumph this season and he looked unruffled and composed. The really serious tests at the Southerns and the National would follow, but for now he looked in great shape. Blackheath packed five in the top ten to win the team prize by a big margin and lift the Invicta Cup; they looked a good outside bet to capture the much-coveted National team title, and, who knows, perhaps Sydney's time to be National champion had come too? Weary legs and cold weather were forgotten as they celebrated a great day's work. Sydney, of course, made little fuss, wiping his glasses and quietly getting changed for the journey back to London.

★★★

Sydney's impressive recent form led to speculation over whether he might be persuaded to come out of semi-retirement and bid for an Olympic team place. The Press Association even reported that a South African club had 'adopted' Sydney and would be sending over food parcels addressed to "Sydney Wooderson, Britain's middle distance hope for the Olympic Games." Durban Athletics Club went on to urge others to do likewise and send food to British athletes struggling with inadequate post-war diets. News that Sydney had retired from international competition evidently hadn't reached South Africa – but this did illustrate the high esteem in which he was held around the globe. Harold Sulin, chairman of DAC, was quoted:

> "This is an example other clubs might follow. Each could similarly adopt a British athlete thus making sure he or she is given an even chance with the rest of overseas competitors from countries with a better stocked larder than Britain."

The London Olympics were by now a mere eight months away and during the build-up there would be considerable debate over whether Britain's team was at a disadvantage because of post-war food rationing. The outspoken Dr Christopher Woodward, an adviser to the GB team, feared GB could become "also rans" because they were clearly undernourished compared to rivals. He went on to accuse officials of generally treating them like children and compelling them to compete in minor events to their detriment. He firmly believed an athlete could achieve only one performance per season at 100 per cent effort. Sydney was asked his views on all this, and pointed out he'd won several important races in one season while surviving on rationed foods. Along with champion hurdler Ron Ede, he firmly disputed the doctor's view that elite athletes only had one top performance in them per year. Ede revealed he and others were currently benefitting from private coaching, free medical attention and food parcels in the run-up to the Games.

Meanwhile Sydney again had to deny interest in competing in the Olympics, and indicated his focus this year centred on the National cross-country at Sheffield. Was he serious about a bid to become national champion at Sheffield? Many correspondents and fans during this period seemed unclear whether Sydney was fully operational these days, or whether he regarded himself as semi-retired. Sydney tried to clarify things in a letter to J. Lewington, a fan based in Devon:

> "This summer [1948] I am not doing any track training, for, as you know, I have really retired. I have changed over to [cross-]country for, except for one or two big races, one can take it less seriously than track running, and at the same time be a help with the club on the team side, besides getting a lot of fun out of it."

★ ★ ★

A fortnight after the Kent champs, a record 21 counties did battle at Horsham for the inter-counties crown and the Daily Telegraph Cup, some 183 runners tackling a slippery seven miles with a heavy plough section and a fence to be surmounted. It was tough going in the wind and rain and even experienced Reg Gosney of Eastleigh fell twice when leading. Sydney led Kent to victory, coming third himself in 42:54. He unselfishly 'packed' with colleagues until the final 400 yards when he went hell for leather for personal glory and got close to leading pair Bert Swindells and Jack Corfield of Staffs. But he'd left it too late and just as they hit the final slope he indicated with a wave of his hand that he was done, and Swindells pressed on to win.

Having tasted success at county and inter-county level, the Southerns and the National were Sydney's next targets, and he prepared with a couple of club events in February. First up was Blackheath's Rowland Cup contest over ten miles at Hayes where, on a wet but relatively mild day, he won in 57:36, followed by a five-mile match against Old Croydonians, Culham College and Cuaco Harriers in much more favourable conditions. The latter featured a catastrophic wrong turn by the three men leading, who were wrongly directed, which helped Sydney and clubmates grab an untroubled victory in 28:38, six of them crossing the line in a tightly-packed bunch and being given joint-first.

The Southern champs were staged on the final day of February in the attractive setting of Aylesford in good weather, and an inspired Sydney chalked up a great win in 55:32. His usual tactics worked perfectly as he stayed in contention without fuss early on, kept an eye on things and accelerated in the latter stages when others began to crumble. Reg Gosney

(Eastleigh) ran heroically but couldn't live with Sydney's final sprint. He'd never looked stronger in a cross-country setting than on this day, and fellow runner Stan Tomlin would later write in *Modern Athletics*:

> "There was nothing of the typical rugged cross country runner about Sydney. His rhythmic running was most unsuited for uncertain winter surfaces. But he had courage to a remarkable degree, and it was a terrific display that brought him [this] Southern title."

It was an enjoyable run at Aylesford which, a few months later, would be chosen as a base by the Finnish team prior to the Olympic Games. The facilities were good, but to make themselves feel at home the Finns would install a sauna – believed to be one of the first ever seen in Britain. They would leave it in place after departing, meaning many a home-grown runner would get the chance to enjoy this Scandinavian experience.

For Sydney, a great day at the Southerns would put him in great heart as focus shifted to the National at Sheffield in March. He was currently flying and would surely never have a better chance of becoming champion, a marvellous way to climax the final months of his celebrated career. To stay sharp and loose for the big day he needed a low-key race in non-treacherous conditions the weekend before – and a run at his old school sounded perfect for the job. The match was a three-way affair between Sutton Valence, Blackheath and the school's old boys Old Suttonians over a familiar five-mile route. A train trip to Maidstone and then by bus to the school was required for the Heathens, although Sydney had agreed to race for the Old Boys' team and not his club. The school emulated Felsted by rigging up a system whereby marshals around the course transmitted news of the race via continuous commentary. Sydney ran at under six-minute-mile pace to win without undue stress, narrowly pipping teammate Jim Scott-Wilson. The following day he ventured down to Hastings to perform the role of Godfather at a christening, at the request of his protégé Tony Weeks-Pearson. In Sydney's honour the baby was given a middle name of 'Wooderson'.

43

King of the Country

THE 61st annual National Cross-country championships at Graves Park, Sheffield, represented the biggest day on Sydney's running calendar for more than 18 months. He will have been aware that winning here would cement his status as the best all-round middle- and long-distance runner Britain had produced to date. Victory would be the culmination of a wonderful career and allow him to retire content in the knowledge he had conquered every self-imposed challenge, apart from those cruelly snatched away by the timing of the war, i.e. Olympic success and a four-minute mile. Importantly, he was currently in great form over the country. His National debut a year earlier had been little more than an experiment, and the dreadful conditions had rendered that Apsley race a near-fiasco. Sydney had recently admitted his relief that getting nervous and worked up before races was a rarity nowadays – but Sheffield 1948 marked a return of those dreaded butterflies.

Blackheath's runners met on St Pancras station on Friday 12 March 1948 bound for Sheffield. After arrival that evening at their hotel, many greedily gulped down second helpings at dinner. They were like excitable schoolboys on an outing, brimful of nervous energy. Some wandered into the city for further refreshment but all returned for bed at a sensible hour. Much of Britain was bathed in thin sunshine the next morning, but race-day Sheffield remained stubbornly cloudy. Several hours were killed by a stroll to nearby shops but the Blackheath boys found little to see, apart from noisy groups of football supporters, in town for an FA Cup semi-final at Hillsborough.

Sydney was relieved when it was finally time to head for the changing rooms at Norton Aerodrome, site of a barrage balloon station during the recent war. It was more than a mile from the starting pens in Graves Park and a fleet of buses would convey the runners across. A bugle sounded at 2pm, the five-minute warning to find a bus and get on board. The 10-mile course was mostly firm, undulating grassland, which indicated a fast race. In terms of leg speed Sydney would have no equal, but his credentials at racing ten miles was a different matter.

Around 400 senior men were allocated starting pens according to their club, at one end of a flat, 600-yard starting straight. After stampeding across here they would funnel into paths leading up several hills, a stretch of plough, some woodland and confrontation with a four-foot fence to clamber over into the grounds of Jessop Hospital. A big crowd arrived to witness the spectacle, paying 1/6d for admission to the park and 6d for a programme. Things went like clockwork, despite doubts over the shuttle-bus system, allowing the traditionally spectacular start to be 2.30 prompt. Someone even had the bright idea of firing the starting pistol from behind the runners, thus ensuring everyone heard it and the poor starter didn't get trampled.

The stirring sight of 400 runners advancing like a colourful whirling horde – all the more spectacular because of the immense width of the start-line – thrilled the Sheffield crowd. Stanley Wooderson was among them, cheering on his brother. Once they'd headed out of sight they began to string out in packs, and after two miles Sydney, wearing No.107, was seen to be running well among a leading bunch. Hitting halfway in around 27 minutes, a group of nine men led, Sydney looking strong in roughly sixth place. As the race wore on, it steadily became clear the winner would come from a group of four: Sydney, Vernon 'Vic' Blowfield (Belgrave), Albert Shorrocks (Halesowen) and Jack Charlesworth (Aylesford PM). By now the dangerous 38-year-old Reg Gosney (Eastleigh) had quit due to tendon trouble.

By the time the leading quartet hit the nine-mile point, Sydney and Blowfield had burned the others off and a great finish looked likely. Presumably worried about Sydney's legendary fast finish, the Belgrave man made a bold move, suddenly shooting into the lead and pounded along at full effort to open a gap of almost 30 yards. At this point the spectators had converged leaving just a narrow funnel for the runners to race along – which raises the possibility Blowfield had thought this was the finish funnel, and had made his surge too soon? Sydney kept his cool and was able to produce his own kick in the final 800 yards, passing his man emphatically. There was no holding him as he then stormed up the cruelly-placed final hill to win by 20 yards from gallant Blowfield in 56:52.

Winning in this fashion on such a course was a massive achievement for a track specialist and Sydney had needed to work harder than ever before for it. It had been a near-perfect performance, beautifully judged, but now he was absolutely shattered like never before. It was a day of great celebration for Blackheath, whose team placing of third was their best yet at any National. They'd even survived an incident when Alan Brent was knocked over mid-race by a stray football. He bounced back up to finish 42nd. Following on from their runners-up spot in the Southerns, this had been the club's best cross-country season yet.

Blowfield was given a time of 56:56, Shorrocks third in 56:59, with Belgrave declared team winners. Fourth-placed Charlesworth, who had been astonished by Sydney's performance earlier in the season at Farningham, was again full of admiration and his verdict reproduced in *Athletics Weekly* is as good a summary as any:

> "There were four of us in contention… we had broken away from the field and had been running bunched together until the last half-mile. We went through a small copse and began to run downhill; the pace really began to hot up and it was becoming apparent it was going to be each man for himself. Sydney had started to open a gap by the time we turned left at the bottom, a short flat piece followed, then it was left again, this time to the finish. Sydney proved his utter superiority up that hill. Blowfield and Shorrocks tried desperately to hold him… I blew up and managed to scramble in fourth. It was my hardest race ever and the other two were equally played out… Sydney just did not know what it was to give up."

Reflecting some time later, Sydney would say: "Sheffield was a new race, a new distance, and I got it right. It was the most exhausting race I ever ran and I never did serious cross-country again after that."

Immediately afterwards, Sydney was one of 12 invited to wear an England vest in the international race at Reading three weeks hence.

Athletics
1/-
THE NATIONAL PUBLICATION FOR GREAT BRITAIN
107
SYDNEY WOODERSON WINNING THE "NATIONAL" AT SHEFFIELD
SEE PAGE 22 FOR DETAILS OF
ATHLETICS PICTORIAL SOUVENIR
FOR THE OLYMPIC GAMES
London, 1948

He accepted and was named captain of the team. His retirement from international athletics in 1946 was not being cancelled, he explained, for he was treating Reading as an exception as it was a team race.

Captaining the England team was no small matter and Sydney prepared with great care for his big day in Leighton Park, giving himself time to recover fully from the battle of Sheffield. The 35th international championships (which in 1973 would morph into the IAAF World champs) was being staged in England for the first time in 12 years. Sydney was proud to skipper his country on home turf but had to steel himself for another gruelling test on tricky ground that would last the best part of an hour. And there was an added problem this time: the best talent from the continent would be gunning for him.

A chilly but sunny day greeted the many visitors to Leighton Park on Saturday 3 April. The venue was an independent Quaker school for around 250 pupils, where a demanding course had been created for this unique day involving three laps of just over three miles each, featuring large ditches, gates and a stile. Sydney led a 12-man England squad whose members represented 12 different clubs and the nine-man scoring team was announced as: Adams, Ashcroft, Blowfield, Carrick, Charlesworth, Christina, Corfield, Downer, Hughes, McMinnis, Shorrocks and Wooderson. Their toughest opponents were thought to be the French, winners on the three previous stagings, even though star man Raphael Puzajon was missing this time.

England paraded to big cheers in their all-white tracksuits, a crowd of 15,206 paying customers in the park. But home fans' enthusiasm began to wane when Belgium's John Doms took the lead at the end of the first lap and few Brits appeared to be putting up a serious challenge. Doms stormed to a relatively straightforward win in 54:05, and the next half-dozen home were all Belgian or French, while Sydney, in his unfamiliar all-white kit, with red rose badge and a huge No.12 below it, was a tired 14th in 55:50. The disappointed hosts finished as third team way back on 114 points, with jubilant Belgium's tally of 46 pipping France by just a single point. Ted Downer of Eastleigh in eighth was the first home nations man past the post in 55:17.

Although England's third place of 1947 was repeated, it was a huge blow to come so far behind the runners-up and statistically it was the country's worst showing since the event began in 1903. Although he didn't express it publicly, Sydney must have accepted his best days were over now – it seems the tough nature of the course disrupted his rhythm, whereas three weeks earlier at Sheffield he'd settled well on the faster going. After the race he mentioned being hampered by a minor leg injury but didn't blame everything on this and added: "I just couldn't get into my stride – I guess the Belgians were just too fast."

Desperate for some sort of follow-up story, the press contingent at Reading again quizzed Sydney about the forthcoming Olympics, and he wearily and politely denied any involvement, explaining for the umpteenth time he felt too old at 34 for the rigours of track racing, and would instead watch the Games from the Wembley stands. He was planning time off work to see as much of the athletics programme as possible.

Sydney was at the stage of his running career where enjoyment and satisfaction were higher on his list of priorities than straining fiercely for high placings. And there were very few events on the calendar that generated more fun and high spirits than the *News of the World*'s annual London to Brighton Relay. On Saturday 10 April, he signed up to run a six-mile leg for Blackheath from the Red Lion hotel at Handcross to the Castle Hotel at Hickstead. Taking the baton from Gordon Monshall, he shrugged off soreness in his leg, a hangover from Reading, to hold on to third place before passing to the team's penultimate runner Jim Scott-Wilson. Anchorman Jack Braughton brought them in on the crowded seafront in third place, breaking Sydney's stage record in the process. The aggregate time of 4:00.05 left them just over two minutes adrift of winners Belgrave and runners-up Birchfield who enjoyed a real thriller, finishing within 11 seconds of each other. This would be Sydney's last competitive action for more than six months.

★★★

As summer 1948 arrived and the London Olympics drew ever closer, Sydney Wooderson stuck to his word and remained inactive following the London-Brighton road relay in early April. He'd made it clear many months ago he wouldn't be running at the Wembley showpiece and no amount of prompting from the press and public would tempt a change of his mind at this late stage.

Sydney could hold his head high and let the younger set fly the flag, his career coming to an end with his becoming arguably the best all-rounder British running had ever produced. He'd proved himself an elite performer over a remarkable range of distances and surfaces – from world beating half-miles up to victory in the notoriously difficult 10-mile English National cross-country. It would be a long time before any runner could rival such versatility and range at top level, among them would be the likes of Steve Ovett (400 metres in 47.4 and a half-marathon in 1hr.05.38), Ron Clarke (a mile in 4:03 and 20 kilometres in 59:22.8) and Rod Dixon (800 metres in 1:47.6 and the marathon in 2hrs.08.59).

On an informal basis Sydney was by now doing his bit for Britain's Olympic hopes by making himself available to middle-distance men for advice and coaching tips. He spoke regularly with Alec Olney of Thames Valley Harriers, for example. He had been approached in 1947 to do this work, but would later intimate that he was unhappy with how it went generally, even going so far as admitting he'd "messed up" the job, presumably a reference to the lack of success British track men would ultimately have at the Games.

While athletics fans contemplated an Olympics without their bespectacled hero, the man himself kept busy at weekends by making guest appearances here and there and maintaining his ritual of long countryside walks. Since the war he had been living in Village Way, Beckenham, in a smart, modern bay-windowed semi, and from here would travel many a mile to give something back to the sport now that he wasn't competing so often. For example, he headed deep into East Anglia one evening for a 'Sportsmen's Service' at Wethersfield Parish Church in Essex where he'd agreed to read the lesson. Another commitment saw him perform an exhibition run over half-a-mile at a special Olympic Year Sports Festival in Hastings, and on more than one occasion at the Methodist Central Hall in Redhill he joined other well-known sportsmen to give talks to the accompaniment of film clips. One Saturday saw him attend Ightham Sports and Social Club's annual gala in Kent at which there was momentary panic when a trophy he was supposed to be presenting was found to be missing. Sydney patiently stood around until it was eventually discovered tucked in a wheelbarrow, covered by a tarpaulin, stowed there to protect it from rain and grubby young fingers!

44

Olympic Torch Controversy

THE summer of 1948 was a hot one in England. The new National Health Service began functioning, Comprehensive Schools were introduced, post-war bread rationing ended, and the sun shone brightly on the London Olympics.

By now Sydney Wooderson, seen as the finest runner the nation had ever produced, quietly slipped out of the limelight, done with serious athletic competition. He would be 34 in August, had recently become romantically attached, and his full-time job these days needed his full attention. He was clear that his only running in future would involve occasional team events over country or road where clubmates might benefit from guidance from a wise old hand.

The time was clearly ripe for the sport of athletics to acknowledge and honour Sydney's immense contribution over a period of nearly 20 years. And, by chance, the perfect opportunity was staring everybody in the face: A 'mystery runner' would be needed to carry the Olympic torch into Wembley Stadium on July 29 to perform the symbolic lighting of the flame to launch the 14th Olympiad.

Sydney would surely be perfect for the job: a proud and patriotic Englishman, an athlete of courage and unprecedented talent at the end of his career, a much-loved, modest and dependable character of immense integrity who commanded respect around the globe. The public wanted him to do it, indeed many were taking it for granted he would be doing it. The press wanted it to be Sydney, fellow athletes wanted it to be him. Surely there could be no other serious candidates?

Alas, just a fortnight before the Games' opening ceremony, a dark cloud loomed on the horizon. Rumours started circulating that the torch-bearer would not be Sydney at all. The *Daily Herald* of July 15 reported:

> "One big decision still remains to be made: Who shall carry the blazing Olympic torch on its final stage into the Arena on July 29? It is whispered that the claims of Sydney Wooderson, now retired, but perhaps the finest runner this country ever produced, are being opposed because the unobtrusive, bespectacled little man does not physically represent the popular international idea of a great athlete – a muscled Adonis. To rule out Wooderson because of this would be carrying showmanship too far. Sydney's figure may not be ideal, but there is nothing wrong with his figures, as any record book will show. Don't let us have a squabble over this. His claims stick out a mile – a record mile."

This, and other newspaper gossip, fuelled the fire over subsequent days. One piece, in the *Dundee Courier*, caused particular surprise, revealing that none other than Lord Burghley – President of the IAAF and chairman of the Olympic organising committee in London – had personally told them the mystery torch carrier would be: "A very tall, fair-haired athlete", and His Lordship also "conveyed the impression it would be a local man." As it was traditional to keep the identity secret until the torch-bearer actually appeared, the paper suggested, with justification, that Burghley might well just be mischievously tossing them a red herring and on the day everyone would find out it was Sydney Wooderson after all – the man "generally recognised as being the greatest British athlete".

Broadcaster and historian Bob Phillips would examine the torch controversy in great detail years later. He wrote:

> "The leader article in The Times of Wednesday 28 July 1948, the day before the Games were to open, loftily turned its attention to the burning (in the literal sense) issue of the moment: 'Even among those who have not become, to use an almost unavoidable phrase, Olympic-minded, there is one event in the Games which has captured the imagination – the carrying of the lighted torch from

distant Olympia to the Stadium at Wembley'. The article concluded emphatically: 'Nearly everyone knows the runner they would like to see'. No name needed to be mentioned because the man in question was the nationally-renowned Sydney Wooderson… there was no doubting his credentials and his aptitude for the task, but unfortunately for him there were other considerations which were kept secret – and, worse than that, he was to receive the shabbiest of treatment at the hands of organising committee members who otherwise had carried out as exemplary a task in the lead-up to the Games as could be hoped for."

As Bob Phillips understood it, Sydney was told beforehand at some point that he would be the final bearer of the torch into the stadium and would light the flame. He arrived on the big day expecting to carry out the privileged task, only to be informed he was not wanted. But this was no last-minute decision for the chosen man had been informed by letter at least three weeks earlier. The letter had stated:

"You should be attired in white, and I would suggest that you use lightweight rubber shoes, spikes not being necessary. The pace round the Stadium would be moderate without being too fast or too slow. It is all part of the 'play' and will require a certain amount of acting to make it effective."

The recipient of the letter turned out to be a young athlete whose abilities, though respectable, were far inferior to those of Wooderson. He was John Mark, a quarter-miler not quite fast enough to qualify for the Olympics himself, but a medical student who did have the attributes of being tall, blond, and muscular – the polar opposite of little Sydney of course. He also had the 'appropriate' background, being current President of Cambridge University Athletic Club, a position none other than Lord Burghley had occupied years earlier. "The brave little solicitor's clerk from Blackheath Harriers had cruelly been passed up at the last moment for an Adonis," concludes Phillips.

Writer David Thurlow delved into archived paperwork which revealed the search for a man who was "tall and blond" had in fact been going on for at least three months before the 1948 Games. The organising committee agreed in June to approach John Mark "subject to him not being included in the British team". Mark was eliminated in the heats of the 440 yards at White City on July 3, meaning he hadn't made the team, so was duly recruited. Sadly nobody had the good grace to inform the overwhelming favourite for the position.

Sydney's reaction to the whole affair is not on record, and, just like John Mark, he would always keep his thoughts to himself. But he did confirm many years later to David Thurlow that there had been conversations about the matter with Lord Burghley and torch relay organiser Bill Collins but he couldn't recall the sequence of events. Of course, there had been a secrecy aspect to consider, but the overall impression all these years later is that the whole thing was handled very badly. To avoid the embarrassment Sydney must have suffered on being left unemployed that July morning, perhaps he ought to have sought clarity earlier himself, but his natural politeness and reticence may well have held him back.

An interesting slant on the whole business would see the light of day nearly 50 years later, courtesy of *The Times*' athletics correspondent Neil Allen. He wrote:

> "For me, deliberately choosing so-called Greek-god figures for an Olympic opening ceremony smacks far too much of a Berlin *ubermensch* feast for the propaganda lens of [Nazi propagandist film-maker] Leni Riefenstahl… I can never forget what happened four years later in Helsinki [1952 Olympics] when a rotund, balding 55-year-old trotted round the track and the capacity crowd bellowed the immortal name of Paavo Nurmi, Finland's track hero as Sydney Wooderson was ours."

Bob Phillips concluded:

> "It is astonishing that the Games organisers, all of them staunch defenders of the establishment faith, should have taken as their model an image created by the country against which they had been fighting for six years, and which had been brought to universal attention by Fraulein Riefenstahl's dramatic but disturbing film of those Nazi-traduced Games. Even so, it was perhaps realistic

> of Queen Elizabeth (later the Queen Mother) to say, as she is reputed to have done, when she was told of the choice of John Mark: 'Of course, we couldn't have had poor little Sydney doing it'."

Fleet Street journalist Norman Giller would recall in 2011 the time he phoned Harold Abrahams, one of the Games organisers, to ask why Sydney was passed over. Abrahams candidly admitted it was because Mark looked like a Greek god who fitted the image of an Adonis running a torch up Mount Olympus. Abrahams added: "Dear Sydney Wooderson did not even enter our minds. He was such a frail man and, believe me, carrying the Olympic torch on that last lap with the arm extended took enormous strength. John Mark carried it out to perfection." Giller recalled further conversations in which he was assured via Oxbridge sources that when Mark made his big entrance into the stadium, the Queen herself (later the Queen Mother) was overheard to say: 'Dear me, what a pity they did not get that dear little Sydney Wooderson to do it'."

There appears little or no mention of Sydney's absence in contemporaneous press reports of the opening ceremony, but it was surely a talking point among the crowd and elsewhere. The media of that era was less inclined to enter into controversy, but the matter has been chewed over a number of times in subsequent years. One additional theory suggested Sydney's polite but firm refusal to compete at the Games himself might have put a few noses out of joint in the corridors of power, helping to sway things against him. On balance, the desire for everything at the parade to 'look good' does seem the over-riding reason for the snub: In his book *Austerity Britain*, David Kynaston says the press of the day also stayed silent about the banning from the parade of the "unsightly" rowing cox Jack Dearlove, who only had one leg. This was the first opening ceremony since the Berlin spectacular, and the GB organisers clearly wanted its parade to be picture perfect.

It did indeed 'look good' on the big day. Just after 4pm on the sweltering afternoon of Thursday 29 July the final flaming torch-bearer did his thing and a choir of 1,200 accompanied by the massed bands of the Brigade of Guards sang the Olympic hymn – Rudyard Kipling's *Non Nobis Domine* – while the flag with its familiar five inter-linked rings was raised. The 85,000 crowd was bewitched.

The athletics programme duly got underway and the next day, sitting high in the Wembley stands, was none other than Sydney Wooderson, accompanied on their first 'date' by his office colleague Miss Pamela Willcocks. Wedded to athletics until now, Sydney's life was changing direction fast, and the young woman beside him would soon become Mrs Wooderson.

45

Misery in Manchester Mud

THERE was mud, rain and wind, the like of which many battle-hardened runners had never experienced before. Even the normally inscrutable Sydney Wooderson was prompted to describe Worsley as the worst cross-country conditions he'd ever run in.

The 168 who ran this 194–9 Inter-Counties championship on the outskirts of Manchester would never forget the experience – Sydney included. The bigwigs at the English Cross-Country Union had made the bold decision to take this showpiece event to new territory – awarding it to the sport's North of England region for the very first time. Worsley was chosen to host the event and a route devised involving four laps of just under two miles each, based at Grange Farm.

On Saturday 15 January, after completing his working week in a warm, oak-panelled London office, Sydney Wooderson jumped on a special breakfast-time train from Euston, along with four colleagues from Blackheath Harriers and dozens of others representing southern counties. They were met at Manchester's Piccadilly station by a fleet of buses which ferried them to Worsley Secondary Modern School. Here the runners were pleased to find what one Blackheath man called "Excellent changing and washing accommodation" – although he did follow up this compliment with a dig about the "traditional Manchester weather" as the rain continued to tip down.

I had to pore over several maps before locating the spot used for the race. It was tricky trying to picture the scene at Grange Farm back in January

1949 as the weather on my visit was warm and dry and there was barely another person in sight as I scanned the horizon – merely an unrelenting buzz of traffic from the point nearby where the M60 and M602 motorways meet.

Although the Inter-Counties race had never been this far north until 1949, the last English National before the war had been on this very course. Runners who recalled that race said conditions were appalling, and ten years later things were even worse. It would be one hell of a slog and the weather was unrelentingly awful. Men were strung out in a long procession, apparently more intent on survival than overtaking people ahead.

Local favourite Ron Williams of Lancashire nicked a dramatic late win, passing the neck-and-neck pairing of Alec Olney (Middlesex) and Geoff Saunders (Lancs). Although Sydney, the reigning national champion, was famously light on his feet, this was a course not even he could enjoy and he trudged home seventh in 49:00. One suspects his motivation on a day like this was not at its highest. His star was clearly on the wane by now; he'd achieved much of what he wanted in running, and at the age of 34 a settled life in the suburbs bringing up a family was beckoning.

Home county Lancashire ran like men inspired – their six scorers all among the first 20 past the post. They won the team prize comfortably, with Sydney's Kent team back in fourth. Sydney was around 45 seconds adrift of the winner and never featured at the front of the race. On the long train journey home he must have contemplated the fact that conditions had been so tough his average pace had been only seven-minutes-per-mile – almost certainly his slowest in any serious race since boyhood.

Nevertheless, seventh was highly respectable in most eyes and his performances so far this season silenced a few doubters and showed he wasn't quite ready to hang up the spikes yet. The campaign had got underway in October 1948 on an unseasonably warm day at Hayes when he was a relaxed 12th in the Blackheath five-mile club race won by Alan Brent from a field of 80. A fortnight later on Oxford University's flat Kennington course, he came fifth for Blackheath in 40:55, 42 seconds behind home winner Pollard. After another break of a fortnight, a sunny day greeted the popular Nicholls Cup mob match on Coulsdon Downs against South London Harriers, for which Sydney arrived late for the start but still managed to come second of 126 in 48:41, albeit a good margin behind SLH's Brian Bowering.

On Saturday 27 November a second trip into academia saw Sydney joint-third with colleague Jack Braughton, beaten by 20 seconds to the post by Cambridge Hare and Hounds' duo Chris Brasher and S. Groton. The hospitable students laid on a splendid tea and Sydney and pals would not arrive home till well after 10pm. A week later Blackheath hosted the Royal Military Academy team from Sandhurst and Thames Hare and Hounds, Sydney claiming eighth in the 7.5-mile contest, almost a minute down on THH winner Peter Curry. Blackheath's Maugham had looked good for victory on this unusually mild and bright afternoon until he made a disastrous wrong turn mid-race. The last action before Christmas 1948 saw Sydney chalk up his first win for nine months, in the annual 7.5-mile mob match against Ranelagh at Hayes for the Davies Challenge Cup. On wet, slippery ground his 44:27 left him 13 seconds clear of Braughton as Heathens took the team prize.

* * *

January 1949 would prove a red-letter month, Sydney getting engaged to girlfriend Pamela Willcocks of Kingston Hill, a secretary at his place of work. The couple decided they would marry at some point in 1950 and only broke the news to family and close friends. However, Sydney's fame inevitably meant it wouldn't remain secret for long, leaking out and making the newspapers a few weeks later. Once the news went public, Sydney revealed a few more details:

> "We met three years ago when I returned from war service to my city office. Miss Willcocks is secretary to one of the partners in the firm of city solicitors for which I work. We actually became engaged on January 16, but only close friends knew about it. It may be about a year before we marry. Pamela comes to see most of my races."

Pamela and her future mother-in-law were among supporters at the Kent cross-country championships at the county police HQ at Maidstone on New Year's Day 1949. The seven-mile route proved tougher than usual due to bitterly cold and stormy conditions. Hailstorms and ferocious wind battered the field as reigning champion Sydney came in fourth in 43:13.

Dick Adams (City of Rochester) took his title, but Sydney was content to lead Blackheath to victory in the team contest. It was one of the toughest tests in living memory, featuring orchards, 100 yards of road, some plough, a track through a wood and lots of roadside grass verge. The wife of Kent's Chief Constable handed over the prizes, but a shortage of refreshments at the end for the weary runners went down rather badly.

As covered earlier, another battle with the elements followed at Worsley, before Sydney was able to taste victory again in the club's Rowland Challenge Cup over 10 miles on Saturday 5 February. He won in 57:28, a good distance clear of Wally Spencer, in a record field of 53. On this brisk, spring-like day Sydney had overtaken Spencer after about eight miles and built a big lead on Fox Hill. There followed afterwards an interesting debate in the clubhouse over how regularly a member had to complete a 10-mile cross-country race to be considered "a true cross country man". The consensus was that one had to be completed at least every three years to maintain that hallowed status.

A week later Sydney and clubmates headed down to Sutton Valence School for the regular race across the fields against teams from the school and Old Suttonians. An excited young spectator that day was pupil Tony Millard, with whom I made contact in 2017. Tony told me:

> "I remember Sydney coming in joint-first with Jim Scott-Wilson – who later married one of the assistant matrons if I recall correctly. The course was 5.3 miles long and the race certainly ended on 'The Lower' and I suspect started from there too, as I remember that we used to run past what we called 'bloody mountains' rugger pitches before joining the road section. I suppose the same course is used even in modern times. We were in awe of Sydney, as I remember being one of many young boys who went down to the Dining Hall to get his autograph! I was in my second term in Bennetts House at the time, and all the runners agreed to sign autographs while taking refreshments in the Dining Hall, and I still have those autographs in my school Blue Book. I left St. Margaret's house in Lent 1953 and went on to follow a career in banking."

Sydney was always made very welcome at his old school, and the same went for the Royal Military Academy at Sandhurst, where he appeared on

Saturday 26 February for the 1949 Southern championships. News of his engagement had made some newspapers that same day, and fiancee Pamela was among the big crowd as 128 teams gathered for the 10-mile showdown. One national daily even snapped a picture for their later editions of the happy couple boarding a train to the race from Waterloo Station. Sydney came 14th in 57:57, around 90 seconds behind impressive winner Alec Olney (TVH). Blackheath were disappointed to finish as low as sixth in the team rankings, but Sydney said afterwards it had been tight and with a little luck they could have won. He issued a rallying call to his clubmates not involved today, urging them to adjust their priorities for future seasons by aiming specifically at the Southerns and National, just like he always had since the war.

46

Transition to Normality

BROMFORD Bridge was never one of Britain's most glamorous or scenic horse racing venues. But it certainly had an interesting 71-year lifespan: Suffragettes burned down its main grandstand, it was used as an anti-aircraft station during the war, and in 1949 humans replaced horses when it hosted the 62nd English National cross-country championships.

Now Bromford Bridge is no more. Lester Piggott, Greville Starkey and other famous jockeys dismounted one wet June evening in 1965 and next day the place closed for good. Birmingham council purchased the site and bulldozers moved in. Nowadays the site is a sprawling housing estate with a long chunk of the M6 motorway thrown in for good measure.

You can still make out parts of where the racetrack went, but you need to look very carefully among puddles and long grass under the overhead cables and the motorway flyover.

I had a run here as part of my Sydney tour, knowing this was for him a swansong of sorts. Although he wasn't quite ready to be put out to grass, he knew this was likely to be the last serious contest he took part in. Having caused a real stir by winning the National at Sheffield the previous year, he lined up as a popular reigning champion and the most famous name among a record pre-entry of nearly 2,000 runners. A record 449 men started the 10-mile senior contest, sent on their way at 2.30 by the Lord Mayor of Birmingham, and wearing the colours of 53 different clubs.

"It was colossal," wrote one correspondent, and the Pathe News commentator with the plummy voice exclaimed: "What a scrum! Just look at 'em!" It took an age for the massive pack to string out and Jimmy Green, editor of *Athletics* magazine, would call for restrictions in future as he believed this size of field was totally unwieldy, despite the good facilities at Bromford Bridge. There were fences to be hurdled, rough tussocky grass and a hill that had a cliff-like descent. The course took them adjacent to, but not actually on, the track used by the horses. However, they did get changed in the stables, one allocated to each club complete with a key for storing clothes and valuables.

After the spectacular sight of the mass start, Sydney was nippy enough to establish a prominent place early on, but after a few miles dropped back. He kept an eye out for clubmates and ran with them to provide encouragement where he could. He came home 45th, modest by his high standards, but no great shock. His salad days were gone and, as if to emphasise this, at exactly the same time some 150 miles to the south 20-year-old student Roger Bannister was setting a new Varsity record at White City, running the mile in 4:16.2. A few weeks later Bill Nankeville would break the AAA championship record with 4:08.8; Bannister and Nankeville were the future, Sydney's golden era was slipping away.

Meanwhile, a thrilling duel at the sharp end of the Bromford Bridge battle saw Leeds doctor Frank Aaron pip North Londoner Alec Olney by 30 yards to become the new English champion. Sydney didn't seem unduly sad about conceding his much-coveted crown. Holding the title for a year had been a wonderful bonus in the twilight of a career that might easily have ended years earlier. He was probably more disappointed about Blackheath failing to finish among the top ten teams, an outcome partly due to Alan Brent being forced to quit mid-race.

Any lingering gloom within the Blackheath camp would be banished three weeks later by the heady atmosphere of the annual *News of the World* London to Brighton relay. At least 40 from the club turned out to run or support, and in fine weather proceedings got underway promptly at midday on Streatham Common.

Sydney, running the seventh leg, was not at his sharpest, but his 31:36 clocking was still highly respectable, and only 42 seconds slower than a new stage record created by the popular veteran Jack Holden (Tipton) that same afternoon. Holden's run took his club from fifth to second, while Sydney made up 20 seconds on the race leaders during his stint. He received the baton from clubmate Holland and was seen smiling broadly as the Blackheath bus chugged past him, its occupants cheering wildly. There was the usual traffic chaos as supporters' vehicles shuttled up and down the route looking for their runners. Sydney passed the baton to Alan Brent with Blackheath by now in 14th place, and they hit the seafront finish-line 11th in 4:05.00, winners Belgrave having recorded 3:57.35.

Sticking to his promise of no more track racing, the London-to-Brighton would ultimately prove to be Sydney's last open race of any sort. He didn't know this at the time, having indicated to colleagues he would probably have another shot at the National in 1950, which would be at Aylesbury. We now know that didn't happen, and all that lie ahead before full retirement would be half-a-dozen closed club races. His 35th birthday and married life were looming large by now, and running was taking a back seat. His young protégé from Hastings, Tony Weeks-Pearson, joined Blackheath around now, and Sydney generously gave up time to help coach this promising young talent.

During the summer of 1949 it was interesting to note that although he'd quit serious track running three years earlier, Sydney still led the all-time British rankings at 1500 metres, one mile, three miles, 5000 metres and 800m/880y. The only distance he'd ever tackled seriously at which he didn't finish 'top of the pile' was the rarely-run two-miles, his attack on that record ruined by injury.

Over the autumn of 1949 he was happy to enjoy the renewed camaraderie of a club cross-country season, albeit finishing well outside the top ten in four of five relatively low-key races. He was 18th at his club's five-mile championship in 30:05, 17th in the mob match with South London Harriers in 49:10, 13th in the contest with Orion Harriers in 46:24, and 23rd in the muddy Blackheath 10-miler in a very steady 75:38.

This campaign and, effectively, his entire running career, drew to a quiet close on Saturday 11 February 1950 where it had all started – at Sutton Valence School. On a day battered by rain and gale-force winds, Sydney came home a relaxed joint-first in 29:39 alongside colleagues Betteridge and Brill in the five-mile contest against the school team.

It wasn't quite a case of slipping quietly out of the sporting spotlight. Sydney would remain in demand for occasional guest appearances and, as cooperative as ever, would rarely turn requests down. He appeared at Ruislip as a special guest at the ceremonial opening of the new Finchley Harriers HQ, joining a pack of about 70 for a steady four-mile spin afterwards. Not long after this, shocking news would filter across from New York that his old rival Jack Lovelock, now 39, had been killed when falling into the path of a subway train near the Brooklyn hospital where he worked.

Speculation inevitably centred on whether Lovelock had taken his own life, but it would emerge the tragedy occurred at a time Lovelock had been feeling seriously dizzy, a symptom said to have resulted from an earlier riding accident. A shocked Sydney paid public tribute, describing the Kiwi as his greatest opponent on the track, following their six intense battles in the 1930s, and added that Lovelock's Berlin victory of 1936 was one of the finest performances he'd ever seen. He said:

> "Lovelock had been a temperamental athlete, suffering terribly from nerves before a race and could build up his peak for only one race per season. After that he seemed to be burned out. He liked to rely on others to set the pace. He would jockey for position on the last lap and rely on his sprint at the end."

Sydney made another celebrity appearance at the National cross-country at Aylesbury in March 1950, as the guest starter of a junior race. Although there appears to have been no public announcement of retirement from all competition by now, Sydney will have known privately it was all over – and must have gazed rather wistfully upon the colourful and noisy scenes at Aylesbury. A world record entry of 1,587 runners had been received for the day's various races, more than 500 of them from senior men. Cross-country was clearly thriving as never before, just as one of its greatest champions was bowing out.

A day or two after Aylesbury, the IAAF issued a comprehensive history of officially acknowledged European track and field event records: Britain held seven of the 58 men's records and two of the 19 women's marks. One of the seven was Sydney's 1:49.2 for the half-mile, run in 1938. Overall, Britain were well behind Sweden, who claimed 24 records, and Germany 11.

In the spring of 1950 Sydney, by now approaching the age of 36, married fiancee Pamela, ten years his junior, at St. Paul's Church in Kingston Hill, Surrey. Born in Weybridge, his bride was the daughter of gardener William Willcocks. Among the guests at the ceremony on Saturday 15 April were officials and colleagues from Blackheath Harriers.

Married life began in a newly-purchased home in Beverley Road, Worcester Park, Kingston. It was convenient for his workplace, the Keene Marsland branch office at Kingston, and not far from Pam's parents. It was a smart, bay-windowed semi in a quiet tree-lined street, typical suburbia and one of many well-ordered yet unostentatious houses that were home to commuters in the 1950s. Interestingly, the house was positioned exactly one mile from Motspur Park, the scene of some of his greatest running feats. It is tempting to think this choice of address was no coincidence, but, on reflection, probably unlikely!

He was embarking on married life as a professional man with a reasonable salary and an unusual degree of national fame, but that of course didn't mean he was especially well off by any means. These were austere times for the vast majority with London still in a mess after the war, both structurally and economically.

In 1950 the capital and its hinterland was a far cry from the colourful, cosmopolitan city it would become. The fifties would soon gather momentum and become a decade of great change, but while Sydney was cutting himself off from active sport and contemplating starting a family, the capital was still a grey place where day-to-day life could be unrelentingly tough. The writer and campaigner Doris Lessing, later a Nobel Prize winner, arrived in London around now for the first time and described what she found:

> "London was unpainted, buildings were stained and cracked and dull and grey; it was war damaged, some areas all in ruins, and under them holes full of dirty water once cellars, and it was subject to a sudden dark fogs… No cafes, no good restaurant, clothes were still 'austerity' from the war, dismal and ugly. Everyone was indoors by ten and the streets were empty… the war still lingered, not only in the bombed places but in people's minds and behaviour."

Times may have been tough generally at this time, but Sydney was not interested in finding ways to make extra money from his fame; even though he no longer competed, he remained determined not to put his amateur status in jeopardy. *Evening News* sportswriter Jack Oaten approached him with the idea of working on an autobiography together, Oaten having been earlier approached by a publisher willing to pay a big cash advance. To his astonishment Sydney turned him down flat, and Oaten would later explain:

> "The amateur spirit held something special for Wooderson, hard to define but always very real. Believing that he had something of great importance to pass on to the next generation, I transmitted the [book] offer, which was backed by a substantial sum in cash. To my lasting regret but intense admiration, Wooderson refused. He wished to keep his amateur status unstained even in retirement."

Confirmation, if it were needed, that Sydney's era as a champion was gone and the new generation had taken over, came on an April evening in 1951 when Roger Bannister, running as a guest at a cool and completely windless Motspur Park, won a three-quarter mile contest in 2:56.8. He comfortably banished Sydney's 12-year-old English native record of 2:59.6 to the history books. Bannister's display prompted press gossip that he was "methodically developing himself into a miler of Sydney's class" and would surely soon be the first man to break four minutes for the mile. Around a year later, another Wooderson record would go up in smoke at White City when 21-year-old Gordon Pirie scythed 8.4 seconds off Sydney's six-year-old three-mile mark of 13:53.2.

For the very last time as a relatively young man, Sydney was tempted to don the competition shoes again when, in October 1951, he joined 74 clubmates for a five-mile spin at the Blackheath cross-country championship at Hayes. He had no pretensions about finishing near the front and concentrated on encouraging others, coming home 47th, more than six minutes behind winner Roy Morley.

A week later, he made another unexpected move, appearing at the 22nd Royal Variety performance at Victoria Palace, London, when he was part of a surprise parade of top British sportsmen for the entertainment of the Queen, Princess Margaret, the Duchess of Gloucester, and two sisters who had recently been nursing the seriously-ill King George

VI. Sydney was seen alongside cyclist Reg Harris, motor racing's Reg Parnell, the Cambridge rowing crew, athlete Macdonald Bailey, footballer Stanley Matthews and champion jockey Gordon Richards.

47

Taking a Back Seat

THROUGHOUT the early 1950s Sydney kept in close touch with happenings at his club, putting in some coaching stints and helping out as a race and event official. On one occasion, Blackheath provided most of the race officials at a National Provincial Bank Sports meeting and when it was decided to stage an 'officials race' – a light-hearted two-lap walk – Sydney couldn't resist stepping up to the start-line, and promptly won the event ahead of clubmate Doug Tingey.

Sydney's efforts coaching Blackheath men supplemented those of the highly-regarded Austrian Franz Stampfl, who hired himself out to an assortment of London clubs (e.g. Blackheath, Belgrave, SLH) over this period and was on a retainer to look after athletes at Oxford University and coached at schools. Stampfl took regular sessions in Battersea Park and at the Duke of York Barracks in Kings Road, Chelsea, where attendance cost one shilling per person. During 1955 Stampfl departed to live and work in Australia.

In May 1953, Sydney's long-standing British mile record fell to Roger Bannister, who clocked 4:03.6 at Iffley Road, Oxford. It led to considerable controversy as regards ratification, as Chris Chataway's presence as a pacemaker meant it had not been a bona fide race. The same could be said of Sydney's record run nearly 16 years earlier as that, of course, had been a specially-formed handicap in which he had 'rabbits' to chase. Whatever the pros and cons of these record-chasing arrangements, Bannister would now admit that beating his hero Sydney's time so emphatically meant the four-minute mile was indeed within his reach. But Bannister was a natural worrier, just like Sydney, and became obsessed with the fear that someone else would get there first.

Later that summer Sydney would get to see the White City cinder track from a different point of view, driven around it in an open-topped car before the start of the inaugural Emsley Carr Mile race. Around 40,000 turned out to see the British Games that day and press photos showed the vehicle circling to much waving and cheering, and behind the driver sat Sydney, by now 38, but looking decidedly middle aged, alongside fellow passengers Gunder Hagg, Joe Binks and Paavo Nurmi. The four legends of the mile signed a red leather-bound book, which contained a history of mile running since 1868, and would be signed by all winners of the Emsley Carr Mile from that day hence. The first winner that afternoon was Gordon Pirie in a magnificent 4:06.8, smashing the stadium record set by Sydney 14 years earlier in 4:07.4.

⋆⋆⋆

As time went by, outside the world of Blackheath Harriers, little would be heard about Sydney apart from the occasional feature in magazines or newspapers that often referred back to his training methods.

Sydney rarely went into much detail when asked how he used to train, preferring to sum things up by saying he did far less, in terms of mileage and frequency of session, than the modern runners were now doing. And with hindsight he was glad that had been the case.

In the pages of *World Sports* magazine in 1955 he revealed his typical summer season training sessions during his early years as a miler would end in September, and in the following month he'd begin cross-country work, with the priority being the Kent county race in the January:

> "During the three months leading up to this race, apart from club runs each Saturday, I would train two or three times on midweek evenings, come hail, rain or sun, and if it was cold would wear tracksuit and gloves. Since these evening runs were on the road, I took good care to wear a heel sponge to prevent jarring. It would raise a smile nowadays, but after the Kent race I used to take a whole month off! I think athletes today might benefit from a

slight relaxation in training like this – not so much for physical but mental reasons. In February I would begin getting ready for the track season.

"The early season track-training was usually at Battersea under the supervision of Albert Hill, whose motto to me was 'Keep it light'. Nevertheless I'd turn out four or even five times a week – and the modern idea of training more than once a day was something that never even occurred to us. As the season approached we stepped it up. It is with some diffidence that I set forth a typical mid-March week: Day 1 – about four miles easy striding, Day 2 – 2 x 440 yards, Day 3 – three-quarter-mile time-trial (never faster than 3:08), Day 4 – 1.5 miles fast striding (say 7 mins), Day 5 – four miles easy striding. On Sundays a walk which would vary according to how much time I could spare from my studies – between 2 and 14 miles.

"I do believe there is such a thing as saturation point in training and if I had to choose between the Chataway method of about 35 miles a week and the Kuts method of nearer 135 miles, I would certainly choose the British way of life!"

Sydney was very conscious how mental tiredness could affect top runners. He admitted to suffering from pre-race nerves, sometimes up to five days before a big race. In 1966 he told Bob Phillips:

"A typical session of mine would be a two-mile warm-up, three-quarter mile time-trial in 3:10, a two-mile warm-down and then off home. I am sure one reason why athletes – like Peter Snell for instance – retire after no more than three or four years' major competition these days is because of the great mental and physical demands made on them. In the 1930s we had perhaps three peaks to aim at during the season – the AAA championships, of course, the European Games if there was one, and one international. Now it's under four-minute miling in May and the same form to be maintained until September. The whole attitude of the sport is much more professional and I'm not sure whether I could have competed under present day conditions."

He often marvelled at the workloads of modern runners and would recall how his policy had always been to rest completely for at least three days prior to a race. He usually managed nine hours of sleep the night before a race and always opted for a light fish meal on the day itself. Interviewed by GB international Bruce Tulloh in 1983, Sydney pointed out:

> "Albert Hill had been coached by Sam Mussabini so we were really using his methods. I would go out and warm up properly, doing two or three miles, and then I would do my 'piece' which might be a half-mile or a mile and a half, or whatever he decided. On the Wednesday before a mile race we would do a three-quarter mile time-trial; if I was aiming at 4.20 on the Saturday I would try to run a 3.15 three-quarter and then rest for three days. I just could not do the kind of training Coe and Ovett are doing now!"

Speaking to writer Alistair Aitken in 1979 he said what training he did in the 1930s and 1940s he considered to be more than most people, but compared to today was very little as he had to combine it with work:

> "To me it seemed quite a lot, but today it probably sounds like nothing at all. I suppose it would be a matter of one to two hours [each session]. It's difficult for me to be objective as I haven't done the [modern, intensive] training but I do feel that they tend to do too much today."

Paavo Nurmi, running superstar of the 1920s, often used to assert that only big, powerful men could hope to make or break running records. By the end of the 1930s Sydney had certainly put that one to bed. In his book *Olympics Cavalcade: Who's Who of 1948*, author A. J. Wallis pondered over where small-framed Sydney got his "astounding" stamina and running power from. The answer, he concluded, was that in proportion to his small build he had abnormal heart and lung capacity. He noted that Sydney's stride measured six feet seven inches, over a foot longer than his height, and over a mile he therefore picked his feet up and put them down again 796 times – three foot beats every second! Sydney told Wallis he added to his running in summer with swimming, golf and tennis, adding:

"I have no room for crazy ideas or cranky notions… no need for special diet, my years in the Army proved that, normally just plain home food is best. Massage is far too overrated – all I need is about one massage throughout a season. I've never smoked and seldom drink – better to do neither. There are no rules on style as each of us has his own individual style which can be improved and modified, but no-one should try to copy others. Hagg and Andersson kick their rear leg well behind above the level of knee, which is condemned in text books, but they still break records."

48

Four Minutes: If Only, If Only...

ALL the speculation over who would be the first man under four minutes for the mile came to a thrilling end in Oxford on Thursday 6 May 1954, and Sydney Wooderson greeted Roger Bannister's historic 3:59.4 with genuine warmth: "It is absolutely wonderful news. I always thought he would be the first to do it."

Had circumstances been different Sydney could have been that man, for it was widely agreed he was robbed of his chance by the intervention of war. It was probably small consolation that *The Times*, reporting Bannister's triumph, called Sydney "the man who had made it possible." By 1939 Sydney had made himself a serious sub-four candidate, building towards a peak with his best years still ahead. But then came war and six years of poor diet, disjointed training and a lack of quality racing. Experts were agreed that he'd been highly unlucky and the prize could have been his had he been born just a couple of years earlier or later.

Sydney's chances of achieving the feat were first seriously aired at a Waldorf Hotel dinner in 1937 when guest speaker and 19th century champion Walter George got to his feet. He told Blackheath Harriers members that young Wooderson would run a mile in four minutes one day "as long as he didn't tear himself to bits" doing cross-country.

Sydney himself is said to have smiled quietly at old Walter's bold prediction – but according to John Bryant, author of the book *3.59.4*, he did confess as early as spring 1938 that he fancied his chances. At the beginning of summer training he'd announced to the world he was hoping to run the first four-minute mile: "It is the ambition of my life to be the first to do it." But where, the press wondered, were the runners to be found to take Sydney around a lap apiece at a level 60 seconds?

When he'd set his 1937 world record of 4:06.4 Sydney had clocked two laps in around 58 seconds each and managed a fast finish, demonstrating that a uniform 60-per-lap shouldn't be beyond him. But, Bryant pointed out:

> "Sadly, as so often with Wooderson, he was to be robbed of the opportunity of running the perfect mile. War cheated him of what should have been his finest athletic hours when the Olympics of 1940 and 1944 were cancelled. The lost years between 1938 and his re-emergence in international competition in 1945 should have been Wooderson's greatest."

In his biography *Chris Brasher – the Man Who Made the London Marathon*, Bryant recalled a 1951 round-table conference of a dozen British sportsmen chaired by Raymond Glendenning of the BBC, who asked what were the prospects of a four-minute mile by a Briton. Roger Bannister piped up:

> "I would say there is a reasonable possibility of our doing it. If you can find the man who can run a mile in 4:04 like Sydney Wooderson, it's reasonable that you will find someone who can go below that when he has someone to run against."

Respected athletics correspondent Jack Oaten of the *Evening News* firmly believed Sydney had it in him to go sub-four:

> "His fastest was 4:04.4... and his was a career interrupted by a world war, with its attendant difficulties of lack of the right food and the right conditions and time for training. Despite this he put up performances which were not to be equalled for another nine years. If only we had been able to have a series of races with the great swedes Hagg, Andersson, Strand and Persson, who were his contemporaries at the end of the Second World War, the four-minute mile would have been accomplished by one of them. In my opinion that one would have been Wooderson."

Sydney's fellow miler Bill Nankeville concurred:

> "Just at the time when he was running into top gear the war came… together with Roger Bannister he was without doubt our greatest miler. With his uncanny stamina and tremendous finishing speed I feel he possibly could have beaten even Roger."

During the 1930s many so-called 'experts' dismissed the four-minute mile as impossible, but during the war Joe Binks was the first journalist to give serious consideration in print to the idea of a man going under four minutes. After Arne Andersson reduced the record to 4:02.6 in 1943, Binks put forward the radical idea of a cooperative international effort to achieve the feat:

> "It would be best to have four or five top-notchers training together before the race and I suggest that running of laps in 60 seconds be practised. Each runner should help the others with pacing and only around the last lap should the competitors go all out to gain an individual triumph."

He proposed Hagg and Andersson would be the major contenders but also recommended that Sydney join them, calling his victory at Ibrox Park in 1943 in atrocious weather one of the greatest miles ever run given all the circumstances.

Barely a month after Bannister finally created history on the Iffley Road track in 1954 and put the matter to bed, Gordon Pirie ran a mile in 4:05.2 at New Beckenham, signalling the fall of another of Sydney's records. He had beaten Sydney's British mile record on a grass track, achieved at Chelmsford exactly eight years earlier. Another year on, as Britain took on Germany on the first day of August in 1955 at White City, the 22-year-old medical student Derek Johnson beat Sydney's British allcomers half-mile record in a sizzling race, clocking 1:48.7.

The records he held were disappearing, his direct involvement in athletics was diminishing, but Sydney still popped up occasionally in the public eye. In the summer of 1955 he agreed to appear on BBC Light Service radio in a special show to celebrate 75 years of athletics, alongside Jim Peters, Chris Chataway and Lord Burghley. A few months later his club acquired a handsome silver cup to commemorate his achievements in the sport and decided it would be awarded annually to the winner of the club's junior one-mile championship.

Journalists still occasionally sought his views on matters athletic, and in late 1956 Bob Ferrier of the *Aberdeen Evening Express* took the long train journey south to meet Sydney at Charing Cross station to discuss the upcoming Olympic Games in Melbourne. He told Ferrier he would have loved to have been there, although the idea of "five days in an aeroplane" would not have been to his liking. Ferrier's article would focus chiefly on Sydney's views on the chances of the British athletes, but he seemed just as preoccupied by the fact that Sydney looked so ordinary and behaved just like any other of the thousands of rail passengers thronging the station that day. His presence gave no hint of his celebrated past.

Family matters were of primary concern these days, wife Pamela giving birth to a son, Philip Sydney, in February 1954 and a daughter Hilary Pamela in November 1957. By the time his offspring were both at primary school their famous dad had begun dabbling in sports journalism, putting his name to a column in the *Coventry Evening Telegraph* – 'Athletics with Sydney Wooderson' – which would appear throughout the 1960s. It featured general chat on the athletics scene in Britain, opinions on performances and prospects, but contained little or no anecdotal content about Sydney himself, and is likely to have been largely ghost-written.

The swinging sixties transformed London, banishing the gloom and austerity suffered by Sydney's generation over the previous two decades. However, there would be unhappy episodes too, Sydney's mum Nettie dying in March 1964 aged 88, having moved out of her Beckenham home several years earlier to live nearby with Stanley and his family. A year or two later Sydney is thought to have fallen out with his superiors at work, leading to him quitting to become a partner at a smaller legal firm, Heath Giles and Co of Stafford Road, Wallington, Surrey. This would be a joint venture with fellow solicitor Derek Gifford in which they were able to use Sydney's famous name to attract business.

The family moved to a more expensive home in Reigate and, with his children at private schools, Sydney found himself working very hard to maintain the lifestyle, and under some pressure from his various responsibilities. Those stress-busting country walks had never been so important.

But by 1968 Sydney had become ill, stoically suffering symptoms for some time before finally consulting a doctor, and being diagnosed with Crohn's Disease. It seems likely the stress and anxiety of his new position at work contributed towards this. Despite the symptoms of his illness, he was determined to remain as active as possible and in 1969 accepted the opportunity to become President of Blackheath Harriers for a second time, his tenure to cover the club's centenary year from April. Anxious to play a full part in this big year, Sydney put his name down for a special centenary relay that was organised at Croydon Arena in South Norwood on Sunday 27 April. It involved teams of runners completing 100 legs of one mile each, and at the age of 54 Sydney donned the black kit one last time and would receive the baton to run the 50th stage for Blackheath.

The opposition was provided by runners from host club Croydon, as well as Belgrave and Cambridge Harriers and Sydney – despite having barely run at all in 20 years, let alone competitively – managed a highly respectable mile time of 6:18 for his four laps of the cinder track (splits: 90, 98, 96 and 94 seconds). Blackheath won the event narrowly in an aggregate time of 8hrs.38:04.6 after a gripping contest saw the lead change hands a number of times in the latter stages. It seemed appropriate the final race of his life would be a mile on a cinder track, and next morning *The Times* featured a large photo showing Sydney in action, looking slim and fit for a man of his age, but with much less hair than in his heyday and deteriorating eyesight that required spectacles with heavier frames and thicker lenses than the old days. There was widespread delight in seeing him in action again that went beyond just the running community, and Sydney remarked with a smile afterwards that he'd received more attention this day than during his days as national champion.

The year of 1969 also saw the death of Sydney's former coach Albert Hill aged 79, who by now had lived in Canada for more than 22 years. If Sydney thought he was on the road to becoming a 'forgotten hero' himself, the case of Hill will have been startling, for this double Olympic champion's passing received scant recognition, his obituary in *The Times* barely filling three lines.

49

A Restless Soul

AFTER Sydney stopped running completely in his mid-thirties he hadn't seemed, on the face of it, to find it difficult adjusting to life without sport. However, his wife would describe him as becoming "a restless soul" in his post-running years.

His fondness for long walks seemed to increase as he got older, but, as most runners know, a nice stroll is no replacement for the adrenalin rush, the sociability and general feelgood factor that running provides. As pointed out repeatedly, Sydney was a noticeably quiet, inscrutable fellow – even for a man hailing from his 'stiff upper lip' generation of Englishmen. So maybe privately he did miss the thrill of victory, the roar of the crowd and the goodwill showered upon him when he pulled on racing kit.

Sydney came from an era when runners rarely continued their sport into middle and old age simply for fun and fitness reasons. The streets of the 1950s and 1960s very rarely hosted 'leisure' runners and any that did slip into public view would attract curious or baffled gazes. The idea of going for a casual jog though Kingston and into the parks would probably have drawn far too much attention to appeal to Sydney.

Whatever his private feelings, Sydney was certainly not one for living in the past, nor did he plan to exploit, or even enjoy, the celebrity status first bestowed in younger years. That was history. His son Philip and daughter Hilary were born several years after the spikes had been hung up for good, so never saw him run. Although they quickly became aware of his fame,

Reminiscing with journalist Neil Allen (centre)
and fellow mile champion Derek Ibbotson.

there would be little or no discussion at the meal table of dad's days as a national hero.

Philip and Hilary kindly took time out to recall memories of their dad for me, and painted a fascinating picture of a quiet, dignified, generous man of integrity. A man completely without ego, who chose to stash his trophies well out of sight and even allowed precious old BBC films of his triumphs to rot away in a shed. Sydney never sought recognition and certainly never wanted fuss. Said Philip:

> "He made a clean break from running when he married our mum, or did so very shortly afterwards. He certainly never carried on running to keep fit, instead preferring the long and frequent walks. However, he did carry on attending Blackheath Harriers events, doing timekeeping, coaching and attending other meetings arranged by groups such as the Boys' Brigade, to present trophies and suchlike. Hence I do I have some dim memories of standing as a child, watching cross-country runners on muddy, foggy Saturday afternoons, standing with Mum and other mothers and wives among the women not allowed in the clubhouse in those days.
>
> "From working at Keene Marsland's solicitors in the city, he was moved to their Kingston office after the war. I think he had a falling out with the company leading to him breaking away in the late 1960s, buying into Heath, Giles and Company in Wallington, Surrey, becoming senior partner. My father was no natural business man, but his name brought in clients with whom he was popular. Anxiety over all this might have contributed to severe illness at this time – for he suffered from Crohn's disease. The consultant told our mum that if he hadn't been so fit he'd never have survived it, but to go through so much for so long before consulting a doctor meant he must have been a masochist!
>
> "Dad was a worrier and tended to keep things bottled up. Even my mum said she often didn't know what was upsetting him. He'd go and shut himself in another room. I think he found it a great strain taking over Heath, Giles and Co. and, looking back, must have had financial worries. He'd taken on the house in Reigate in the mid-

1960s which cost a lot more than the one just sold, and he had us two children at private schools. By 1968 he was ill. The diagnosis of Crohn's disease was followed by enduring a difficult operation.

"Character wise, he was very private. He never talked about his achievements or told anecdotes around them. But Dad was still always scrupulously polite with his fans, although not enthusiastic. Wherever we went as children, people would see the surname and ask: 'Any relation?' Thus, he was made a fuss of, but sometimes taken up by dubious hangers-on, because he was far too nice to say no, and also far too modest to want to take centre stage. He was invited to be the Liberal candidate for Sutton constituency, but turned it down.

"I think he had a small motorbike at one stage and I also remember him driving home in a new green Standard 10. It meant we were the proud owners of one of the first cars in the road. Dad had also owned the first TV in our road. All the neighbours apparently piled in there to watch the Coronation. I was born in 1954 and though they never admitted it, I think I was named after Prince Philip, and when Hilary came along was named after Edward Hillary, who climbed Everest. Edward Hillary also happened to be related to a branch of the Wooderson family who'd moved to New Zealand.

"As for all Sydney's trophies, they were never on display but crammed in a metal box, stuffed away in the attic. However, before getting married, when he was still living at home, his mother used to proudly display them, highly polished, in a big bow-fronted Regency cabinet, which I think Dad ended up giving to the rag and bone man! Old BBC films of his races were left to rot away in rusty canisters piled in our garden shed.

"I remember a day when the BBC came to interview him – I must have been seven or eight. There were two enormous grey and green vans, like furniture vans, with a generator and cables snaking across the pavement. I was kept out of the house, so it stayed a mystery to me, but it's possible the BBC presented him with those film reels of his famous races after this interview instead of a fee – which, knowing my dad, he'd almost certainly have refused. He never played the film clips – we didn't have that sort of projector. They were left in their metal cases to rust in an old wooden shed with no lock, just full of tools and junk – and it leaked! I guess when they moved from Reigate, he dumped them, if not before. He always liked clearing things out, much to Mum's dismay.

"Dad never talked about the foreign travel he'd done in order to run his great races – certainly not to us. In his last years I did ask him about the Berlin Olympics, but his only memory seemed to be of getting lost on the way between the stadium and where he was sleeping. No memories of Berlin itself. Only after he died did I find his photo album containing little black-and-white pictures – one of which showed Hitler and Goering, saluting from up on their podium.

"Walking was his release and also a hobby. He wouldn't have referred to doing walking for fitness but would have called it taking exercise. He would get restless sitting down. Every weekend Dad would go walking, when possible on both Saturday and Sunday. Quite often Mum would go with him. I accompanied him more often than Hilary and quite often he and I would go out before Sunday lunch. It was the time when I could talk with him. We had some good conversations, on books we'd read or politics. He had a very liberal attitude, despite being so constrained in himself.

"And on family holidays, you guessed it, we walked and walked! I only realised how unusual this was when I started telling friends. It was a case of getting up, and having a pre-breakfast walk; after breakfast, take sandwiches and go on a long cliff walk. Get back, have an evening meal and go for an evening walk. Mum called him a restless soul. He had a general love of nature, preferring the country to town, but wasn't one to stop and stare, like our mum, to look at the birds and flowers. She'd got used to going on walks as well, what choice did she have, after all? But she liked to stop and stare, sit on a bench, draw a sketch. Not with him. It was always, 'What's round the next corner?'

"Regarding other hobbies, he was a good photographer in the 1950s and 1960s, but gave it up in the 1970s. He had an interest in architecture – cathedrals, castles, churches and the like. He always loved reading and his favourite was Thomas Hardy, although he did have a quote from Shakespeare for any occasion. He listened to Beethoven and Haydn. He was also a very good gardener, creating a garden in every house he owned, and also liked visiting gardens and joined the National Trust.

"He took us on regular holidays, to Cornwall, Devon and Wales, and in the late 1960s we had a driving holiday to Austria as well as a trip to Paris. Later, he was a frequent visitor to Italy while I [Philip] was living there, but he wasn't confident on the Continent. He preferred his English food. He always continued to follow sports news in the papers and on TV, though showed no enormous admiration for any one athlete.

"Sydney was very close to his mother, but she was a reticent person too. His mother and father had a distant marriage, my grandfather living in Camberwell, at least during the week. It was his second marriage and I don't think he ever got over the loss of his first wife. He became fascinated with spiritualism, trying to get in contact [with her]. My grandmother [Sydney's mother Nettie] had started off as a sort of governess for the two girls from the first marriage. It was she who had the link with Kent – for her parents [the Tindalls] owned a hotel in Tenterden and her father was an accountant for the Wooderson firm. Nettie attended and supported him at many of his races, but it wasn't a case of acting as a sort of personal manager – maybe his brother Stanley was more supportive in that way.

"Sydney first met our mum Pamela in his London office just before the London Olympics, and going to the Games turned out to be one of their first dates together. On getting married she gave up her job and never returned to work, though did help type out legal documents for him in the early days of Heath, Giles and Co. To start married life they moved to Worcester Park, near Kingston – I recall him saying it wasn't easy finding a house so soon after the war. He found that one in Beverley Road so bought it, probably wanting somewhere not too far from my mum's parents in New Malden. Next they moved to Reigate in 1965, and when he retired headed for Cornwall in 1980. They found that a bit remote, so moved to Dorset in 1985 to be closer to friends and family.

"Thanks to the Crohn's disease he was on drugs for the rest of his life, and these took away his vitality, but other than that, he kept his health, and was only incapacitated for the last few years, losing his eyesight and suffering from an extreme form of Parkinson's. Thus he could no longer read or enjoy his country walks. But Dad was a stoic. He never complained. Instead he spent many hours listening to BBC Radio 4 and talking books."

The Blackheath and Bromley Harriers' HQ.

50

The Finish-Line

SYDNEY retired as a solicitor in the late 1970s and he and Pamela moved from commuter-belt Reigate to Cornwall, seeking to enjoy their remaining years in tranquil and pleasant surroundings. However, the far south-west corner of the country would prove a little too remote and before long they moved again, this time to the riverside market town of Wareham, Dorset.

Settling here meant they were much nearer to son, daughter and grandchildren. Here they could also be visited regularly by Stanley, and thus the two brothers' countless outings on foot together continued well into retirement. Stanley's daughter Jill recalled:

> "Sydney was a very pleasant uncle. He was so modest about his running and hardly mentioned it. We were aware of his fame as it was publicly well known when we were young. It was assumed all of us children would be good at running just because Sydney and Stanley were! He found it embarrassing to talk about his success and with his shyness, making speeches was torture for him. At one birthday party staged for him he even went out of the room when we watched a video of his sporting history compiled by a friend!"

Sydney followed sport via newspapers and TV but had no particular favourite team or individual. However, he expressed huge admiration for

Seb Coe who broke three world records in just 41 days during summer 1979. Coe's new world mark in the 800 metres at Oslo's Bislett stadium saw him become the first British holder of this record since Sydney's great run of 1938. This prompted an outbreak of media interest in Sydney, who told James Coote of the *Daily Telegraph*:

> "I could not keep up with the intense competition they go in for nowadays. It is incredible that Coe should break these two records in such a short time – my ideal would have been three hard races per season."

Speaking to sportswriter Alistair Aitken that summer, Sydney made some interesting points about changes during the 30 years since he'd been at the top of his game:

> "These days the top athletes don't seem to regard cross-country in the same way as we did… we used to have packs that went out together – the fast pack, the slower and slow packs and everybody kept with their pack under the one leader of each. But nowadays they come up to run on a Saturday from the club HQ and go out in ones-and-twos just as they like, and sometimes don't bother at all if they are racing on the Sunday."

Meanwhile, the *Sports Argus* carried a feature in which comic actor and 'national treasure' Norman Wisdom revealed he'd been a huge fan of Sydney Wooderson and had been a regular at White City around the time Sydney held world records. Wisdom had also followed in the great man's footsteps by running in Army championships: "I used to take running quite seriously and am quite proud of the fact I once finished seventh in the Southern Command cross-country when I was in the Army," he said.

In summer 1987, shortly before his 73rd birthday, Sydney made a guest appearance at Crystal Palace stadium to mark the 50th anniversary of his world mile record. A special old-fashioned handicap mile was staged as part of the Miller-Lite meeting, to commemorate Sydney's great run of 1937. It proved a real thriller for the curious crowd with Steve Crabb winning in 3:51.76 as a pack of eight finished in a dramatic rush. Sydney was photographed chatting with Seb Coe and told reporters he was amazed to see present-day elite runners doing the mile up to 20 seconds quicker than his old 1937 record:

> "I suppose we had pacemakers of a different kind in my day, but it was not so blatant as today as we had these handicap races. There was never so much fuss about records, although there was always a sense of achievement when you broke the British record."

Asked about the old stories that he used to refuse expenses payments back in the pre-war days, Sydney explained:

> "I decided to run at Ibrox Park and paid my own fare to the meeting, but afterwards I was slipped an envelope that contained £12. At the time it was a fortune for me but I was strictly an amateur and I sent it back as soon as I could. I even paid for the postage despite the fact that I was earning only £3 a week as a solicitor's clerk at the time. I wanted to stay an amateur and this would have been an infringement of the rules."

When Sydney's 75th birthday came along in 1989, Blackheath's *Gazette* featured a special article to mark the occasion, describing how he nowadays kept occupied down in Dorset by walking, theatre-going, reading and maintaining his and Pamela's sizeable garden. Athletics historian David Thurlow also used the anniversary to create a 56-page illustrated booklet about him, *Forgotten Champion*, published in conjunction with the British Sports Association for the Disabled.

Richard Liston of the *Daily Telegraph* persuaded a reluctant but unfailingly polite and cooperative Sydney to do an interview and asked whether the old champion harboured regrets about the cruel way in which he lost six of the best years of his career to the war. Sydney was philosophical:

> "Sport closed up once the bombing started and... I think one realised that we had to win the war, so one just accepted it. Quite frankly you wondered if you were going to be alive at the end. Even though I lost out on two Olympic Games and had retired when the 1948 Games came along, I can't really regret it. Obviously I

> would have liked to have broken four minutes for the mile, and won an Olympic title, but that's life. I had a good time from 1934 to 1939… I'm quite proud of still holding the record for the number of consecutive wins in the AAA mile."

Although he preferred to lead a quiet life in Dorset, Sydney could occasionally be persuaded to put on his best suit and turn out if a special athletics anniversary was taking place. The May 1994 event in London to mark 40 years since Bannister's four-minute mile required considerable cajoling from club colleague and friend Tony Weeks-Pearson before he agreed to go. Weeks-Pearson recalled accompanying Sydney from Wareham to the bright lights of London's West End, the last leg of the journey involving a cab ride along the Mall to the Grosvenor House Hotel. Sydney was by now nearly 80 and, typically, was nervous and uncomfortable at the prospect of receiving lots of attention and having to meet and greet a mix of old acquaintances and complete strangers. It appears this discomfort and the painfully slow London traffic combined to cause an uncharacteristic tantrum, as Weeks-Pearson would recall:

> "According to the media cliches, Sydney was not supposed to do 'passionate', much less 'furious', but at that moment I thought he was about to do both! 'I've a good mind to turn around and go back home,' he told me convincingly. From me, there were convincing consolations about his public's disappointment if he did that…"

Fortunately Sydney contained his urge to order the taxi to do a U-turn and would go on to enjoy the night's festivities. Celebrated milers Bannister, Cram, Coe, Snell, Morceli, Jazy, Walker, Landy, Ryun, Elliott, Bayi, Ibbotson and Andersson would be called on stage, but before that a seated Sydney was afforded a standing ovation when footage of him was shown on a large screen. Weeks-Pearson recalled seeing him enjoy having cups of tea poured for him by Olympic golden girl Mary Peters and then, not only autographing a Blackheath centenary book, but mischievously sealing it with a kiss!

Colin Welland, director of the film *Chariots of Fire*, was among those present who tentatively asked for Sydney's autograph: "He was my boyhood hero," he explained. Sydney dutifully scribbled away until after

Sydney (right) at home with brother Stanley.

midnight, quietly amazed to be the centre of attention among so many stars. By breakfast time the following morning he was on a train back to Dorset, grateful for all the tributes, but privately rather glad the fuss was over.

An 80th birthday party for Sydney was staged by Blackheath at the Hayes clubhouse and attended by about 200 people. All in all, 1994 would prove quite a year, but would end on a sad note when Sydney's older brother Alfred died in November at the age of 83.

In *Athletics Weekly* the following year, Trevor Frecknall echoed the views of many when he queried Sydney's baffling omissions from New Year's and Birthday Honours Lists. Frecknall wrote:

> "Just about the most enduring mystery in post-war British athletics is why Sydney Wooderson has never been knighted. He so typified the stature and spirit of war-torn Britain it was taken for granted by his friends and admirers that Royal recognition would follow. They're still waiting, while Wooderson spends his 82nd year in contented retirement with his wife in Dorset. His eyesight is bad now, but he still goes for daily constitutionals of two miles to clear his mind."

It did indeed seem as if formal recognition was long overdue, and before long the Olympic gold medallist and London Marathon founder Chris Brasher, a persuasive and charismatic figure, put his not inconsiderable energy into a campaign to have Sydney honoured. Meanwhile, Sydney was visited at home prior to his 85th birthday by author/historians Peter Lovesey and David Thurlow, who wanted him to name his six best races for a proposed article in *Track Stats* magazine. Returning from a walk with his brother, Sydney sat down and went through his career highlights, but was unable to narrow it down to six races, and eventually settled on these seven:

- Public Schools mile, White City, April 1933
- Southern AAA mile, Guildford, June 1934
- AAA mile, White City, July 1935
- Inter-club handicap mile, Motspur Park, August 1937
- Army/RAF/AAA/USF meet, White City, August 1945

- European Championships 5,000 metres, Oslo, August 1946
- English National Cross-Country, Sheffield, March 1948

Another project timed to coincide with Sydney's 85th birthday was completed by Somerset-based athletics historian Michael Sheridan who published a comprehensive list of Sydney's races. He produced the booklet *A Gentle Cyclone* with the help of club and school documents and Sydney himself, detailing more than 250 events featuring Sydney between 1929 and 1969.

In December 2000, more than half-a-century after his last race, Sydney was finally recognised on the New Year's Honours list, awarded an MBE for services to Blackheath Harriers and to athletics. Brasher's campaign had been successful. Sydney told Tom Knight of the *Telegraph* it was a huge surprise as his achievements had taken place so long ago, and confessed that returning to the limelight would be a big ordeal. He was nearly blind by now but was comforted by the knowledge a royal aide would accompany him at the presentation and he would have friends at his side at the reception. He added mischievously:

> "It obviously took them a long time to make up their minds. What annoys me is that actors and actresses get these honours two-a-penny. It's very nice – not that it means anything. I'll be glad when it's over really."

Sydney probably wasn't intending to sound curmudgeonly, it was merely his dislike of fuss surfacing again.

A few months later, in March 2001, Sutton Valence School named its new Sports Hall in his honour and despite warning them in advance of his poor health, Sydney was able to attend the grand opening ceremony. It took place on the final day of term at which the traditional 'baton race' was staged, an event that must have brought back memories for its most famous participant. In return for their gesture, Sydney presented the school with the trophy he'd won as an 18-year-old at the 1933 Public Schools championships. He was pleased to have defied his failing health and made it to the event, but generally his enforced inactivity in recent times had become a source of great frustration for a man with such love for the great outdoors. An active mind in an unwilling body was very upsetting for him, according to his son-in-law William.

Sydney Wooderson MBE, flanked by Roger Bannister and Chris Brasher.

* * *

By 2006 Sydney and Pamela were living in the Anglebury Care Home in Wareham and it was here, four days before Christmas, that Sydney passed away. He was 92.

The cause of death was formally certified as two-fold, firstly old age and secondly the effects of Parkinson's and Crohn's disease. Many obituaries were published in subsequent days, particularly substantial articles appearing in the *Times, Telegraph* and *Independent.*

Sydney's funeral took place at the Church of Lady St Mary, Wareham, on Thursday 4 January 2007. Befitting a man who didn't like a lot of fuss and attention, his gravestone here is simply marked, making no mention of his MBE or his international sporting fame.

The day after the funeral, Sir Roger Bannister was among those who paid warm tribute on BBC Radio. A special 'service of thanksgiving and celebration' in Sydney's honour would be staged later in 2007 at West Wickham Parish Church, organised by Mike Martineau, past president of the Blackheath club. A highlight of the day was a wonderful eulogy given by Tony Weeks-Pearson, the long-standing clubmate and family friend who had been coached by Sydney.

Weeks-Pearson said Sydney had been a great all-rounder, but as a human being rather than a sportsman. He pondered whether Sydney had actually made deliberate use of his media image as a small and frail runner to come up with a "Blackadder-ish cunning plan" thus leaving opponents confused and baffled. He said calling Sydney 'frail' had been ridiculously wide of the mark:

> "His was a free, tough mind, forthright, independent, enlightened and progressive in his views and judgement. All these qualities went with an unwavering loyalty to his valued wife and talented family, also to countless others such as his coach and friend Albert Hill". He also suggested perhaps Sydney shared something of the melancholy of his favourite author Thomas Hardy: "It would be surprising if anyone who had served in the London Fire Service and the British Army in the Second World War did not come out of all that with some such effect on their make-up."

Before the reception that day, Blackheath's clubhouse was formally named in Sydney's honour in a ceremony involving Philip and Hilary Wooderson, who read out poems they had composed for the day. The memorial service was attended by 21 international athletes (14 of them Olympians) and many messages were received from famous names unable to get there. Steve Ovett sent condolences and revealed Sydney had been a childhood hero of his. Lynn Davies, president of UK Athletics, said Sydney had been a gigantic inspiration to an entire generation wearied by the Second World War – his athletic achievements were legendary and it had been an honour and privilege to have known him. Lord Seb Coe called Sydney the senior partner in a very exclusive club.

The club had previously gathered at the same church to celebrate its centenary in 1969, on a day when Sydney, president for that year, gave a reading "Let us now praise famous men…" and now the club had returned to praise the life of the club's most famous man, who had been a member for 75 years.

Generations have passed through the ranks of the now-renamed Blackheath & Bromley Harriers AC since Sydney Wooderson's heyday, but the club remains immensely proud of him. He can be seen on the walls, not only in yellowing photographs but by way of a framed portrait in oils by 1930s artist George E. Dafters.

It is a measure of Sydney's ability that the club's all-time record for 800 metres in early 2018 (set by Chris McGeorge) was only 1.5 seconds quicker than Sydney's best of 80 years earlier. He was a pure amateur, squeezing training between work commitments and using facilities and equipment far less helpful that today's. In a tribute on the club's website, Dr Greg Moon recalled:

> "I asked Sydney if he regretted not being an athlete today, as his performances would have made him very rich. Without hesitation he responded that he loved his time in the sport; it was a hobby, relaxation and highly enjoyable. Today he would be a full-time athlete; it would be his job and he would have to get out of bed in the morning and run as work. That would have lost much of the fun. No, he regretted nothing."

SYDNEY CHARLES
WOODERSON
1914 - 2006
PAMELA LUCY
WOODERSON
1925 - 2014
together again walking free

Sydney Wooderson's main records, in chronological order:

April 1933, White City – First schoolboy to run sub-4.30 mile (4:29.8)
June 1934, Belvedere – Kent senior mile record (4:27.8)
August 1934, White City – Equalled UK mile record (4:13.4)
August 1935, Ibrox Park – UK mile record (4:12.7)
June 1936, Chelmsford – UK mile record (4:10.8)
July 1937, White City – AAA champs mile record (4:12.2)
July 1937, Paris – UK 1500m record (3:51.0)
August 1937, Ibrox Park – UK three-quarter-mile best (3:00.9)
August 1937, Motspur Park – World mile record (4:06.4)
August 1938, White City – UK half-mile record (1:50.9)
August 1938, Ibrox Park – UK 1500m record (3:49.0)
August 1938, Motspur Park – World 800 metres record (1:48.4)
August 1938, Motspur Park – World half-mile record (1:49.2)
September 1938, Paris – European Champs 1500m record (3:53.6)
September 1938, Oslo – UK 1500m record (3:48.7)
May 1939, White City – Inter-Counties mile record (4:07.4)
June 1939, Fallowfield – World three-quarter-mile best (2:59.5)
July 1939, White City – AAA champs mile record (4:11.8)
August 1940, Ibrox Park – Scottish all comers mile record (4:11.0)
September 1945, Paris – French all comers 1500m record (3:48.9)
September 1945, Gothenburg – UK 1500m record (3:48.4)
September 1945, Gothenburg – UK mile record (4:04.2)
July 1946, Dublin – Irish all comers two-mile record (9:05.0)
July 1946, White City – UK three-mile record (13:53.2)
August 1946, Oslo – UK 5000m record (14:08.6)

Blackheath past-president Mike Martineau (left) and
author Rob Hadgraft with the portrait of Sydney by George E. Dafters.

Acknowledgements

The author is grateful to all those who helped with research, offered encouragement, and passed on cuttings, data, images and words of wisdom. This, in no special order, included:

Philip Wooderson, Hilary Taylor, Jill Gunn, Simon Amos, Mike Martineau, John Turner, Peter Lovesey, Bob Phillips, Kevin Kelly, David Thurlow, Cameron Bowie, Alex Wilson, Colin Kirkham, Central Library Bromley, Central Library Bexleyheath, Alexander Turnbull National Library of New Zealand, The British Library, Norman Brown (Royal Pioneer Corps), National Union of Track Statisticians (NUTS), Will Radford and Sutton Valence School, John Davies, Andy Milroy, Stuart Mazdon, Mike Fleet, Professor Matthew Taylor, Patrick Calnan, Mel Watman, Jes Cooban, Robert Holderness, Blackheath & Bromley Harriers AC, Tony Millard, Dave Cordell, Chris Haines, Trevor Vincent, Kevin O'Sullivan, Chris Tobin, George Brose, Francine Payne, Keith Morbey, Tim Johnston, Hugh Barrow, Brian Boulton, Roger Robinson, Ferdie Gilson and Ian Vaughan-Arbuckle.

The images reproduced were either from private collections, or property of the author.

Bibliography

3:59.4 by John Bryant (Arrow, 2005)

A Gentle Cyclone: The Running Career of Sydney Wooderson by Michael Sheridan (SP, 1998)

Albert Hill – A Proper Perspective by Greg Moon (SP, 1992)

All Out for the Mile by George Smith (Forbes Robertson, 1955)

As If Running on Air by David Colquhoun (Craig Potton, 2008)

Austerity Britain 1945-1951 by David Kynaston (Bloomsbury, 2007)

Beer and Brine: The Making of Walter George by Rob Hadgraft (Desert Island, 2006)

Borrowed Time by Roy Hattersley (Little, Brown, 2007)

British Athletics 1950 by Michael Sheridan (SP, 2004)

British Athletics 1951-1959 by Michael Sheridan (SP, 2008)

Centenary History of the Blackheath Harriers by DK Saunders & AJ Weeks-Pearson (SP, 1989)

Chris Brasher: The Man who Made the London Marathon by John Bryant (Aurum, 2012)

Conjuror on the Kwai by Fergus Anckorn (Pen & Sword, 2016)

Conquerors of Time by Lynn McConnell (Sports Books, 2009)

First Four Minutes by Roger Bannister (Putnam, 1955)

Four Minute Mile by Tim Hartley (Mortons, 2014)

Hitler's Olympics by Christopher Hilton (Sutton, 2008)

Honour of Empire, Glory of Sport by Bob Phillips (Parrs Wood, 2000)

In the Long Run by Jim Peters & Joseph Edmundson (Cassell, 1955)

Lovelock by James McNeish (Hodder & Stoughton, 1986)

My Life in Athletics by Mel Watman (SP, 2017)

Official History of the AAA by Peter Lovesey (Guinness Superlatives, 1979)

Out in Front by George Gretton (Pelham, 1968)

Ross by Norris McWhirter (Churchill, 1976)
Running Round the World by Jack Crump (Robert Hale, 1966)
Sport and the British by Richard Holt (Oxford University Press, 1990)
Sydney Wooderson and Some of His Great Rivals by Guy Butler (Vail, 1948)
Sydney Wooderson: Forgotten Champion by David Thurlow (SP, 1989)
The 1948 Olympics by Bob Phillips (Sports Books, 2007)
The Austerity Olympics by Janie Hampton (Aurum, 2008)
The Impossible Hero by Dick Booth (Corsica, 1999)
The Legend of Lovelock by Norman Harris (Nicholas Kaye, 1964)
The Lonely Breed by Ron Clarke & Norman Harris (Pelham, 1967)
The Miracle of the Mile by Bill Nankeville (Stanley Paul 1956)
The Perfect Distance by Pat Butcher (Weidenfeld & Nicholson, 2004)
The Perfect Mile by Neal Bascomb (Collins Willow, 2004)
The Thirties – An Intimate History by Juliet Gardiner (Harper, 2011)
Today We Die a Little by Richard Askwith (Yellow Jersey, 2016)
Tomorrow You Die by Andy Coogan (Mainstream, 2012)
Twin Tracks by Roger Bannister (Robson, 2014)
Who's Who of British International Athletes 1945-1960 by Michael Sheridan (SP, 2010)

Newspapers, periodicals and newsletters consulted:

All Sport (Sweden), Athletics, Athletics Weekly, Blackheath Harriers Gazette, Coventry Evening Telegraph, Daily Dispatch, Daily Express, Daily Herald, Daily Mail, Daily Record, Daily Telegraph, Egyptian Mail, Eighth Army News, Horse and Hound, Kentish Times, Liverpool Echo, London Evening News, Look and Learn, Lyons Sports Sheet, Modern Athletics, Morning Post, New York Journal, Newcastle Evening Chronicle, News of the World, Pioneers Calling, Punch, Sporting Chronicle, Sporting Record, Sports Argus, Sunday Mirror, Sunday Post, Sunday Times, The Bystander, The Crusader, The Independent, The Oldie, The Stagbearer, The Tatler, The Times, Track Stats, West London Observer, World Sports.

The sports centre at Sutton Valence School.

About the Author

Born in Bedfordshire in 1955, Rob Hadgraft was a news reporter, sportswriter and publications editor for 26 years before turning freelance in 2000 to focus on writing books and features about sporting history. This is his 20th book, a sixth biography of a champion runner of yesteryear after acclaimed studies of Alf Shrubb, Walter George, Louis 'Deerfoot' Bennett, Arthur Newton and Jim Peters. Rob, married and based in North Essex, has been a keen club runner himself for 35 years, completing around 1,100 races. Unlike the subject of this book, he has been unable to retire gracefully from the sport!